The
Empowered
Writer

The Empowered Writer

An Essential Guide to Writing, Reading, and Research

K.M. Moran
Eric Henderson

FOURTH EDITION

OXFORD
UNIVERSITY PRESS

OXFORD
UNIVERSITY PRESS

Oxford University Press is a department of the University of Oxford.
It furthers the University's objective of excellence in research, scholarship,
and education by publishing worldwide. Oxford is a registered trade mark of
Oxford University Press in the UK and in certain other countries.

Published in Canada by
Oxford University Press
8 Sampson Mews, Suite 204,
Don Mills, Ontario M3C 0H5 Canada

www.oupcanada.com

First Edition published in 2010
Second Edition published in 2014
Third Edition published in 2017

Library and Archives Canada Cataloguing in Publication
Title: The empowered writer : an essential guide to writing, reading and research / Kathleen Moran,
Eric Henderson.
Names: Henderson, Eric, 1951- author. | Moran, K. M., 1955- author.
Description: Fourth edition. | Revision of: Henderson, Eric, 1951-. Empowered writer. | Includes
index.
Identifiers: Canadiana (print) 20210136103 | Canadiana (ebook) 2021013612X | ISBN 9780190165710
(softcover) | ISBN 9780190165741 (EPUB)
Subjects: LCSH: English language—Rhetoric. | LCSH: Report writing. | LCSH: Academic writing.
Classification: LCC PE1408 .H388 2021 | DDC 808/.042—dc23

Cover image: © iStock/SolStock
Cover and Interior design: Laurie McGregor

Oxford University Press is committed to our environment.
Wherever possible, our books are printed on paper which comes from
responsible sources.

Paperback printed by Marquis, Canada

1 2 3 4 — 25 24 23 22

Brief Contents

Contents

PART TWO Essays

PART THREE Research

PART FOUR Grammar

Readings

From the Publisher

Oxford University Press is pleased to present the fourth edition of *The Empowered Writer*. Now in full colour, this text is a four-in-one guide covering rhetoric, research, and grammar with integrated readings. This approach gives students a detailed yet widely applicable and accessible guide for developing skills in writing and research.

Tailored specifically to college and university students in undergraduate composition courses, this text offers an effective method for developing skills in research, writing, and personal and business communication. Key principles are illustrated through sample professional and student essays and reinforced through classroom-tested exercises that encourage students to empower themselves as writers in training, to participate actively in honing their skills, to make informed choices, and to think critically about how and why they write.

This revised edition features essays on topics relevant to students in Canada, including the environment, mental and physical health, and Indigenous peoples. New EAL notes highlight unique and difficult features of the English language to help improve the reading and writing skills of students new to the language. Additionally, the documentation chapter (Chapter 12) includes the latest documentation styles including the spring 2021 updates to the MLA style guide (9th Edition).

We hope that, as you browse through the pages that follow, you will see why we believe *The Empowered Writer* remains the most exciting and innovative textbook for Canadian students of writing and composition.

Exceptional Features of *The Empowered Writer*

Abundant exercises. Well over a hundred exercises designed to be completed individually or in groups provide students with ample opportunity to practise and refine their skills. Exercises include

- post-reading questions
- chapter review questions
- documentation exercises
- grammar exercises

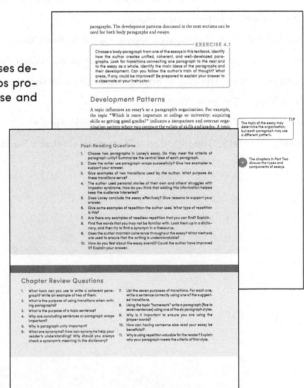

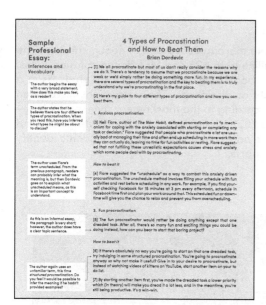

High-interest professional essays. Accessible selections cover topics of particular interest to students—including the environment, mental and physical health, productivity, and cultural differences. Marginal annotations highlight techniques for students to follow or avoid.

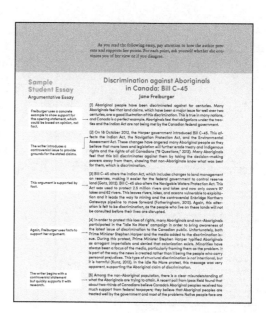

Sample student essays. Numerous examples of student writing, many of which are new to this edition, illustrate important rhetorical techniques and demonstrate to students that their best work can stand alongside the work of professionals.

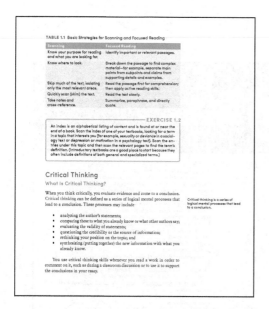

Critical-thinking focus. The authors encourage students to think critically about their plans and purposes for writing in order to structure their work and to conduct research effectively.

Helpful marginal notes. New EAL notes provide additional information to readers on difficult and unique features of the English language. Other marginal notes include writing tips, content summaries, cross-references to related material in other chapters, and a running glossary that reinforce important ideas. Boldfaced key terms are defined in the margins, and the definitions are compiled in a glossary.

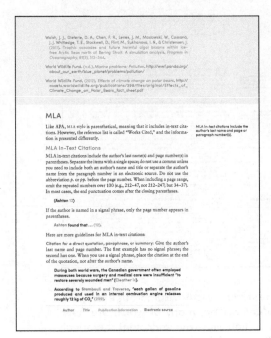

Updated and thorough coverage of documentation. The authors outline both APA and MLA documentation styles, making the book a valuable resource for students in a wide variety of disciplines. The instructions have been updated according to the most recent style manuals, including the 2021 9th Edition of the MLA style guide, and citations are now colour-coded to help students identify the various parts.

Checklist for EAL writers. Students of English as an additional language will benefit from this appendix, which clarifies common idiomatic words and phrases and matters of usage that native English speakers often take for granted.

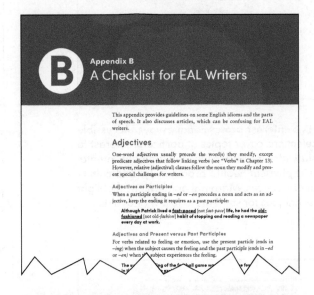

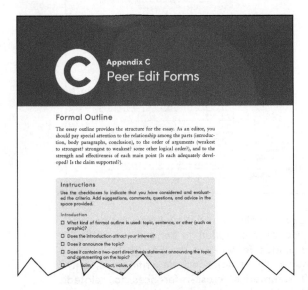

Peer editing forms. These forms help students to evaluate the work of their classmates.

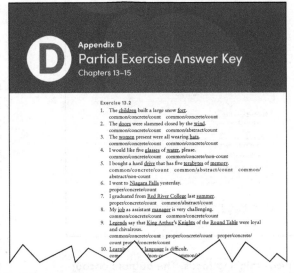

Partial answer key. Answers to most of the grammar exercises allow students to check their progress. Unanswered exercises can be assigned as graded coursework.

Online Resources

The Empowered Writer is supported by additional materials for both instructors and students, all available on Oxford Learning Link (OLL), www.oup.com/he/Empowered4e.

For Instructors

- An **instructor's manual** features learning objectives, key terms, group work and take-home assignments, in-class writing assignments, and additional resources for each chapter.
- A comprehensive **test bank**, capable of integrating with the instructor's own learning management system, provides hundreds of questions in multiple-choice, fill-in-the-blank, short-answer, and essay formats.
- **PowerPoint slides** for each chapter provide key information from the text for instructors to use and build on for their own courses.

For Students

- A **student study guide** includes self-grading practice quizzes, consisting of multiple-choice and short-answer questions; a practice mid-term exam; and a practice final exam.
- A collection of **grammar quizzes** for students tests their skill level and competencies.

Preface

There are many books currently available that help students learn how to write at the college or university level. The fourth edition of *The Empowered Writer* differs by taking a more academic approach to the subject, while addressing the same material. For example, the student samples are genuine, coming from students who have taken courses with us or our colleagues. These samples are either actual essays, summaries, or excerpts, not pieces that follow a journalistic style. Many of the professional essays also follow the rules set out in this text. While a few of the samples use a journalistic style of writing, students generally are not asked to read about how to write an essay and then asked to analyze a piece that does not follow the same stylistic rules they have been learning.

Critical thinking is an essential skill for any successful writer at this level, and so the term is introduced and explained in detail from the outset, in Chapter 1. The application of critical thinking is then stressed throughout the following chapters. Students are also introduced to the differences between expository writing and argumentative writing, and clear examples, often with annotations, are provided so that the readers can see the differences. In addition, an extensive section about research and how to properly integrate and present sources in an essay outlines the most current practices used in APA and MLA documentation.

Writers at this level are typically required to use a more elaborate writing style than they have been accustomed to using. Unfortunately, many students take this to mean using more words, rather than choosing the most accurate words or phrases. The later chapters help students build on grammar rules they already know, so that their grammatical structures reflect a higher level of writing. A section about style will help students learn to write clearly and concisely, developing a skill that is valued in the workplace.

We have included a chapter to deal exclusively with summary writing, both as a stand-alone task and as a means to incorporate research material in an essay. Again, the student summaries that we have included to illustrate the concepts discussed are genuine, having come from students we have taught. Several of these summaries relate to the full-length essays found in *The Empowered Writer*, so learners can try their hand at summary writing before comparing their product with what other students have produced in the past.

Finally, the book includes chapter objectives, extensive exercises, and chapter summary questions. The new edition also includes post-reading questions at the end of the sample professional and student essays designed to help students connect content with technique. By involving the student and encouraging the completion of these exercises, we hope that students will apply what they have learned often enough that writing no longer seems an irksome task but a satisfying one.

Acknowledgements

I would like to thank all my students who have helped make this book possible. You have made this journey so much fun! I would also like to thank those whose continued support has made this edition possible. While there are too many people to mention, a special thanks goes to my students who have allowed me to use their essays, as well as to Will Bahr, who keeps my life organized while I lose myself in the manuscript.

K.M. Moran
July 2021

The authors and publisher would like to acknowledge the following reviewers, along with those reviewers who wish to remain anonymous, whose thoughtful comments and suggestions have helped to shape *The Empowered Writer*:

Anne Ginn, St. Lawrence College

Linda Harwood, Selkirk College

Amy Hodgson-Bright, Lethbridge College

Amelia Horsburgh, Vancouver Island University

Jeremy Jackson, Medicine Hat College

John Muise, The University of New Brunswick & St. Thomas University

Kathryn Pallister, Red Deer College

Christine Pryce, Georgian College

Amanda Quibell, Georgian College

Laura Schechter, University of Alberta

Dorothy Woodman, University of Alberta

PART ONE
Writing and Reading

1 Basic Skills Development

By the end of this chapter, you should be able to

- understand the roles of writing, thinking, and reading in creating and understanding texts;
- use three reading strategies to understand texts;
- apply the CARS test;
- use critical thinking methods to engage with texts; and
- apply strategies for reading unfamiliar words and improving vocabulary.

The writing process involves more than just writing words. This chapter will explain how writing is connected to thinking and reading. You will explore the importance of thinking critically when you read and write. You will also examine how to infer word meaning and expand your vocabulary.

▲ Photo: tttuna/iStockphoto

An Integrated Approach

As you continue your studies, and later, when you graduate to the work force, you will be required to express yourself in writing. You will need to organize your thoughts logically, choose your words carefully, and create documents that inform and persuade. The practical strategies in this text ensure that what you write will clearly convey your skills and knowledge to your readers.

 Chapter 2 discusses writing for the workplace.

> **TIP**
>
> Good writing involves organizing your thoughts logically, choosing your words carefully, and crafting documents that inform and persuade.

Writing and Thinking

Writing is inseparable from thinking. First, you have an idea, then you translate your idea into words that make sense to you. After writing your words down, you edit your words until they reflect exactly what you meant to say.

Exercise 1.1 asks you to write about something you enjoy. This book will help you go from this simple exercise to writing complex research papers and will show you how the process is similar for all types of writing.

EXERCISE 1.1

Write about a skill or hobby that you enjoy—do not stop to edit yourself. When you've finished, answer the following questions.

1. Do you have a reason for doing this activity? Has this reason ever changed?
2. How have your interests in this activity changed over time?
3. How would you write this piece if you wanted to convince someone to try your activity?

Writing and Reading

Reading and the writing process are closely connected. When we read, we interpret the writer's thoughts using our own knowledge and experience (see Figure 1.1). This includes our knowledge of words, our understanding of the world, and our emotions. By studying the works of other writers, we improve our own writing.

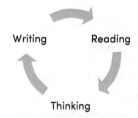

FIGURE 1.1 The critical writing cycle

When you read, you not only read the words, but you also look at how writers present their ideas. Is the writer expressing an opinion, or are the writer's ideas supported by research and facts? Read this paragraph and then consider the questions that follow:

> **Music was far more creative in the 1980s than it is today. The punk and prog rock movements had expanded into new wave, which mixed influences of both genres. Sounds and instruments were driven by evolving technology. Musicians experimented with sounds more than at any other time, and music videos brought a whole new element to music. Fans not only could hear the music but could also see the musicians. These stars became trendsetters, the likes of which have not been seen since. Pop music of the 1980s was, of course, the usual drivel that has been produced by every generation and is analogous to today's cult of rap and hip hop, which all sounds unimpressively alike.**

1. Why did the writer use specific words? What words express the author's opinion? What statements are supported by research?
2. What did the writer mention that you already knew? What didn't you already know about the subject?
3. Did the writer state anything that you disagree with? If so, why do you disagree?
4. Are the writer's statements logical?

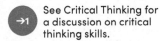
See Critical Thinking for a discussion on critical thinking skills.

By examining writing in this way, you are beginning to develop critical reading and thinking skills.

When you read critically, you identify the writer's purpose in writing, the intended audience, the writer's style, and the specific strategies used to communicate meaning or tone. Analyzing a work in this way will help you improve your own writing.

You will also note when the author is being subjective (expressing an opinion) rather than objective (informing using verified research). Authors often include their opinions, such as in the first sentence in the paragraph about 1980s music. There is no factual basis for the statement; it is simply based on how the author feels. To be objective, the author would need to include researched data, such as sales numbers, to prove this point. Facts, statistics, or secondary sources are required to back up your opinion so that your writing is not completely subjective.

Reading Strategies

Active readers examine words and how they combine to inform, persuade, or evoke memories or emotions.

The following two paragraphs begin an article about procrastination.

You know the people who walk confidently into an algebra test without trying to burn last-minute formulas into their brains? They may seem like homework cyborgs, but they're real, and you can become one of them—once you learn to keep procrastination under control.

The first step: Understanding that procrastination isn't caused by laziness! Most of us put things off to avoid negative emotions—from awkwardness to boredom to anxiety. But the truth is, you'll save yourself tons of stress if you outsmart those sneaky feelings that get in your way—and it's easier than you think.

Kaminski, M. (2015, October). Why can't I stop procrastinating? *Choices, 31*(2), 14–15. http://choices.scholastic.com/story/why-cant-i-stop-procrastinating

The expressions "homework cyborgs" and "burn last-minute formulas into their brains" are invented by the writer, but you knew what they meant because you thought critically about the wording. You analyzed it for meaning and made personal connections, remembering fellow students who seem to do nothing but study and others who study frantically at the last minute.

If you continued to read the article, you could make certain inferences and conclusions based on the writer's statements and the way they were presented. For example, Kaminski discusses typical types of procrastinators. While not specifically stating what type of procrastinator you may be (if you are one), you could make an inference by connecting your experience with one of the types described in the essay. As you read on, you could test the author's logic and consistency and compare it to your own experience by asking questions such as the following:

Inference is a conclusion we make based on the evidence presented; the corresponding verb is *infer*.

1. Are the claims logical? Does the writer support them with proof? Does the writer link ideas in an understandable way?
2. Are they valid, considering what you know about the subject?
3. Is the information reliable?
4. Does the author provide enough proof in step 1 for you to agree with the beginning of the piece?

When you ask these kinds of questions, you are responding critically to a work. You are evaluating the validity and logic of the claims and deciding if the evidence supports the author's arguments.

As you write assignments, you repeat this cycle:

- You read a text.
- You think about it critically.
- You write about your thoughts, making them clear and concrete.

To further your understanding, you might restart the cycle by rereading the piece, rethinking it, and perhaps clarifying your thoughts some more

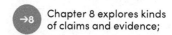 Chapter 8 explores kinds of claims and evidence;

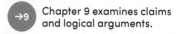 Chapter 9 examines claims and logical arguments.

by writing about them again. Responding to essays and thinking about the writers' conscious choices help you develop and improve your own writing skills.

TIP

Reading at the college and university level means reading–thinking–writing, where you

1. focus on understanding;
2. use critical thinking to test the validity of the statements; and
3. analyze and evaluate the work, considering the methods and strategies that the writer uses to make it effective (or not).

Selective reading is a reading strategy with a goal, such as scanning for main points or reading for details.

Scanning is a reading strategy in which you look for key words or sections of a text.

Focused reading is a close and detailed (i.e., word-by-word) reading of a specific, relevant passage.

The thesis statement is the main point of your essay, or what you are trying to prove.

→10 Chapter 10 explores various research strategies.

College and university courses require different types of selective reading, such as scanning and focused reading, that help you look for specific information.

Scanning is reading with a purpose. When you scan, you read for the main points or to identify another specific feature. If you want to know the subject of a reading, you will scan the introduction or look at the first sentence of each paragraph (this is often a topic sentence that tells you what the paragraph is about). Texts, like this one, break large chapters into smaller pieces using headings and subheadings. Use these to look for your information. The table of contents or glossary will help your search for key words.

Focused reading concentrates on smaller blocks of text. Sentences are read carefully for detail and sometimes for tone or style.

Scanning and focused reading are often combined. For example, following these stages will help you conduct thorough research:

1. *Scan for material that relates to your topic*: Begin by scanning catalogue entries, journal indexes, book contents pages and indexes, reference books, and other types of sources in order to find materials to support your essay topic.
2. *Scan for usefulness*: Once you have located most of your sources, scan them to choose those that will be the most useful for your purpose.
3. *Scan for main ideas*: Scan individual articles, books, and websites to identify the main ideas.
4. *Focus to find details that support the main ideas*: Read for details and evaluate how they fit with your thesis statement or with the ideas of other writers.

Scanning and focused reading are deliberate reading strategies. Ask yourself specific questions as you read to get as much from the text as possible. Table 1.1 outlines some basic tactics for scanning and focused reading.

TABLE 1.1 Basic Strategies for Scanning and Focused Reading

Scanning	Focused Reading
Know your purpose for reading and what you are looking for.	Identify important or relevant passages.
Know where to look.	Break down the passage to find complex material—for example, separate main points from subpoints and claims from supporting details and examples.
Skip much of the text, isolating only the most relevant areas.	Read the passage first for comprehension; then apply active reading skills.
Quickly scan (skim) the text.	Read the text slowly.
Take notes and cross-reference.	Summarize, paraphrase, and directly quote.

───────────────────────────── EXERCISE 1.2

An index is an alphabetical listing of content and is found at or near the end of a book. Scan the index of one of your textbooks, looking for a term in a topic that interests you (for example, *sexuality* or *deviance* in a sociology text or *depression* or *motivation* in a psychology text). Scan the entries under this topic and then scan the relevant pages to find the term's definition. (Introductory textbooks are a good place to start because they often include definitions of both general and specialized terms.)

Critical Thinking

What Is Critical Thinking?

When you think critically, you evaluate evidence and come to a conclusion. Critical thinking can be defined as a series of logical mental processes that lead to a conclusion. These processes may include

Critical thinking is a series of logical mental processes that lead to a conclusion.

- analyzing the author's statements;
- comparing these to what you already know or what other authors say;
- evaluating the validity of statements;
- questioning the credibility or the source of information;
- rethinking your position on the topic; and
- synthesizing (putting together) the new information with what you already know.

You use critical thinking skills whenever you read a work in order to comment on it, such as during a classroom discussion or to use it to support the conclusions in your essay.

→1 See "Responding Critically and Analytically through Questions" for tips on becoming a careful reader who asks important, relevant questions.

Because critical thinking involves many related activities, such as examining an issue and getting more information from other sources, it can take some time. When you plan the timeline to complete your project, ensure that you set aside enough time for you to complete this stage of the process.

Applying Critical Thinking

When you read an essay or a book or evaluate a real-life situation, you review what you have read or experienced and then infer the meaning. When you infer, you arrive at a probable conclusion based on your evaluation of what you read or see.

EXERCISE 1.3

Consider the following situation:

> You and a group of classmates have agreed to have an online meeting to discuss a class project. At the agreed time, one group member does not join the meeting. When you see Joseph at school the next day, you ask why he did not participate. He tells you that he had no internet connection at home last night.

What can you infer from his statement? Is there more than one possibility? Which is the most likely? What could you say or do to ensure that your conclusion is the most probable one? Use the following headings to complete your answer.

Possible inferences

Probable inferences

How to ensure that your inference is correct

As a critical thinker, you question assumptions, including your own; test the evidence; and accept or reject the conclusions after careful analysis. When questions arise, the critical thinker seeks answers within the text but may also consider relevant personal experience or outside sources. For example, in the situation described in Exercise 1.3, you might ask others who live in Joseph's neighbourhood whether they had internet problems.

When analyzing an argument, you must evaluate all the writer's claims and look for failures in logic or misuse of emotion. You should also think about points that writers don't raise. Are they avoiding certain issues?

Fact-based writing can produce contradictory findings. For example, two researchers investigating the connection between video games and violence may find very different, yet credible, conclusions. What can account for the conflicting results? Do the authors mention the contradictory results or only their own? Answering these questions requires critical thinking.

Reading and Critical Thinking

When a writer makes a claim that experts have debated for years—for example, that cats are smarter than dogs—readers will question it. Making the best inference from the evidence presented requires considering several factors:

- *Writer's credibility*: Is the writer a trusted expert? What is the nature of their expertise? Could they have a bias, such as hating dogs?

- *Nature of the thesis or main points*: Specific points are stronger and often easier to prove than general ones. For example, there are many different dog breeds, so can a writer make claims for the intelligence of all dogs?

- *Basis of the statement*: A claim may depend on one particular definition of a term. For example, there are various ways to define *intelligence*. Those who think a dog is more intelligent may point to trainability as the definition of intelligence, while cat fanciers may point to adaptability or independence.

- *Method*: How does the writer attempt to prove their point? Do they use fact or opinion?

- *Support*: A credible writer provides evidence. You must evaluate the writer's evidence and the way it is presented. What kind of evidence does the writer use? Do they rely too much on one kind of evidence or one source? How many sources are used? Are they current (recent studies may be more credible than older ones)? Does the writer ignore some sources (e.g., those that find dogs more intelligent than cats)?

- *Conclusion*: Has the evidence supported the writer's claim? You will consider how weaker points affect the validity of the findings. Are there any gaps or inconsistencies in the chain of reasoning? Is the writer's conclusion logically supported?

> **TIP**
> Note the use of *their* and *they* in these sentences. Since we don't know which gender pronoun would be correct for the writer being discussed, it is advisable to use the plural form of the pronoun in order to stay gender neutral. For more information about pronoun usage, check Chapter 15.

 Chapter 7 examines thesis statements.

EXERCISE 1.4

We use critical thinking and inferences in our everyday lives. For each of the following scenarios, choose the best inference from the list and justify your choice.

1. You get a text from your friend at 9:00 pm. She broke her leg and she is at the hospital waiting for emergency surgery. She asks you to come and visit her. However, when you get to the hospital the next day, she is not there.

   Inferences:

   a. You mistakenly thought she would be in the hospital for at least one day.

   b. Your friend was playing a trick on you.

   c. The hospital has lost her information.

   d. No inference is possible. (What further information is needed?)

2. Trevor and Juan are roommates. Trevor suggests that they subscribe to Apple TV and split the cost. Juan says he is not interested. Trevor then suggests subscribing to BritBox. Juan says he is not really interested in British TV. Finally, Trevor suggests Netflix. Juan says he just isn't interested in watching movies.

Inferences:

a. Trevor is pressuring Juan too much.

b. Juan wants to use another service.

c. Juan doesn't have enough money to help with this cost.

d. No inference is possible. (What further information is needed?)

3. It is Todd's roommate's turn to cook dinner. When Todd gets home, his roommate is glued to the TV and the kitchen looks untouched. "Wow! Something smells great," enthuses Todd.

Inferences:

a. Todd has a poor sense of smell.

b. Todd is sarcastically voicing his displeasure.

c. Todd is trying to give his roommate a hint that he should start dinner.

d. No inference is possible. (What further information is needed?)

4. Brad is helping Kodi train for the 600-metre race by recording his time after every complete circuit of the track. Kodi does the first circuit in 60 seconds and the second in 65.

Inferences:

a. He will probably do the third circuit in about 55 seconds.

b. He will probably do the third circuit in about 65 seconds.

c. He will probably do the third circuit in about 70 seconds.

d. No inference is possible. (What further information is needed?)

EXERCISE 1.5

In the following blog post, Lawrence Cunningham uses critical thinking to analyze the book publishing industry and its future, where the use of digital reading devices is steadily increasing. Using your critical thinking skills and ability to make logical inference, read the essay and answer the post-reading questions.

Where Are the Books?

[1] Books have lined the shelves of the offices of all my colleagues at every school where I have worked. In my early days of teaching, or when spending a term as a visitor, I'd wander into a learned neighbor's office to get acquainted. The titles and content of those books announced a person's intellectual background and interests. They were instantly and extensively a topic of earnest discussion. If my interlocutor should be interrupted by a call or an assistant popping in, I'd amuse myself by grazing over the titles, scanning the shelves that added up to an inventory of

knowledge. On their shelves and mine, students attending office hours would likewise find easy icebreakers.

[2] When visiting the homes of friends, especially new friends but longer-term friends as well, it has always interested me to see what books are stacked on their shelves, in the living room, the study, along hallways. At parties, these books have been great conversation starters, fountains of discourse and debate. You could even pick them up and hand them over, citing the passage on a given page where you recalled a point being made particularly well.

[3] My wife and I, when house hunting the last time around, inspected two dozen apartments before falling in love with the homey charm of the one where we live now. As an anonymous broker showed us through the absent homeowners' place, we'd scan the stacks of books that gave a sense of the people who lived there—lovers of art history, a denizen of Wall Street, devotees of history, biography, the Civil War. Stephanie and I would joke, when viewing that rare apartment empty of books, that the absence of books was an absence of warmth and that we would not trust the people who lived there. "Where are the books?" we'd ask in bewilderment as we rode down the elevator, never to return.

[4] Today, with reading so often done and "books" acquired digitally, stored in pixels on hand-held devices, we see fewer new titles gracing the offices of colleagues and teachers, the homes of friends. No longer on display, they can no longer be conversation pieces. The average age of books on shelves is rising steadily and even these [are] becoming anachronistic. Shelves are given over to decoration, clocks, cups, bells, photographs. My wife and I wonder, "What will our kids think, 10 or 20 years from now, when they see an apartment without a single book in it?" Maybe nothing. We would be horrified.

[5] But exactly what the future holds is uncertain. One of my recent books, *The Essays of Warren Buffett*, is selling briskly in both print and digital, though with vastly more sales in print than digital, yet it costs $35 in print and half that in digital. Time will tell.

Cunningham, Lawrence. "Where Are the Books?" *Minding Our Campus: Reforming Our Universities*, 26 Mar. 2013, https://www.mindingthecampus.org/2013/03/29/where_are_the_books/.

1. Why do you think Cunningham feels it is important to have icebreakers, such as book titles, when meeting new colleagues?

2. What does the word *interlocutor* mean? Why do you think Cunningham uses this rather than a similar word?

3. What does the author's opinion of books and the vocabulary he uses tell you about his perception of his audience?

4. Arrange the following items from most to least important: Cunningham's credibility, the credibility of the blog that published the post, Cunningham's support for his claim, and your own or your friends' experiences with books. Give reasons to support your answer.

5. Cunningham states that he would not trust people who did not have books in their houses. Do you feel the same way? How does his opinion affect your view of him and how you feel about the blog post?

Responding Critically and Analytically through Questions

Reading for college or university involves pre-reading, first reading, and second reading.

Pre-Reading

Pre-reading helps you decide whether a particular source will help or support your research. Some articles may contain an abstract, which is a concise summary of the article and states the writer's hypothesis, method, and results. Reading abstracts can help you find the articles that are most relevant to your own reading or research interests. Ask yourself the following questions when working at the pre-reading level:

→5 Chapter 5 discusses how to write abstracts.

TIP

By reading each word of a work's title carefully, you can often determine whether it will be useful to your research.

- *What does the title tell me?* Non-fiction titles tell you what the book is about and often its organization and tone. A title may also indicate whether the author plans to tell you about the topic or only argue some aspects of it. You should not decide whether a source will be useful to your research solely by its title, but it is a good starting point. For example, what assumptions can you make about works with the following titles?

  Smith, Pamela J. *Global Trade Policy: Questions and Answers.* Wiley-Blackwell, 2013.

  Natural Resources Canada. *Canada's Changing Climate Report.* Canada in a Changing Climate, 2019, https://www.nrcan.gc.ca/ maps-tools-and-publications/publications/climate-change-publications/canada-changing-climate-reports/canadas-changing-climate-report/21177.

Both titles contain words that inform their readers whether the author is discussing or arguing a topic. The title of the first book suggests that the author will answer specific questions. The second indicates that the report looks at climate change from a distinctly Canadian perspective.

- *How long is the text?* You should make sure you have time to complete your first reading of an article or abstract in one sitting to get a sense of the whole. With a longer essay or a book, you can do this with individual sections or chapters.
- *Who is the author?* What are their credentials? Are they featured in your textbooks or mentioned by your instructor? Are they associated with an academic institution or organization? What else have they written?
- *What are the author's profession and nationality?* Are any other important or defining characteristics given, such as experience in the field?

- *Do they belong to or have affiliations with a specific organization, group, or community?* Will the bias of that group have an influence on the author's work?
- *Why was the work written?* Was it written to convince readers of a particular opinion or point of view? If so, how will this affect the way you use it?
- *Is the work divided into parts?* Are there headings and subheadings that tell you about content or organization? In articles, extra spacing between paragraphs usually indicates divisions. In a book, look for chapter titles and subheadings within individual chapters.
- *When was the work written?* Generally, you will want to look for the most recent research to support your thesis. but sometimes, a recent date means that the book is only a reprint of a much earlier edition. If the book has been revised since it was first published, the new updates may make it especially useful. Essays that appear in an edited collection were probably first published earlier than the collection itself (though essays are sometimes commissioned for a volume and would then bear the same date).
- *Who are the work's readers?* Who was it written for? If it is an essay, what publication does it appear in, and what does this information tell you? If the article appears in a scholarly journal, one in which the articles have been evaluated by knowledgeable peers, the article is likely a reliable resource for your project.
- *If it is a book, who is the publisher?* Is it an academic or a university press? Again, if you are writing a research essay, a scholarly publication might be a more reliable source than a book aimed at a wide, non-specialized audience.
- *What is the level of language used?* If the language seems difficult or specialized, you may have to do a little background reading or research. You will read this material more slowly, defining words by their contexts wherever possible and making sure that you have your dictionary handy.

→ 1 See Word Meanings for coverage of word meanings.

- *Is there an abstract that summarizes the entire essay?* Usually, an abstract precedes an essay. In a book, the preface, introduction, or foreword might give you a summary. The editor of an essay collection often summarizes the essays in an introduction or a foreword.

EXERCISE 1.6

Many of your textbooks include references to journal articles, books, and other media. These may be found in the notes, bibliography, or suggestions for further reading (perhaps at the end of each chapter). Choose two journal or book titles from a textbook in your favourite subject, analyze them word by word, and describe what you think each is about.

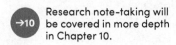 Research note-taking will be covered in more depth in Chapter 10.

Tone is the writer's attitude (e.g., subjective, objective, formal, or informal) to the subject matter.

Jargon is language that is specific to a field or a group.

→6
→9
Chapters 6 and 9 cover kinds of essays in more detail.

First Reading

In your first reading, you read for content and general impressions. If you own the book, you can underline or highlight passages that interest you and write notes in the margins. If it is a library book, invest in sticky notes to do the same. If it is an e-book, many devices offer the ability to comment and highlight.

When reading, remember to ask questions that will help you read critically. The questions below will help you get started. Eventually, using these questions will become part of your reading routine:

- *What does the introduction tell me about the topic?*
- *Is the author's tone clear?* Tone is the writer's attitude to the subject matter—for example, subjective, objective, formal, or informal.
- *What kinds of words are used?* Is the vocabulary level simple, sophisticated, general, specific, or specialized?
- *Is jargon used?* Jargon consists of words and expressions used in a particular discipline or among members of a group. This vocabulary may not be understood by people outside the group and you may have to expand your vocabulary to understand the material thoroughly.
- *What kind of writing is it?* Is the work persuasive, expository, personal, narrative, descriptive, or a combination of different kinds?
- *Do I understand what the essay or chapter is about?*
- *Is the thesis clear?* Do I agree or disagree with it?
- *Can I identify the main points?* For example, are they in paragraph topic sentences?
- *Are the points well supported?* Is there always enough detail provided?
- *What kinds of sources does the writer use?* Are sources listed in footnotes, endnotes, or parenthetical references? Are the sources credible?
- *Is the text easy to follow?* Can you determine word meanings from the context or should you use a dictionary?
- *Does the author ever express reservations or doubt?* Do they appear to contradict themselves?
- *Does the author seem to change their argument at any point?* Do they explain the change or support it with evidence?
- *Does the work shift its focus?* If so, is there an apparent reason for it?
- *Is there a distinct concluding section?* Does it address the questions raised in the introduction?

———— EAL

When you read a piece for the first time, this is referred to as skimming. This means you are reading to get the general idea of what the writing is about. (Scanning, on the other hand, is reading to find specific points in the text.) When you are skimming, do not worry about translating words you do not understand. Just make note of those words, either by highlighting or making a star beside them. During the second reading, you can take time to look up words. However, before you use your dictionary, try to understand the meaning based on the topic of what you are reading.

Using the same material from Exercise 1.6, choose five of the reading routine questions in "First Reading" (above) and further analyze the book or journal. Write a short description (no more than one or two sentences) for each question and, if relevant, provide examples. Would either title be appropriate for use in an essay? Why or why not?

In the following essay, the marginal annotations provide a reader's responses in a typical first reading.

Bear Cub: Rogue Wildlife Is Par for the Course on Canada's Northernmost Green
Eva Holland

Sample Professional Essay
First Reading

[1] It was morning by the time a golfer discovered the carcass. Massive and partially devoured, the moose lay dead on the fairway. The night before, the ungulate had wandered out of the shelter of the trees lining the green, and a grizzly bear had taken it down right there on the manicured grass. Not much can shut down the Dawson City Golf Course during its short summer season, which starts as soon as the ice breaks up and the ferry can go back on the water. But in 2013, a bear-versus-moose death match did just that. Management closed the course for 36 hours while conservation officers disposed of the carcass and set traps in case the grizzly returned to claim his leftovers.

> Notice the use of the author's language. The word *par*—a golf term— may entice golfers to read this article.

> The author uses a synonym for animal so that her writing does not become repetitive. She assumes that, even if readers do not know the word, they will be able to understand it based on the previous sentence.

[2] Located at 64 degrees north, just half a day's drive south of the Arctic Circle, the course is the most northerly natural green in Canada. Here's how you find it: First, follow dusty, tourist-heavy Front Street until it dead-ends at the Yukon River, which is so silt-choked it looks like chocolate milk. Nudge your pickup onto the open-deck ferry and feel the vessel shudder as it fights the current to cross. Next, wind up a hill out of the valley on a narrow paved highway that'll take you to Alaska if you keep going. Instead, turn left, following the blue signs marked with a stick-figure golfer in mid-swing. Dodge the six-inch-deep ruts that mar the dried-mud-and-gravel surface. Engage your four-wheel drive, if you've got it. The chewed-up road climbs along a cliff edge before it slopes down into dense boreal forest. Suddenly, the tall, spindly spruce trees part, and fairways appear on the left and right like an oasis.

> The author places her thesis in the middle of the paragraph. What is her purpose in doing so?

> The author uses directions much like residents of rural Canada do. What effect does this have on the readers?

> Why is the fact that this is a boreal forest important?

> Why does the author compare a golf course in northern Canada to a desert oasis?

[3] Early last June, a rust-riddled Ford F-250, its bed loaded with grey-brown silty dirt, sat parked at the edge of the green at Hole 3. Under a high early-summer sun that wouldn't set until nearly midnight, a man with a shovel walked from the green to the truck and back again, scooping earth from the pile and scattering it across the half-grown grass.

> The author uses many words that create a visual image for the readers, making it much easier to identify with what is being described.

[4] Aside from encounters with rogue wildlife—a moose that likes to stomp holes in the eighth green; a black bear that spent the summer of 2014 outside the crew's quarters—maintaining the greens is the toughest part of running the course, which is used mainly by locals. Yukon winters mean temperatures below −40 degrees for days at a time, and each spring thaw reveals dead brown patches.

> Here the author is supporting the thesis, which is about the challenges of maintaining a golf course that is so far north.

Again, the author is supporting the thesis.

[5] Matt Smith, slight and dark-haired with a deep tan, is the superintendent of grounds; sanding the greens gives his newly seeded grass a fighting chance. Down south, at a big corporate golf course, he'd have spreaders and sanders—machines to help with the job. But here, he does it by hand, spreading the loose soil, raking it smooth, then flattening it with a drum roller. Smith gathers the soil himself from a spot on the side of the road just down the hill, loading it into a Bobcat and carrying it back to the truck. "Ideally, I'd be using a coarse sand," he says. But he'd have to truck it in from Whitehorse, a six-hour drive away. "You've gotta work with what you got, right?"

Why does the author make a distinction between fresh water and non-potable water? What is non-potable water?

Why does the author include this fact?

[6] To keep the course running, Smith has to make sure that an array of aging machines remains functional. The facilities run on solar power—with a diesel generator as backup—and fresh water is trucked in. (He pumps the non-potable water for the sprinkler system from the marsh below the eighth and ninth holes; last summer, when a valve for the main suction line fell off into the muck, Smith spent three hours swamp-diving to retrieve it.) He's used to having a gun on hand: there's a 12-gauge for shotgun starts or in case of a bear or moose emergency.

The author ends the piece by re-emphasizing how much work is involved in keeping the course open.

[7] Smith's main concern, though, isn't facing down megafauna. The real mischief-makers are the ravens, who swoop down and snatch balls as helpless golfers look on. (Rule number 10 on the scorecard reads, "No penalty if you lose a ball to ravens.") On that June morning, Smith finishes raking, slams the truck's tailgate shut, and throws his rake and shovel on the ever-shrinking pile of dirt in the bed. Then he slides into the driver's seat and rumbles on through the rough.

Holland, E. (2016, February). The bear cub: Rogue wildlife is par for the course on Canada's northernmost green. *The Walrus*. http://thewalrus.ca/bear-club. Reprinted with permission from Eva Holland.

EXERCISE 1.8

Choose one of the articles that you used in Exercises 1.6 and 1.7. Using the strategies discussed in the section "First Reading," read through the article and make annotations based on the most relevant items in the bulleted list. Examine the points you have noted and identify the strongest ones by asking these questions: Are there particular arguments or statements that you feel are stronger than others? Are there any sections that you feel weaken the essay? Are there any words you do not understand based on the context? If so, do you need to look them up in a dictionary?

→3 →4 Chapters 3 and 4 discuss specific writing strategies, such as analogy and narration.

Second Reading

In your second reading of a work, you apply critical and analytical skills. To develop such skills, ask yourself these questions as you read:

- *What specific strategies does the writer use to draw me into the work from the beginning?* For example, do they use questions, a quotation, an anecdote, narration, a description, or an analogy? Is their chosen method effective?

- *Is the author's purpose in writing clear from the start?*
- *Who is the intended audience?* Is the choice of words always appropriate for this audience?
- *Why does the writer use the tone that they do?* Is the target a specific or a general audience?
- *Does the author try to persuade you to change your mind about something?* Or does the author explain or explore a topic, describe something, or tell a story?
- *Is the main point of the work announced in the introduction?* What is the thesis statement? Can you put it in your own words?
- *How are the points supported?* What kinds of evidence are used? Does the writer use examples, illustrations, facts, statistics, authorities, personal experiences, or analogies?
- *How does the writer organize the work?* Is one method used more than any other—for example, comparison and contrast, definition, cause and effect, narration, description, or division?
- *Does the author appear reliable and fair?* Is the language judgmental?
- *How are the main points arranged?* Is the strongest point placed near the beginning, middle, or end? Is the most effective order of points used?
- *Does the work depend more on logic or on emotion?* Do you relate to the images the author creates with words, or do the facts give you more information?
- *Does the writer appeal to a set of values or standards?* Does the author support or question a particular attitude or standard of behaviour?
- *Are there any lapses in logic?* Does the writer assume that you understand their ideas when, in fact, you need more information?
- *If the points are not always clear, why not?* Does the work contain specialized language, insufficient background, poorly constructed paragraphs, faulty or ineffective writing style, or inconsistencies or contradictions in the argument?
- *Is the conclusion effective?* What makes it effective or ineffective? Does it accurately wrap up the essay or does it leave you feeling that something is missing?

Critical thinking is more than just reacting to the text and either agreeing or disagreeing with the author. When you think critically, you delve deeper into the topic and examine your feelings, impressions, and values.

Thinking critically applies to how you read and react to social media, too. Do you trust everything you read? Do you share a post before finding out whether it is true or not? Do you look at the source of the post to see if there is any bias in the writing? Remember that what you post on social media never disappears, so you need to think carefully before re-posting. Doing research to find the truth behind the post helps you spot misinformation that may wrongly influence others.

> **TIP**
> A bias is revealed in the language an author uses. Sometimes the language used is emotional or obvious, such as a phrase like "Why would anyone do this?" Other times, the language is more subtle. When reading, always ask yourself what point of view the writer is trying to make you believe.

When you think critically, you look for overgeneralizations, assumptions, and broad statements that are unsupported by research. What is your initial reaction to the statement "Everyone hates Nickelback, but everyone loves Neil Young"? Seeing the word *everyone* should make you wary of an overgeneralization. If *everyone* hates Nickelback, how has the group reached international audiences and sold millions of albums? Neil Young is in his seventies, so how relevant is he to your generation? Whom did the author consult to generate this kind of statement? Has the author simply assumed that everyone thinks the same way? When you think critically, you are cautious of such broad statements and always question them before accepting them to be true.

Finally, there is a simple test you can apply to anything you read to reveal a bias or to examine the reliability of what is written. The CARS test is designed to help you establish fact from fiction.

- C *means credibility*: Who is the author? What organization does the writer work for? What is the source of your information? Is it a .com site or an educational site? What research supports the claims the author makes? For example, while Wikipedia has a lot of good, reliable information, it is not always credible because we often do not know who wrote the material.
- A *means accuracy*: Is the information you are reading up to date? Is the information true? Is it detailed and complete?
- R *means reliability or reasonableness*: Does the information in the article agree with your other research sources? Are the sources the writer uses reliable, or is the information just opinion? Does the author make overgeneralizations, such as "All Canadians eat maple syrup"?
- S *means support*: When the author uses statistics, does the author state where these came from? What research has the author used?

Using the CARS test for anything we read helps us develop critical thinking skills that can be used in all areas of life, including school and work.

Word Meanings

TIP

Avoid online dictionaries that are not affiliated with a reputable publisher; the sources are often not cited and the definitions may not be accurate.

The texts you read now may be more challenging than what you are used to. A reliable, current dictionary—whether in print or online—is necessary to help you understand these books and articles. However, looking up every word you do not understand is time-consuming and interrupts your train of thought. You could miss important points. When reading, you need to find a balance; you must know the exact meanings of some important words but only approximate meanings for many others.

First, try to determine meanings through context clues (the surrounding words) or similarities with words you already know. Then, use a dictionary to confirm a guess or when you have no idea what a word means. If an author thinks the typical reader won't know a certain word, they may define it, use a synonym, or rephrase it to make the meaning clearer. The author may also let the surrounding words clarify the meaning and connotation of the unfamiliar word.

A synonym is a word that means the same thing as, and can therefore replace, another word.

Connotation means the feeling or an idea that a word creates.

— EAL

When looking up a word in a translation dictionary, do not stop there. Always do a reverse translation. The first words you may be given do not always match the true meaning of the word in English. You might also want to go a step further and check the word in a thesaurus. A thesaurus can be helpful because it will show you similar words. In this way, you can build your vocabulary.

Let's look at a few examples. Specialized words, such as words borrowed from another language or culture, are defined for general audiences:

The *waribashi* (disposable wooden chopsticks) are provided for free at many Asian restaurants.

Particularly important concepts may be given an expanded definition:

The theory of culture shock—the cycle of liking, disliking, and then accepting the new culture one is in—is widely accepted among linguists and social researchers.

Even in highly specialized writing, the author may define terms the reader might not know:

If records cannot be located or will definitely not be available anywhere because of the patient's circumstances, children without adequate documentation should be considered susceptible and should receive age-appropriate vaccination. Serologic testing for immunity is an alternative to vaccination for certain antigens (e.g., measles, rubella, hepatitis A, diphtheria, and tetanus).

Immunization Action Coalition. (2018). *Vaccine safety.* http://www.immunize.org/askexperts/vaccine-safety.asp

Rather than being stated directly in a clause or phrase, a definition can be implied in the following sentence:

Ruttenbur and the soldier have a joint house and property in the game, even though the soldier is married in real life. Such in-game polygamy is common.

Thompson, C. (2012, September 12). Game theories. *The Walrus.* http://thewalrus.ca/game-theories/

When a writer doesn't define a word, you may be able to infer its meaning by looking at the words around it and at the idea they are trying to express. In the following example, the statement after the dash helps to clarify the cause of PTSD:

> **Post-traumatic stress disorder (PTSD) is a mental health condition that's triggered by a terrifying event—either experiencing it or witnessing it.**
>
> "Post-Traumatic Stress Disorder." *Mayo Clinic*, 2019, https://www.mayoclinic.org/diseases-conditions/post-traumatic-stress-disorder/symptoms-causes/syc-20355967.

What follows a word may suggest its meaning, not by defining or rephrasing but by expanding or illustrating through examples:

> **He has a lot of chutzpah—his exaggerated swagger, his condescending tone, and his overinflated ego all point to this.**

EXERCISE 1.9

Using context clues, your knowledge of similar words, or a suitable dictionary, write a one-sentence definition for each italicized word in these two passages. If you determine the meaning through context or other clues, look up the word in a dictionary and compare your definition with the "official" one.

1. In *virtual* spaces, questions of moral behavior seem to have been passed over entirely, perhaps because, until recently, few games have been specifically designed to allow people to virtually participate in morally *reprehensible* behavior. The record-breaking sales of the Grand Theft Auto series guarantee that this will soon change. Such a huge market for the game has shown that there is a collective desire to *immerse* oneself in virtual *misbehavior*.

   Tuplin, Andrew. "Virtual Morality." *Adbusters*, 11 Oct. 2008, http://www.adbusters.org/article/virtual-morality/.

2. Sadly, *segregationist rhetoric* has consistently *hijacked* the debate over black-focused schools, overshadowing what's really at stake. *Proponents* of the concept say it bears no resemblance to segregation, and that they can't afford to worry about the political *optics* when they have the chance to do something—anything—to address the crisis in black education in not only Toronto but the country as a whole.

   Wallace, Andrew. "The Case for All-Black Schools." *This Magazine*, 8 Jul. 2009.

Reading carefully to determine both the immediate context and the main idea of the sentence or passage can help you determine a word's meaning. If you are still in doubt, look up the word. By examining a word's denotations (dictionary definitions) and at least one of its connotations, you are well on the way to making it part of your writing vocabulary.

Denotation is the literal meaning of a word.

Improving Vocabulary

Broadening your vocabulary is essential for you to be able to express your ideas skillfully and coherently. Each profession has its own specialized vocabulary that you will learn as you progress to your final certification. Your instructor may explain these new words, or they may be defined in the glossary of a textbook.

Reading also broadens your vocabulary by introducing you to new words. Consider online vocabulary-building games such as crossword puzzles, Scrabble, and Boggle. Check your thesaurus (included in most word processing software) to discover synonyms for words you already know and to add variety to your writing. Just make sure the meaning is appropriate by checking it in a dictionary.

Once you have learned new words, it is important to use them so that they become part of your vocabulary. Some people keep a word journal to record new words and their meanings. Practise using your new words as often as possible so that they become part of your everyday vocabulary.

Brian Dordevic includes many inferences in his essay about procrastination. He expects you to be able to link his ideas to the thesis without him explaining how they relate. While reading, try to identify the main points that appear to be inferences and decide whether they are clear or if direct statements would be better. Also note any words that are unfamiliar to you.

EXERCISE 1.10

Before reading this article and answering the questions that follow, practise pre-reading and answer the following questions.

1. What information does the title convey?
2. How long is the article?
3. Who is the author? What do you know about him?
4. Is the work divided into parts? What does this tell you?
5. What is the level of language used? Is there any specialized vocabulary you can see?

EXERCISE 1.11

Now do a first reading of the article. Underline or highlight passages that interest you. You may also write comments, thoughts, criticisms, etc., in the margins. Then answer the following questions.

1. What are your impressions of the information presented?
2. What is the tone of the article?
3. Who do you think the intended audience is for this article?
4. Do the points seem well supported?
5. Does this article pass the CARS test?

Sample Professional Essay:

Inferences and Vocabulary

The author begins the essay with a very broad statement. How does this make you feel, as a reader?

The author states that he believes there are four different types of procrastination. When you read this, have you inferred what types he might be about to discuss?

The author uses Fiore's term *unscheduled*. From the previous paragraph, readers can probably infer what the meaning is, but then Dordevic goes on to explain what *unscheduled* means, as this is an important concept to understand.

As this is an informal essay, the paragraph is very short; however, the author does have a clear topic sentence.

The author again uses an unfamiliar term, this time *structured procrastination*. Do you feel it would be possible to infer the meaning if he hadn't provided examples?

4 Types of Procrastination and How to Beat Them
Brian Dordevic

[1] We all procrastinate but most of us don't really consider the reasons why we do it. There's a tendency to assume that we procrastinate because we are weak or we'd simply rather be doing something more fun. In my experience, there are several types of procrastination and the key to beating them is to truly understand why we're procrastinating in the first place.

[2] Here's my guide to four different types of procrastination and how you can beat them.

1. Anxious procrastination

[3] Neil Fiore, author of *The Now Habit*, defined procrastination as "a mechanism for coping with the anxiety associated with starting or completing any task or decision." Fiore suggested that people who procrastinate a lot are usually bad at managing their time and often end up scheduling in more work than they can actually do, leaving no time for fun activities or resting. Fiore suggested that not fulfilling these unrealistic expectations causes stress and anxiety which some people deal with by procrastinating.

How to beat it

[4] Fiore suggested the "unschedule" as a way to combat this anxiety driven procrastination. The unschedule method involves filling your schedule with fun activities and rest before scheduling in any work. For example, if you find yourself checking Facebook for 15 minutes at 3 pm every afternoon, schedule in Facebook time first and plan your work around that. This scheduled fun or downtime will give you the chance to relax and prevent you from overscheduling.

2. Fun procrastination

[5] The fun procrastinator would rather be doing anything except that one dreaded task. After all, there's so many fun and exciting things you could be doing instead, how can you bear to start that boring project?

How to beat it

[6] If there's absolutely no way you're going to start on that one dreaded task, try indulging in some structured procrastination. You're going to procrastinate anyway so why not make it useful? Give in to your desire to procrastinate, but instead of watching videos of kittens on YouTube, start another item on your to do list.

[7] By starting another item first, you've made the dreaded task a lower priority which (in theory) will make you dread it a lot less, and in the meantime, you're still being productive. It's a win-win.

3. "Plenty of time" procrastination

[8] Many people find it difficult to start a project when they know the deadline is a long way off. This type of procrastination is clearly visible in students who often struggle to start an essay earlier than a few days before the deadline.

[9] You may also have tasks that don't have deadlines. Take a look at your to-do list. Chances are you have at least one item that you've been putting off for weeks if not months. It's something you want to do, you know it will make things better in the long run, but you keep putting it off.

How to beat it

[10] Professor of Psychology and Behavioural Economics at Duke University Dan Ariely experimented with getting his students to set their own deadlines.

[11] Ariely gave his students three assignments and let them set their own deadlines. He hypothesised that students would choose the last day of term for the deadlines as this would give them the most time to do their work (and procrastinate). In reality, the majority of students chose earlier deadlines and got better grades than those who left their work until the last minute.

[12] The implications? By setting yourself deadlines and announcing them publicly, you will not only be able to get your work done, but you'll do a good job of it. Try setting deadlines and telling your friends, family and co-workers about them. This public commitment should keep you on track and motivate you to meet those deadlines.

4. Perfectionist procrastination

[13] Perfectionists are always striving for the best and, as such, are constantly criticizing their own work. For some perfectionists, the fear of failing, or producing work to a low standard, can be so overwhelming they never actually get around to starting anything.

How to beat it

[14] Philosopher and professor emeritus at Stanford University John Perry thinks procrastinating can actually be a good thing for perfectionists. "As long as they have a lot of time to do a task, they fantasize about doing a perfect job. Leaving it till the last minute is a way of giving oneself permission to do a merely adequate job. Ninety-nine per cent of the time a merely adequate job is all that is needed."

[15] Try looking back at the last five jobs you completed. Were they all perfect? Probably not. Were they sufficient? Chances are you're already working to a high standard so stop giving yourself a hard time. Identifying times when you didn't do the perfect job, but the consequences were the same as if you did, will help you to overcome your perfectionist routine and stop procrastinating.

Dordevic, B. (n.d.). *4 Types of procrastination and how to beat them.* Alpha Efficiency. https://alphaefficiency.com/4-types-procrastination-beat/

The author uses both headings and topic sentences in this essay. The headings can help you determine which paragraph you could find most helpful if you don't have time to read the whole essay.

The author is providing information from a scientific study to support his credibility. If this were an article in a journal, he would be required to provide proper citations so that you, as the reader, could find and read this study yourself.

Dordevic again uses a quotation from a credible source to support his point.

This is only half of the essay that Dordevic wrote, and so it does contain the author's conclusion. How would you craft a conclusion for this half of his essay?

Post-Reading Questions

1. Is the introduction effective?
2. What is the author's purpose in writing this?
3. Why does the author use the tone he does?
4. Does the author try to change your mind about something?
5. How are the author's points backed up?
6. Does the article depend more on logic or emotion? What is your proof?
7. Does the author appeal to a set of values or standards?
8. Are the points clear?
9. We do not get to read the author's conclusion to this essay. How does the lack of a conclusion affect how you view the article's information?
10. What vocabulary did you learn in this article that you could include in your own speaking and writing?

Chapter Review Questions

1. Using the examples in Exercise 1.4 as a model, create your own situation and a list of possible inferences.
2. How does improving your reading skills affect your essay writing?
3. What are some differences between first and second readings?
4. What are some differences between scanning and focused reading?
5. What role does critical thinking play in essay writing? In reading?
6. What is the CARS test? Why is it useful?
7. How can you identify author bias?
8. Why should you be careful about what you post on social media?
9. What are some effective ways to build your vocabulary? Are there others that were not mentioned that you could suggest to your classmates? Describe them.
10. Why is improving your writing skills important?

2 The Writing Situation

By the end of this chapter, you should be able to

- identify the purpose in the writing process;
- understand how to write for a specific audience; and
- write for the workplace.

To write a strong essay, you need a clear understanding of why and for whom you are writing. This chapter outlines the factors you need to consider when refining your purpose and audience. You will also learn essential tips for writing in the workplace.

▲ Photo: Anson0618/Shutterstock

Writing Purpose

Purpose is your reason for writing, as well as how you approach the task.

Before you begin writing, you need to think about your purpose. The following questions will help you focus your reason for writing your essay. If you are still uncertain about your writing purpose, ask your instructor:

- Did you choose your own topic or were you given one? If the latter, does the topic need narrowing?
- What form will your writing take? Response, essay, research proposal, lab report?
- Does the assignment ask you to learn something new or does it ask you to apply material you already know?
- Will your essay inform, explain, argue, tell a story, describe, analyze, compare and contrast, or summarize? If the assignment includes a specifically worded question or statement, pay particular attention to verbs such as *evaluate*, *assess*, *summarize*, *explore*, *explain*, *argue for or against*, *discuss*, or *describe*. Each term indicates a different purpose for the assignment.
- Will you be using your own ideas based on memory, observation, opinions, readings, or class or group discussions?
- Will you need to research your topic? Where will you find your resources? How much time will you need to do your research?
- Should your language be formal, like that of most academic disciplines? Will informal language, such as contractions, be acceptable?
- Will you be submitting work in progress, such as pre-writing assignments, a self-survey, a proposal, an outline, a plan, or a rough draft?
- Is there a word limit? Will marks be deducted if you write more or less?
- How much time have you been given for the assignment? An in-class-essay exam would require a different assessment of purpose than that of an essay assigned weeks in advance.

Answering these questions is a good way to understand an assignment's requirements. Consider using these questions to create a self-survey such as the sample one in Table 2.1. Using such a self-survey will help keep you on track.

EXERCISE 2.1

Using Table 2.1 as a guide, create a self-survey for a current or recent writing assignment. Identify the questions relevant to the task, write your responses, and briefly state what you know and what you need to find out to satisfy the writing purpose.

TABLE 2.1 Self-Survey Table

Question	Response	Where to Begin/What Needs to Be Done
Choice of topic?	Was given category (technology); need to narrow topic	I'm interested in smartphone gaming apps, but I need to make the topic more specific; brainstorming works best for me.
Kind of writing?	Formal research essay	I will start with online research and ask the librarians for help.
Main activities?	Mainly informing and explaining, but I'll be summarizing the results of studies and relating statistics	I need to reread the sections in the text on exposition and summarizing.
Specific skills?	Analyzing, synthesizing, and summarizing; evaluating will be important because there are a lot of strong opinions about technology	We're just starting to cover research, so obviously I need to become familiar with research methods and what's involved in synthesizing information from diverse sources.
Language?	Formal language, which means no contractions; I need to know if I can use developer slang	I'm not always sure what is formal versus informal usage; I'll read the text and ask my instructor.
Sources?	Three secondary sources are required; need to think about CARS (credibility, accuracy, reasonableness, and support); need to use APA citation style	I'm not sure how many studies have been done on the topic. I will begin by looking for apps' history, books/websites on apps; talk to friends who develop apps? Because the topic is current, I likely won't be using many books, but I will use some online sources, especially publishers' web pages; I'll need to check if these are considered reliable sources.
Work in progress?	1) proposal; 2) outline; 3) first draft; 4) final draft; note dates for peer editing in the syllabus	I know that I will be asked to submit an informal proposal, explaining my interest and knowledge about the topic; by this point, I hope to have narrowed my topic.
Length requirements?	About 1,000 words	Can I go over without penalty? How strict is the word count? Right now, it looks hard to do in 1,000 words, which is why I need to work on narrowing the topic right away.
Time requirements?	We have four weeks before the final version is due, with due dates for the stages of the project	I need to create a schedule to visit the library and begin research; I think I'll need to spend a lot of time on my outline since it will be graded.

A Is for Audience

Almost everything is written for an audience—your readers. For example, a novel will look and read much differently than a text for one of your courses. Each is written for the people using it. Student writers must also write their essays for a particular audience or reader.

Audience refers to your intended readers and their expectations.

Audience-Based Writing

Audience-based writing focuses on the reader, not on the writer. When you write, you need to consider who your audience is and where their interests and values lie.

If your instructor allows you to use informal wording, you can address the audience directly by using the pronoun *you*. You may also be able to discuss events by using *I*. Here are two essay introductions that use an informal style:

- Do you enjoy using social media?
- When I chose a roommate, I was looking for someone who was fun. I should have looked for someone who could pay the rent.

However, in formal writing, these pronouns are usually replaced with *one* or nouns such as *reader*. The reader is rarely addressed directly. The following statements are formal:

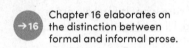
Chapter 16 elaborates on the distinction between formal and informal prose.

- Many students are required to complete at least one humanities credit in order to graduate.
- When examining the steps required to complete the project, one should pay close attention to what needs to be done first.

EXERCISE 2.2

Choose one of the sample essays in this book and, in point form, analyze it for the following:

- Is the writing formal or informal?
- Are there places where the writer has changed from one type to the other?
- How does the style of writing affect the way you feel about the piece?
- Does the style increase the writer's credibility, as discussed in Chapter 1, in the discussion of CARS in "Second Reading"?
- Who is the audience?

Audience-based writing must be error free and have a clear meaning. Ideas need to be expressed directly and concisely. Your work should have no obvious lapses in logic, nor should you assume a reader knows something just because you know it. You may have to define certain terms or clarify specific points. It is best to assume that the reader knows a little less about the subject than you do.

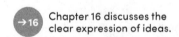
Chapter 16 discusses the clear expression of ideas.

Readers should not have to fill in gaps. Take this sentence:

Of all the bills-of-lading submitted, only 20 per cent had errors.

The writer should have helped a general reader by giving additional information, such as what a "bill-of-lading" is and what the errors were.

Rewrite the following sentences, adding detail for the audience wherever necessary.

1. Of the 1,500 students enrolled, only 750 actually completed the ECE course.

2. In order to borrow money interest free from the World Bank, nations must prove they are "developing" and not rich.

3. Most of the items that people place in recycling containers are actually sent to the dump.

4. Organic products have become *de rigueur* for foodies.

5. Rural access to high speed internet has become a pressing political issue.

6. Hipsters believe that they influence fashion trends.

7. The typical order at Tim Hortons is a "double double."

8. Wearing a bathing costume at the theatre is verboten.

9. An ISBN is required to order that book.

10. Cloud computing is becoming the norm.

Audience Factors

Consider the following basics about an audience when you prepare to write:

- *knowledge*: background, expertise, or familiarity with the topic
- *interest level*: extent of interest or potential interest
- *orientation*: the attitudes and emotional or ethical positions that define a typical reader

By thinking about these factors, you improve your ability to engage your audience. Suppose you want to explain a particular skill that you are an authority in. You must first consider how much your readers know about it. At college or university, you are writing for your instructor; therefore, you are writing to show the knowledge you have learned about a topic from your research or experience. Other times, you are writing for people who do not have as much knowledge as you do to help them learn about the topic.

Meeting audience expectations means providing enough information so that they will hear and understand you. For example, if you don't meet their expectations of using familiar terms or explaining unfamiliar ones, they may not pay attention to your points.

Many of the articles found on the databases your college or university subscribes to are written for an audience of experts. For example, the *Journal of Management* is written for people in business, and most of its readers are familiar with the terminology, or jargon, used in its articles.

Using these databases, find an article written for a specialized audience and one on the same topic for a general audience (you might try searching magazines or newspapers). Compare the writing styles. How are different words used to convey the same information? For example, in articles about the use of language, which term would be used for a general audience: *discourse* or *conversation*?

While taking this course, your primary audience is your instructor. Therefore, it's important to follow the directions for the assignment. For example, if you are required to include a title page with the instructor's name and course number on it, omitting this information would be failing to meet required expectations. Pay careful attention to the presentation of your essay, using the proper font size and type.

However, secondary readers, such as other faculty members or future employers, may read your writing as well, especially if you plan to create an e-portfolio to include with job applications. Try to write with this larger audience of potential readers in mind.

The following essay was online, so the paragraphs are shorter than those in an academic essay and the author also included headings. However, the author has followed the basics, such as keeping the purpose and audience in mind and using topic sentences.

TIP

An audience can vary in its attitudes toward the subject, the writer, or the thesis; these attitudes can range from very positive to very negative.

Sample Professional Essay
Purpose and Audience

Listen to Your Gut: Rewards and Challenges of Intuitive Eating
Lisa Petty

The author uses the word *atwitter*. This term was chosen because most people are familiar with the Twitter app. The word also refers to birds singing together. Therefore, the author is using a metaphor as a tool to engage the audience, showing that the number of dieting strategies on the internet is like listening to a flock of birds singing together.

[1] The internet is constantly atwitter with the latest diet strategies—what works, what doesn't, and what to try next to shed that stubborn weight. That food has shifted from being a basic survival need to a potential source of health problems seems counterintuitive. Is intuitive eating the answer to weight woes?

EAL

A metaphor is used in literature to show a similarity between things that seem to be unrelated, but a quality or trait can link them together.

Unhealthy food relationships

The author is using informal language, such as contractions like *don't* instead of *do not*.

[2] A variety of reasons may explain why our hunt for the perfect diet is perpetual. Research has shown that restrictive diets don't lead to long-term healthy weight. While this may, in part, be because reducing food intake is not sustainable over the long term, unresolved unhealthy relationships with food may also be involved.

[3] Consider the influence of societal pressure to look a certain way, an influence that has many young people severely cutting calories while they're also experiencing rapid body change at puberty and young adulthood. Eating behaviour fueled by body image concerns sets up a pattern of disconnecting from hunger cues and body needs that can persist well into the middle years.

[4] Negative body image has been associated with disordered eating, including anorexia and bulimia, as well as overweight and obesity. Once these patterns have been established, it's very difficult to override them. But it is possible.

Tapping into body wisdom

[5] Intuitive eating is based on the premise that the body has an innate wisdom about the quantity and type of food required to maintain an appropriate weight and achieve nutritional health. Intuitive eating has been associated with less disordered eating, more aspects of positive body image such as body appreciation, and improved emotional functioning.

[6] Essentially, intuitive eaters eat when they're hungry and stop when they're satisfied. No food is off-limits unless it's restricted by a specific health issue such as a food allergy or diabetes, for example, and intuitive eaters eat what and when they choose. In other words, intuitive eaters don't consider the potential impact that a food might have on body weight.

[7] This isn't to suggest that intuitive eaters aren't concerned about their health. On the contrary: people with higher body appreciation tend to focus on body function (what the body can do and feel) rather than body image (appearance) when making food choices.

[8] My own research showed that the mid-life women in my study made food selections based on how it made them feel physically and mentally. For example, they might skip dessert before an important meeting if they've noticed that sugar zaps their energy.

[9] In theory, then, intuitive eaters will instinctively choose a variety of foods in the right amounts to help them meet their nutritional requirements and to help them feel good in their bodies. Some folks are naturally intuitive eaters or easily make the switch to this type of eating, while others might have a more difficult time with it. What's going on?

Mixed signals

[10] The body's goal, always, is to achieve allostasis or balance. When it comes to eating, a multitude of mechanisms are at work to sensitize us to food cues when energy reserves are getting low.

[11] For example, the appetite hormones ghrelin and leptin and other circulating molecules are directed by the hypothalamus, which is the control centre in the brain. These hormones are secreted in response to changing.

[12] Significantly, there are substantial and stable individual differences in interoceptive sensitivity that are evident in neuroimaging of the insula. Perhaps not surprisingly, studies show that our level of interoceptive sensitivity is associated with awareness of hunger and satiety cues, as well as whether we eat for hunger or for emotional or external reasons.

The author is assuming that the audience knows the names of eating disorders, but does not go into detail by further distinguishing them, as a writer of a peer-reviewed journal article would have to.

In the first sentence, the author is using words that not everyone is familiar with, such as *premise* and *innate*. However, the author then explains the topic sentence in the rest of the paragraph, making it easier for the audience to understand the point without having to use a dictionary.

The author mentions their own research, but does not give any details, so either the reader must accept these comments as fact or the reader will have to search the internet for the relevant research.

[13] Some research suggests, however, that the insula might be more finely attuned to emotion or external stimuli than to internal cues, which may play a role in overeating. Interoceptive sensitivity has also been shown to decline with age.

[14] Lower interoceptive sensitivity has been observed in anorexia, binge eating, overweight, and obesity, as well as depression. On the other hand, intuitive eating is associated with higher levels of interoceptive sensitivity.

> The author has introduced vocabulary that many people will not be familiar with, showing the readers that the author expects them to have more knowledge about biology than the average audience member would.

Sensitivity training

[15] Amping up interoceptive sensitivity can be a challenging process, not only because we may have unconscious food programming, but also because we may jump to conclusions about what body sensations to expect when we're hungry, for example, or what the sensations we experience might signal.

[16] We also may have trained ourselves to ignore physiological responses like hunger, stress, and pain. Mindfulness therapies may be useful in helping to re-establish the mind–body connection.

[17] Mindful eating is the cousin of intuitive eating and includes the same principles for food selection but adds the component of meditation. Taking time to focus on the eating experience allows mindful eaters to notice whether foods are fresh or of good quality, and to assess whether they want to continue eating them.

> The author does not end with a concluding paragraph, which would help the reader more clearly understand the main points of the essay.

[18] Research has shown that even without specific training in mindful eating, mindfulness practices such as meditation may encourage people to control portion sizes, experience less uncontrolled eating, and increase the likelihood of choosing fruits over sweets as a snack—without once thinking about calories. Intuitively, it makes sense.

Lisa Petty, PhD. Alive: https://www.alive.com/health/listen-to-your-gut/. Excerpted from alive magazine, #451, May 2020. Published by Alive Publishing Group. Reproduced by arrangement with the Publisher. All rights reserved.

Post-Reading Questions

1. What is the author's purpose? Does it change in the article?
2. Who is the primary audience? What do you think the expected age range is? Explain.
3. Who would be a possible secondary audience?
4. The author starts the essay using non-specialized language, but then begins using highly technical language. Why do you think the author did this?
5. How do you think the author views the audience? Do you think the author believes that readers will view the topic positively, neutrally, or negatively?
6. Is the language throughout the essay formal or informal? Explain.
7. Does the author explain points well enough? Could any explanations be improved?
8. If the author had included more information about her research, such as when and where, would this have added to her credibility?
9. The essay focuses on the benefits of intuitive eating. Do you believe there are other positive or negative points that are missed?
10. Explain whether you feel the author judged the primary audience correctly.

Writing for the Workplace

Workplace writing has a specific audience with particular expectations. People can be overwhelmed by the number of messages they receive at work each day. They need to be able to scan a message quickly to determine its importance. Therefore, your writing must be clear and concise. By meeting this expectation, your audience saves time and is more likely to understand and respond to your message.

Depending on your job, you may be asked to write case studies, blog posts, tweets, emails, or reports. While these types of writing seem very different from essays, many of the same basic principles apply. Critical thinking skills help you decide on the purpose, the audience, the tone, and the content.

Purpose

The purpose of your message will dictate whether you want to use an informative or persuasive approach. It is important to understand how your audience will feel about the message you are sending before you choose your approach.

If you are informing employees of a straightforward policy change, such as switching from cheques to direct deposit on payday, the informative approach works best. However, if you are announcing new start times for shifts, you will use the persuasive approach that considers your audience's possible negative reaction to the news. You need to help your readers understand the issue and persuade them to accept the change. Taking time to understand your audience will help you avoid any misunderstanding that could damage your relationship with your readers.

Primary and Secondary Audience

Always consider your primary and secondary audiences when composing a message. Many business messages are read by people who are not necessarily the intended audience. For example, you may send your supervisor an email requesting that desks be rearranged to facilitate greater communication and collaboration between employees. That message may be forwarded to a senior manager, which means you now have a secondary audience. The message may also go to your colleagues, another secondary audience. You need to consider all potential audiences when you write your message.

A further consideration is whether the message is going to people in your department or to a more general audience. This understanding will help determine what vocabulary to use. If you work in the sales department and are discussing "early adopters" with other salespeople, you do not need to define this jargon; however, if you are writing to people who do not know the term, you will have to explain that it refers to customers who are quick to buy new products. It is important to tailor your message to your audience: if your readers already know words that you define, they will become bored; if you do not define words that are new to them, they will become overwhelmed. Either way, they will stop reading, and no message is effective if no one reads it.

Tone

Tone is also important. The tone of your message conveys your attitude toward your audience. You want your message to be polite, respectful, and considerate of your readers' time and interest. Think of how you would react if you were given your own message.

In business writing, you always need to consider the limited time that your reader has for reading your email. You need to get to the point in the first paragraph. This may appear to be very abrupt or even rude, but this is the standard for good communication in North America. Here are two sample replies to a request from your manager:

> **Thank you so much for your kind invitation to the meeting and for your request that I present my report on first-quarter earnings. As you requested, I have enclosed a draft copy of my remarks for your perusal and comment. I hope that the draft will meet your needs and look forward very much to hearing from you with your comments. (61 words)**

Revised for clarity and conciseness:

> **I'm looking forward to presenting the earnings report at the meeting on Thursday. Please let me know if you require any changes to the attached draft. (26 words)**

The second response is shorter by more than half, but it is still polite and includes the information that the manager needs to know: 1) you will be at the meeting, and 2) you've sent the draft report they wanted to see.

Never compose a message in anger; if you feel you must reply to a message that upset you, make sure that you have calmed down before responding.

When you are composing business documents, organization and clarity are key factors, just as when you are writing an essay. Your reader has limited time and wants you to get to the point quickly. Take time to create a rough outline or write a quick draft in Word first. Ensure all the points you want to make are covered and check that you are supplying all the information you have been asked for. It is easy to ignore this step with emails because you feel you need to reply right away. However, having to send a second email because you forgot something will waste everyone's time and create a poor impression of your communication skills.

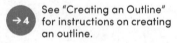

See "Creating an Outline" for instructions on creating an outline.

Dear Sam,

Thanks for sending me the May 2020 report so quickly. I appreciate the summary you sent along with it.

I have a few questions that I require answers to.

1. How recent are the statistics you cited on p. 15?
2. Who participated in the research discussed on pp. 52–70?
3. Did you really mean "in-house" on p. 83?

I need the answers to these questions by June 22 at 5:00. The final draft of the report will be sent to shareholders on July 1, so the changes need to be made before June 24.

I can be reached at ext 5234 between 9:00 and 4:30 daily. You can also email me.

Thanks,

Kim

Kim Wong
Vice-President, Customer Care
ABC Corp.
123 Valley Rd.,
Anywhere, Alberta L2L 2L2
1-800-438-2929 ext 5234

TIP

Paragraphs in workplace writing are often shorter than academic writing so that readers can view the content quickly.

Note the clear, concise writing. However, the necessary details are there for the reader to fully understand the points.

The writer gives a specific date and the reason for this. Again, the reader knows when, exactly, the information is required. Leaving a vague date, such as "next week" could lead to misinterpretation.

For email, adding a signature is important, especially for messages that go to readers who are not part of the company.

EXERCISE 2.5

1. What are three characteristics of writing for the workplace?
2. What are the dangers of not understanding your audience?
3. What is the difference between a primary and a secondary audience?
4. If a message is not clear and concise, what problems can occur?
5. What tone will the audience expect you to have?
6. Draft an email to your instructor explaining that you will be missing a class next month to attend a conference relating to your special area of study.

Chapter Review Questions

1. Why is it important to understand your audience?
2. Why is it important to have a clear purpose in mind when writing?
3. How can the tone of your writing affect your audience?
4. Why will your reader appreciate your being concise in your writing?
5. Why is it important to know how much previous knowledge your reader has about the subject you are writing about?
6. When might you use jargon in your writing?
7. How do you decide whether to use formal or informal language in your essay or report?
8. The marketing manager asks you to write a case study that explains how your company's product solved a problem and saved money for a client. Who might be a secondary audience for this case study?
9. Would you choose the informative or persuasive approach to writing a message to your employees asking for their feedback on a recent workplace seminar? Explain your choice.
10. Would you choose the informative or persuasive approach to writing a message to your employees asking for volunteers to organize the company picnic? Explain your choice.

3 Paragraph Essentials

By the end of this chapter, you should be able to

- construct an effective paragraph;
- write coherently;
- choose techniques to improve paragraphs; and
- apply five paragraph styles where appropriate in an essay.

Like an essay, a paragraph needs to be constructed in a way that leads the reader logically to its conclusion. If any element is missing, such as the topic sentence, the paragraph could lack unity and coherence and you could lose the reader's attention. Paragraphs must also be connected to each other in a way that helps the reader follow the essay's points. In this chapter you will learn how to create unified and coherent paragraphs that keep the reader's interest.

▲ Photo: fotogestoeber/Shutterstock

Introducing the Paragraph

A well-organized paragraph will

- introduce the topic of the paragraph;
- develop that topic with evidence; and
- summarize the paragraph.

The beginning of a paragraph, or topic sentence, announces what is to follow. Without a clear topic sentence, the supporting points will lack force and the paragraph will not be cohesive. The middle of the paragraph develops the main point, often using sources to support the topic. The ending provides a satisfying conclusion and usually acts as a summary of the paragraph's main idea.

Topic Sentence

The topic sentence introduces the main idea in the paragraph. Therefore, it often expresses a general, rather than specific, idea. The other sentences in the paragraph support or expand on the main idea, providing more focused details. The topic sentence is usually the first sentence in the paragraph because it provides a logical starting point and makes the paragraph easy to follow.

The thesis statement in an essay serves a similar function, providing a logical starting point for the argument that the remaining paragraphs will prove.

The **topic sentence**, usually the first sentence in a paragraph, introduces the paragraph's main idea.

 See Chapter 7 for an expository essay template and Chapter 9 for an argumentative writing template.

EAL

When you are reading professional writing, the topic sentence may not always be obvious. Accomplished writers may put the topic sentence elsewhere in the paragraph; however, when you are first writing to North American standards, your instructors expect you to follow the rule of placing the topic sentence first in the paragraph.

EXERCISE 3.1

In each set of sentences, choose which one makes the best topic sentence.

1. Topic: locavore movement

   a. In small communities, stores often use local products to produce their own wares.

   b. Eating locally is a good way to sustain the local economy and farming community.

   c. For example, on Vancouver Island, most grocery stores sell dairy products from Island Farms and other regional dairies.

2. Topic: smartphones

   a. Recent studies have found that the brain cannot handle all the multi-tasking we try to do.

b. We interrupt our meals, leave conversations, and tune out of meetings to answer our smartphones.

c. Smartphones dominate the lives of many people in society today.

3. Topic: the importance of nature on well-being

a. Nature helps reduce stress.

b. All people need to be exposed to nature regularly.

c. Interacting with nature often helps people reduce stress levels.

Concluding Sentence

In a stand-alone paragraph, your concluding sentence will show how the ideas you presented in your paragraph supported the topic and have resulted in a logical conclusion. When you write essays, each paragraph's concluding sentence connects back to your essay's thesis to show that your supporting paragraph has done its job.

You may have been taught to end a paragraph by writing a concluding sentence that leads to the topic of the next paragraph. Doing this for every paragraph will become tedious for the reader. To add variety, you can use another technique called paragraph wrap.

Paragraph Wrap as Conclusion

Using a paragraph wrap is a satisfying way to conclude a paragraph as it reminds the reader what the paragraph was about. It is especially effective in a longer paragraph where the reader might lose track of the main idea. Remember that the wrap reinforces the main idea's importance by using different words. This is very similar to the conclusion in your essay.

In the following paragraph, the writer successfully wraps the main idea, which is introduced in the first (topic) sentence:

A **wrap** is the last sentence of a paragraph that sums up the main point and recalls the topic sentence.

> **If politicians focused on the issues that mattered to the public, rather than spending energy attacking each other, the public might be more engaged in democracy and the election process. Many Canadians are interested in health-care spending, climate change, social welfare programs, and drug use. Politicians could present their specific aims in those areas and also discuss what funds will be needed to address these issues. Realistic budgets could be presented. Then, Canadians could make well-informed decisions at election time. Instead, most politicians just spend time attacking each other or the opposing parties. This does little to present facts and preys on the fears people have. This way of campaigning appeals to few people, and thus turns voters away from the whole process. It would be best for democracy if politicians addressed facts, rather peddling conflicting opinions.**

Transitions between Sentences

Transitional words and phrases guide the reader from one sentence to the next, showing the relationship between them. Note the use of *then* and

A transition is a word or phrase that connects ideas from one sentence or paragraph to the next.

TIP

Transitional FANBOYS words (*for, and, nor, but, or, yet,* and *so*) should never be used to begin a sentence. They should be used only to connect two main ideas within a sentence.

 Chapter 14 discusses transitional words and phrases further.

instead in the above paragraph. *Then* introduces a sentence that describes what could happen next. *Instead* introduces a sentence that demonstrates a contrast to what should occur. Some of the most useful transitions and the relationships they express are listed in Table 3.1.

Transitional words and phrases can be overused. Too many can clutter the paragraph and the essay. Avoid wordy transitions such as *in spite of the fact that, due to the fact that, first and foremost, in conclusion,* and *in the final analysis,* which can be expressed more concisely as *in spite of, due to, first,* and *finally.*

You must write with the reader in mind and leave no gaps in the logical development of your ideas. Transitional words act like a GPS for your readers, guiding them from the beginning of your paragraph or essay to the end. Your reader must be able to follow your logic every step of the way. In the following passage, the writer has left something out, and no transitional word alone can bridge the gap:

> **There are so many ways people can get information now. Blogs, social media posts, and online newspapers are numerous. Is everyone qualified to report on the news?**

The writer quickly moves from a generalization about getting information to examples without connecting the two ideas. This leaves a gap in the logic of the paragraph. The author needs to connect all the ideas, including the last question.

> **There are many sources of information that people can access now because of the internet. For example, blogs, social media posts, and**

TABLE 3.1 Transitions

Purpose	Examples
Limit	*admittedly, although, it is true that, naturally, of course, though*
Show cause and effect	*accordingly, as a result, because, consequently, for this reason, if, otherwise, since, so, then, therefore, thus*
Illustrate	*after all, even, for example, for instance, indeed, in fact, in other words, of course, specifically, such as*
Emphasize	*above all, assuredly, certainly, especially, indeed, in effect, in fact, particularly, that is, then, undoubtedly*
Show sequence or addition	*after, again, also, and, as well, and then, besides, eventually, finally, first . . . second . . . third, furthermore, in addition, likewise, next, moreover, or, similarly, too, while*
Contrast or qualify	*after all, although, but, by contrast, conversely, despite, even so, however, in spite of, instead, nevertheless, nonetheless, on the contrary, on the one hand . . . on the other hand, otherwise, rather (than), regardless, still, though, whereas, while, yet*
Summarize or conclude	*finally, in conclusion, in effect, in short, in sum (summary), so, subsequently, that is, therefore, thus, to summarize*

online newspapers are so numerous that it is difficult to choose which source to use. Therefore, readers need to question who is actually qualified to report the news.

Connecting Paragraphs by Using Transitions

In an essay, your reader must be able to follow your thoughts from one paragraph to the next. Because a new paragraph introduces a new topic, it is important to use transitions to help the reader connect the ideas in different paragraphs. A transition, which can be a word, phrase, or clause, can occur at the end of a paragraph as a wrap or at the beginning of the next paragraph as part of the topic sentence.

 See "Transitions between Sentences" earlier in the chapter.

When connecting paragraphs, avoid the kinds of transitions used to connect sentences within paragraphs, such as *for example, consequently, moreover.* They are not usually strong enough to connect one paragraph's main idea to the next one.

TIP
When making connections between paragraphs, avoid brief one-word transitions, which are too weak to link paragraphs.

One way to create a transition topic sentence is to begin the sentence with a dependent clause that refers to the previous paragraph. The following example begins with a dependent clause (underlined) before introducing the paragraph's topic (italicized). The dependent clause acts as a transition, showing that the previous paragraph focused on the fostering of independence through home-schooling. The independent clause introduces the new topic.

→ 13 Chapter 13 focuses on sentence construction.

> **<u>Although the qualities of independence and self-motivation are important in a home-schooled education,</u> *its flexibility enables the child to learn at his or her own pace, matching progress to the child's natural learning processes.***
>
> Student writer Marissa Miles

The <u>dependent clause</u> provides a clear reference to the topic of the preceding paragraph: independence and self-motivation. The *independent clause* introduces the topic of the current paragraph, which is children learning at their own pace.

> **Another crucial function of genetic engineering is its application to the pharmaceutical industry.**
>
> Student writer Neil Weatherall

This topic sentence leads readers to the new topic by reminding them that the essay's focus is on the critical functions of genetic engineering. This sentence explains that the author is going to introduce the reader to another function after discussing a different one in the previous paragraph.

In the first topic sentence example, the writer reminds the reader of what was discussed in the previous paragraph and tells them that the current paragraph will add new information. In the second topic sentence, the writer reminds the reader of the topic of the entire essay and how this

Chapter 4 discusses the various ways to develop a main point in a paragraph or throughout an essay.

paragraph is supporting that topic. Either method for making the transition to a new topic and paragraph is effective.

A unified and coherent paragraph develops one central idea and contains sentences that connect logically to each other.

A unified paragraph focuses on one central idea that is announced in the topic sentence and that all sentences relate to.

Paragraph Unity

Each paragraph should focus on one central idea announced in the topic sentence. Placing your topic sentence at the beginning anchors the main idea of the paragraph. In a unified paragraph, all sentences relate to the main idea being presented.

An essay should contain one idea per paragraph. In your rough draft, you may not always follow this principle. Therefore, an important question to ask when revising is whether each paragraph contains one main idea.

During revising, you may see that one paragraph is much longer than the others. You can often find a logical place to divide the paragraph into two shorter ones. Use logical transitions to combine very short paragraphs, which may appear underdeveloped on their own.

> **TIP**
>
> There is no perfect paragraph length. Some instructors give students an ideal range—such as between five and eight sentences—to ensure that each paragraph is sufficiently developed. Paragraphs can be longer. The aim is to keep paragraphs, including your introduction and conclusion, roughly the same length.

EXERCISE 3.2

In each of the following paragraphs, one sentence is off topic, affecting the paragraph's unity. Identify this sentence and explain why it doesn't belong.

1. Youth councils aren't unique, but listening to them is, says [Ian] Soutar, who makes a pointed jab that Justin Trudeau's youth council wasn't heard when they protested publicly over the government's $4.5 billion purchase of the Trans Mountain Pipeline. The party is trying to pave way for ever younger voters, literally. In 2018, May tabled a private member's bill that proposed to lower the voting age to 16, arguing that people that age are allowed to work, drive, and pay taxes. (In late September, NDP leader Jagmeet Singh proposed a similar lowering of the voting age.) The Greens are also working to ensure younger representation within its leadership, Soutar notes, pointing to the 43 Green Party candidates who are 29 or under—15 per cent of the slate. "We've got a tremendous number of kids not old enough to vote knocking on doors," May tells *Maclean's*. They are so dedicated and work so hard.

   Kingston, Anne. "How Millennials Could Power Elizabeth May's Greens." *Maclean's*, 7 Oct. 2019.

2. Multi-tasking has become one of the biggest myths of the twenty-first century. Everyone is expected to do it, as evidenced by the number of jobs requiring this skill. However, multi-tasking is not possible for humans. When that happens, the brain takes time to catch up to the new task. People, instead of being more productive, are actually losing valuable time. This can be seen when one tries to talk to someone playing a game on a smartphone, especially if asking questions. What actually happens is that the brain quickly switches between tasks. Often, responses barely relate to the question asked. If people are to be productive, it's time to stop buying into this myth.

Paragraph Coherence

It is often easy to identify a paragraph that contains off-topic ideas, but identifying a paragraph that lacks coherence may be more difficult. In a coherent paragraph, each sentence is skillfully connected to the next so that they stick together and convey a single idea.

A coherent paragraph is easy to follow because its sentences are connected to each other.

Here is the opening of an essay about the need for more research about the gig economy in Canada. Although the ideas are quite simple, the paragraph is difficult to follow. Try to determine why this is the case.

> **The gig economy has come to Canada. Jobs are easier to find. Jobs are often only contracts though.**

Now consider a rewritten version of this paragraph. Why is it easier to follow?

> **The gig economy has become part of the work world in Canada. In some ways, jobs have become easier to find, because of the number of companies advertising for people with specific skills. However, many of these gig jobs are only offered on a contract basis.**

Part of the problem in the original paragraph is that ideas are just placed on the page with little additional context. The careful use of repetition and transitions in the second example helps the words and ideas stick together. The writer has expanded on these ideas and added transitions, such as *however*, to connect ideas.

In another example, coherence is achieved largely through the use of repetition, rhythm, and parallel structures, all of which are discussed in the following sections.

> **Sailing can open your senses in a way that other sports cannot. The feel of the wind on your face, the warmth of the sunshine wrapping itself around you, and the motion of the waves bring you closer to nature than if you were sitting on shore. The quiet and solitude can lead to mindful reflection and inner peace. Perhaps this is why sailing has been romanticized for centuries and sports such as jogging have not.**

Word Choice

Often, more than one word can convey a similar meaning. As a writer, your task is to choose the best word within the context of your sentence, paragraph, or essay. Whenever you use a word that is not part of your everyday vocabulary, you should confirm its meaning by looking it up in a dictionary. Asking someone else to read your essay and circle unclear words can also help you choose better words. If you are using a thesaurus to look for similar words, you need to make sure the word you choose does indeed have the same meaning. Again, look the new word up in a dictionary.

TIP
Understanding the meaning of words is important to your writing. Poor word choice will prevent your reader from understanding your essay's message.

Chapter 1 discusses strategies for learning word meanings.

Translation dictionaries are helpful when looking up words that you may not know in English. However, do not rely on the translation dictionary to give you the appropriate word. Once you choose a new word, do a reverse look-up with the dictionary. Put the English word into your translator and see what the word means in your native language. It is also a good idea to look up the English word in an English-language dictionary and then examine the meanings. This will also help you make sure you have chosen the correct word. Often, translation dictionaries do not consider the context of what you have written, and the incorrect choice of words can confuse, or even worse, amuse, your audience. This will affect your credibility as a writer, and then your reader may ignore the well-crafted argument you make.

Logical Sentence Order

Through your writing, you share your thought process with your reader. To ensure your reader's understanding, your sentences and paragraphs need to be arranged in a logical order. If your ideas do not connect logically, the paragraph will be incoherent. Asking someone else to look for gaps in logic can help you write a better essay.

Repetition and Synonyms

Repeating key words or phrases in a paragraph reinforces your main idea and helps your reader understand it. Use alternative words and expressions, such as synonyms, to aid understanding. If you use a thesaurus, check a synonym's dictionary definition to ensure that the word is appropriate and matches your intended meaning. For example, you can write that "Professor Smith was *certain* that the experiment would work." A synonym for *certain* is the word *particular*, but replacing *certain* with *particular* in this sentence would not make sense.

Remember that selective repetition is not the same as being repetitious, which occurs when you needlessly repeat a word or an idea.

Parallel Structures

Experienced writers also use parallel, or balanced, structures to achieve coherence. Charles Dickens often employed this strategy: "It was the best of times; it was the worst of times" (*A Tale of Two Cities*). Parallel sentences can also repeat structures to make the ideas clearer, such as "In order for students to remain healthy, they should eat well, exercise regularly, and sleep enough."

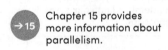

Chapter 15 provides more information about parallelism.

Find the logical gap in the following passage and add a linking sentence or phrase to make it coherent.

Electric and hybrid vehicles seem to be the future of transportation around the world. Little research has been done to determine how detrimental the batteries are and how to dispose of them. They are a step in the right direction though.

Coherence through sentence order

Examine the following sentences. Then, with a partner or in a group, add transitions to make the paragraphs unified and coherent. Transitions may be used to combine sentences or to introduce a sentence in a way that relates it to the previous one. Remove the one sentence that doesn't belong.

1. I was a child. My mother and I went strawberry picking. We both loved fresh strawberries right from the field. They were so delicious and sweet. She taught me how to choose the ripe ones. Not too ripe. They would spoil quickly. I wanted a puppy. We would have toast with fresh strawberries in the morning. We made jam together. I have grown my own strawberries. They don't taste as good. The ones I picked with my mom were the best.

2. Studying for final exams is hard. You have to review everything studied during the semester. One of my high school teachers taught me a great study method. Three weeks before the exam. Spend one week reviewing your notes. Make notes about information you don't remember really well. Make cheat sheets. Spend the next week reviewing that information. Make possible test questions. Don't worry about sports. The week before the exam, test yourself with the questions you made. Study for one hour each night. You will do well on your exams.

Coherence through transitions

Fill in the blanks in the following paragraph by choosing the appropriate transition from this list:

above all

but

for example (could be used twice)

in fact

moreover

unfortunately

Note: One transition has been given to you, and one should not be used in the paragraph.

Massive energy consumption is having a negative impact on the planet. _____, in 2019, Western Europe suffered many severe weather incidences. *Unfortunately*, these changed weather patterns are not an isolated occurrence. _____, almost every credible scientist today believes that the Earth is facing a climate crisis due to the emissions of greenhouse gases from cars, planes, and coal-burning power plants. Ninety per cent of the energy used in the US comes from fossil fuels: oil, coal, and natural gas, _____ problems arise from other sources, too. _____, nuclear power plants leave radioactive by-products, making storage difficult. _____, dams built to produce hydroelectric power are not much better as nearby populations must be relocated and the surrounding habitat is destroyed.

The following paragraph features repetition (in *italics*) and transitions (in **boldface**) to show you how the author built a coherent paragraph.

Over the centuries, the practice of *medicine* has changed. In Europe, in the twelfth century, people were bled to release negative humours. **In the Victorian era**, drugs like morphine and opium were used to *treat* infants with colic and even women who were deemed too emotional. **Along the way**, many aspiring salesmen sold homemade *remedies* claiming to *cure* everything from baldness to toothaches. There were also many herbal *elixirs* that were passed down through generations that seemed to work. Indigenous people too used many plants found in the wild to create *curatives*. **Over time**, *medicine* came to be ruled by science, and people developed a lot of *faith* in it. **Unfortunately**, in the late twentieth century people began to lose *confidence* in modern medicine. **Therefore**, they turned to more holistic treatments. However, those *practising* traditional medicine and those *providing* holistic medicinal treatments can never seem to accept that both types may provide relief to patients who need it. Both sides will often discount the other entirely. It is time that science returned to the study of nature so that patients can have a true idea of what works from the natural world and what is better treated in the more "traditional" sense. If both sides could work together, the practice of medicine will continue to *evolve*.

1. Identify the topic sentence, the repetitive devices, and transitions in this paragraph.

2. Do you think that the writer made a good choice of synonyms? Why or why not?

3. Based on the text, what topic do you think will be developed in the next paragraph? Give evidence to support your answer.

4. Are there any transitions that could be changed to make the piece more coherent? Give examples.

5. Are there any ideas that are unclear? Explain your answer.

6. Is the paragraph logical? Explain your answer.

7. Is there anything that could be added to increase the writer's credibility? Explain your answer.

8. Is there anything in the paragraph that disrupts the unity? Explain your answer.

9. Do you feel the paragraph is coherent? Explain your answer.

10. Is the paragraph unified? Explain your answer.

Identify the topic sentence, the repetitive devices, and transitions in the paragraph below. This is taken from the middle of an essay about the television show *The Sopranos*. Based on the transitions, what do you think the previous and following paragraphs are about? (Carnegie, Morgan, and Rockefeller made their fortunes through exploitation. They were among a group of wealthy men in the 1920s nicknamed "the Robber Barons.")

> In a sense, mafia films have always provided a critique of capitalism, beginning with the Depression-era classics *Little Caesar* (1931) and *Scarface* (1932), when the cruelties and dysfunctions of the system were obvious. During the economic crises of the 1970s, *The Godfather* (1972) and *The Godfather: Part 2* (1974) depicted the American Dream and criminal enterprise as essentially one and the same. It's a rationale that Tony Soprano has internalized, as is clear from the way he defends his line of work to his therapist, Dr. Melfi: "The Carnegies and the Rockefellers ... the J.P. Morgans—they were crooks and killers too, but that was a business, right? The American Way?" Even more than other works in the mafia genre, *The Sopranos* shows us criminality woven into the fabric of everyday life, as we overhear Tony's "respectable" neighbour Dr. Cusamano eagerly gathering insider trading tips at his own backyard barbeque.

Giavannone, Aaron. "We're All the Sopranos Now." *Maclean's*, 21 May 2020, https://www.macleans.ca/opinion/were-all-the-sopranos-now/.

Paragraph Purpose

Each of the paragraph styles below is created to serve a distinct purpose. They are used in an essay as body paragraphs to relate your supporting evidence to your thesis, and they offer variety that will interest your audience. Each one of these paragraph styles can also be extended as a pattern for an entire essay, as shown on the list in "Development Patterns" in Chapter 4.

Analogy

An **analogy** is a comparison between two objects that share a characteristic. The analogy helps the reader understand the original object. For example, you could compare fast food to the fast pace of modern society.

An **analogy** is a comparison that helps the reader to better understand the original object.

The following excerpt uses the analogy of a desert to stress the importance of water management in North America.

Imagine a hot, torturously dry desert. Throughout this arid wasteland, no life exists—not a tree, shrub, or animal alive. Though to many residents of Europe and North America this scenario may seem highly abstract and incomprehensible, it is the reality faced by many equatorial nations, such as China, Africa, Saudi Arabia, and parts of India. Residents of these nations have developed a keen understanding of the importance of water, and how best to manage it to enable a basic level of existence. However, residents of nations more endowed with water, such as Canada, seem largely indifferent to such a reality.

Student writer François Beaudet

Description

Description adds concrete, physical detail to an essay.

Description can be used at any point to add concrete, physical detail, but it should play a limited role. Try to evoke the five senses in your descriptions; for example, describe a hamburger from the top bun through its condiments and the meat to the lower bun, the smell of fried onions, the sizzle of the burger on the grill, the taste of the mustard and tomato, the roughness of the napkin as you wipe away the dripping ketchup from your chin. Concrete details help your reader "live" the experience.

This paragraph describes Fallingwater, a house designed by Frank Lloyd Wright.

Hoffman presents a visual image so that readers can imagine the building, even if they have never seen it.

When Wright came to the site he appreciated the powerful sound of the falls, the vitality of the young forest, the dramatic rock ledges and boulders; these were elements to be interwoven with the serenely soaring spaces of his structure. But Wright's insight penetrated more deeply. He understood that people were creatures of nature, hence an architecture which conformed to nature would conform to what was basic in people. For example, although all of Fallingwater is opened by broad bands of windows, people inside are sheltered as in a deep cave, secure in the sense of hill behind them. Their attention is directed toward the outside by low ceilings; no lordly hall sets the tone but, instead, the luminous textures of the woodland, rhythmically enframed. The materials of the structure blend with the colorings of rocks and trees, while occasional accents are provided by bright furnishings, like wildflowers or birds outside. The paths within the house, stairs and passages, meander without formality or urgency, and the house hardly has a main entrance; there are many ways in and out. Sociability and privacy are both available, as are the comforts of home and the adventures of the seasons. So people are cosseted into relaxing, into exploring the enjoyment of a life refreshed in nature. Visitors, too, in due measure experience Wright's architecture as an expansion of living.

Hoffman, D. (1993). *Frank Lloyd Wright's Fallingwater: The house and its history* (2nd rev. ed.). Dover.

Definition

Defining a topic not only tells the reader what you will be talking about but also helps you understand your topic better and organize your main points. You will often define in your opening paragraph, so that your audience is clear about the meaning of the terms you will use in your thesis and in your essay. If your topic is about the dangers of fast food, you need to define *fast food* for you and your reader. Does it mean a Big Mac or microwave meals? Both could be considered fast food. An entire essay can be focused on defining one term and expanding on that definition with examples that support the definition. In Chapter 6, definitions are used by John Jacobs in his expository essay.

In the following example, the writer concisely defines *cloud computing* and compares it to limited network computing to expand the definition.

> **Cloud computing is a technology that allows users to access information and documents without being tied to one computer or network. These clouds also allow users to share documents, and anyone can make changes as the need arises. Networks established within companies require users to log in to the company network where data is stored in order to access documents. Storage is often limited on these networks, and documents are difficult to update by many different users. Cloud computing, on the other hand, means that people can access many different networks and systems, and users can share documents with others easily. Multiple people can access shared documents and make simultaneous changes. Also, storage space can be increased, for a fee, as the user's needs increase. No longer is a person tied to one computer or network.**

Example/Illustration

Using concrete examples is a way of supporting a point and clarifying an abstract idea. Examples can often be combined with other methods, such as cause–effect, cost–benefit, or comparison and contrast (see "Development Patterns" in Chapter 4). If you were using the cause–effect method to develop the point that fast food saves valuable time (an effect), you might talk about the convenience of drive-throughs at fast-food restaurants. Examples are very important in most writing, whether they are brief expansions of a point or more fully developed explanations.

> **Brief expansion:**
>
> **Plagiarism can be the result of fear of failure, not understanding the materials being studied, lack of time management, or the attitude that everyone does it, so it's okay.**
>
> **Fully developed explanation:**
>
> **As long as there has been school, some students have cheated. Before the internet, cell phones, and smart watches, students wrote information on their shoes, on their clothes, on small bits of paper**

Defining a topic tells your reader what you will be discussing in your essay, helps you understand the topic better, and helps you organize your main points.

Using concrete examples is one of the best ways to support a point and clarify an abstract idea.

tucked away, and even on their skin. Many older people claim it was much harder to cheat when they were students, as they didn't have technological equipment to help them. For teachers, the age-old solution to needing to cheat is just to study.

Narration: How Can It Be Told?

Narration (the telling of a story) can be an effective way to introduce or reinforce your topic.

A story can lend drama to an argument or illustrate a point. Narrating an incident, or even including some dialogue, can be an effective way to introduce or reinforce your topic. Narration is used in personal essays but can also be used in other types, as in the following sample about the legendary origins of the Earth. Because description and narration are generally considered informal, ask your instructor before using them extensively in a formal essay.

> In the beginning, in the Sky World, a pregnant wife asked her husband to fetch delicacies she craved. But she wanted the bark of a root of the Great Tree in the middle of Sky World, which none were permitted to touch. Finally, however, he gave in, and scraped away soil to bare the root of the tree. Underneath was a hole, and as the woman peered down into it, she fell through. The birds helped transport her as she fell, and the great Sea Turtle received her on his back. Here, on the Sea Turtle's back, she planted bits of roots and plants she had brought from the Sky World. And she walked across the turtle's back, planting, praying, and creating the Earth that we know as Turtle Island.

Crystal Links. (n.d.). *Iroquois story of creation.* https://www.crystallinks.com/iroquoiscreation.html

Personal: Why Should It Affect Me?/ How Does It Affect Me?

A personal paragraph focuses on an aspect of the writer's life or a relevant experience.

A personal paragraph focuses on an aspect of the writer's life or a significant experience that illustrates the thesis of an essay. In a successful personal paragraph, the writer is able to make their experience seem relevant to the reader. However, don't use this method in a formal essay. This paragraph style is typically used in personal essays or when writing an opinion or argumentative essay.

To present your personal experience with fast-food restaurants, you might consider your childhood visits to them, when the busy, exciting atmosphere was more important to you than the food. Student writer Brian Gregg begins his personal/expository essay on college binge drinking with a recent personal experience; such an approach would be particularly appropriate if his audience were mostly college or university students.

> Exam time is approaching at my college, and stress levels are at an annual high. For this reason, when Friday night arrives, I know I will be drinking—and I definitely will not be alone. Last weekend, my friends and I went to a typical residence party. If I can remember correctly, there were about 15 people noisily crowded into a room the size of a large closet, and many more were herded in the hallways. According to a study in the *American Journal of Public Health*, today's North American college students have the highest binge

drinking rate of any group, even when compared to their peers who do not go to school; furthermore, alcohol is associated with many social problems on college campuses and is the most widespread and preventable health issue for the more than six million students in America (Wechsler et al., 1995, p. 921).

The essay "Everything You Need to Know about Impostor Syndrome" was written for a general audience; its purpose is to show the readers that feeling like an impostor is common but can be avoided. When reading the piece, consider whether the author meets the criteria for good paragraphs. Are the points linked logically? How successfully does the language help you better understand the article? Note how the author has included definition, example, narrative, and description in this essay.

Everything You Need to Know about Impostor Syndrome

Sydney Loney

Sydney Loney

Sample Professional Essay
Good Paragraphs

[1] Tara Sutton is an award-winning war correspondent and documentary filmmaker from Toronto. She has a master's degree in journalism from New York's Columbia University, and she was the first foreign reporter to enter Fallujah, Iraq, after the siege in 2004 to document human rights abuses during the Iraq War. She's also given talks all over the world. But, sometimes, Sutton feels like a fraud.

> The author introduces the topic with a real-life example that many people can understand or sympathize with, creating interest.

[2] "When I was in Iraq, I was the only video journalist and I was freelancing," says Sutton. "Everybody else had security experts and crews and flak jackets, and I didn't have any of that stuff. I'd lie there at night thinking, 'You're so useless. You don't know what you're doing. Why are you even here?' I always felt so inferior, like I wasn't as qualified as everyone else."

What Is It?

> Loney uses headings to notify the reader what is coming. This technique is often used in longer essays and reports so that readers can identify sections of interest quickly.

[3] Though impostor phenomenon, or impostor syndrome, as it's commonly called, was first identified in 1978 to describe high-achieving people who dismiss, minimize, or ignore evidence of their abilities, Sutton only recognized the symptoms in herself after reading an article about it in *The New York Times*. Since then, high-profile people—from Mike Myers (who famously said, "I still expect that the no-talent police will come and arrest me") to Facebook COO Sheryl Sandberg—have publicly admitted that they had a problem.

> In this paragraph, the author defines impostor syndrome.

[4] In an article published in the *International Journal of Behavioral Science*, research estimates that 70 per cent of us will, at least once in our lives, fear being exposed as frauds, no matter how successful we are. "People who feel like impostors have a hard time internalizing and owning their accomplishments and, instead, ascribe them to things like luck, timing, connections or computer error," says Valerie Young, the author of *The Secret Thoughts of Successful Women: Why Capable People Suffer from the Impostor Syndrome and How to Thrive in Spite of It*.

> The writer introduces statistics about the syndrome and includes quotes from an expert, balancing the anecdotal examples from the previous paragraphs.

[5] These feelings are especially common for students and people in creative fields such as writing, acting, and music. "You're judged subjectively and are perceived as being only as good as your last book, film, show or assignment," says Young. "You have to continually prove yourself in ways you wouldn't if you were in an accounting department or in customer service." That self-doubt is also more common among women, minorities, and people who grew up poor or working class. "Whenever you're in a group for whom there are stereotypes about competence, you're more susceptible," says Young.

How to Make Impostor Syndrome Work for You

[6] Alicia Liu first blogged about her brush with impostor syndrome in 2013, and she has revisited the topic several times since. The Canadian computer programmer, who now lives in San Francisco, wrote about how feeling like a fake made her reluctant to speak up for fear of sounding stupid. "The stakes were even higher because I was the only female engineer on nearly every team I've been on, so I felt I was representing my gender," she wrote. "I quietly avoided doing things I didn't think I'd be good at, even though the only way to get better is to do them." That's one of the problems with impostor syndrome—it can hold you back from learning. It may even make you overprepare, which "leads to unnecessary work and potential burnout," says Liu.

[7] But Pamela Catapia, a registered clinical counsellor in Vancouver, says there can be benefits to feeling this way. "If you have impostor syndrome, you're likely a caring, conscientious, talented person who has both the desire and the capacity to improve the world," she says. She points to her clients as evidence; many of them tell her they feel like impostors, but, for the most part, they're actually extremely competent with unrecognized or underutilized leadership skills.

[8] While Catapia admits that impostor syndrome can lead to procrastination, self-sabotage, anxiety and overwork, she says it is possible to make those feelings work for you. The secret is to recognize the good and the bad of impostor syndrome—and hang on to the good. "If overpreparing for things is working, keep that strategy. But if you're feeling burned out and exhausted, dial it down," she says. Young agrees. "I don't like to hear people say 'stop being a perfectionist,' because that's not helpful. You do things because you're getting something out of it. So I ask people, 'What's the good part about being a perfectionist that you want to keep?' If you care deeply about the quality of your work—not everyone does—keep that part, but let go of any shame you might feel over minor and very human imperfections."

[9] Sutton credits impostor syndrome with helping her become a better journalist, though she didn't realize it at the time. "The benefit of feeling that way is that I asked so many questions. I had no assumptions that I knew what was going on," she says. "It also led me to do a lot more listening than talking."

[10] There are still days when Sutton's self-doubt resurfaces, especially when it comes to public speaking. "Whenever I start to write a speech, I feel like I don't have anything to say. Now I know it's just a feeling, but in the beginning, I believed it was true."

Make Peace with Your Inner Critic

[11] Though impostor syndrome can push us to achieve, it can also do more harm than good, leading to anxiety, procrastination and burnout. Here's what to do if the negatives start to outweigh the positives.

1. Know That You're Normal

[12] We often assume that struggling with confidence in a new situation is proof that we're impostors, says self-help speaker and author Valerie Young. But those feelings are normal. "Of course you're going to feel off base at first," she says. "If you're starting a new job, instead of thinking, 'I don't belong here,' try, 'This is going to be hard for a while. This is new for me, and mastering or taking on new things is hard.'" She adds that, unless you're a narcissist, you should have feelings of self-doubt every now and then. "If it's your first time doing something, you haven't had time to develop the confidence that comes from prior experience."

2. Put It in Context

[13] Consider why feelings of inadequacy are there in the first place, says computer programmer Alicia Liu. "It's not merely a personal issue—though impostor syndrome is too often framed as purely personal. For me, it also reflected the discrimination and stereotyping in the tech industry and wider culture." Your own experience may be rooted in childhood or exacerbated by dismissive co-workers or cultural stereotypes. "You need to sort through your beliefs about yourself and your talents and to examine which belong to you and which came from others," says clinical counsellor Pamela Catapia. "Think about the beliefs that protect, guide and encourage you to grow versus the ones that shame and control you and keep you stuck." When you acknowledge how other people's attitudes might be holding you back, it's easier to feel worthy and confident.

3. Change Your Mind

[14] "If you want to stop feeling like an impostor, you have to stop thinking like one," says Young. "This means reframing the way you think about competence, failure and fear. If you get an assignment that feels beyond you, instead of thinking, 'I have no idea what I'm doing,' the reframe is, 'Wow! I'm really going to learn a lot,'" she says. And remember, your body doesn't know the difference between fear and excitement—sweaty palms and a dry throat come from both. "As you're walking to the podium or going to meet with your boss, just keep thinking, 'I'm excited.' The best part is that, over time, you will be."

Loney, Sydney. "Everything You Need to Know about Impostor Syndrome." Canadian Living, Nov. 2016, http://www.canadianliving.com/life-and-relationships/money-and-career/article/everything-you-need-to-know-about-impostor-syndrome. Reprinted with permission from Sydney Loney.

The writer recalls the previous discussion before continuing with advice for handling impostor syndrome.

By separating the main points of advice with numbered headings, Loney draws attention to them and makes it easier for readers to retain the information.

Notice that Loney repeats the credentials of the people quoted, reinforcing their position.

The article uses a description of how fear and excitement feel plus examples of stressful situations with which the reader can easily identify.

The article ends on a positive note, which reiterates the point that impostor syndrome can be overcome.

Post-Reading Questions

1. Choose two paragraphs in Loney's essay. Do they meet the criteria of paragraph unity? Summarize the central idea of each paragraph.
2. Does the writer use paragraph wraps successfully? Give two examples to support your answer.
3. Give examples of two transitions used by the author. What purpose do these transitions serve?
4. The author used personal stories of their own and others' struggles with impostor syndrome. How do you think that adding this information helped keep the audience interested?
5. Does Loney conclude the essay effectively? Give reasons to support your answer.
6. Give some examples of repetition the author uses. What type of repetition is this?
7. Are there any examples of needless repetition that you can find? Explain.
8. Find five words that you may not be familiar with. Look them up in a dictionary, and then try to find a synonym in a thesaurus.
9. Does the author maintain coherence throughout the essay? What methods are used to ensure that the writing is understandable?
10. How do you feel about the essay overall? Could the author have improved it? Explain your answer.

Chapter Review Questions

1. What tools can you use to write a coherent paragraph? Write an example of two of them.
2. What is the purpose of using transitions when writing paragraphs?
3. What is the purpose of a topic sentence?
4. Why are concluding sentences or paragraph wraps important?
5. Why is paragraph unity important?
6. What are synonyms? How can synonyms help your reader's understanding? Why should you always check a synonym's meaning in the dictionary?
7. List the seven purposes of transitions. For each one, write a sentence correctly using one of the suggested transitions.
8. Using the topic "homework" write a paragraph (five to seven sentences) using one of the six paragraph styles.
9. Why is it important to ensure you are using the proper words?
10. How can having someone else read your essay be beneficial?
11. Why is using repetition valuable for the reader? Explain why your paragraph meets the criteria of that style.

Paragraph and Essay Development

By the end of this chapter, you should be able to

- identify organizational patterns for writing paragraphs and essays;
- apply the stages of essay writing;
- develop an essay through substantial paragraphs; and
- combine organizational methods within an essay.

Well-developed essays are built on unified, coherent paragraphs and written with a specific audience in mind. Your audience expects a logically developed essay and an appropriate level of language that communicates your ideas clearly. In this chapter you will learn strategies for pre-writing, researching, organizing, and composing your essay. You will also explore the organizational patterns that will help you develop your ideas and connect with your audience.

▲ Photo: locrifa/Shutterstock

Developing Your Essay

As discussed in Chapter 3, an effective paragraph is

TIP

A unified paragraph or essay focuses on one topic. A coherent essay provides logical connections so the reader can follow the writer's train of thought. Well-developed writing contains supporting information organized in a consistent pattern.

- *unified*; it focuses on one topic.
- *coherent*; it makes sense and provides logical connections so the reader can follow the writer's train of thought.
- *well developed*; it contains supporting information that is organized in a consistent pattern and thoroughly expands a point.

The same applies to an essay: an essay focuses on one topic, with each body paragraph explaining a particular part.

EAL

> Western logic is based on making a statement and then providing proof that the statement is well supported and relevant. Providing proof and relevance is necessary in most Western writing.

The following paragraph from an essay about the opioid crisis clearly illustrates these concepts. The author connects the crisis to those affected, showing unity. Repeated words, such as *people* and *Canadians*, and synonyms, such as *crisis* and *issue*, provide coherence. Finally, the paragraph is well developed, as it illustrates the origins of the opioid crisis before discussing the common attitudes of people toward addicts, which get in the way of finding a solution, the essay's main focus.

> **Chronic pain sufferers have been offered opium-based drugs for over a century. However, when it was discovered that these drugs were highly addictive and sought after by others for their psychoactive components, doctors stopped prescribing them and turned to older, and often less-effective medications. Those who used opioids were set adrift and forced to use the black market to obtain relief. The opioid crisis now affects people from small towns to large cities. People of all ages are dying daily. Unfortunately, not many people are willing to tackle this issue, and some wish to pretend that this will not affect them, other than seeing users on the street or finding needles and other drug materials on the streets or in parks. Users are now forced to the edges of society where those not wishing to engage in the issue can mostly ignore it—except to complain about the homeless addicts in the community.**

The development pattern determines how an essay or a paragraph will be organized.

Choosing the appropriate development pattern for essays and paragraphs is one of the keys to writing a successful essay. For example, if you are writing an essay to persuade an audience who may not agree with your point of view, you could use your less controversial arguments in your first body paragraph and move to the more controversial ones in later paragraphs. The development patterns discussed in the next sections can be used for both body paragraphs and essays.

— EXERCISE 4.1

Choose a body paragraph from one of the essays in this textbook. Identify how the author creates unified, coherent, and well-developed paragraphs. Look for transitions connecting one paragraph to the next and to the essay as a whole. Identify the main ideas of the paragraphs and their development. Can you follow the author's train of thought? What areas, if any, could be improved? Be prepared to explain your answer to a classmate or your instructor.

Development Patterns

A topic influences an essay's or a paragraph's organization. For example, the topic "Which is more important at college or university: acquiring skills or getting good grades?" indicates a comparison and contrast organization pattern where you compare the values of skills and grades. A topic such as "Solutions to the problem of homeless people" could use the problem–solution pattern in which a problem is defined and solutions offered.

Asking the questions in Table 4.1 will help you choose which pattern will work best for your topic. Each question will guide your choice of development pattern. If your topic is "fast food," you could use any of these methods to develop it. Further explanations of the more commonly used patterns of development follow Table 4.1.

TIP

The topic of the essay may determine the organization, but each paragraph may use a different pattern.

The chapters in Part Two discuss the types and components of essays.

TABLE 4.1 Questions and Patterns of Development

Question	Pattern of Development
What is it?	Definition
When did it occur?	Chronology (time)
What does it look like?	Description
How can it be told?	Narration
How do you do it? or How does it work?	Process ("how to")
Why should/does it affect me?	Personal
What kinds/categories are there?	Classification/division
What causes/accounts for it? What is the result/effect?	Cause–effect
What is the answer?	Question–answer
How can it be shown?	Example/illustration
How can it be (re)solved?	Problem–solution
What are the advantages/disadvantages?	Cost–benefit
How is it like something else?	Analogy
How is it like and/or unlike something else?	Comparison and contrast

Chronology: When Did It Occur?

Chronology means tracing a topic's development over time.

A chronological pattern shows development over time. When did fast food first appear? When did it truly begin to affect people's lives? Tracing the evolution of fast food in the last 25 years might provide the audience with an appreciation of how the industry has changed.

The following paragraph uses chronology to discuss the evolution of the telephone:

> Alexander Graham Bell is known as the inventor of the telephone. His experiments with hearing devices led to his invention. The telephone revolutionized communication, but only if one was home to receive a call. Messages taken by other family members could often be lost or forgotten, which is why some families had bulletin boards or notepads beside their phones. Early phone users had to dial the operator in order to place a phone call to someone. These operators then manually plugged lines into a large board to connect callers. (They could also listen to the call and catch up on the latest "news" in the community.) Eventually operators were replaced by electronic connectors, but the problem still remained of missing the message if you weren't home. In 1950s, a Japanese inventor, Kazuo Hashimoto, created answering machines. Now, even if one wasn't home, messages could be left. However, more was to come. In 1973, Martin Cooper from Motorola used the first cell phone (Loeffer, 2019). These early cell phones were large and cumbersome, but gradually became smaller and more convenient. These phones allowed people to be connected to the world all the time. The development of the telephone and the subsequent technologies have allowed people to remain connected, no matter where they are.

References

Loeffer, John. "The History behind the Invention of the First Cell Phone." *Interesting Engineering*, 25 Aug. 2019, https://interestingengineering.com/the-history-behind-the-invention-of-the-first-cell-phone.

"Kazuo Hashimoto: Japanese Inventor." Peoplepill, https://peoplepill.com/people/kazuo-hashimoto/.

Process: How Does It Work?

Explaining a process focuses on the steps in a sequence.

See Chapter 6 for a description and sample of a process essay.

A process essay explains the step-by-step stages of a process. The steps are listed in chronological order. Using the fast-food topic, you could describe the process of making burgers from the time a customer places an order to the time they receive the food.

The following is a process paragraph.

> When you change a tire on your vehicle, the first thing to ensure is safety. The car or truck should be moved to the side of the road, well away from traffic. The jack, often found on top of the spare tire, is removed from the trunk and then placed under a sturdy part of the vehicle near the flat tire, to allow access to the tire. The ground must be level so that the jack does not fall over when the vehicle is raised. The next step involves loosening the bolts on the flat tire with a lug wrench, also found with the spare. Once the bolts are loosened and the jack is on a level surface, use it to lift the car, so that access to the

flat tire is possible. The flat tire is then removed and replaced with a new tire. The bolts are put back on and tightened slightly with the lug wrench. Once this is accomplished, the jack can be lowered, and the bolts tightened further. Place the old tire, the jack, and the lug wrench inside the vehicle, and drive carefully down the road.

Classification/Division: What Kinds Are There?

In classification or division, you begin with many items—for example, commonly known members of the animal kingdom—which you organize into more manageable groups: mammals, birds, fish, reptiles, and amphibians. Each category could in turn be organized into still smaller units. For mammals, these groups could be rodents, primates, and carnivores. Fast-food burgers can easily be classified into hamburgers, chicken burgers, fish burgers, or veggie burgers. The differences could be analyzed by applying the same criteria to each category.

Classification focuses on a large number of items that can be organized into more manageable groups.

Division breaks the subject into parts for better understanding of the whole.

In division, you are concerned with the whole instead of the individual parts. You break a subject into parts in order to better understand or explain the whole (the subject). For example, to illustrate how essay structure works, you can divide it into introduction, body paragraphs, and conclusion. The paragraph on cloud computing (see "Definition" in Chapter 3) uses division to explain the difference between types of data saving.

Cause–Effect: What Is the Cause? What Is the Result?

You can use the cause–effect method to organize an entire essay or to analyze a main point in one or more paragraphs. Cause–effect might focus on one effect, which would be the result of one or more causes. For example, someone's successful athletic career could be the result of good coaching, hours of practice, dedication, determination, a supportive family, etc. On the other hand, you could focus on one cause and consider one or more effects, such as a diet of fast food (cause) resulting in obesity, high blood pressure, and higher cholesterol levels (effects). Cause–effect studies are particularly common in the sciences.

A **cause–effect** essay or paragraph might focus on one effect, which would be accounted for by one or more causes, or focus on one cause and consider one or more effects.

The antecedent–consequent organizational method uses time–order relationships in a similar way. For example, many people will be reflecting on their lives before and after the COVID-19 crisis. The following excerpt discusses one cause for stress in first-year students.

The **antecedent–consequent** organizational method includes an antecedent (a preceding event, condition, or cause) and its consequence (result).

> **A major cause of stress in first-year students is the need to establish a new social base. Students not only find themselves among strangers but also often have to rely on these strangers for moral support. Consequently, friendships tend to be forged rapidly but superficially. When students inevitably find themselves dealing with mid-terms, assignments, and an increasingly heavy course load, they need close friends and family for support but are forced to turn to these new acquaintances instead. Intense friendships may be formed during such times, but often the stress is insurmountable, leading students to give up and head home.**

Student writer Alexis Parker

┌─ **TIP**
│ *Antecedent* means something
│ that comes before. You could
│ look at this pattern as "A
│ happens and then B follows."
└─

Question–Answer: What Is the Answer?

The question–answer method involves posing questions and explaining their answers. Questions such as Who? What? When? Where? Why? and How? can be applied to almost any topic.

The question–answer method is effective when you ask a question in the topic sentence and answer it in the paragraph. Questions such as Who? What? When? Where? Why? and How? can be applied to any topic. Posing a relevant question engages the audience because it invites an answer. For the topic of fast food, a question might be "Why are different fast-food restaurants always built so close to each other?"

In the following excerpt, the writer poses two questions, which suggest the essay will focus on technological advances.

> **Are electric cars the solution to pollution? Are self-driving cars an effective way to reduce congestion on city streets and highways? With the world's climate warming rapidly, we need to try new ideas rather than relying on what has been done in the past.**

Problem–Solution: How Can It Be (Re)Solved?

The problem–solution method of development could focus on a problem, a solution to a problem, or both a problem and a solution.

The problem–solution pattern could focus on a problem, a solution to a problem, or both a problem and a solution. A problem with fast food is its nutritional value; proposing ways to make it healthier combines this development pattern with example/illustration. In business, this is the typical pattern of a case study. You begin by describing a problem that a customer had, and then you show how your company's product provided a successful solution.

In the following sentences, the author states the problems of and suggests an alternative solution to fast food.

> **The problem with fast food, either from restaurants or the microwavable meal aisle, is the lack of nutrients and the high sodium content. While many students are often too tired to cook when they come home, there are ways to have a nutritious, home-cooked meal. Purchasing a slow cooker gives the student the option to add ingredients to the pot in the morning, to turn on the machine before class, and to come home to a delicious meal.**

Cost–Benefit: What Are the Advantages and Disadvantages?

Cost–benefit analysis involves studying a topic's pros and cons.

Cost–benefit analysis can be applied to almost any topic and begins with analyzing it to determine its advantages and disadvantages. You could apply this method to fast food by weighing the benefits, such as convenience and price, against the costs in terms of long-term health issues. In an expository essay, the analysis approaches the pros and cons objectively. However, if you are writing an argumentative or a persuasive essay, you will choose to emphasize the importance of one over the other, for example, that the costs to people's health far outweigh the benefits of consuming fast food. If you took the opposing position, you might begin with benefits, as student writer

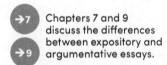

Chapters 7 and 9 discuss the differences between expository and argumentative essays.

Jutta Kolhi does in her argumentative essay on genetically modified organisms (GMOs).

EAL

> An argumentative essay does not mean to have an argument. It means that you are presenting your point of view and then convincing the reader that your point of view is valid. The goal may be not to change your reader's mind but to introduce them to a new way of thinking.

Some scientists believe that releasing GMOs into the environment could reduce pesticide use since crops could be genetically modified to produce a toxin against the pests. Unfortunately, such a toxin could have adverse effects on other organisms, such as the pollinator species of the plant. Some believe that genetic engineering could reduce hunger in Third World countries by allowing more food production. However, after growing genetically modified crops, the farmer would be unable to save some seeds to grow more crops because the seeds that GMOs produce are sterile, forcing the farmer to buy new seeds every year—an unrealistic expense. Furthermore, introducing GMOs in Third World countries would be risky, as most countries have limited resources and few safety measures in place for controlling GMOs.

Comparison and Contrast: How Is It Like and/or Unlike Something Else?

Comparison and contrast essays explain the similarities and differences between two things. When you compare and contrast, you first look for logical criteria for comparison. In arguing that one fast-food restaurant is better than another, logical criteria would be prices, food quality, cleanliness, and staff friendliness.

The following paragraph compares the cultures of Canada and the United States.

While these countries together occupy most of North America and were initially settled by Europeans, the two countries differ in a number of ways. Though both countries hold free elections to choose their representatives and leaders, the United States is a federal democratic republic and Canada has a parliamentary system. The US also waged a revolutionary battle to escape from Britain's rule, but Canada remained part of the British Empire after Confederation and eventually chose to become part of the Commonwealth. The US has distinct cultural divisions even today between its North and South, while Canada tends to be divided by language, religion, and east-to-west regions. The final difference that many mention is that the US is a cultural melting pot, while Canada celebrates diversity. Therefore, while these countries share a continent, the makeup of the countries is different.

Comparison and contrast involves finding logical criteria for comparison and then analyzing their similarities and differences.

 See Chapter 6 for a description and sample of a comparison and contrast essay.

Look at the topic "video games." Your topic sentence depends on the development method you choose. Here are some examples:

- *Definition*: Players of video games manipulate images on a screen using hand-held technology.
- *Chronology*: The first video game, Pong, was invented in 1958.
- *Description or narration*: The lights in the room are dimmed, the screen is alive with colour, and Jess begins her adventure to rescue Zelda.
- *Process*: For serious gamers, the first step to enjoy gaming is choosing the best computer.
- *Personal*: When I was in school, I looked forward to riding on the bus, so I could play games on my phone.
- *Classification*: Video games are rated for various audiences, such as "Everyone," "Teen," and "Mature."
- *Cause–effect*: Many people believe that playing video games results in isolation and addiction.
- *Question–answer*: What makes fans loyal to one particular game franchise?
- *Problem–solution*: To combat parental resistance to long hours of gaming, teens need to remind parents of the benefits of gaming, such as increased memory, improved cognition, and improved mental well-being.
- *Cost–benefit*: Though video games are expensive, they provide hours of entertainment, escape, and new challenges to overcome.
- *Analogy*: Playing video games is like having a vacation in the fantasy world of your dreams.
- *Comparison and contrast*: The loyalty that gamers have for their favourite games is very similar to the dedication of today's fans for the singers and bands that they follow.

With these examples in mind, write at least three different topic sentences for three items in the following list. Use a different organizational method for each sentence.

    animal rights

    carbon taxing

    climate change

    evolution of trolling

    exercise

    hacking

    organ transplants

    privacy

    public speaking

    sports violence

stress

technology

text messaging

the LGBTQ2+ movement

vaping

Essay Writing

To write an interesting, informative essay, you must consider your audience, as discussed in Chapter 3. You also need to decide how to make the essay logical and easy to follow for your readers. You need to use writing patterns that will help you organize your essay into a unified, coherent, and well-developed whole. Therefore, you need to understand not only paragraph development but also the stages involved in developing your essay so that you choose and develop ideas that will connect with your audience.

Stages in Essay Writing

An essay consists of an introduction containing a thesis statement, body paragraphs, and a concluding paragraph that restates the thesis. To help your audience understand the ideas you want to present in your essay, you need to carefully choose and organize your supporting material. Essay writing requires five stages:

Body paragraphs are the middle paragraphs of an essay that help prove the thesis by presenting facts, arguments, or other support.

1. *pre-writing (inventing)*: finding a topic and developing a thesis statement
2. *researching*: finding background information and supporting evidence (this could involve intensive library resources or simply examining and explaining your knowledge about a topic)
3. *organizing*: determining the order of points; outlining
4. *composing (writing drafts)*: putting your ideas in paragraph form and rewriting for clarity and coherence
5. *revising (final draft)*: editing for EETS (see "Revising the Final Draft" below), ensuring correct formatting, and proofreading

You should always plan for enough revision time to ensure that your writing is mechanically correct, using the proper font type and size and correct page set-up. Instructors may have a preferred font type and size, such as Arial 12, but generally, you will follow the standard page set-up found in word processing programs. Essays are usually double spaced, so you need to set that up before you begin composing your drafts.

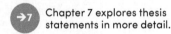

→7 Chapter 7 explores thesis
statements in more detail.

TIP

Pre-writing helps you clarify your thoughts about a subject, generate useful ideas, create your thesis, and discover your main points.

A **subject** is a broad category that contains several possible topics.

A **topic** is narrower, or more focused, than a subject.

A **thesis statement** is even more focused because it makes a specific comment on the topic or tells the reader how you will approach it.

Pre-Writing

Pre-writing strategies help you clarify your thoughts about a subject and enable you to think of useful ideas. Pre-writing often helps you generate a possible thesis statement and discover your main points.

If your instructor hasn't given you a topic, the pre-writing stage begins with finding one. You need to recognize the difference between a subject and a topic. A subject is a broad category— such as modern technology, climate change, alternative energy sources, the internet, and changing weather patterns—that contains many potential topics. A topic is narrower, or more focused. Examples include the pros and cons of using Zoom, the increased threat of forest fires in northern Canada, wind turbines and their impact on farming, three search engines you should use instead of Google, or climate change and its impact on fluctuating weather patterns.

A thesis statement is even more focused because it makes a specific comment about the topic or tells the reader how you will approach it. Sometimes a thesis is developed by considering a cause and an effect; for example, "the lack of censorship from the social media networks causes the spread of misinformation," "climate change causes forest fires," "the pandemic caused artists to find creative ways to reach their audience."

A thesis can also be discovered by choosing a topic and asking "What three things about this topic will be of interest to my readers?" If you begin with the subject of food and then narrow that subject to edible insects, you must still ask "What about edible insects will be interesting to my readers?" After brainstorming and some more research, you learn the following: raising insects requires less land and water than other proteins sources such as cattle and pigs, insects emit less greenhouse gas, and edible insects have excellent nutritional value. Now you can form a thesis that focuses on edible insects and explains what you will be telling your readers about the topic: "More people should start to consider insects as a food source because raising them uses less land and water and results in fewer harmful greenhouse gases, and edible insects offer excellent nutritional value."

Figure 4.1 visualizes the relationship among subject, topic, and thesis, and Table 4.2 offers examples of each category.

A look at the first example in Table 4.2 will help illustrate the differences. The writer wants to write about popular music. This is a subject because it covers a wide range of ideas and interests. You could take this subject of popular music and brainstorm many topics, such as the origins of hip hop, learning to play electric guitar, music streaming services, favourite musicians, concert experiences, etc. This writer chose the topic "popular music of the '60s," but discussing 10 years of music is still too big a topic for an essay. What about '60s music could be of interest to a reader? Is there a cause and effect that could be explored? Finally, the writer develops a thesis: "The popular music of the '60s was influenced by the politics of the time, including civil rights unrest, a rising demand for women's rights, and anti-war protests." This thesis has narrowed the topic of popular music to popular music in the 1960s and narrowed the focus again to look at this

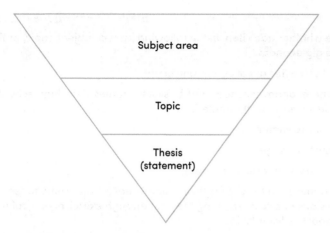

FIGURE 4.1 Subjects versus topics

music through the lens of politics. The thesis also contains a comment that narrows the essay's focus to only three political issues: civil rights, women's rights, and anti-war protests. Now, the writer has a clear focus for research and knows how the essay will be structured with paragraphs relating to the three political issues.

TABLE 4.2 Subject, Topic, and Thesis

Subject	Topic	Thesis
Popular music	Popular music of the '60s	The popular music of the '60s was influenced by the politics of the time, including civil rights unrest, a rising demand for women's rights, and anti-war protests.
Censorship	Censorship in the digital age	Censorship of misleading information is the responsibility of the owners of social media networks.
Social media	The amount of information available on social media	Social media helps conspiracy theorists spread misinformation.
The pandemic	The livelihoods of people affected by the pandemic	While protecting themselves and others, musicians used their creativity to reach their audience, including filming virtual concerts, teaching music online, and performing in outdoor spaces with a socially distanced audience.
Climate change	The effects of climate change	Forest fires in California and western Canada are a direct result of climate change.
Food	Year-round fresh fruit and vegetables	Having fresh fruit and vegetables in grocery stores year-round has negative effects on the economy, the environment, and transport infrastructures.
Stress	Student stress	Organization, planning, and networking can help first-year students who are stressed by the number of assignments and projects that are part of their programs.

Decide whether each item in the following list is a subject, topic, or thesis.

1. The gig economy

2. First semester at college or university

3. Home economics, shop, and business studies help high school students become well rounded.

4. Favourite winter sports

5. Climate change

6. Jazz has an interesting history.

7. Students need to care for their mental health by learning to recognize the signs of stress, ensuring they get enough exercise, and cultivating supportive friendships.

8. Pets

9. Therapy pets

10. The benefits of gaming include increased creativity, enhanced visual-spatial skills, and improved problem-solving.

TIP

All pre-writing strategies could be considered meeting places between you and your topic. Because they are designed to "free up" your thoughts and feelings, don't hesitate to experiment or vary these methods.

Questioning is a pre-writing strategy that helps you create a possible thesis as a specific question or series of questions that you will try to answer.

Pre-writing strategies will help you develop your topic. Pre-writing involves questioning, brainstorming, freewriting, or mind mapping.

Though you may not have used any of these before, by trying them now, you may find that some of these work for you.

Questioning

Questioning is often a good strategy for an expository (or explanatory) essay in the sciences and social sciences. Your thesis can be a specific question or series of questions that you try to answer. These questions are often turned into statements for your final version of the thesis.

Asking yourself the following questions will help you find a subject, which you can then start to narrow down into a topic:

- Where do my interests lie? What are my hobbies, leisure pursuits, reading interests, extracurricular activities? Even if you choose a familiar topic, you will still need to do research.
- What would I like to learn more about?
- Are sufficient sources available? As well as checking journals, the internet, and library resources, you can also use questionnaires, interviews, experts, statistics, etc.
- What topic might other people like to learn about? What topic could benefit society or a specific group (for example, students at my college or university)?
- Can I think of a new angle on an old topic? For example, "screen time can be beneficial rather than problematic, as most claim."

Once you have determined a subject, you can learn more about it by asking the traditional journalistic questions (Who? What? When? Where? Why? and How?). Let's say your subject is "roommates." Your questions might look like this:

- Who are the best (or worst) roommates?
- What are the qualities of an ideal roommate?
- When is the best time to start looking for a roommate?
- Where can you find a roommate?
- Why are roommates necessary (or unnecessary)?
- How do you get along with a roommate?

From your questions, you could narrow your topic to "four qualities of an ideal roommate" or "why having a signed roommate agreement is a good idea." To create a thesis from one of these topics, you need to explain what you are going to tell your reader about the topic, for example:

- The ideal roommate is responsible, tidy, flexible, and honest.
- Having a signed roommate agreement helps roommates organize chores, outline responsibilities, and avoid arguments.

Brainstorming

Brainstorming is an effective idea generator that can be done alone or in groups. In collaborative projects, all participants can give input.

When brainstorming, you write any words, phrases, or sentences that you associate with a subject. Write any ideas that you think of, and do not stop to edit ideas. Do this for 5 to 10 minutes. When you stop writing, go through your ideas and see if there are ways to connect or group them. These connections may need more brainstorming, or they could form one of the supporting paragraphs of your essay. If you still feel you do not have enough ideas, repeat the steps until you have enough ideas for your essay.

Brainstorming can be combined with other pre-writing methods. For example, after asking the journalistic questions about roommates, you could brainstorm answers to "What are the qualities of an ideal roommate?" If you narrow your answer to three or four qualities, brainstorm about each of them to find examples and further ideas that could be used in your body paragraphs.

Brainstorming is writing words, phrases, or sentences that you associate with a subject without stopping to edit your ideas.

Freewriting

In freewriting, you write without stopping for a span of time, usually 5 to 10 minutes. If you don't have a topic, freewrite to see where your thoughts lead you. You can also begin with a specific topic. If you start writing about something else, don't edit your ideas. Don't worry about spelling or grammar either. Just allow your ideas to flow. There is no need for any punctuation or capital letters.

Freewriting means writing without stopping. It is important to let your ideas flow without editing or censoring them.

Your purpose is to keep writing without lifting your pencil or pen from the page or fingers from the keyboard. Another suggestion is to hide what you are writing by sliding a blank page over what you have written as you go or blocking your view of the screen. This prevents you from wanting to go back and edit what you've written before your time is up. If you get stuck, write anything, such as "I can't think of anything to say," "What's the point of this?" or even "Blah blah blah" until another idea or association comes to you.

If you find freewriting beneficial, you can follow it with a looping exercise where you underline potentially useful words, phrases, or sentences. Choose the best one and use it as the beginning point for another round of freewriting. You can also summarize the most useful phrases into a sentence and use it as your starting point.

Looping involves underlining potentially useful words, phrases, or sentences and choosing the best one as a focus for more freewriting.

Although freewriting is mostly used for pre-writing, you can use it any time in the writing process to

- break through writer's block when you feel you have nothing to say;
- help you discover thoughts or feelings you might not have known about—this feature makes freewriting helpful for personal essays; or
- narrow a topic using looping and, sometimes, come up with a thesis and main points.

In the following freewriting and looping sample, the writer discovers a potential thesis for an essay. In this case, writing for five minutes yielded a topic that was complete enough to serve as a thesis statement (shown by double underlining):

> <u>**Bureaucracy can be very disturbing you can get parking tickets**</u> **even when there is <u>no parking left and you are forced to park by the yellow line</u> and you think you'll be gone early enough in the morning where was the bureaucracy when you needed them to make the decision in the first place and it can also lead to you having to take english 100 over again because you didn't get the B- required for the elementary post-degree program even though <u>you feel your writing should be at least a high B</u> or A average and the teacher says just be more clear and some comma errors and gives you a mediocre mark <u>who's to say that the best teachers are the ones who get the A average</u> because I <u>think the best teachers are the ones who know what it's like to struggle because they have learned hard work and they have also learned patience</u> these two things are the most important things being a teacher or they are up there anyway.**
>
> —Y.M.

Choosing to freewrite on the subject "bureaucracy," Y.M. began with a complaint about parking, which triggered a complaint concerning a mark in a previous English course. The student continued to follow this train of thought while complaining about the poor mark. This led the student to consider the qualities of a good teacher, claiming that being a good teacher has nothing to do with marking or education but with the idea of having to struggle and overcome obstacles. This slant on what makes a good teacher becomes a starting point for developing a thesis. Y.M. could test this claim by finding evidence to support it.

Mind Mapping

Mind mapping helps you see ideas and connections graphically. Unlike questioning, brainstorming, and freewriting, mind mapping is spatial and enables you to see the connections among your thoughts. On a blank piece of paper, write down and circle your topic and then think of related words or phrases, which you also record and circle, connecting each with the word or phrase that inspired it.

The pre-writing strategy of mind mapping involves circling words and phrases and connecting them to other words. Doing so allows you to see the relationship among thoughts.

Figure 4.2 is the result of a group mind mapping exercise that began with the subject "vitamins" and produced the potential thesis statement, "Because of media hype and the promise of good health, more people than ever are taking vitamins before they really know the risks involved." The dotted lines in the figure represent other possible connections, which you can often find in this method.

FIGURE 4.2 Mind mapping diagram about the subject "vitamins"

Mind mapping allows you to form distinct groups of related words and phrases, which can help you develop your main points and provide a structure for your essay. It is often useful for starting an argumentative essay, which needs logical connections.

After your pre-writing stage, you probably will have enough ideas and have made enough connections to determine your topic. You may also be ready to express your thesis.

Thesis Statement

The thesis statement tells the reader the main point of your essay or what you will be attempting to prove. This statement has two parts: the topic and the comment. For example, in the thesis "Car manufacturers frequently develop new models based on consumer tastes and the economy," "Car manufacturers . . . models" is the topic and "based on . . . economy" is the comment. The comment tells the reader how you will be discussing the topic, or what your focus will be. If you were writing an essay about Macbeth as a tragic hero, your thesis statement could be: "Macbeth shares three characteristics of classical tragic heroes: he has a tragic flaw, he falls from greatness, and his death results in a return to order." The reader of this statement knows from the comment portion that the body paragraphs of the essay will explain Macbeth's flaw, his fall from greatness, and how his death brings about a return to order.

— EXERCISE 4.4

The following topics are arranged from broadest to narrowest. Indicate the ones that could be turned into an effective thesis.

1. Species extinction

   Threatened species in Canada

   Threatened species in Canada's Arctic

   Threatened polar bear habitats in Canada's Arctic

   Threatened polar bears living near Coats Island in Hudson Bay

2. Smartphones

   Use

   Apps

   Popularity of gaming apps

   The need for friends to complete quests on gaming apps

3. Nutrition

   Dieting

   Fad diets

   The keto diet

   Lack of essential nutrients while on the keto diet

Research

Research is an important component of post-secondary-level reading, thinking, and writing. Once you have narrowed the topic or developed a research question for your essay, you can begin researching. As you learn more, you will be able to refine your narrow topic into a thesis and also decide what evidence will be necessary to support that thesis and make your argument clear to your readers.

If your essay is research oriented, you will find much of your supporting evidence in the written and electronic material in your library or resource centre. You could also use interviews and surveys for first-hand experiences and opinions. Note that interviews or surveys for school essays usually need to be approved by a school ethics committee. Speak to your instructor first if you plan to use these resources in your essay.

TIP

Research can come from personal interviews or published sources, such as newspapers or journals.

→10
→11
Chapters 10 and 11 discuss the research process.

Organization

Organization helps your readers understand your content and follow your argument. Building an outline is an essential step in writing organized, successful essays. Your outline helps you see where you need more supporting material, where an argument needs to be stronger, and the most effective way to arrange your ideas. Finding this out halfway through your first draft can be disheartening.

An outline also saves you time and prevents you from getting off-track as you draft your essay. An outline can also help you decide which organizational pattern (discussed earlier in this chapter in "Development Patterns") you will use for the essay and paragraphs.

Your outline may change over time as research reveals new information, but it is extremely important that you do not skip this step if you want to write a well-organized, articulate paper. You will probably develop your own outline style, and there are different ways to do this.

Your outline can be as simple or a detailed as you wish. Some people just create bullet points of the thesis, the topic sentences and supporting ideas, and a concluding point to wrap up the essay. Other people create a more detailed outline with all the ideas and body paragraphs more or less complete. Other writers jump in and create a draft of their essay and then go back, examine what was written, and reorganize ideas into an outline.

An **outline** is a representation of your points and supporting material. Creating an outline is an essential stage in essay writing, enabling you to see the arrangement of your ideas before you begin a draft.

TIP

An outline written before or during the first draft should be considered an organizational aid that can be altered or adapted as your thinking changes or as you come across new evidence.

→11
You will find an example of an outline in Chapter 11.

EXERCISE 4.5

Look at the outline for "The Cost of Buying Happiness" in Chapter 11 and then read the essay (also in Chapter 11). Do the paragraphs follow the outline? How do you think the outline helped the writer?

Organizing an Outline

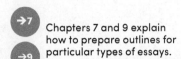
→7
→9
Chapters 7 and 9 explain how to prepare outlines for particular types of essays.

An outline is a vertical map of ideas and supporting information. Your main points are the headings; under each, you list ideas connecting to them, such as support, examples, and evidence.

Although the outline typically proceeds from general points to specific ones, you also need to decide how you are going to develop your main point and the order in which you are going to place your body paragraphs. There are several ways to order your points logically:

- *Climax order*: Begin with your weakest, or least important, point and proceed to the strongest, most important.
- *Inverted climax (dramatic) order*: Begin with your strongest point and end with your weakest.
- *Mixed order*: Begin with a moderately strong point and follow with the weakest argument before concluding with the strongest.

The number of main points and the strength of the opposing argument are factors that can help you determine which method is best for your topic.

Creating an Outline

Here are some general guidelines for making an outline:

1. Use pre-writing techniques to decide on your topic and narrow your focus to create a working thesis.
2. Divide the outline into an introduction, body paragraphs for support and development, and a conclusion.
3. Plan for a minimum of five paragraphs unless told otherwise or your essay is very short.
4. Ensure that you have only one main idea per paragraph.
5. Ensure that the main points are ordered logically and effectively for the audience.
6. Divide each paragraph's main idea (topic) into supporting points (at least two per paragraph) that develop the topic of the paragraph.
7. Design your outline to graphically show the relationship between main ideas and their points of development (or subpoints.) You can indent subpoints or assign alternating letters and numbers to show the level of development (e.g., I, A, 1, a).

Composing: Writing Drafts

Getting words on paper in sentence and paragraph form is the most challenging stage for most writers. Your outline will guide you through writing your first draft.

When you begin your first draft, don't worry if your introductory paragraph is incomplete. You will go back later and expand this paragraph once you are satisfied with the conclusion of your essay. For now, write your thesis statement and begin the first paragraph.

Start with the topic sentence of your first paragraph and then create sentences to explain your topic. Include the support (such as examples, anecdotes, or statistics) for each idea and craft a concluding sentence. Repeat this process for each body paragraph.

Once you have completed them all, draft a concluding paragraph. This conclusion can be a summary of everything that you have said in the body of the essay. Finally, you can turn to writing the introduction.

Remember that these paragraphs are just your first draft. To meet your audience's needs, work on this draft many times, adding and deleting sentences and reorganizing paragraphs for emphasis. When you begin to write, your ideas may branch beyond what you originally planned in your outline. This does not mean the outline is useless; it helps you develop your ideas and keeps you focused on the main topic and how to develop it.

TIP

In the first draft, your focus should be on putting your ideas in sentence and paragraph form. Later drafts will strengthen your structure and content.

Composing on the Computer

You can create your outline and write your first draft either on paper or on a computer. Both systems have advantages. Some people write a draft on paper so that they can use colours and can draw circles and lines between similar ideas. Others feel that using pen and paper increases their creativity and that a blank screen is too intimidating.

Drafting on a computer can save time because you can add or revise ideas quickly. You can use editing tools such as Track Changes and Comments to make notes as you go along. You can also cut whole sections and place them elsewhere for emphasis or to build a stronger argument. However, remember that computers crash, files get lost, and printers run out of ink.

Keeping Copies

It is important to keep copies of your drafts. Create a system that works best for you. For example, save a clean copy on your hard drive at various stages and label it clearly so you can find it in case you need it later. You should also save a clean copy of your outline.

TIP

When you are writing your document, it is important to keep copies of previous drafts.

Many students work from their outline file, adding details and creating a draft of their essay. To do this with your writing, copy your outline into a new file, save it with the new draft number, and work from this version so that you retain a clean outline.

After finishing this first draft, you can repeat the process, so you have a new document. Creating new files as you progress allows you to revert to an older file and start again on a fresh copy if you decide you don't like the changes you made or if you find that you cut information you didn't want to delete.

Make sure that you regularly save your work. Set up autosave so that the computer regularly saves your material. You can also save your work in a cloud storage system. Ask your librarians or IT department staff for suggestions. Backing up your document in the cloud allows you to work on it anywhere you have a device and internet access. You can also save your document to a USB stick or an external hard drive, or email it to yourself so that you have a backup in case your computer crashes. This happens more regularly than you may think.

Most colleges and universities give students access to the school network, so you can save documents there. This is cloud storage and you can access your files from anywhere. Never save your document to a school computer's desktop. This material is regularly wiped from school computers.

Revising the Final Draft

Creating drafts, especially the final draft, is probably the most ignored stage of the writing process (besides creating an outline). Your early drafts are usually rough attempts to put your thinking into words. You need to closely examine your essay's strengths and repair any weaknesses. The acronym EETS will help you follow all the parts of the revision process. This process could involve any or all of the following:

- Examine purpose and audience
- Examine logic and clarity
- Test support
- Spend time fine-tuning

Examining Purpose and Audience

Does the essay fulfill its purpose and address your intended audience? Do all of your body paragraphs support your thesis? Are your ideas presented in the best order to convey your message to your audience? Have you chosen the correct organizational patterns? Is the language formal enough for your audience?

Examining Logic and Clarity

If you are unsure of whether your essay is logical, ask a friend to read it and comment where arguments are incomplete or do not make sense. This can help you find lapses in logic that may confuse the reader.

If the essay's structure seems strong, look at each paragraph as a mini-essay, with a topic sentence, a well-developed main idea, and a concluding thought. Is each paragraph unified, coherent, and adequately developed? Did you use the right organizational pattern? Are paragraphs roughly the same length, or are some too short or long?

Try reading the essay aloud. If you had to reread sentences or stumbled over awkward passages, these areas need to be rewritten for clarity.

You need to be objective when evaluating your writing, so leave time between completing your draft and revising it. When you've spent time on a project, it's easy to read what you *think* is there rather than what you have actually written. Again, ask someone else to read your paper and focus their

---

TIP

Usually, the early drafts are essentially rough efforts to put your thinking into words.

TIP

Getting someone else to read your paper can give you valuable input, especially if they can point to any unclear passages that you need to revise.

---

reading by asking them to look for unclear or confusing passages. This is not the time to look for spelling mistakes, grammar errors, and typos.

Testing Support

Your body paragraphs should reinforce your thesis and support your points. If some ideas seem undeveloped, go back to your notes or earlier drafts to find more supporting material. Check that all your points are as strong as they could be.

Examine the examples, explanations, or research used. Do these really provide strong enough support for your ideas? Are there better supports to use? Have you used the supports properly? Do your sources pass the CARS test? Chapter 11 explains how to use research in an essay.

TIP
The CARS test is used to ensure you are using sources that are good enough for college or university writing. CARS stands for credibility, accuracy, reliability (or reasonableness) and support. Chapter 1 discusses the CARS test.

Spending Time Fine-Tuning

In the fine-tuning stage, you shift focus to individual sentences and words. Make sure that each sentence is free of spelling and grammatical errors, that you have chosen the correct words, and that you have used appropriate transitions between sentences and paragraphs. Check for sentence variation. Can you combine short, simple sentences into longer, more complex ones, or can you use different sentence types to make your points more interesting?

TIP
The final draft usually focuses on four main stages: **E**xamining purpose and audience, **E**xamining logic and clarity, **T**esting support, and **S**pending time fine-tuning (EETS).

Finally, print out your final paper and proofread it carefully. Look for typos; spelling, grammar, and punctuation mistakes; faulty sentence structure; and mechanics errors. If you have been asked to follow a formatting style, this is the time to make sure your headings and spacings meet the required standard. Grammar- and spell-checker software will help, but you also need to do a close reading yourself; if you type *form* instead of *from*, the spell-checker will not identify this as an error—but your instructor will.

→16 Chapter 16 explains efficient writing and editing strategies, as well as proofreading guidelines.

The best way to accomplish this step is to read your essay from the end to the beginning. Start at the last sentence and then read each of the preceding sentences one at a time. When you read from the top to the bottom, your brain will often fill in errors. By reading from the bottom up, each sentence becomes a single statement, and it is easier to find errors this way.

Applied to formatting, mechanics includes margin size, spacing between sentences, font size and type, and page numbers; applied to writing, it includes abbreviations, capital letters, hyphenation, and numbers.

The Critical Response

A critical response assignment requires you to use your active reading skills to analyze an essay you have never seen before. Your response will demonstrate effective critical thinking and your ability to analyze the writer's purpose, audience, and strategies. Depending on the nature of the assignment, you may be able to use your own perspective on and/or experience about an issue.

The main function of a **critical response** is that you critically think about a text and respond by sharing your views with others.

Your critical response shows your readers that your evaluation of the author's thesis and success in developing it is valid and well supported. A critical response often clarifies your thoughts or reveals your feelings

5 9 Summarizing skills are an important asset when writing a critical response. Chapters 5 and 9 examine how to summarize others' work.

about an issue, but you should not force your opinions on the reader. A critical response needs to engage with the reader, so you can share your own views.

Below are some of the objectives and conventions of response writing. Pay careful attention to the guidelines you're given, as they can vary greatly from instructor to instructor and from assignment to assignment:

- Your first sentences could include an overview or generalization about the text or the central issue(s) it raises.
- If your reader is unfamiliar with the text, briefly summarize its main ideas (or its plot, if the text is a literary work or a movie).
- Include a thesis statement that briefly indicates your approach to the essay, topic, or issue.
- Don't forget that you are primarily reacting to and analyzing a text. If you use personal experience or observation, it should help support a point but never replace analysis.
- Unless your instructor requires it, you don't need to research the topic.
- The length of a critical response can vary, so follow your instructor's guidelines for word count.
- In addition to analyzing what is in the essay, you can consider what is not there. What has the writer left unsaid?

→1 Chapter 1 provides a more complete list of questions applicable to a wide range of readings.

The following questions are often relevant to a critical response:

- Does the author appear reasonable? Do they establish a claim and support it logically throughout? Are there failures in logic?
- Does the author succeed in making the issue relevant to the reader? Does the author appeal to the reader's concerns and values? How do they do (or not do) this?
- Is the tone inviting, openly challenging, or neutral?
- Is the order of points appropriate? Are all points well supported?
- What, specifically, would strengthen the writer's argument?
- Does the essay appear free of bias? Is the voice objective? If the author openly declares an opinion, is it a good strategy?
- Does the author acknowledge the other side of the argument? How do they respond to the opposing viewpoint (e.g., fairly, effectively)?
- Does the author make emotional appeals? Are any extreme or manipulative?

Read Cathy Gulli's essay about putting young offenders in solitary confinement, followed by a student's critical response. After reading the latter, discuss with a classmate whether it satisfies the requirements of a critical response. Make a list of what you liked about the response and what you think could be improved.

Why Do We Still Put Young People in Solitary Confinement?

Cathy Gulli

[1] As the provincial advocate for children and youth in Ontario, part of Irwin Elman's job is to watch out for young people detained in a youth justice facility, which is essentially a jail for anyone aged 12 to 17 who is serving time, or awaiting trial or sentencing. There are 20 across the province, and they all operate under the same legislation and the Ministry of Children and Youth Services. At any point during their stay in custody, young people have the legal right to call the provincial advocate. Elman has fielded many complaints, but even he is alarmed by the serious violations exposed in a landmark report compiled by his office and released this week on the use of solitary confinement.

[2] "It's a Matter of Time: Systematic Review of Secure Isolation in Ontario Youth Justice Facilities" reveals a startling portrait of injustices and indignities occurring within some of the very institutions intended to uphold the rule of law and respect for human rights. Among the most egregious offences that have happened since 2009, the earliest year studied: young people have been confined for days or weeks longer than is prescribed by provincial law or supported by international research; the use of isolation has increased among the youngest, most vulnerable, subset of detainees, those aged 12–15; youth have endured "dehumanizing conditions" inside the cells such as extreme temperature fluctuations and waiting hours for staff to dispose of their bodily waste; they have been denied their legal rights to access a lawyer or the provincial advocate—and have been taunted as "sissies" by staff for such requests.

[3] Solitary confinement is a lawful practice in Canada, albeit an increasingly controversial one. It is supposed to be used as a last resort to manage behaviour, especially physical aggression; once a threat has ended, youth must be released. In Ontario specifically, the Child and Family Services Act states that individuals under 16 cannot be confined for more than 8 hours in one day or 24 hours in a week; those older than 16 cannot be held for more than 72 hours unless approved by a provincial director. And yet, the report shows that, in 633 cases, young people were held in isolation for more than 24 hours. Three-quarters were confined for between 1 and 3 days; one-quarter was held for 3 to 17 days. (There was a decrease in the use of solitary confinement across all facilities from 1,021 in 2009 to 701 in 2014; that may reflect the fact that fewer youth have been placed in custody.)

[4] Elman realizes staff in a crisis situation only have a few tools and strategies to use, including isolation, but he is convinced that prolonged isolation is never warranted. "If your hope is to help young people turn their lives around, on what planet does anybody think that putting them in a room with very little in it for days in a row is going to help?" he says. "It makes no sense."

[5] In compiling the report, the advocate's office obtained data from the Ministry of Children and Youth Services and interviewed young people at all 20 justice facilities. (The information pertains to April 2009 to March 2010, and the calendar years of 2013 and 2014.) Many of the youth described "inhumane" conditions. Some said they weren't able to shower, or that the water temperature fluctuated between extreme hot and cold. Some were not given blankets at night; any bedding was taken away during the day. They felt degraded when receiving food through a slot in the cell door. Books were prohibited. Eighty youth were denied a Bible or prayer mat. One told the advocate that solitary confinement turns youth

Gulli adds this explanation to clarify the meaning for the audience.

Here Gulli states the focus for the essay.

Based on the preceding words, what does the word *egregious* mean? Why did Gulli use this word rather than a better-known one?

Notice that the author uses a word that many understand to show how the youth are viewed by those in authority. How does this choice affect you, as the reader?

Gulli uses facts to support this point so that you, as the reader, know that this argument is based on facts, not just an opinion.

Note that, in a formal essay, you need to provide a concluding sentence. Do not end with a quotation.

Gulli has a specific opinion about this treatment. Can you think of a counter-argument? Critical thinking involves looking at both sides.

"into crazy, mad, angry people." Another described hearing "kids go crazy—yelling, punching walls until their knuckles bleed cause they can't take it anymore."

[6] These revelations are especially distressing given the arguments against solitary confinement by experts in human rights, child welfare, medicine, and neuroscience. The United Nations says solitary confinement, which it defines as isolation for more than 22 hours, should be "absolutely prohibited" in youth under 18 and individuals who are mentally ill. "Prison psychoses" syndrome is now established by researchers as a consequence of solitary confinement, and can cause problems including "perceptual distortions, paranoia . . . and self-harm."

The author cites a well-known source to support this argument regarding solitary confinement.

[7] In its journal last year, the Canadian Medical Association argued that "other options" should be explored for handling young inmates, citing the potential "long-term or permanent" health effects, including altered brain activity, "depression, phobias and personality changes, which may affect the offender's ability to successfully reintegrate into society upon release."

Again, Gulli cites a doctor associated with a well-known Canadian university. Is the intended audience Canadians only? Why or why not?

[8] To Dr Jean Clinton, a professor and youth psychiatrist at McMaster University who has consulted on child welfare, "solitary confinement is a guaranteed exacerbation of trouble." Many young people in custody have endured childhood maltreatment; they may be developmentally delayed, or have a mental illness or learning disability; many have experienced racism or multi-generational trauma as descendants of residential school survivors (black and Aboriginal youth are overrepresented); some have fetal alcohol spectrum disorder, or suffer from an addiction. At the same time, the brains of adolescents are not fully formed, says Clinton, so "leaving them inside a cell with nothing in it but their anger and repeating thoughts" sets them up for more problems.

[9] Youth have a "biological drive for sensation-seeking," she says, and interacting with others helps to form the neural pathways that create identity. Without positive stimulation and relationships, their brain development is stunted. Gratefully, the opposite is also true, says Clinton: "Neuroplasticity means that this is an amazing opportunity for change and growth."

[10] That is the view of Stephen de Groot, a former professor of social work at the University of Manitoba, who has developed a "relationship- and strengths-based approach" for facilities. The goal is to teach young people how to "emotionally and socially self-regulate" partly by staff modelling that behaviour. That can occur in ways as simple as eating lunch together, and as significant as having youth set personal goals to achieve. "Just by changing the focus [of their time in custody]," he says, "we see differences in kids' behaviours."

Is this a fair representation of the opposite side of the argument? Is the author biased? Why do you feel this way?

[11] But change doesn't come easily. Since 2010, de Groot has worked with both the Ministry of Children and Youth Services and many of the justice facilities cited in the advocate's report to implement his relational approach, "but there's a lot of resistance to it." That's because staff often feel their control is being taken away; some say their safety is at risk—perhaps justifiably so: they do not wear protective gear or possess weapons; their "de-escalation" tools come down to communication, restraints, isolation, and physical strength. "We do have staff who are injured," says Diane Irwin, executive director at St Lawrence Youth Association (SLYA), a justice facility outside of Kingston, Ontario, "sometimes severely."

[12] At SLYA it has taken two years and "many long, long sessions" with de Groot for the entire staff to "buy in," says Irwin. Today, she says they have seen success, with youth more comfortable in custody, and staff saying their job is easier; there have only been two youth grievances, and no one has quit. Solitary confinement is

still used, but that happens less often and for less time; that decision is now made by a team, including a supervisor. "My biggest point to our staff is if our ultimate goal is to help youth be productive citizens and not reoffend, you want them to pay attention to your teachings. And they're not going to if they don't respect you and if you don't have a relationship with them."

[13] The recent changes at SLYA speak to the variability between how facilities operate. The advocate's report showed that, while serious problems with the use of solitary confinement have occurred at some justice facilities, others have rarely held young people in isolation. That reveals "a lack of safeguards that would ensure a child within one facility would be cared for in the same ways as a child in another," says Kim Snow, a professor and child welfare researcher at Ryerson University who analyzed the report's data. There also appear to be no indicators to suggest that young people who are more prone to aggression are relegated to certain facilities. That alone is evidence that alternatives to solitary confinement exist.

> Gulli places the negative before the positive here. Does that affect how readers will feel about how different facilities operate?

[14] For its part, the ministry has appointed an expert panel to review its residential services, which includes justice facilities; the findings will be reported by the end of the year. It remains to be seen whether the advocate's recommendations, including a ban on the use of solitary confinement for more than 24 hours, are adopted. In response to several specific questions from *Maclean's*, the ministry replied vaguely that it "will review [the] thoughtful and important recommendations." In the meantime, Elman says the stunning misuse of solitary confinement is akin to sentencing a young person twice: "When you put them in an institution and control every moment of every day, they're punished," he says. "You don't need to make it any worse."

> The author creates doubt in the reader's mind and then uses the word *vague* to describe the ministry's response. How does the word choice affect readers' view of the ministry?

Post-Reading Questions

1. Has Gulli clearly supported the ideas presented in this essay? Give examples of passages that support your answer.
2. What type of audience is Gulli writing for? Is the level of language appropriate for this audience? If not, what could be changed?
3. What was the purpose for writing this piece? Did Gulli achieve it?
4. How could Gulli be more objective in this piece? Choose at least two of the points presented and reword them to show less bias.
5. What organization pattern(s) did the author use?

Response to "Why Do We Still Put Young People in Solitary Confinement?"

Julianny Vahlis

Sample Student Essay

Critical Response

[1] Solitary confinement is inhumane for young people in Canada while in Venezuela people are being killed by young people. This is a topic that needs to be treated wisely. It is a fact that taking basic rights from young people is inhumane, but the law should not take it easier on them either. Elman states that, "If your hope is to help young people turn their lives around, on what planet does anybody think that putting them in a room with very little in it for days in a row is

> Note that Vahlis looks at both sides of the argument.

Here Vahlis uses both the argument quoted in the original article and presents views based on personal experience and beliefs.

going to help?" I do not know if solitary confinement is going to help, but those youth need some kind of disciplinary action. There should be consequences for their actions. There should be a way to help these people, but also a way to protect the people that work around them. "We do have staff who are injured," says Diane Irwin, executive director of one of the facilities outside Kingston, Ontario.

Again, Vahlis draws from personal experience. How could this argument be made stronger?

[2] In my country, the law protects children and teenagers, so what happens when youth make minor offences in Venezuela? Nothing happens because, according to the law there, children and youth should not go to prison and if they do go, it is for a short period of time. I would not like Canada to become a country where young offenders are protected but citizens who might never commit a crime are not.

What solution do you think Vahlis would suggest?

[3] In the article, Dr Jean Clinton states that solitary confinement is a guarantee of trouble. In my personal experience, not giving them any kind of disciplinary action guarantees a bigger offence after coming out of prison. In my experience, this becomes a never-ending cycle because the law feels sorry for the minor, the minor does not change, and the cycle continues. The problem needs a solution. When I was in my country, I was robbed by a 13-year-old. This caused me feelings of sadness, disappointment, and anger. It is not that I wanted human rights taken from him, but I wanted some kind of justice or solution.

Vahlis obviously feels very strongly about this topic. Do you agree or disagree with the final statement? Why?

[4] I believe that it is good to apply relationship-based methods for improving behaviour, as Professor Stephen de Groot is doing in Ontario; however, responsibilities should also be given to these youth to show them the cost of their actions. I do not want to be hard with what I say. I just want to point out a reality that Canada might face if youth do not face consequences for their actions.

Post-Reading Questions

1. Has Vahlis written a good response? Give specific examples to support your thoughts.
2. What specific points has Vahlis chosen to address from the original essay?
3. What, if any, important points should the author have included? What, if any, should Vahlis have excluded? Explain.
4. How has the perspective of the original article influenced Vahlis's response?
5. Are there any areas in this critical response essay that are unclear, or did Vahlis judge the essay's audience appropriately? Give examples to support your answer.

As you read the following essay, look for the different organizational methods that the authors use to develop the piece. Do they rely on one more than on the others? Pay attention to how the authors link ideas both within and between paragraphs.

If Corporations Have Legal Rights, Why Not Rivers?

David Suzuki and Rachel Plotkin

[1] A popular sign at climate marches reads, "System Change, Not Climate Change."

[2] What does system change look like? Environmental crises such as climate disruption and plastic pollution have led many to suggest it means moving from a perpetual-growth economic system to a circular one, reforming land management to co-management with Indigenous Peoples and shifting from extractive, polluting energy sources to renewables.

[3] Our society is constantly evolving its ideas and approaches. There are no doubt systems changes that have not yet been dreamed of. But in considering how to make systems more equitable and sustainable, one change underpins all others: a change in our relationship with nature.

[4] The Western relationship is one of dominance. Government agencies that manage ecosystems are called "natural resource" departments, inferring that nature is a resource for human exploitation. Every inch of the planet has been petitioned for human ownership. The mainstream view is that nature is property, not a living, generative force. It's a perspective upheld by our legal systems. People "own" farm animals, we can legally deplete the ocean of fish, and when private companies drain public aquifers for profit, communities must go to court to challenge them.

[5] Under Western legal systems, the concept of "personhood" includes rights, powers, duties and liabilities. In many countries, corporations are recognized as having legal "personhood" and accompanying rights as well. Recently, as a reflection of Indigenous leadership and world views, the legal rights of personhood have in some instances been extended beyond people and corporations to nature itself.

[6] In New Zealand, after centuries of advocating for a river they identified as their life force, the Māori negotiated a treaty settlement with the government recognizing that the Whanganui River, or Te Awa Tupua (which refers to the entire river system "and all its physical and metaphysical elements"), has the rights of a legal person.

[7] According to David Boyd, author of *The Rights of Nature: A Legal Revolution that Could Save the World*, this recognition, formalized in law in early 2017, means that, "In short, the Whanganui River is no longer owned by humans but by itself, Te Awa Tupua." The law puts the interests of the river first and contains safeguards against privatization and harm, and enables citizens to sue government and corporations on the river's behalf.

[8] When the legislation passed—with support from all political parties—New Zealand Green Party co-leader Metiria Turei said, "Our environment, however we want to describe it, is our ancestor and from where we come, and, therefore, we owe our environment everything—our life, our existence, our future. The law slowly is starting to find ways—clumsy and not perfect by any means, but it is slowly trying to find ways to understand that core concept."

Sample Professional Essay

Paragraph Development

Why do you think the authors chose to start the essay with a single statement, rather than a full introduction?

The authors use repetition between the end of the second paragraph and the beginning of the third in order to help the reader transition from one paragraph and thought to another.

The authors use definition in this paragraph by making the statement about dominance, and then explaining what they mean by giving clear examples of this dominance.

The authors are not neutral in the essay and their bias is against the Western idea of ownership of nature.

If you do not know the term *Maori*, what can you infer it means based on the previous paragraph?

[9] New Zealand offers an introduction to an unfolding story. Numerous initiatives worldwide are aimed at bestowing legal personhood and accompanying rights to nature, including rivers, forests and mountains. New Zealand has since given the same rights to a 2,000-square-kilometre former national park known as Te Urewera and to Mount Taranaki.

[10] Unfortunately, in addition to being clumsy, some of these laws contain loopholes government can use to override nature's rights. Enforcement in many regions has also proven to be a challenge, especially when changes to mainstream resource extraction practices are required.

[11] Some Indigenous experts also point to significant limitations with the Western concept of "legal personhood," especially when viewed alongside Indigenous laws. Anishinaabe-Métis lawyer and law professor Aimée Craft said in an email, "Indigenous laws tell us that *nibi* (water) is living—it has life and can take life. Recognizing the agency and spiritedness of water is distinct from the concept of legal rights of water or personhood. Indigenous legal orders can provide insight into the mechanisms by which we can honour our responsibilities to water, in all of its forms."

[12] The Western relationship with nature has led to climate and biodiversity crises. System change does not happen overnight. But it has begun, and this is a source of hope. As many Indigenous Peoples worldwide have articulated, we come from nature and are kin to it. We don't own it. To develop new systems of sustenance and respect, we must move collectively beyond seeing nature as merely something to exploit.

Suzuki, David, and Rachel Plotkin. "If Corporations Have Legal Rights, Why Not Rivers?" *David Suzuki Foundation*, 11 Mar. 2020, https://davidsuzuki.org/story/if-corporations-have-legal-rights-why-not-rivers/. © 2021 David Suzuki Foundation

Post-Reading Questions

1. In the introduction, the authors use the term *climate disruption*, rather than *climate change*. What difference does this make to you, as a reader? Is this explanation needed? Why or why not?
2. Explain how the authors maintain paragraph unity.
3. How do the authors develop the paragraphs in this essay? Give examples of the methods they use.
4. As noted, the authors have a bias against the idea of owning nature. How does this bias affect your reaction to this essay?
5. What is the overall organization pattern in this essay? Be prepared to explain your answer.
6. Who do you think the audience is for this essay? Explain your answer.
7. From the essay, prepare an outline. Use either point form or a more formal approach.
8. Are there places in the essay that the authors could have strengthened their argument?
9. Are there any areas that the authors could have improved clarity?
10. David Suzuki is a well-known Canadian scientist and environmental advocate. Do you think a less well known author would have been a better choice as a co-writer? Explain your answer.

Chapter Review Questions

1. What are some of the characteristics of effective paragraphs?
2. Why is supporting information important in paragraphs?
3. What is the difference between a topic and a thesis?
4. Using the topic "homework," use one pre-writing method to generate ideas for an essay.
5. What are the five stages in essay writing? Why is each important?
6. What is a critical response assignment?
7. What acronym can you use when revising your final draft? What is each step?
8. Which ways would you choose to make sure that your work is saved?
9. Why is it important to save previous drafts of your work as separate documents?
10. What strategy can you use to be more objective when revising your work?
11. List three organizational methods used for both paragraphs and essays and explain when it is appropriate to use each.
12. Can more than one development pattern be used in an essay? Why or why not?

5 Summarizing Other Writers' Work

By the end of this chapter, you should be able to

- write a summary;
- write a paraphrase; and
- create an abstract and an annotated bibliography.

Summarizing another author's work is common both in school and at work. Summarized material can be integrated into essays and reports and add variety and credibility to your writing. To manage the daily influx of information that relates to your employer's business, your manager may ask you to summarize this material so that key points are available for clients and your fellow employees. This chapter will help you learn how to write summaries, paraphrases, abstracts, and annotated bibliographies.

▲ Photo: Rawpixel.com/Shutterstock

What Is a Summary?

A summary is a short overview or outline of a longer piece of writing. You can write a summary of a sentence, a paragraph, or an entire essay or report. The summary, written in your own words, must include its main idea(s) and not add anything that isn't in the original.

You may already have experience in summarizing your thesis and main points in your writing when you write the conclusion of an essay, for example. In Leman Koca's essay "How to Improve Memory"—reprinted in Chapter 6—the author summarizes the thesis and main points in the concluding paragraph. The thesis states: "Although it is a common problem in this century, it is simple to improve memory by following these three steps: being examined by a doctor, reducing stress levels, and training the brain."

(The concluding paragraph is broken into two sections here.)

In summary, being examined by a doctor, reducing stress levels, and training the brain are three important steps to improve memory. If people are having trouble with their memory, they need to take it seriously and solve this problem by following these mentioned suggestions.

People should not neglect to take care of their memory and strive to live a good life with beautiful memories.

When you write an essay, you might also include a summary of another writer's work to

- use a source's main idea(s) as background information;
- contrast with or support a point of your own (e.g., show how it is similar to or different from the other writer's position); and
- explain the other writer's position as it relates to your thesis.

Summary writing skills can be used in the following ways in essays and stand-alone exercises:

- to summarize an essay or a passage from a textbook for a professor to ensure you understand the writer's ideas
- to briefly summarize a text to construct an annotated bibliography for a research paper
- to summarize an author's words in a paraphrase rather than using direct quotations

All these activities have one thing in common: you are presenting someone else's ideas. Therefore, you must clearly understand the material you summarize and carefully represent the original work.

A summary is a shorter rewritten version of an original work.

Here the author reminds the reader of the thesis that was being explored in the essay.

Here, the author wraps up the essay with a clincher that gives advice about living with beautiful memories.

TIP

Although you may have summarized your thesis and main points in your own essays, an important writing skill is knowing how to summarize the ideas of other writers.

→11 Chapter 11 discusses summarizing secondary sources.

To summarize, you need to use your own words and sentence structures. When using a translation dictionary, check what the word is in your own language. Then translate the word you find from your own language and see what it is in English. This will help to ensure you are using the correct word. A thesaurus can also help you choose a different word. Just make sure you are using the correct word, as words often have a variety of meanings. For example, if you search a synonym for *gift*, you may see the word *allowance*. To many Canadians, an allowance is not a gift, but a monetary reward for doing work your parents have told you to do. So, for many Canadians, *allowance* is not the same as *gift*.

How to Write a Summary

Summaries may seem similar to the book reports you wrote when you were younger, but they differ in two ways: 1) summaries do not analyze what you have read; 2) they do not make recommendations.

Along with the qualities listed above in "What Is a Summary," a well-written summary

- retains the meaning of the original piece;
- includes the subpoints (if it is a longer summary);
- omits examples and illustrations, unless they are very important;
- uses the same order as the original;
- keeps the original's relative importance of ideas; and
- uses concise wording.

Follow these steps when writing a summary of any length:

1. Read the entire work to learn its purpose, thesis statement, intended audience, purpose, etc. The title should signal the content of the piece, and headings will direct you to the main points.
2. Read the piece again and write down its major points in your own words.
3. Read both the article and your summary again to make sure you have stated every point that the original author intended without adding any personal bias.
4. Make sure you have used your own words. Create your own sentence structures and use synonyms. Using the other author's structure and language is considered plagiarism.
5. Edit and proofread your summary before you submit it.

Plagiarism is the intentional or unintentional use of someone else's work as if it were your own.

 Chapter 11 discusses plagiarism.

Summary Length

A summary is always shorter than the original work. The length can range from one sentence to several paragraphs or even pages, depending on the purpose of the summary. Short summaries capture only the most important points. An entire paragraph could be summarized in one sentence because you have omitted the material that is not important to your audience. Your manager at work might ask you to write an extended summary of an entire report to share with others. Often, instructors will tell you that the length of an extended summary should be no more than 30 per cent of the original. This chapter includes summaries of various lengths, accompanied by related exercises.

TIP

Summary length is dictated by the intended use. A summary can be as brief as a sentence or two or can be a longer extended summary.

→5 See the section "The Extended Summary" later in this chapter for more on extended summaries.

Summarizing the Source Material for Essays and Reports

When you summarize another writer's work and use it in your own writing, you must always credit your source. During the research stage, write summaries of the ideas presented by your sources and carefully record the direct quotations you plan to use in your final project. Summarizing a source's content helps you avoid too much direct quotation.

Save this information along with the information you need to identify the source, such as author's name, URL, publisher, publication date, etc. This practice can save you from having to find the sources again when you begin writing.

Summaries and Argument

If the purpose of your essay is to persuade the reader rather than present facts, you still need to distinguish between fact and opinion. Read the following opening to a professional essay.

> **Though some historians tentatively trace this belief [that it's bad luck to open an umbrella indoors] back to ancient Egyptian times, the superstitions that surrounded pharaohs' sunshades were actually quite different and probably unrelated to the modern-day one about raingear. Most historians think the warning against unfurling umbrellas inside originated much more recently, in Victorian England.**
>
> **In "Extraordinary Origins of Everyday Things" (Harper, 1989), the scientist and author Charles Panati wrote: "In eighteenth-century London, when metal-spoked waterproof umbrellas began to become a rainy-day sight, their stiff, clumsy spring mechanisms made them veritable hazards to open indoors. A rigidly spoked umbrella, opening suddenly in a small room, could seriously injure an adult or a child, or shatter a frangible object. Even a minor accident could provoke unpleasant words or a minor quarrel, themselves strokes of bad luck in a family or among friends. Thus, the superstition arose as a deterrent to opening an umbrella indoors."**
>
> Wolchover, Natalie. "The Surprising Origins of 9 Common Superstitions." Live Science, 19 Sept. 2011, https://www.livescience.com/33507-origins-of-superstitions.html.

In this piece, the author is offering a new theory for why the superstition of opening umbrellas indoors evolved. Note that he is not saying that his theory is correct, only that many historians agree with his idea. If you do not read this piece carefully, you could give the reader the wrong impression when writing your summary. Here is an example of a distorted summary:

> **Wolchover states that all scientists agree with Charles Panati that the superstition about opening umbrellas inside originated once modern umbrellas were invented, not from ancient Egyptian times.**

Chapter 9 discusses the difference between fact and opinion.

However, you could correctly acknowledge the author's argument this way:

Wolchover states that a large number of scientists agree with Charles Panati that the superstition about opening umbrellas inside originated once modern umbrellas were invented, not from ancient Egyptian times.

Using Signal Phrases

A signal phrase tells your reader that what follows is information you are sharing from another source. Choose a signal verb that reveals whether the writer is explaining or arguing—verbs such as *prefer*, *believe*, *claimed*, and *argued* suggest that the source is expressing an opinion, whereas *says*, *states*, *described*, and *found* do not.

Using appropriate verbs or phrases such as *according to* shows the writer's attitude toward the subject. However, do not characterize their stance as negative or assume that the writer has a bias. A summary should represent, not judge. The writer may be opinionated, but when representing those views, you should not express your own bias or opinion.

A signal phrase indicates that what follows is taken from another source. When you summarize, be specific but not detailed, and use your own words but the writer's ideas. Do not be vague or distort the writer's meaning in any way.

 Chapter 11 examines signal phrases in more detail.

Sample Sentence Summaries

The following summaries show how to condense a paragraph into a sentence or two. This type of summary is useful when you want to include key ideas in your essay but do not want to quote extensively. Bear in mind that your instructor may require more detail.

Sample 1:

Helen Thompson was one of the first women to obtain a PhD from the University of Chicago. Her thesis, *The Mental Traits of Sex* (1903), illustrates the main arguments in the similarities tradition. These include the importance of overlap between genders, the requirement of highest methodological standards to demonstrate difference, the search for social explanations of difference, and the demonstration of the specificity of difference.

Kimball, Meredith M. "The Worlds We Live In: Gender Similarities and Differences." *Canadian Psychology/Psychologie canadienne*, vol. 35, no. 4, 1994, pp. 388–404.

Summary:

Helen Thompson's 1903 thesis, *The Mental Traits of Sex*, shows the importance of scientific and social study of the similarities and differences between men and women.

Sample 2:

It is time for some perspective. With the growing urgency of climate change, we cannot have it both ways. We cannot shout from the rooftops about the dangers of global warming and then turn around and shout even louder about the "dangers" of windmills. Climate change is one of the greatest challenges humanity will face this century. It cannot be solved through good intentions. It will take a radical change in the way

The summary begins by noting the author, the date of publication, and the title to show where the information came from.

The summary points out the two types of studies that the author used to make her conclusions.

Notice how the author of the summary uses different words and a different sentence structure to state the main points.

we produce and consume energy—another industrial revolution, this time for clean energy, conservation, and efficiency.

Suzuki, David. "The Beauty of Wind Farms." *New Scientist*, vol. 186, no. 2495, 2005, p. 20.

Summary:

In order to fight climate disruption, people have to choose to become actively involved and not complain about the necessary changes.

Because this summary does not have a signal phrase, it will need to be followed with an in-text citation as shown in the sample and summary in Exercise 5.1

EXERCISE 5.1

Using the criteria discussed in this section, analyze the following sample from Kimball's essay and evaluate its summary. Write a summary using the criteria correctly.

Sample:

> Throughout the history of feminism, from Wollstonecraft to the present, two views of gender differences have been advocated (Cott, 1986). In one, similarities between the sexes have been emphasized, whereas in the other, women's special characteristics that differ from men's have been emphasized.

Summary:

> The history of feminism, from Wollstonecraft to the present, shows two different views of gender differences (Cott, 1986). Similarities between the sexes are highlighted in one, but women's special characteristics have been spotlighted in the other.

EXERCISE 5.2

Choose a paragraph from one of the readings in this textbook and summarize it in one or two sentences.

The Extended Summary

An extended summary applies the criteria discussed so far, but it is longer than a few sentences. Because of its length, you may have to use some words from the original to get the information across clearly. You must place quotation marks around any phrases—more than three consecutive words—that you cite directly. Phrases like "climate change" and "Black Lives Matter," for example, as well as jargon, cannot often be rewritten without losing the meaning.

Extended summaries are approximately 10–30 per cent of the length of the original. If the work you are summarizing requires more expertise than your audience has, you may need to write more or add a few transitions to make the summary easy to follow. Add no more than is necessary for clarity.

TIP

An extended summary applies the rules for summarizing to an entire work or a main part of it. Although it is too long to use in an essay, this type of summary shows your ability to identify key ideas and put them in your own words. You must also decide whether to include all the main ideas or only the most important ones.

How to Write an Extended Summary

Use these seven steps to write an extended summary (you will recognize some of the instructions from the steps to writing any summary):

1. Read the work to learn its purpose, thesis statement, intended audience, etc. Take note of the author, their professional credentials, and any other sources used.
2. Reread the article, noting its major points, the most important subpoints, and/or key examples. From these points, write an outline using your own words.
3. Read the article and your outline to make sure you have not missed any of the main points.
4. Following your outline closely, write a summary that includes the thesis statement and all the main points. If you are writing a summary of a specific length and have room for more than the main points, pick the most important subpoints or supporting ideas to reach the required length.
5. Check your wording against the original to ensure that you have

    • avoided using the original writer's wording;
    • accurately reworded the writer's points;
    • matched the order of the points to the original;
    • checked for bias in the writer's work and in your summary; and
    • put quotation marks around phrases and words taken directly from the original.

6. Create a title for your summary using the following pattern: Summary of ["Title of Essay,"] by [Name of Author]. After listing these elements in the title, you may not need to mention them again.
7. Edit and proofread your summary.

TIP
Ensure that your summary is in your own words and that you have put quotation marks around words and phrases taken directly from the source.

Begin by doing step 1 all at once. Minimize distractions, as you want to make sure you understand the writer's meaning. Take a break—a few hours or, if you have enough time, even a day—before beginning the next step. If the work is short and you feel you can concentrate well, you can move on to step 2 immediately. When you can, leave time between steps. When you come back to a work after being away for a while, you will find errors more easily.

An extended summary should contain the work's thesis statement and the main ideas. Generally, the thesis statement appears in the introduction of the original, and the main ideas are often the topic sentences of major paragraphs. However, this might not be the case. Furthermore, since not every paragraph will contain a main idea, the number of paragraphs in the original might not match the number of points in your outline.

Extended Summary Samples

Let's look at samples of extended summaries. The first is preceded by the original essay and the summary's outline.

The $15 Minimum Wage Movement Rises Up

Janet Nicol

[1] The fight for a $15-an-hour minimum wage in British Columbia is a fight for women's rights, according to organizers of the campaign. Women make up the majority of those who perform low-wage work across Canada.

[2] "These are not young people living in their parents' basements," Irene Lanzinger, president of the BC Federation of Labour, said about minimum-wage earners. "These are parents, single mothers and new Canadians."

[3] Women make up 63 per cent of workers on minimum wage in British Columbia. Last year, the federation launched its Fight for $15 campaign in partnership with local family-advocacy and anti-poverty groups. The coalition has held rallies and other events to raise public support for the cause. Campaign leaders met with the province's Liberal Premier Christy Clark and Minister of Labour Shirley Bond.

[4] In September, minimum-wage earners in British Columbia received an increase of 20 cents, and now earn $10.45 an hour. British Columbia has the second-lowest minimum wage in Canada after New Brunswick, yet the province has the highest cost of living. Lanzinger said she is "at a loss to explain" the government's unwillingness to make a significant change. "The government wasn't feeling the public pressure," she said. "We were astounded at the small amount."

[5] During the recent holiday season, campaign coordinator Denise Moffatt dressed as the Christmas Grinch on downtown Vancouver streets to draw attention to what she says is the province's stingy stance. Coalition members also handed out lumps of coal to shoppers, letting them know workers were being "scrooged" on the minimum-wage issue by government.

[6] "The increase would make a huge impact on women," Lanzinger predicts, "and would represent a positive economic impact because the wages would go back into the economy. In the past 15 years, BC has been among the worst provinces for child poverty. Poverty has a long-term cost on our education, health care and the criminal justice system."

[7] "Young workers have always been engaged in this issue," Lanzinger added. "They approached our executive to suggest the campaign, which lines up with other fights across Canada and American cities. We thought, if that's what it takes to lift people out of poverty, we'll do it."

[8] The Alberta government is committed to a $15-an-hour minimum wage, to be phased in over three years. According to Statistics Canada, more than 820,000 Canadians work at or below the minimum wage. This represents 5.8 per cent of all workers. Newfoundland and Labrador has the highest proportion of employees working at minimum wage (9.3 per cent), while Alberta had the lowest proportion (1.3 per cent). US cities including Seattle, San Francisco, and New York City have passed laws with timelines for designated employers to implement a $15-per-hour minimum wage.

[9] Contrary to claims by the business lobby, consumers would not end up paying much more if wages go up, Lanzinger believes, because costs are spread over many customers. "Wouldn't consumers want to know the workers serving them are making a decent wage? I have yet to encounter a good argument against this campaign."

[10] British Columbia also should develop a poverty-reduction plan, Lanzinger adds. "Raising the minimum wage is part of the solution. We also need to raise welfare rates and have a social housing plan."

[11] The high cost of child care is another barrier for single mothers entering the workforce. Even at $15 an hour, many workers will continue to struggle to make ends meet, Lanzinger admits, which is why the federation envisions the next step as a "living wage" campaign. "That's way down the road though," she said. "Right now the government has to deal with poverty."

Nicol, Janet. "The $15 Minimum Wage Movement Rises Up." Herizons, Winter 2016, pp. 6–7.

When you choose the main points to summarize, paraphrase them (put them in your own words) as you construct an outline. Remember that the final summarized version must be in your own words and that direct quotes must be placed in quotation marks.

Outline:

[1] Women in British Columbia are fighting for their rights by asking for a $15 minimum wage.
[2] Women make up more than half of the minimum-wage workers in British Columbia.
[3] Only New Brunswick has a lower minimum wage, yet British Columbia is the most expensive place to live in Canada.
[4] Irene Lanzinger, the president of the BC Federation of Labour, believes that a higher minimum wage would improve the province's economy because higher minimum wages mean more money in the economy.
[5] Lanzinger believes that a higher wage would mean less poverty and fewer costs to society.
[6] The campaign for higher wages for women has joined with other young workers who are affected by minimum-wage jobs in order to help eliminate poverty.
[7] Statistics Canada shows that just under a million workers receive minimum wage or less.
[8] Costs for goods and services would not rise very much if minimum wage were $15, as the increased costs would be absorbed by many customers.

[9] Lanzinger also believes that the BC government should reduce poverty with a many-pronged approach, which includes higher minimum wage.

[10] In the future, child-care costs should also be investigated, but poverty is the immediate issue.

Nicol's article features many illustrations, such as the passage that discusses minimum wage in other provinces and discusses cities that have passed legislation to improve pay. Much of the information in the article is evidence that supports the writer's thesis and does not need to be included in the summary. Because some passages simply elaborate on the main points, the summary avoids repetition by not including them:

Summary of "The $15 Minimum Wage Movement Rises Up," by Janet Nicol

Women in British Columbia are campaigning to increase minimum wage to $15 an hour, which they believe is part of the rights women should expect. In British Columbia, women make up more than half of the minimum-wage workers, and only New Brunswick pays less for minimum wage, yet British Columbia is the most expensive place to live in Canada. This means that many people live in poverty.

The president of the BC Federation of Labour, Irene Lanzinger, believes that a higher minimum wage would be very beneficial to the province's economy, as more money would be in circulation. Lanzinger also feels that more money would reduce poverty and would improve other social problems. In order to help promote the increase in minimum wage, the campaign joined with other workers who are also affected by this issue. These two groups represent some of the Canadians who work for minimum wage or less. These Canadians make up just less than 6 per cent of workers.

While some argue that the costs for goods and services will increase due to a higher minimum wage, Lanzinger disagrees as the increased costs would be absorbed by many customers. In the future, Lanzinger would like to see a many-pronged approach taken to reducing poverty in British Columbia, including examining costs for caring for children, but the current government focus needs to be on the poor.

Our next sample summarizes an essay from Chapter 12.

Summary of "Polar Bears: Bright Outlook or Grim Future," by Adam Cook

In this essay, the author looks at the future of polar bears, which, while not endangered, are threatened by human activity. Humans have hunted these animals for a variety of reasons, and this activity is causing many problems, such as decreased habitat and fewer cubs being born. Hunting has also reduced the food sources that these bears rely on.

Air and water pollution has also contributed to the declining numbers of polar bears. Not only does the pollution kill various marine wildlife,

but it also results in polar bears not being able to obtain enough food because their food sources are dying. Finally, climate change has a direct impact on the polar bears, as they need ice to hunt and build up their store of fat and nutrients. However, the ice is not lasting as long as the bears need it to. For females, this ice is extremely important, for without food caught while on the ice, their cubs will not survive. Without changes to human behaviour, the polar bears will die out.

Other Ways to Summarize

When you present another writer's ideas in an essay or a report, you use a paraphrase of the writer's words—you summarize in your own words what the author has said. Two other formats for summarizing the content of an author's work are abstracts and annotated bibliographies.

Paraphrase

A *paraphrase* restates the source's meaning using only your own words and sentence structure. Paraphrase when you want to cite a small amount of material that is directly relevant to your point. Include the entire original thought but rephrase it.

A paraphrase is usually about the same length as the original work. You normally paraphrase an important part of a text, perhaps a whole paragraph or two. A strict paraphrase is entirely in your own words. Because a paraphrase includes information from the source and is about the same length as the original, it is unlike a summary, whose main purpose is to condense the main ideas of the original while keeping its basic meaning.

EAL

> When you write a paraphrase, you use your own sentence structure. A paraphrase is not written using the original author's sentence structure and merely changing a few words. Doing this only shows that you can use a thesaurus. The purpose of a paraphrase is to demonstrate that you understand the material and that you can explain it using your own words and sentence structure. A good writer uses paraphrases and short summaries in an essay more than direct quotations, as paraphrasing and summarizing show the audience that you have done enough research to really understand the material you are using to support your ideas.

TIP

A summary is shorter than the original, but a paraphrase is approximately the same length.

 See Chapter 11 for more on paraphrasing, using direct quotations, and citing.

The following example illustrates the differences between summarizing and paraphrasing. The original paragraph is from student writer Barclay Katt's "Tail of Opposites" (see Chapter 6). The paraphrase follows the same development of the paragraph that was used in the original, but the words are not directly quoted. The summary reduces the content of the paragraph to one sentence.

Most people have been struck, at one time or another, by the way pet owners come to resemble their pets. It is strange why this is so, and never the other way around—that pets come to look more like their owners. For some reason, the face of the cat or dog is more

transferable to the human face than the human face is to that of the dog or cat. Here, it must be admitted that the dog owner is at an advantage. As there are far more breeds of dogs than of cats, the observer cannot help but be impressed by the infinite variety of possible faces of dog owners—from pushed-in pug to the full-blown majesty of Irish wolfhound.

Summary:
Many have noticed that people who own pets often look like their animals, but this comparison is found more often with dog owners than cat owners (Katt, 2017, pp. 134–5).

Paraphrase:
It has often been observed that those who own pets look like their animals. However, pets seldom resemble the people who own them. Perhaps this is because people see animals in human faces, but not humans in animal faces. People who own dogs are compared most often to their pets because there are more kinds of dogs than cats. Therefore, people can see many types of breeds in human faces, such as a pug or an Irish wolfhound (Katt, 2017, pp. 134–5).

EXERCISE 5.3

Paraphrase the paragraph you summarized in Exercise 5.2.

Abstract

An abstract is an overview of your purpose, methods, and results. An abstract appears before the beginning of the essay; it is placed after the title and author notation and before the introduction, enabling readers to decide whether they wish to read the whole piece. Write it after you have finished your essay or at least after you have formed your conclusions.

You will often find abstracts at the beginning of papers in peer-reviewed journals and can search for them in the databases at your school library. Abstract length varies: an essay abstract is generally 75–100 words; an abstract for a scientific paper is at least twice as long; and some are even longer. A writer will often incorporate key phrases or even complete sentences from the full work into the abstract.

Reading abstracts can help you determine whether an article will be useful for your essay. However, do not use the abstracts alone; scan the whole article to ensure that it relates to your topic.

An **abstract** is an overview of your purpose, methods, and results. It can include key phrases or even whole sentences from the full work. Not all the material needs to be reworded.

TIP
Articles in peer-reviewed journals have been evaluated by experts before publication.

1. Using your school's databases, find articles with abstracts. Choose two articles that you find easy to understand by scanning the contents.

2. Read the abstract for one article and then read the complete work.

3. Read the second article without looking at the abstract first.

4. Compare your understanding of the two articles. Was it easier to understand the first or second article?

5. Write a one-paragraph abstract for the second article and then compare it to the actual one. How do they differ?

Annotated Bibliography

An annotated bibliography summarizes similar works in the field of study. It includes a concise version of the content, focusing on the thesis statement and major points or findings, and can also include an appraisal of the study's usefulness.

Because an annotated bibliography may contain hundreds of entries, each one must be brief. If the entry refers to a book-length study, the main points may take the form of major section or chapter headings. Sometimes, it also includes an appraisal of the study's usefulness or contribution to the field.

An annotated bibliography is an expanded bibliography that often accompanies a large project, such as a book, dissertation, or other major study that requires detailed research. It summarizes the material in each of the source documents and includes a concise version of the content, focusing on the thesis statement and major points or findings.

The following is a sample annotated bibliography entry of Sandy Crashley's "The Cost of Buying Happiness: Why Less Is More" (see Chapter 11).

> **Crashley discusses the minimalist movement and the tiny house movement in relation to how society views success. The author examines both movements, and then discusses the characteristics of each. Crashley cites studies that show the effects of a consumer-oriented society. Information from a variety of sources is effectively integrated into the paper to support the author's points. Crashley uses logically ordered subtopics to present a successful overview of the benefits to individuals when they eliminate needless possessions. [77 words]**

Create an annotated bibliography using the articles from Exercise 5.4.

Summarizing at the Workplace

Preparing a summary is not only a classroom activity. While at work, you may be asked to summarize information for colleagues or your manager. You may be asked to attend a seminar or conference and report on what you learned. You obviously will not give people a very detailed account of the event or give your opinion about how valuable it was. Instead, you will need to apply the same rules you learned here and relate the important information.

Read the following memo and write a summary to present to your instructor. Try to keep the summary length to 10 per cent of the original.

MEMO

TO: Juan Alexandros, District Supervisor

FROM: Gail Fromme, Human Resources Manager

DATE: 12 November 2020

SUBJECT: CHANGES TO WORKPLACE ASSESSMENTS

As of 1 January, we will be implementing a new system to evaluate the managers in each district. This new evaluation includes the latest in psychological testing, which we feel will better predict who will succeed as a manager and whom we need to eliminate.

I will be sending out the new forms within the next few days, once our legal team has vetted them. Please do not share these forms with the staff, as district supervisors will be the only ones using them.

The company would like you to inform the managers that changes will be made to the yearly evaluations. Please notify them that the new evaluations will include

1. feedback from the staff they manage;
2. a minimum of 15 hours on-site supervision by the district supervisor;
3. a self-evaluation, which will be compared to the staff feedback; and
4. a visit to head office to meet with an evaluation team.

Once you receive the new evaluation package, which will include all the necessary new forms and detailed instructions, please read everything carefully. Any questions you have will be answered at the training session we will be having in mid-December. In the meantime, feel free to call me at ext. 267 between 8:30 and 4:00, Monday to Thursday.

The following article contains summarized information. While reading, note whether the author uses adequate transitions between ideas and between what is summarized and what is new material. Also, think about how she summarizes other works to add credibility to her ideas.

Almost a Million Canadian Kids in Poverty Is an Acute Emergency
Elizabeth Lee Ford-Jones

Sample Professional Essay
Summarizing

> The author's thesis or main idea is set out immediately in her title.

[1] Hundreds of thousands of Canadian children are growing up without enough.

[2] UNICEF's most recent report on child well-being in rich countries ranked Canada 17 out of 29 countries assessed, scoring 27th in child obesity, 22nd

in infant mortality and 21st in child poverty rates. Sadly, this isn't news. The House of Commons resolved to eradicate child poverty in 1989, but in late 2013, Statistics Canada reported that 967,000 children in this country still lived in low-income homes.

[3] These numbers don't simply represent difficult childhoods; they mark a huge group of Canadians who are growing up without the supportive environments they need to develop into healthy adults. They will carry the stress of early adversity throughout their lives.

[4] In 2009, my colleagues and I began a new elective in social pediatrics based out of the Hospital for Sick Children so that medical students could see first-hand the social realities of impoverished Canadian children. The students visit the homes of poor families, sometimes with social workers and infant nurse specialists, and witness the unsettling ways that social environments impact the health of patients.

[5] The stories they report back from the field are deeply troubling, particularly for a country as wealthy as Canada. The students see the impact of neighbour-hoods that lack positive activities for children, food insecurity, long parental work hours at low-wage jobs combined with long public transit times, and the near impossibility of accessing services such as eye examination, expensive corrective lenses, and dental work for their kids. The students see what parent-ing low on hope looks like.

[6] In one case, McGill University medical student Maya Harel-Sterling visited an inner-city Canadian mother of 18 years of age who had given birth to a frail baby girl in her bathroom after keeping her pregnancy a secret. In her reflection published by *Paediatrics and Child Health*, "How Did You Sleep Last Night? Have You Eaten Today?" she describes the crowded apartment with four other residents and no room for the baby to crawl or play. The mother sleeps on the floor.

[7] In another household, an elderly grandmother cares for the children while their mother works evenings as a cleaner and their dad drives a pizza delivery truck. The kids spend much of the time with the television on—not a jot of stim-ulation there.

[8] Mounting evidence in the field of social epidemiology shows that poverty limits the futures of children, especially babies, who lack living environ-ments with family support and opportunities to learn and be active, mentally and physically. We won't resolve this problem without providing access to jobs that pay a living wage and appropriate community supports for every Canadian.

[9] In the April 2014 issue of the *Journal of the American Medical Association*, Neal Halfon, a child health researcher at the University of California, wrote that child poverty levels are persistently high. He wrote that these trends were not due to temporary ups and downs in business but to major shifts in the structure of the economy, which he calls "structural deficits."

[10] The results, including a lack of adequately paying jobs and proper training for skilled work, leave low-income families ill-prepared to give their children the strong start they need for healthy development. This is a problem in both

the United States and Canada. Low-income children, especially minorities and Aboriginal people, are growing up with an increased risk of preventable diseases—diseases both medical- and mental health–related that arise as a result of their early living conditions and will affect us all.

Even in a non-academic essay, a writer needs to start with a topic sentence so that the readers know what the paragraph will be about.

[11] We can address this triad of problems: unacceptable levels of stress ("toxic stress"), which affect cortisol production and set a path of learning and disease problems; lack of access to comprehensive health services; and fundamental disadvantage, including poverty. There are pilot programs in place, but services must be broader and readily available.

[12] Where do we start? What was once considered "a long emergency"—with outcomes manifesting some years later in the life trajectory as ill-health and lack of contribution to society—ought now to be recognized as an acute emergency. Societal structures must change so that the lottery win of life doesn't fall to only a small percentage of families.

The author begins her final paragraph with a question that is linked to her thesis. She then uses the rest of the paragraph to answer her question and to restate her view that the number of Canadian children living in poverty is an acute emergency.

Lee Ford-Jones, Elizabeth. "Almost a Million Canadian Kids in Poverty Is an Acute Emergency." The Toronto Star, 8 Sept. 2014, http://www.thestar.com/opinion/commentary/2014/09/08/almost_a_million_canadian_kids_in_-poverty_is_an_acute_emergency.html.

Post-Reading Questions

1. Was it easy to understand when the author switched between new ideas and the summary of others?
2. How did the summarized parts of this article add to your understanding of the author's argument?
3. Do you think the author gave enough information from the UNICEF report? Why or why not?
4. Is Ford-Jones's point of view clear? What are the author's feelings about poverty in Canada? Use examples from the article to support your idea.
5. Why do you think the author chose to write an article like this rather than a typical summary as outlined in this chapter?

Chapter Review Questions

1. What are the key characteristics of a summary?
2. What steps can you follow in writing an extended summary?
3. When would you write an extended summary?
4. What is the difference between summarizing and paraphrasing?
5. Why would you use a summary or paraphrase in an essay?

6. What are two key points to remember when writing a paraphrase?

7. What is an abstract?

8. Why is an abstract helpful?

9. What is an annotated bibliography and when is it used?

10. Why would you use summary skills at work?

PART TWO
Essays

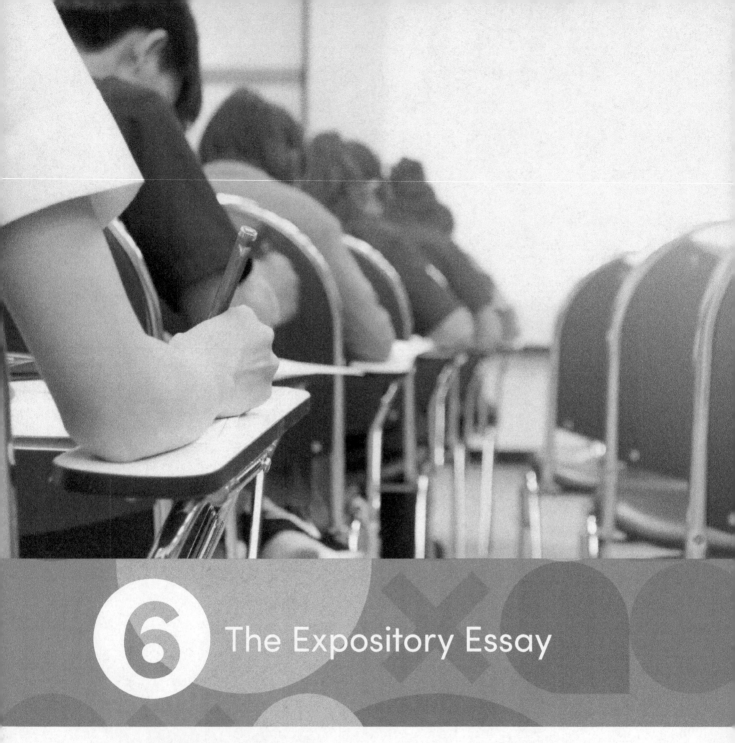

6 The Expository Essay

By the end of this chapter, you should be able to

- organize expository essays; and
- write an effective in-class essay.

All essays have a specific purpose. In order to write the type of essay your audience expects, you need to recognize these different purposes. In Chapter 9, you will learn how to write an argumentative essay. This chapter will focus on the strategies you need to write expository and in-class essays.

How to Write Various Expository Essays

This chapter focuses on the following types of expository essays: process, comparison and contrast, and in-class (or examination). Each discussion includes a sample essay.

The Process Essay

In a process essay, you tell your reader how to do something, for example, how to install a printer, detail a car, or prepare to host a webinar. You take the reader through the steps of the process in logical order so that they can achieve results that are similar to yours. This is a structure that you will use often in business to explain how to use a new product or system to your clients or fellow employees.

The introduction for a process essay is brief and direct. It provides background information or includes preparation instructions, such as listing equipment needed for the activity. It must include a clear thesis statement that says how you are planning to explain the process.

When preparing your outline, briefly list the steps and then go back and 1) make sure they are in logical, chronological order, and 2) fill in the details of each from beginning to end. Review them again when you are finished to make sure that you have left nothing out.

You may also include what not to do in a process. For short processes, put more than one point in a paragraph. For example, if you are describing how to select a computer, you can include researching online and asking opinions in one paragraph.

Your conclusion can focus on the importance or benefits of the activity or highlight common mistakes, reinforcing the value of having the proper tools or taking safety precautions.

Possible process essay topics include explaining how to

- choose an ideal pet;
- create a web page;
- give a Zoom presentation;
- organize a social or an educational event for a group you are involved with; and
- prepare for a test.

←4 Each type of essay described in this chapter follows the same principles of paragraph organization described in Chapter 4.

→9 See Chapter 9 for more on argumentative essays.

How to Improve Memory
Leman Koca

Sample Student Essay
Process Essay

[1] "I know this person, but from where?", "Did I turn off the stove before I left?", "What was the number of. . . ." Especially now, people frequently say these kinds of things. Maybe having a busy lifestyle, relying on technological devices, and using social media weaken people's memory today. Having a weak memory and being forgetful causes some serious problems in life. Although it

Koca gives background information so that the reader can identify with her topic. The author ends with her thesis and the steps required to be successful. Note that her supporting paragraphs follow in the same order as the steps listed in the thesis statement.

Note that the writer begins her paragraph with the transition "the first step," which helps the reader easily understand that this is the first step among many.

Koca uses parallel structure (repeating a sentence pattern) to introduce each action the reader should follow in order to complete the process. Parallelism is discussed in Chapter 15.

In concluding the paragraph, the author reminds the reader of the crucial steps involved for the first part of the process.

The writer gives concrete examples to help the reader fully understand the step she has given for the process.

Koca repeatedly states the process's purpose. Repetition can be as effective as using obvious transitions, as discussed in Chapter 3.

While the paragraph wrap is short, it is an effective review of the content.

is a common problem in this century, it is simple to improve memory by following these three steps: being examined by a doctor, reducing stress levels, and training the brain.

[2] The first step for a forgetful person is being examined by a doctor. By having a blood test, the person can learn if they lack vitamins or omega-3. Some studies argue that understanding the interaction between vitamins and omega-3 fatty acids can help in the understanding of brain deficiencies (Rathod et al., 2016, p. 23). Therefore, a patient who suffers from weakened memory should take vitamin B12 capsules or omega-3 supplements regularly or follow a nutritional diet plan that is rich in vitamin B12 and omega-3 such as nuts, fish, beef, eggs, and dairy products. Additionally, patients should have a blood test by an endocrinologist to learn whether they have any thyroid problems. According to Seyedhosseini Tamijani et al. (2019), "thyroid hormone treatment alleviates the impairments of neurogenesis, mitochondrial biogenesis and memory performance induced by methamphetamine" (p. 74). A patient with a thyroid condition will most likely require taking a hormone treatment. As can be seen, being examined for vitamin and fatty acid deficiencies and having your thyroid treated will make a big impact to solve forgetfulness.

[3] The second step to improve memory is reducing stress levels. First, the person needs to take time for any kind of exercise to decrease the levels of stress. Sing and Sachdev (2020) declared in their study that with one-month middle-intensity physical activities, good results were obtained with a considerable increase in reducing stress levels. Implementation of aerobic exercises moderately in the long term reduced stress and enhanced perception (p. 1). For example, going for a walk on a trail or by the seaside, participating in a fitness class, or practicing yoga are good options to reduce stress. Second, the person should take some time for hobbies like painting, reading, dancing, or whatever the person is interested in to diminish stress levels. Leisure activities have benefits for mental health among the middle-aged group, especially when they are with others (Takeda et al., 2015, p. 10). For instance, painting will support concentrating on beautiful images and help to get rid of unnecessary worries. If people feel extreme stress, it is likely that they will forget many details in their daily life. Thus, reducing stress levels and making the brain relax through exercising and spending time on interests are good tips for people who complain of weakened memory.

[4] The final step is training the brain to enhance memory. To begin with, a person can consider playing brain games as an enjoyable method of training the brain. This is important because O'Shea et al. (2019) claimed, "overall, it appears that 'brain games' may modestly benefit aspects of cognition and aspects of mood in patients presenting with MCI" (p. 42). For instance, many free apps can be downloaded to electronic devices, or many brain games could be bought such as word puzzles, Sudoku, chess, and similar games from any stores. Next, the person can try to learn new skills such as learning a new language or learning how to play a musical instrument. Mansens et al. (2018) discovered that "making music at least once every two weeks and especially playing a musical instrument is associated with better attention, episodic memory and executive functions in older adults" (pp. 964–971). For example, when people attempt to learn a new language, they need to memorize new words and this will help them to expand their memories effectively. If people follow these steps, they might prevent Alzheimer's and similar neurological diseases. Thus, training the brain is quite an important step to improve memory.

[5] In summary, being examined by a doctor, reducing stress levels, and training the brain are three important steps to improve memory. If people are having trouble with their memory, they need to take it seriously and solve this problem by following these mentioned suggestions. People should not neglect to take care of their memory and strive to live a good life with beautiful memories.

The first part of the concluding paragraph effectively summarizes what was stated in the process essay. The author also includes a note of caution but continues with the positive outcome of following her process.

References

Mansens, D., Deeg, D. J. H., & Comijs, H. C. (2018). The association between singing and/or playing a musical instrument and cognitive functions in older adults. *Aging & Mental Health, 22*(8), 964–971.

O'Shea, D. M., Wit, L., & Smith De, G. E. (2019). Doctor, should I use computer games to prevent dementia? *Clinical Gerontologist, 42*(1), 3–16.

Rathod, R., Kale, A., & Joshi, S. (2016). Novel insights into the effect of vitamin B12 and omega-3 fatty acids on brain function. *Journal of Biomedical Science, 23*, 1–7.

Seyedhosseini Tamijani, S. M., Beirami, E., Ahmadiani, A., & Dargahi, L. (2019). Thyroid hormone treatment alleviates the impairments of neurogenesis, mitochondrial biogenesis and memory performance induced by methamphetamine. *Neurotoxicology, 74*, 7–18.

Singh, M., & Sachdev, S. (2020). Correlation between general intelligence, emotional intelligence and stress response after one month practice of moderate intensity physical exercise. *Journal of Exercise Physiology Online, 1*, 38.

Takeda, F., Noguchi, H., Monma, T., & Tamiya, N. (2015). How possibly do leisure and social activities impact mental health of middle-aged adults in Japan?: An evidence from a national longitudinal survey. *PLoS ONE, 10*(10) Article e0139777.

Post-Reading Questions

1. When you looked at the essay's title, what did you expect to learn from the author?
2. Were your expectations met? Give evidence to support your answer.
3. Does the author use argument in this piece? If so, where?
4. How do the paragraphs follow the organization patterns you have studied?
5. How could Koca have organized this essay differently?
6. Does the author use any words that are unfamiliar to you? Did you need to look them up in a dictionary? If not, why?
7. Did the author include any new ideas in the concluding paragraph? If so, what are they?
8. What essay prompt do you think Koca was given?
9. The author used research for this paper. Do the sources pass the CARS test? Explain.
10. Does the author use emotion in this essay to encourage people to adopt her point of view?

The Comparison and Contrast Essay

Comparison and contrast can be used as the primary organizational method in either an argumentative or an expository essay. This approach can be more challenging than others, so consider using the four-step approach:

1. Make sure you can actually compare topics. It is not possible, for example, to compare the American health-care system to the Canadian educational system.
2. Make sure the topic is manageable. Comparing high school education in two provinces is manageable, but comparing it between Canada and the United States is not.
3. Carefully choose at least three areas of comparison for your main points. Make sure each is logical and manageable.
4. Choose either the block or point-by-point method of organizing your essay.

Point-by-Point Method

The point-by-point organizational method applies one point of comparison to each subject for each paragraph. In the following outline, the numbers represent your points of comparison and "A" and "B" the items you are comparing:

1. Point of comparison

   A: Subject of comparison
   B: Subject of comparison

2. Point of comparison

   A: Subject of comparison
   B: Subject of comparison

3. Point of comparison

   A: Subject of comparison
   B: Subject of comparison

Block Method

In the block organizational method, consider all the points that relate to your first subject (your first block of material). Then consider all the points that apply to the second subject (your second block). Place the points in the same order. Here is an example:

A: Subject of comparison

   1. Point of comparison

2. Point of comparison
3. Point of comparison

B: Subject of comparison

1. Point of comparison
2. Point of comparison
3. Point of comparison

Let's apply the two methods to the instruction "Compare and contrast the benefits of home cooking to the benefits of dining out."

Point-by-Point Method: Home cooking versus dining out

1. Nutrition

   A: Home cooking
   B: Dining out

2. Ease

   A: Home cooking
   B: Dining out

3. Impressions on friends

   A: Home cooking
   B: Dining out

4. Cost

   A: Home cooking
   B: Dining out

Block Method: Home cooking versus dining out

A: Home cooking

   1. Nutrition
   2. Ease
   3. Impressions on friends
   4. Cost

B: Dining out

   1. Nutrition
   2. Ease
   3. Impressions on friends
   4. Cost

Tail of Opposites: Meow, Meow, or Woof, Woof?

Barclay Katt

[1] For most people, it is an easy choice. In fact, it is not really a "choice" at all: it is simply the way it is. There are "cat people" and "dog people" in the world, and neither group speaks the language of the other. They are as separate as curds and whey, and when a cat person meets a dog person on neutral turf, the result is a war of words in which the fur is sure to fly. It seems that each group disdains the other; in many other ways, each doggedly or cattily proclaims its separate identity.

[2] Just by walking into a house, you can tell whether the owner is a feline fancier or a canine connoisseur. (The fact that you have made it to the front door tells you something; have you ever heard of a watchcat?) The cat owner will show you to the elegant living room. Elegant? Cat owners possess the most costly furniture, but it is invariably armoured by ugly plastic coverings with, perhaps, a swath of towels wrapped around sofa ends. The dog owner will conduct you swiftly to the humble kitchen table. En route, you will notice the unmistakable "odeur du chien." But in the kitchen, cooking odours will mingle with those of dog, disguising the latter, though not erasing them completely.

[3] Talk to these two different groups of people, and you will again notice a difference. It is not that cat people are snobbish or that they believe themselves superior; the tilt of their noses has nothing to do with it. But there is one thing that they will expect of you: unremitting absorption in the object of their affection—Kitty. You had better be prepared to spend much of your time gazing in adoration at the magnificent specimen. You must also suffer the fastidious attentions of the cat, if it deigns to give them—even if the tribute takes the form of the kneading of its knife-like claws on your thigh.

[4] It is not that dog people are crude or that they have no concern for social graces. But there is one thing that they will expect of you: conviviality, even to the point of garrulousness. Be careful not to turn away from your host too often (resist the temptation to find out where that annoying series of yips is coming from). Dog owners are famous back-slappers, jabbers, and unapologetic probers of your person. But they will never ask you to share the virtues of their pet and will suddenly lose their warmth if you show too much interest. They are possessive of the bond and discourage interlopers.

[5] Most people have been struck, at one time or another, by the way pet owners come to resemble their pets. It is strange why this is so, and never the other way around—that pets come to look more like their owners. For some reason, the face of the cat or dog is more transferable to the human face than the human face is to that of the dog or cat. Here, it must be admitted that the dog owner is at an advantage. As there are far more breeds of dogs than of cats, the observer cannot help but be impressed by the infinite variety of possible faces of dog owners—from pushed-in pug to the full-blown majesty of Irish wolfhound.

[6] Perhaps it is due to these differences that dog owners and cat owners do not seem able to abide one another; they just never can see eye to eye on anything—or whisker to whisker, for that matter—especially where it concerns the superiority of their own pet. Certainly, the day that cat people and dog people do agree on something will be the day that world peace is finally possible.

Post-Reading Questions

1. Identify the thesis statement in this essay.
2. Identify the organizational method used for comparing.
3. As a member of the intended audience, are you persuaded by this point of view? Give reasons to support your answer.
4. Identify any unfamiliar vocabulary and add those words to your vocabulary journal (discussed in Chapter 1). Could different words have been used as effectively?
5. Would another organizational pattern be as effective as the one Katt uses? If so, which one?

The In-Class (or Examination) Essay

You will probably have to do in-class writing while in college or university. This type of essay requires you to demonstrate your knowledge of a subject and your writing skills, as well as your ability to think, read, and write under pressure.

You may be able to use a text, notes, or a dictionary, or it may just be you, a pen, and some paper.

An in-class, or examination, essay usually tests recall. It also assesses other important qualities, such as organization, time management, critical thinking, and adaptability.

 Chapter 1 discusses critical thinking.

> **TIP**
> In-class writing tests your recall, organization, time management, and adaptability skills.

> **TIP**
> It is important to prepare for in-class writing with realistic expectations: the goal is to distinguish essential information from the rest and focus on what you need to know.

Recall

For an in-class essay, you need to know the terminology of your subject and remember information from lectures, textbooks, and discussions. You also need to know the basics of essay format and structure. If you are asked to write a summary of a text, you will need to know how to summarize; if you are asked to write a critical response to an essay, you will need to know how to analyze and think critically.

An in-class essay tests the application of facts more often than it does the simple recall of basic details. In psychology, you may need to know about B.F. Skinner and his theories of behaviourism, but for the essay, you need to know whether you have to show the impact of this psychological theory or whether you need to explain how behaviourism works.

Organization and Time Management

1. Set time limits.

You may have to write more than one essay in the exam time, so before you begin to write, spend a few minutes calculating how much time you will spend on each one and stick to those time limits. If you find yourself taking too much time on a question, jot one or two points in the margin to follow up on if you have time and move on to the next question.

2. Read the instructions before you start.

Carefully, read every word and underline key words or phrases to reinforce their importance and to keep them in mind as you write. If you misread the question or the prompts and don't follow instructions, you will lose valuable time and marks. This is especially important when the question makes a distinction of some kind: "Answer *three* of the following five questions"; "Respond to *either* question 1 *or* question 2." Pay attention to the verb used to introduce or frame the question—*discuss*, *compare and contrast*, and *explain* give three different instructions.

TIP

When writing an essay, pay close attention to the verb that introduces the question. Words such as *discuss, compare and contrast*, and *explain* provide different instructions.

3. Create an outline.

Creating a brief outline is vital for success in essay tests. This outline will help you remember important points you need to make about the subject. Because of the high stress of these types of tests, memory recall can be weak. By creating your outline, you can refer to it as you complete each paragraph and know that you are answering the question well.

4. Review your answers.

Plan for at least five minutes per question to review your answers after you've finished writing. Check that you haven't left out anything that was asked in the question and that your ideas are in logical order. Proofread and, if necessary, add transitions that will help the reader follow your argument.

Critical Thinking and Adaptability

To answer the exam question properly, decide what the question is asking and focus on strong, well-chosen points and supporting details to develop your answer. A common weakness of in-class essays is the tendency to generalize or to be too broad. You need a manageable topic that can be discussed in a limited time. Use the following questions to help you narrow the focus by examining your knowledge first:

- What do you know about the topic from your experience and studies?
- What have you learned from others' experience with this topic?
- How can you explain the topic using your own knowledge or skills?

TIP

Examples and illustrations turn the general and abstract into the concrete and specific.

Finding where you are knowledgeable is the key to narrowing the topic and to using your strengths.

All essays benefit from examples and illustrations as these support your points. Examples and illustrations will also turn the general and abstract into the concrete and specific. Details are essential. Consider using a pre-writing technique, such as questioning or brainstorming, to generate detail.

Chapter 4 discusses pre-writing.

Look at the following topics. For three of them, write a brief outline of how you would develop the topic in a 90-minute essay. At the end of Chapter 7, after you have learned more about how to write an essay, your instructor may ask you to write an essay based on one of your outlines.

1. Discuss age restrictions for using tobacco products.
2. Explain the effects social media can have on your life.
3. Explain the mental health services available for students today versus in the 1990s.
4. Discuss the cost of a post-secondary education for provincial versus international students.
5. Discuss whether it is better to live at home or live on your own while in school.
6. Explain why reading is important.
7. Describe the difference between high school and college or university.
8. Discuss the difference between open-source and proprietary software.
9. Discuss different ways to affect climate change.
10. Define public transportation and explain it in your area.

Identify which type of expository essay best fits each of the following topics:

- respective audiences for online games (such as *MineCraft* and apps like *Bubblepop*)
- how robots or smartphones are changing the way we live
- using Macs or PCs for school
- the value of networking for job hunting
- the value of friends
- the importance of managing stress

The following expository essay uses a number of organizing processes, such as definition and description. The author uses clear examples to explain his points. He includes very clear descriptions so that the readers can visualize what is being discussed, which improves their understanding. The examples also add to his credibility. Remember that essays, whether expository or argument, can use a variety of organizational patterns and can even have different organizing patterns in individual paragraphs.

One Giant Paw Print Stirs an Age-Old Debate: How Big Can a Wolf Be?

Michael Fraiman

A man in the Northwest Territories spotted giant wolf tracks, 7½ inches long. Anything longer than 5½ inches is Amarok territory—the legendary lupine of Inuit folklore.

Sample Professional Essay

Expository Essay

The author has created a thesis statement that is separate from the essay itself.

Fraiman is using the introduction to generate reader interest. He uses the last sentence to introduce the focus of the essay.

[1] Years ago, on a dark December morning, Ron Doctor was driving alone through the snowy hinterlands of the Northwest Territories when he spotted something odd in the thick, fresh snow. He couldn't get a good look, so he drove home and returned to the scene during his precious four-hour window of sub-arctic daylight. The second visit confirmed his suspicions: these were giant wolf tracks, 7½ inches long.

[2] "Holy smoke," the veteran wildlife officer thought to himself. "This is unreal." He'd never seen a wolf track that big.

[3] Doctor gauged the distance between each print—six or seven feet. Head to tail, the beast itself could be as long as eight. He laid his left hand next to the feral vestige and snapped a photo, impressing friends and family, and eventually—out of the blue in January—getting posted to CBC North's website and going semi-viral on Twitter. "We know there's wolves around," he says. "But that size—nobody's ever seen a track that size."

Fraiman provides enough detail so that the reader can visualize where, exactly, this event takes place.

[4] Doctor lives in Tulita, a remote hamlet of 477 people nestled at the junction of the Great Bear and Mackenzie rivers. The legendary Mackenzie is the longest waterway in Canada, whose basin is home to the Mackenzie Valley wolves, among the largest gray wolves in North America. Females can reach 100 lb., but males routinely top 120. Their prints extend 5½ inches. Anything longer is sasquatch territory.

Note the definition the author provides so that the reader can learn the term used in Inuit folklore but also understand the meaning of those words.

[5] Or, more accurately, Amarok territory. That's the legendary lupine of Inuit folklore—a godlike creature who kills lone hunters at night. Most wolves are not Amarok. Sources are foggy on the biggest wolf ever caught, but an Alaskan hunter once bagged a 175-lb. one. That was in 1939, and a few 140-pounders have been caught since. But unlike the mythical Inuit wolf lord, none of them stalked human prey. "It's amazing to me that wolves don't attack people more often," says Dean Cluff, a regional biologist for the North Slave Region of the Northwest Territories. "Because they certainly could. If they knew how weak we were, they would."

[6] Instead, wolves prefer to compete with their Inuit neighbours for moose and caribou. The latter presents a problem because Canadian caribou are heading toward extinction. In the spring of 2020, the government of the Northwest Territories spent more than $320,000 to snipe wolves from a helicopter to protect the Bathurst and Bluenose-East caribou herds. (This is not unique; during the winter of 2019–2020, British Columbia spent almost $2 million to cull 463 wolves from caribou regions.) In 2015, the territory began awarding $200 for each wolf carcass delivered to its Department of Environment and Natural Resources.

The author begins the paragraph by explaining where the wolf carcasses are, but then goes on to explain to the audience why it is difficult to determine a wolf's size, thus helping the reader understand that the size of the paw print found is not an indicator of the size of the wolf.

[7] Many of those dead wolves wind up at Cluff's office in Yellowknife. Equipped with a master's degree in zoology and decades of experience studying wolves, Cluff has amassed a collection of hundreds of wolf carcasses—scientific samples from which he should, theoretically, be able to determine a wolf's size without seeing the animal in person. But hunters don't treat them with consistency. Some carcasses are skinned, some not; others are missing tails or paws. What's more, wolves can pack away 20 lb. of food in their stomachs, making weight comparisons hard (was the animal full when it was shot?). In the winter, when prey is easier to catch, they grow fatter. There are simply too many variables.

In an academic essay, facts and statistics need to be supported with citations and references.

[8] So Cluff is chiselling away at his own solution. "I have a whole bunch of femurs from all these carcasses that I'm going to weigh," he explains. Cluff has asked around, but he's never found a formula for determining wolf weights based on bones, the way paleontologists extrapolate dinosaur data from fossils. If such a formula does exist for wolves, "it's certainly not widespread," he says. "There's not much of a need for this, I suppose. But I want to be able to do that, so I think I can make that contribution. It's just taking time."

[9] Cluff has seen Doctor's photo, but a print alone is even less useful than a femur. So this literal bigfoot wolf is free to run wild in our imaginations, ballooning to monstrous sizes; humans may fear its murderous capacity, marvel at its strength or scapegoat it for the extinction of a whole other species, downplaying the roles of climate change and mining development and shrinking habitat. In Farley Mowat's 1963 book *Never Cry Wolf*, in which he describes the lives of wolves in northern Canada, he blamed shrinking caribou numbers not on stigmatized wolves, but on stubborn humans: "We have doomed the wolf not for what it is, but for what we deliberately and mistakenly perceive it to be—the mythologized epitome of a savage ruthless killer—which is, in reality, no more than a reflected image of ourself."

[10] Meanwhile, a modern-day Amarok, impossibly large yet invisible to humans, may roam Canada's tundra in search of prey. Cluff, for one, isn't afraid. To him, they mark a thriving ecosystem. Wolves signify life. "If you've got wolves," he says, "you've got real wilderness."

> The author does not use a formal concluding paragraph for this essay. However, he does end with a thought-provoking idea to help the reader think about this topic further.

Fraiman, Michael. "One Giant Paw Print Stirs an Age-Old Debate: How Big Can a Wolf Be?" Maclean's, 22 Feb. 2021, https://www.macleans.ca/society/environment/one-giant-paw-print-stirs-an-age-old-debate-how-big-can-a-wolf-be/. © 2021 & Used with permission of St. Joseph Communications. All rights reserved.

Post-Reading Questions

1. Who do you think the audience is for this essay? Justify your answer with relevant quotations from the article.

2. Do the author's methods for developing paragraphs work for this essay? If so, why? If not, how would you have organized the ideas?

3. What are some of the organizational patterns he uses?

4. The author uses many examples of wolf carcasses that are given to Dean Cluff. Why do you think he does this?

5. Why do you think the author uses the Amarok in this essay?

6. Do you think the author uses appropriate examples for the essay? Are there other examples you might have added?

7. List some facts the author uses to illustrate his essay. Explain why you think he chose them.

8. Does reading the article evoke any emotion in you? Do you think this was the writer's intent? Explain.

9. Does this essay have enough detail? What would you add to make it more complete?

10. Explain why this is an expository essay.

Chapter Review Questions

1. Why is it important to pay attention to prompts in an essay question?

2. What are the benefits of including research in an expository essay?

3. What are two ways you can use for a comparison and contrast essay?

4. Is there any advantage you can see to using one method over another in this type of essay?

5. When would you write a process essay?

6. Why should you review the steps in a process essay?

7. What are the important steps to remember when you write an in-class essay?

8. Why should you add examples and illustrations to essays, especially in-class essays?

9. Why is it important to narrow an essay topic? What questions could you ask to help focus your topic?

10. Why is it important to revise and edit your essays before submitting them?

7 Introductions, Thesis Statements, and Conclusions

By the end of this chapter, you should be able to

- structure an expository essay;
- introduce an essay;
- create an effective thesis statement; and
- write an effective conclusion.

The requirements for essays at the college and university level are more advanced than those at the high school level. In this chapter, you will learn how to draw your audience into your essay effectively and to keep them engaged through to your conclusion.

The Expository Essay Template

As noted in Chapter 4, it is important to use an outline to help you write a unified, coherent, and well-developed essay. A template (such as the one in Table 7.1) will help you organize your thoughts into paragraphs. Templates can be expanded or contracted as necessary to include the number of paragraphs required for your essay. Similarly, you can change the number of points required to support your topic sentence. Some topics may need only two, while others may require more. Some points may also need expanding using more explanation or illustration with quotations, paraphrases, or personal observation.

Table 7.2 provides part of a completed template for an essay on eating disorders. The first body paragraph, which has more than three points, uses definition to give the reader the necessary background to understand

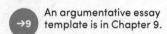

→9 An argumentative essay template is in Chapter 9.

TABLE 7.1 Expository Essay Template

Essay Section	What to Include	Explanation
Introductory paragraph with thesis statement	Usually this paragraph begins with general statements about the topic and concludes with the thesis statement.	Use the opening sentences of the paragraph to introduce your reader to the topic. Make sure that your thesis statement includes at least three ways in which you plan to explore or prove your thesis. Depending on the complexity of the assignment, you may have more or fewer than three. 1. 2. 3.
Body paragraph 1	Topic sentence Point 1 Explanation/illustration Point 2 Explanation/illustration Point 3 Explanation/illustration Concluding sentence	Your topic sentence is an expansion of the first item listed in your thesis statement. Support the topic of your body paragraph using paraphrases, quotations, and statistics from your research or use personal observations if appropriate. The amount of support material required will depend on the scope of the assignment. Use this paragraph's concluding sentence to summarize your support material and relate it to the topic or thesis. The concluding sentence can also lead the reader to the next paragraph.
Body paragraph 2	Topic sentence Point 1 Explanation/illustration Point 2 Explanation/illustration Point 3 Explanation/illustration Concluding sentence	The topic sentence in this paragraph refers to the second point listed in the thesis. Make sure that this topic sentence *includes a transition* from the topic of the previous paragraph to this new topic. Support the topic of your body paragraph using paraphrases, quotations, and statistics from your research or use personal observations if appropriate. Use this paragraph's concluding sentence to summarize your support material and relate it to the topic or thesis. The concluding sentence can also lead the reader to the next paragraph.

Essay Section	What to Include	Explanation
Body paragraph 3	Topic sentence Point 1 Explanation/illustration Point 2 Explanation/illustration Point 3 Explanation/illustration Concluding sentence	The topic sentence in this paragraph refers to the third point listed in the thesis. Make sure that this topic sentence *includes a transition* from the topic of the previous paragraph to this new topic. Support the topic of your body paragraph using paraphrases, quotations, and statistics from your research or use personal observations if appropriate. Use this paragraph's concluding sentence to summarize your support material and relate it to the topic or thesis.
Concluding paragraph	A general summary of the main ideas from the preceding body paragraphs. The concluding sentence is a clincher.	This paragraph summarizes your evidence and shows how it proved your thesis. To conclude, add a clincher—an idea, concept, or thought that the reader can take away from reading your essay.

TABLE 7.2 Expository Essay Template: Eating Disorders

Introductory paragraph with thesis statement	General statements about eating disorders and people's perception of them. Maybe ask a question: Do you know someone with an eating disorder?	
	Thesis: Eating disorders fall into several types and are becoming more prevalent among young people, affecting them both medically and psychologically.	
	Supporting ideas	1. it's important to understand the different types of disorders
		2. why they are on the rise, or at least seem to be
		3. medical and psychological impact
Paragraph 1	Topic sentence	When people think of eating disorders, they often think of teenage girls or runway models who starve themselves, but that is only one of the many disorders.
	Subpoint 1	Anorexia nervosa—most known
	Illustration	Find medical definition from journals and explain whom it affects and its side effects
	Subpoint 2	Bulimia (binge and purge)
	Illustration	Find medical definition from journals and explain whom it affects and its side effects
	Subpoint 3	Compulsive overeating
	Illustration	Find medical definition from journals and explain whom it affects and its side effects
	Subpoint 4	Selective eating
	Illustration	Find medical definition from journals and explain whom it affects and its side effects
	Conclusion	There are many different types of eating disorders, but they all have the same outcome.

the rest of the essay. The next body paragraph could use chronology to establish an increase in eating disorders over a certain period. The final paragraph may use a cause–effect pattern. Remember that you don't need to use full sentences or have fully developed ideas at this stage. Ideas introduced here can also be modified or moved later. At this point, the main purpose is to write your ideas down and organize them.

Note that this first body paragraph begins with a topic sentence that tells the readers that the author is going to talk about various kinds of eating disorders. This introduces the first of the supporting ideas that the author has outlined in the thesis. The subpoints in this paragraph list the disorders and explain them. The concluding sentence refers to the thesis, alluding to the mental and physical harm caused by these disorders.

The author will follow the same pattern for the second body paragraph. The first sentence will make the transition between the two topics, for example: "Though much is known about the variety of eating disorders, what needs to be understood now is why more and more people are affected by them." This sentence relates to the descriptions of the eating disorders in the first paragraph and introduced the second supporting idea about the rise in numbers. The supporting details in this paragraph will include statistics to show the increase in the number of cases.

The first sentence of the third paragraph will also be a transition sentence, for example: "The rise in the number of people affected by eating disorders has forced medical professionals to focus closely on the physical and mental harm that these disorders can cause." This sentence connects the information in paragraph two about the increase in cases to the new paragraph that will focus on the mental and physical impact of eating disorders. The supporting points in this paragraph will include information from medical and mental health experts about the impact of the disorders.

If you are the type of student that does not use an outline, treat the first draft that you write as a brainstorming session. Then, review your paper and create an outline from it. As you go through your draft, you may see how certain ideas fit more coherently in another paragraph. You may also discover that you need additional information to support or clarify a point for your reader. To ensure that your readers can follow your train of thought, use logical connections between your ideas.

EXERCISE 7.1

Create a template for one of the following essay topics.

1. The challenges of online learning
2. How to alleviate stress during the first year of college or university
3. How millennials and Gen Zs are different from boomers
4. The advantages of having a diploma or a degree
5. How the rise of social media has led to increased written communication
6. How stress affects the body

7. What the world was like prior to the internet
8. How research is done on your library databases
9. The disadvantages of a gig economy
10. How students survive the rising cost of living

The Essay's Introduction

Every essay starts with an introduction. In fact, even if this term is not used, almost everything you read begins with a preview of what follows, including books, articles, sales material, and even your résumé. In an essay, the introduction's job is to present the main idea (thesis) and introduce the essay's organizational pattern.

An introduction is the opening of a document that presents the main idea (the thesis statement) and the main organizational pattern.

How to Create Reader Interest in the Introduction

The introduction should create reader interest and assure readers that they are being addressed by a knowledgeable and competent writer. You should avoid using quotes in the introduction, unless you are using a dramatic approach introduction, as mentioned below. You want to save supporting evidence for the body of your essay to convince your reader that you are credible and have done the necessary research to support your point of view.

EAL

Point of view generally means one of two things in an essay. It can mean the grammatical point of view: using first, second, or third person. It can also mean how you feel about or present a topic in your essay. This can be shown in your position in an argument essay, or it can be shown by your bias in an expository essay.

TIP

Your writing needs to catch and maintain the reader's attention and interest. Reader interest is especially important when you are writing for an instructor. If your essay is entertaining and thought provoking, your mark will probably be higher than if it is mundane.

Reader interest can be created through three different organizational patterns.

Logical Introduction

The logical approach follows the pattern of an inverted pyramid. The paragraph begins with a broad, general statement and ends with a narrow, specific statement, which is your thesis statement.

Figure 7.1 illustrates this method.

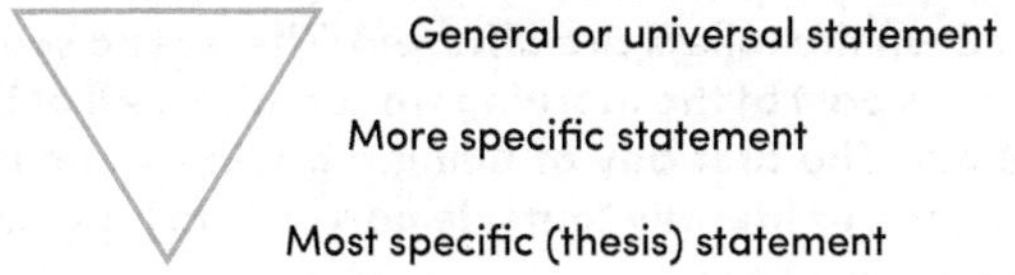

The logical approach moves from a broad to a narrow focus.

General or universal statement

More specific statement

Most specific (thesis) statement

FIGURE 7.1 Structure of paragraph introduction

In the following introduction, the writer begins with a general claim and gradually brings the subject—clean energy—into focus. This development is important for general readers who may not know much about the topic. Pay close attention to how the writer also creates reader interest.

> **For centuries, humans have needed energy to produce goods. It began with a simple fire to cook food on. Once technology began to evolve at a rapid pace, better forms of energy production were needed, such as coal power to produce steam for the Industrial Revolution. Coal continued to be widely used to produce energy, but it led to severe air pollution. Newer forms of cleaner energy were needed. Hydroelectric power was created, which led to the building of dams and flooding land. Nuclear power was invented, but the problem of disposing of spent fuel cells remains problematic. Today, in order to create a less polluted and less damaged environment, many people are turning to clean energy produced by wind farms and solar panels.**

The paragraph begins with a general statement before making specific connections between energy created in the past, which polluted and damaged the environment, and the clean energy produced today.

The author introduces issues from the past and explains the problems they caused.

In the thesis statement, the writer announces the essay's main point, the most specific sentence.

Another kind of logical approach begins by mentioning something familiar to the reader and proceeding to the unfamiliar. The following opening illustrates this approach:

> **While the intelligence quotient (IQ) has long been a useful tool to determine one's intelligence, a development in the study of human intellectual experience has expanded to include one's emotional state. It is called emotional intelligence, or EQ.**
>
> Student writer Chin-Ju Chiang

Dramatic Introduction

The dramatic approach can be used in various ways. You can begin with an interesting quotation (but not a citation from a dictionary), a thought-provoking question, a personal experience, an illuminating statistic, a description of a scene, or a brief narrative such as an anecdote.

Unlike in the logical approach, you begin with something specific, a detail or incident that surprises or intrigues your reader. Your objective is not to shock or startle. In the excerpt below, the student writer creates a scenario that enables the reader to experience an unfamiliar martial art as she did.

In the dramatic approach, the essay's opening is meant to catch the reader's attention in an interesting or thought-provoking way. An anecdote is an incident or event that is used because it is interesting or striking.

> **Imagine what it would be like to wake up one day and not understand anything around you. People are moving their mouths and making strange sounds, but you can't understand what they are saying. Instead of toast or cereal for breakfast, you are presented with rice, a raw egg, soy sauce, and seaweed. People bow instead of shaking hands. The dress code requires a suit and tie. Shoes are not worn inside buildings, so slippers are provided that are never big enough for your feet. Even the toilets are different. There is no seat. You just squat. Exercise is part of the morning work routine. All of this occurs before 10:00 am. The first day of being a *gaijin* (pronounced guy-jean)—a foreigner, or literally "outside person"—in Japan is exciting, yet challenging.**

The writer evokes a detailed scene in order to interest the reader, using both descriptive detail and narration (telling a story).

Putting the reader in the place of the unknowing spectator, the writer continues to evoke the scene, arousing the reader's curiosity and suspense.

The writer concisely defines *gaijin* in the thesis statement. Note that the writer's use of personal experience is a strategy designed to create reader interest. The essay will probably make use of the writer's personal experience coupled with research to explain significant aspects of being a foreigner.

EXERCISE 7.2

Rewrite the above paragraph, about being a foreigner, using the logical approach. (You might have to do some research on the topic.)

Mixed Approach

You can also use a mixed approach to attract interest:

- *Dramatic–logical*: You could begin with a question and then use the logical approach to develop the rest of the paragraph.
- *Logical–dramatic*: You could use a "reversal" strategy, beginning with a general statement before dramatically turning the tables and arguing the opposite. Student writer Grace Beal employs this strategy in her essay on the use of fur in today's society.

Since the beginning of time, people have depended on fur. Cavemen wore animal skins as clothing; furthermore, after killing an animal, such as a buffalo, the flesh would be eaten and the bones would be used in tool-making. They used as much of the animal as possible because of their spiritual beliefs and because, with few other resources, it made sense to waste as little as possible. Wearing fur in that age was a necessity: it was warm, practical, and readily available. Today, it is a far different story. Fur is part of the upscale fashion industry, but killing wild animals for their skin extends beyond fur fanciers; it is a luxury product for many different consumers today, such as car owners with leather upholstery. There are more than 40 different animal species that are killed for their skin, and not a single one needs to be.

The writer makes a general statement.

Using the logical method, the author adds detail, becoming more specific.

The author reiterates the main point before contrasting the caveman's needs with those of society today.

In the thesis statement, the writer forcefully announces the argumentative claim: killing animals for their fur is now wrong.

EAL

Notice that some of these introductions begin with using the second person. Make sure you know whether you can use this in your essay before you begin writing. Many academic essays must be written in third person.

Some academic articles do not use any of these introduction types. Instead, they may begin with a direct and concise statement of the problem or purpose and may even include the study's findings. This is often the case with scientific articles designed for those with specialized knowledge of the subject.

The approach you choose should be relevant to your topic, purpose, and audience. For example, if you were arguing in favour of euthanasia or another issue with a built-in emotional aspect and knew your audience opposed it, a strong, emotional opening could alienate readers.

Other Functions of the Introduction

Aside from creating reader interest, the introduction serves three other important functions:

← 4 Chapter 4 discusses paragraph development and essay development.

- *Announces your topic and the main points*: The thesis statement gives the main points of the essay and must have two parts: the topic and a comment on it (see "The Thesis Statement: Simple versus Expanded" later in this chapter).
- *Introduces the writer*: The introduction is your first chance to establish credibility, presenting yourself as being knowledgeable about the topic as well as being reliable and trustworthy. You show your credibility by writing well and by appearing rational, fair, and in control.
- *Indicates how the writer plans to develop the main points*: Organizational patterns include narration, chronology, comparison and contrast, and cause–effect.

Features of the Introduction

The Opening Sentence

In the logical approach, the introduction usually builds to the thesis. Like the thesis, the opening sentence needs to be written carefully. An ineffective opening may be too general or abrupt, obvious, overstated (making a false universal claim), or irrelevant, as shown in these examples.

Too general:

> **Since the beginning of the twenty-first century, many historic events have occurred around the globe, especially in Europe, Asia, and America.**

Why is this too broad? Does the phrase beginning with *especially* help to make it more specific? How can the statement be made more effective?

Too abrupt:

> **Changes need to be made to our province's driving laws to address driving while using marijuana.**

Why is this statement too abrupt? Would it be less so if it were placed somewhere else in the introduction?

Obvious:

> **As the population continues to rise around the world, the need for transportation will also increase.**

What makes this statement too obvious? What changes would make it more appropriate as an opening?

Overstated:

> **Everyone these days has a computer, tablet, or smartphone.**

TIP Be wary of making "everyone" claims unless your statement truly applies to everyone.

Many people in the world, even in Canada, do not own a computer, tablet, or smartphone. There are few situations satisfied by the "everyone" claim. How can the statement be improved?

Irrelevant:

Few people know that sea otters can live to the age of 15 years.

This opening could be effective if the statement fell into the "believe it or not" category, but it doesn't. How would you rewrite it?

Starting your essay in any of the above ways will cause your reader to question your abilities as a writer. An ineffective opening is like receiving a weak handshake when first meeting someone. You want your opening sentence to create the best first impression possible.

Writing a strong introduction requires time and patience. Sometimes what you really want to say doesn't become clear until after you've written your first draft. In fact, some instructors believe that the introduction should be written last.

> **TIP**
> If you have problems writing an introduction, consider writing the rest of the essay first.

EXERCISE 7.3

In groups, consider the following opening statements and discuss what makes them ineffective. Think about what the topic of the essay might be and then revise them to make them more effective and interesting.

1. Time is money.
2. Text messaging is convenient, but it is too overwhelming.
3. Canada became a country in 1867.
4. I guess we would all own an electric car, if we could.
5. There are many issues with health care in Canada, including hallway medicine.
6. Nuclear energy is, without a doubt, the worst form of energy possible.
7. Why not travel as much as you can?
8. The movement away from organized religion is due to the politics of religion not changing as quickly as society's values.
9. Everyone watches sports.
10. No one in Canada is a better author than Margaret Atwood.
11. Most youth today will not rise above their parents' socio-economic status.
12. A penny saved is a penny earned.
13. Students cheating is just a fact in school today.
14. Who was the Joker, really?
15. Doping is a part of sports—no ands, ifs, or buts.

The Thesis Statement: Simple versus Expanded

A simple thesis statement reveals the essay's topic and makes a comment on it. Here is an example:

Life in residence at the University of the South Pole (topic) helps prepare one for life after university. (comment)

An expanded thesis statement gives the topic and adds more detail, such as the essay's main points. It answers questions such as "How?" or "Why?" to

A simple thesis statement announces the topic and makes a comment on it.

 Chapter 8 discusses thesis statements based on facts, claims, and values.

An expanded thesis statement gives more detail, such as the main points that will be covered in the essay.

account for or justify the main idea. This example addresses the question "How does life in residence prepare one for life after university?"

Life in residence at the University of the South Pole (topic) helps prepare one for life after university (comment) by making a student independent, by reinforcing basic life skills, and by teaching one how to get along with penguins. (details listing the three ways in which this university prepares the student for life)

The three body paragraphs of this essay would each deal with one of the items listed in the comment portion of the thesis statement. The body paragraphs will also follow the same order as the items were listed; in this case, the paragraph about student independence would be the first body paragraph.

Here's an example of a topic, followed by a simple thesis statement and an expanded one that answers the question "Why?"

Topic:

School uniforms

Simple thesis statement:

Making school uniforms mandatory has many advantages for students.

Expanded thesis statement:

Making school uniforms mandatory has many advantages for students, as they eliminate distractions, encourage a focus on academics, and reduce competition based on appearances.

A simple thesis statement may be sufficient for a short essay, such as one of fewer than 500 words. It can be used in an expository essay in which you attempt to answer a question or solve a problem. Check with your instructor for specific guidelines about simple versus expanded thesis statements.

Effective Thesis Statements

An effective thesis statement should be specific, interesting, and manageable:

- *Specific*: The thesis informs the reader about what will follow.
- *Interesting*: The thesis attracts the reader to the topic and the essay.
- *Manageable*: The thesis introduces a topic that can be successfully explored in the space of the essay.

An unclear thesis statement may confuse rather than inform. For example, the following thesis statement doesn't clearly express the main points of the essay.

Pets are important in that they can unify and heal and are an inevitable part of human nature.

This statement leaves the reader unclear as to the writer's exact meaning. As an expanded thesis statement, it needs to be more detailed and precise, so it doesn't confuse the readers. Note that the revised thesis statement uses

TIP

Remember the acronym SIM (specific, interesting, and manageable) when creating a thesis statement.

parallel structure when listing the three points that will be discussed in the essay. They follow the same grammatical pattern: "bringing people . . . , helping them . . . , enabling them . . ." Another parallel wording for the example could be "Pets are important because they *bring* people together, *help* them recover from an illness or depression, and *enable* them to express important human values, such as love."

This revised thesis is more effective:

Pets are important in bringing people together, helping them recover from an illness or depression, and enabling them to express important human values, such as love.

When you revise your essay, your thesis needs to reflect the essay's main point accurately. In this example, we don't know whether the essay is about excessive dieting or body image:

Many youth are obsessed by dieting today due to the prominence our society places on body image.

This thesis does not tell the reader precisely what points the author intends to discuss in the essay. The writer needs to narrow the topic to one specific area, such as three popular diets and the health issues they can create or youth concern with body image and the rise in eating disorders and anxiety among young people.

Never begin an essay by saying, "This essay will . . ." That is the purpose of your thesis statement. Consider these examples.

Ineffective:

This essay will examine the phenomenon of online gambling and argue in favour of strict government regulation of this growing industry.

Revised:

Online gambling is of increasing concern to governments and should be subject to strict regulations.

Remember that your thesis may change as you write your outline or draft and uncover areas about your topic you weren't aware of before. Don't be afraid to go back and change it after you have finished your outline or first draft.

> **TIP**
>
> When you use an expanded thesis statement, you must express your main points in parallel structure. (see "The Parallelism Principle" in Chapter 15).

EXERCISE 7.4

1. Using the three SIM criteria for effective thesis statements, evaluate the effectiveness of the following statements for an essay on aliens, and rewrite the statements that need improving.
   a. It is probable that aliens built the pyramids.
   b. It is clear that aliens are responsible for many of the world's problems today.
   c. Everyone is curious about the possible existence of aliens.

2. Which of these simple thesis statements is best for an essay on how computers influence people? Rate each according to whether it is specific, interesting, and manageable. Be prepared to explain your decisions.

   a. The computer is one of the most entertaining pastimes we have.
   b. Violence found in computer games is affecting children by increasing the number of shootings in schools.
   c. The computer has helped change the way we live compared to the way our grandparents lived 50 years ago.
   d. Computers take away our free time by creating a dependency that is very hard to escape from once we are hooked.
   e. TV is losing its influence because of the increasing popularity of computers.
   f. A computer is a great babysitter for preschool-age children.

3. Write an effective thesis statement on the topic of the computer's influence, using any pre-writing technique you feel comfortable with and making sure that you follow the three requirements of a good thesis statement.

4. Identify the following thesis statements by type and make the simple ones expanded.

   a. Regular, moderate doses of stress not only are inevitable in today's world but also can be good for you.
   b. As consumers, we must keep ourselves informed about the activities of the industries we support.
   c. Although poor waste management has already had a significant impact on the planet, the Canadian government needs to create better recycling chains, to encourage people to reduce the amount they purchase, and to better educate the public.
   d. Education is viewed as a benefit to individuals, but too much education can have negative results.
   e. Many people misunderstand the concept of multi-tasking.

A Thesis Statement Checklist

Use the following checklist when writing thesis statements:

1. Have you written a complete thesis statement, not just a topic?
2. Does it have two parts? (simple thesis statement)
3. Have you included your main points in the order they will appear in your essay? (expanded thesis statement)
4. Are there enough details for the reader to understand your main points (i.e., is the statement clearly phrased and not confusing)?
5. Is the single focus of the thesis clear (i.e., the statement isn't vague and doesn't straddle multiple topics)?
6. Is it worded objectively and not self-consciously (i.e., by mentioning the writer or the essay itself)?
7. Have you arranged your main points in a parallel structure?

In groups, choose a topic from the list and use a pre-writing technique to formulate a simple thesis statement with the three criteria discussed in this chapter.

aliens	nature
elections	skateboarding
clothes	stress
streaming services	alienation
Tinder	psychology
ghosts	taboos
humour	(the) gig economy
indie rock	fake news
justice	recycling
karma	xenophobia
laughter	bike sharing
online shopping	meditation

Exchange your statement with another group's and evaluate theirs according to the three SIM criteria. Give one mark for each; half marks are allowed. When all the groups have completed the evaluation process, discuss the ratings and the reasons behind them. Revise your thesis statement according to the feedback your group receives.

Use another pre-writing technique to come up with three main points, and reword the simple thesis statement so that it is an expanded one. Exchange the statements again and evaluate them based on points 4–6 in the checklist above. Again, discuss the ratings with the other groups.

Introduction Length

In general, an introduction should be no more than about 15 per cent of the essay's length, but you should check with your instructor for specific guidelines. The length will also depend on whether you decide to include the main points of your essay (expanded thesis) or background information.

Evaluate the following introductory paragraphs according to the criteria discussed in the previous pages. Does each function as an effective introduction? Specifically consider the following:

- Which method(s)—logical, dramatic, mixed—did the writer use to create reader interest?
- Is the opening effective? What makes it effective or ineffective?
- Identify the thesis statement. Is it specific, interesting, and manageable? Simple or expanded?

See Chapter 4 for a review of essay organizational patterns.

- Has the writer established credibility?
- Is the essay's main organizational pattern apparent?
- Does the paragraph length seem appropriate?

1. Feminism is not about taking away men's rights. It is about creating an equal world so that both men and women can reach their true potential. In the past, when women got married, they had to give their property to their husbands. They could not vote. They had to perform domestic chores, even if they loathed them. As recently as the 1950s, women had to take their husband's name upon marriage and were often addressed using both the husband's first and last names. Women could not get their own credit cards, much less have a career. The first wave of feminism changed much of this, but a lot of inequality still exists. The fight must continue for equal pay for equal work, fair value for their money, and court systems that defend their rights.

2. What is it about the Italian Mafia that fascinates millions of people? Could part of the answer lie in Hollywood's depiction of a 5' 9", 275-pound Italian named Bruno Francessi who drives a black Cadillac, wears $3,000 silk suits, and claims to have "two" families; or is it the way the media creates celebrity status for Mafiosi people and events? The media and film industry portray a mobster's lucrative lifestyle as the result of thoughtless killings, a regimen of violence and corruption. But to fully understand the mob lifestyle, one must understand how mobsters operate—not what they appear to be on the surface, but the structure, conduct, and economic realities that created their power and enable them to maintain it. As someone who lived close to this power, I know that behind the media perception lies a fundamental belief in and adherence to a system. (Student writer Dino Pascoli)

3. Scams are more of a threat in Canada with the rise of the internet and robocalling. Often the elderly and new Canadians fall victim to this. The newspaper and online media often report incidences of seniors losing their life savings or new Canadians believing they must pay for whatever service is being offered, such as paying back taxes. The people who commit these crimes rely on the victims being uneducated or afraid of authority. In order to combat this crime, people need to be better informed about what organizations like immigration, Revenue Canada, and banks do to collect money and information.

4. Because of sites like Facebook, identity theft is on the rise. What may seem like a fun game can actually be used to collect data about individuals. Many people click on games like "Who were you in a past life?" or "What cartoon character are you?" The most dangerous of all are the ones asking seemingly innocent questions: "How many tattoos do you have?" "How many children do you have?" "How many times have you been married?" Companies and identity thieves mine the internet for information like this. It is important for everyone to be cautious about sharing personal information so that it is harder to steal an identity.

5. Why does my cell phone not work? Why do I get radiation poisoning when I travel by plane? Why is the light switch not working? These are the kinds of questions we ask ourselves when solar flares are striking

the Earth. Solar flares originate from the sun. Every 11 years, the sun switches its magnetic poles, causing the magnetic fields to twist and turn in the atmosphere above sunspots, which are eruptions on the sun's surface. The magnetic field seems to snap like a rubber band stretched too tightly. When one of these fields breaks, it can create energy equal to a billion megatons of TNT exploding. The magnetic fields seem to flip and reconnect after they break. Solar flares occasionally head toward the Earth, and even though we are 150 million kilometres from the sun, these flares can reach us in fewer than two days. While the Earth is experiencing a solar flare, multiple problems can occur—from malfunctions of orbiting objects to disruption in power systems and radio signals. While the flares can produce these problems, they can also create the most beautiful and unusual auroras seen around the world. (Student writer Nicholas Fodor)

EXERCISE 7.7

Evaluate the following introduction based on whether the opening is successful, the writer creates interest and appears credible, and the thesis statement is effective. Rewrite the paragraph, correcting any weaknesses you find. You can add your own material or ideas, but try not to increase the length (approximately 130 words).

Something drastic needs to be done about obesity among teenagers today! Over the last decade, there has been a disturbing trend toward teenage obesity. Teenagers today would rather lodge themselves in front of the TV or play video games for hours on end than get some form of physical exercise. This problem becomes pronounced in high school because physical education is not compulsory in most schools. However, PE classes have a lot to offer. Participation can reduce the risk of heart failure, improve overall fitness, promote good health habits, improve self-discipline and skill development, boost self-confidence, increase academic performance, and enhance communication and cooperative skills. Obesity is an alarming trend among high school students today and should be a concern to both students and their parents.

The Essay's Conclusion

Functions of the Conclusion

The conclusion is the final paragraph of an essay. It recalls the thesis statement and summarizes the discussion in the supporting body paragraphs. It asks the reader to reconsider the thesis based on the evidence presented in the essay. Unlike an introduction, it often works from the specific to the general (see Figure 7.2). An effective conclusion often includes a clincher statement—an idea to remain with the reader.

The **conclusion** is the final paragraph of the essay that sums up what was said in the body paragraphs.

Introduction

Conclusion

FIGURE 7.2 Introduction–conclusion inverted pyramid

Your conclusion should be expected because you have prepared the reader for it, but it should not be a boring restatement of the thesis. This simple restatement conclusion leaves the reader unsatisfied and wondering if you didn't leave enough time to complete the essay properly, got tired of the subject matter, or couldn't be bothered to write an interesting ending.

Spend as much time on your conclusion as you do the other parts of the essay because it will leave a lasting impression with your audience. You want your audience to be left with positive opinions about your logically developed ideas and your professional writing skills.

Two Kinds of Conclusion

The introduction and conclusion are not identical bookends with the body paragraphs in between. The conclusion emphasizes the importance of the thesis in two ways:

A circular conclusion reminds the reader of the thesis. A spiral conclusion restates the thesis and leads the reader beyond it.

- A circular conclusion restates the thesis with different words that stress its importance, perhaps suggesting an action if you are arguing for a practical change to result from your ideas. Reminding the reader of the thesis "closes the circle" by bringing your audience back to the starting point of your essay. This type of conclusion shows *how* the thesis statement has been proven and does not simply repeat it.
- A spiral conclusion suggests a specific way that the thesis could be applied, asks further questions, or proposes other ways of looking at the problem. It refers to the thesis but then also leads the reader to think beyond it. It might point to results of the thesis that suggest action on the part of the reader or further research. Do not introduce new material to support your thesis in the conclusion.

Sometimes the conclusion includes personal reflection, such as considering the way your thesis has affected you or people you know. This kind of conclusion, however, belongs in personal and argumentative essays rather than in expository ones. If you have not used personal experience in the essay, do not use it in the conclusion.

When writing your conclusion, avoid

- restating the thesis statement word for word;
- mentioning a new point (the conclusion rewords the thesis and the main points of the essay in an interesting way but *does not* introduce something new);
- giving an example or illustration to support your thesis (examples only belong in your body paragraphs); and
- writing a conclusion that is much longer than your introduction (exceptions are essays that include a lengthy "Discussion" section).

Read your introduction and then your conclusion to check that it is complete and relates to your introduction in a satisfactory way.

EXERCISE 7.8

Consider these sets of paragraphs, which form the introduction and the conclusion for three essays. Is it clear from the introduction what the writer will be discussing? What kind of introduction does the writer use? Is it clear from the conclusion what the writer discussed? What kind of conclusion is each writer using?

Explain how the two paragraphs in each set are connected and what sets them apart. Consider strengths and possible weaknesses. Remember that the paragraphs should not only function as effective specialized paragraphs but also display unity, coherence, and development.

1. An expository essay
Topic: Preparing financially for the future

Introduction:
If you examine the Canadian public as a whole, most do not save money. Canadians live in a thriving consumer culture. Unfortunately, as many young Canadians graduate from college and university with high levels of debt, they are often moving into an unsure economic future. Therefore, it is important that they learn the basics of sound financial planning, as many have never been formally taught the theory, and many parents do not set a good example. This financial advice should come from a licensed professional who can sit down and analyze a person's needs and help set up a savings plan. Without this professional advice, graduates may fall into the trap of confusing what they need with what they want and falling further into debt.

Conclusion:
Learning the basics of financial planning is a skill that many young people do not have. Determining how money should be budgeted will lead to a more secure financial future. Learning the difference between needs and wants is crucial, as is knowing the importance of saving money. With a realistic action plan, many of the young graduates can effectively pay off their debt and yet live comfortably, which is the goal of most people.

2. An argumentative essay
Topic: Indigenous rights

Introduction:

Canada has a history of racial discrimination toward the Indigenous people who were here long before the first Europeans arrived. As more immigrants arrived, the Indigenous people were pushed onto reserves, which had, and continue to have, many problems, such as a lack of quality medical care and clean water. Despite numerous advocates, the discrimination continues. Indigenous people have repeatedly been shown that they are not as important as those of European descent. They are mocked for being lazy, they are ignored when loved ones go missing, and they are repeatedly betrayed by the government.

Conclusion:

While conditions improve for the Indigenous population, including acknowledgement of their land, and the harm of the residential schools, Canada still has a long way to go in order to recognize these people as equals. More attention needs to be paid to their basic human rights. Colonial racism continues and it must be eliminated. Solutions need to be found to help repair the damage done in the past, and Canadians need to move forward and embrace the cultures and languages of the Indigenous Peoples just as we do for the people who choose to move to Canada and call it home.

3. An argumentative essay
Topic: Smoking and organ transplantation

Introduction:

The atmosphere grew tense in the cramped hospital room as eight-year-old Marla looked up through frightened eyes, trying to be strong for her mother. Everyone was trying to be hopeful, but Marla instinctively knew that she would not be getting a heart transplant in time; the waitlist was long, and an organ match was unlikely. Although Marla was an otherwise healthy girl, there were others on the transplant list who were ahead of her, though not all of them had as good a prognosis. Due to the scarcity of organ donations in comparison to many in need, serious debates have arisen concerning the suitability of some potential heart and lung recipients. Some feel that everyone should have equal right to a transplant and that there should be no pre-conditions relating to what they see as lifestyle choices, such as smoking. Others advocate that smokers should be refused transplants on medical or moral considerations since smokers are more likely to experience complications after surgery. Given the current crisis of long waitlists and variable success rates, lung and heart transplant candidates should be required to quit smoking at least six months prior to surgery in order to reduce smoking-related complications and maximize transplant success.

Conclusion:

The scarcity of organ donations and the length of waitlists have placed an increasing obligation on the part of health-care professionals to ensure the best outcome for their patients. Denying transplants to those who refuse to quit smoking may appear to discriminate against smokers and their lifestyle choice. However, doing so would result in better odds for post-transplant success and would involve the most efficient use of limited health-care services and resources. In short, health authorities should move to institute clear guidelines on pre-surgery smoking restrictions for the benefit of both individuals and the health-care system.

Extract source: Student writer Annie Gentry

The sample professional essay for this chapter is relatively short; therefore, the introduction and conclusion are brief. While you read, ask yourself how the author could have done more to help the reader understand the points being made in the essay.

Alouette Anniversary
Hillary Windsor

[1] Fifty years ago this autumn, after many small steps, Canada took one giant leap into the future.

[2] The successful launch of the Alouette-I satellite on 29 September 1962 made Canada the third nation (after Russia and the United States) to design and build its own satellite and signaled to the world that our country was going to be a player in the space age.

Sample Professional Essay

Introduction and Conclusion

The author uses the transition *but* to link paragraphs.

[3] But it wasn't all smooth sailing straight into the stratosphere for the Ottawa-based research and design team, led by the late John Chapman under the auspices of Canada's Defence Research Telecommunications Establishment (later to become Communications Research Centre Canada). Although the team had world-class engineers and scientists working on the project and believed it would succeed, others weren't so sure.

In an academic essay, a paragraph must include more than a quotation.

[4] "We were certainly confident," says Colin Franklin, chief electrical engineer of the Alouette-I. "But NASA considered the project too ambitious for the technology at the time. No one believed, outside of ourselves, that it would last."

[5] The public perception of the task facing the team was not much better. Franklin recalls reading an article published shortly before the Alouette's launch that stated all the possible things that could go awry during takeoff and highlighted the amount of money being "wasted" on the project. Still, the team was undeterred. "I remember looking at that article," says Franklin, "and it had absolutely no effect on us."

[6] Despite their assuredness, launch day at the US Pacific Missile Test Range in California was filled with a degree of uncertainty. Franklin, now 84, remembers the moment the team received word of the satellite's successful send-off into orbit aboard a Thor-Agena rocket. "There was a huge sigh of relief when it was working," he says. "And then there was jubilation."

Though this is an expository essay, Windsor has also expressed opinions, which are indicated by using words such as *only* and *exceeded all expectations*.

[7] From start to finish, the entire Alouette-I project took only 3.5 years to complete, but it exceeded all expectations. Designed with a nominal lifespan of one year, it spent an impressive 10 active years collecting valuable data about the ionosphere before being decommissioned. Its immediate success kick-started the move to build and launch three more Canadian satellites over the next nine years—Alouette-II, ISIS I and ISIS II—and put Canada in the spotlight.

The acronym ISIS stands for International Satellites for Ionospheric Studies. This acronym has been used since the 1960s in Canada.

[8] "The creation, launch and incredible success of the Alouette gave Canada an international reputation for excellence in satellite design and engineering," says Franklin, adding that at the time, no one on the team realized the long-term significance. "We were not aware that we were doing anything more than successfully building and launching the program. It was just a huge engineering challenge and an exciting program to be on."

[9] In 1987, Communications Research Centre Canada designated the Alouette-I as one of the 10 most outstanding achievements in the first 100 years of engineering in Canada—a notable tip of the hat that put the satellite in the same company as CPR's transcontinental railway network, the St Lawrence Seaway, and the CANDU nuclear power system.

[10] For many, the satellite's launch remains an iconic moment in Canadian history, shot through with personal meaning. Former astronaut Steve MacLean, the current president of the Canadian Space Agency, recalls hearing about it when he was just seven years old. "My dad worked at the National Research Council, so he made sure we remembered stuff like that," he says. "I collected stamps at the time, and a Canadian stamp with a picture of the Alouette on it came out. It's kind of a symbolic thing for me."

The author skillfully switches from a focus on the past to the future possibilities for Canada.

[11] MacLean says that it's hard to predict what the next 50 years have in store for Canada's space industry but hopes that satellites will, in the next five years, provide communications parity for the country, especially in the North.

[12] For his part, Franklin—who's faced down naysayers before—doesn't like to set expectations or limits on what people can accomplish: "People have been spectacularly wrong about forecasting the future before."

[13] In other words, the sky's the limit.

Windsor, Hillary. (2012, July/August). "Alouette Anniversary: Celebrating 50 Years of Canada's Role in Space." *Canadian Geographic*, July/August 2012, http://www.canadiangeographic.ca/magazine/ja12/canada_50_years_in_space.asp.

Post-Reading Questions

1. Is the essay's thesis statement effective? How could it be improved?
2. How could Windsor have created a more effective introduction?
3. What type of introduction does the author use?
4. Does the author use the SIM idea for creating an effective introduction?
5. How do the paragraphs differ from what you learned in Chapter 3?
6. Does the introduction prepare you for what is in the body of the essay?
7. How could the conclusion be expanded into a full paragraph?
8. Given what you have learned about introductions and conclusions, how could the writer have improved both?
9. Do you believe the last sentence was an effective clincher?

Chapter Review Questions

1. Why is a clear thesis important?
2. What is the difference between a simple thesis statement and an expanded thesis statement?
3. Why should you never start an introduction with an overly broad or obvious statement?
4. What does SIM stand for in an introduction?
5. Why is a strong introduction important?
6. Why does an essay need a conclusion?
7. What are three things that should not be in a conclusion?
8. Why is it important to save quotes for your body paragraphs, rather than your introduction and conclusion?
9. Why is a well-written conclusion as important as a well-written introduction?
10. Why is a clincher often a good thing to end an essay with?

8 Claims, Evidence, and the Analytical Model

By the end of this chapter, you should be able to

- choose the claim that is appropriate for your essay topic;
- choose evidence to support a claim; and
- increase credibility with the reader.

Every essay you write must have a thesis supported by solid, clearly linked evidence so that the reader can easily follow your logic. In this chapter, you will learn how to present a claim and to defend it with appropriate evidence that increases your credibility.

▲ Photo: Vtmila/Shutterstock

Kinds of Claims: Fact, Value, and Policy

Two main elements are used in all essays.

- *claim*: a statement of fact, value or opinion, or policy (thesis statement)
- *support for the claim*: evidence and the writer's credibility in presenting that evidence

When you are reading or writing an essay, begin by identifying the claim about its topic.

Most topics can be explored through a claim of fact, value or opinion, or policy. In an expository essay, the claim is presented as factual. In an argumentative essay, you are expressing an opinion or trying to persuade your reader. Therefore, the claim is typically presented as value, opinion, or policy. If your essay topic was homelessness, your claim could be one of the following:

Factual claim:

Because of the unsettled economic climate, the prevalence of homelessness is increasing in most Canadian provinces.

Value or opinion claim:

In a society of excess, the indifference to the problem of the homeless is an indictment of its way of life.

Policy claim:

To solve the problem of homelessness in our city, council needs to increase the number of permanent shelters, erect temporary shelters in downtown parks, and educate the public about this escalating social problem.

Claim of Fact

A factual claim uses empirical evidence. Evidence-gathering methods of observation and measurement are used. A factual claim can be proven by facts and figures, such as statistics, or the findings of relevant studies.

Claim of Value

A value or opinion claim is an ethical claim that appeals to a principle or a moral system; values might be based on religion, a philosophical world view, or social and cultural background. It is supported by the understanding that a certain standard of good or bad, right or wrong, fair or unfair, is accepted.

A claim is the assertion about your topic that appears in your thesis statement.

 Chapter 7 discusses effective and ineffective thesis statements.

---TIP

All essays can be written in either first person, using *I, we,* etc., or third person, using *the author, they,* etc. This is seen in these examples. Ensure you know which your instructor requires.

A factual claim is proven by facts and figures or the results of relevant studies. The term *empirical* refers to a claim being based on observed or measured data.

A value or opinion claim is an ethical claim that appeals to the reader's principles or moral system.

--- EAL

As a claim of value can be culturally based, claims need to be argued logically so that the reader can understand your point of view, even if their culture is not similar.

Claim of Policy

A policy claim is usually a call for action to fix a problem or improve a situation.

A policy claim usually calls for some kind of action to fix a problem or improve a situation. Although this type does not need to be based on a claim of value, it often is. For example, a proposed change to a law that gives people more control over something in their lives may be rooted in a claim of value. The argument might be that the change will produce a more democratic society and greater individual freedom.

EXERCISE 8.1

The 10 thesis statements listed here contain claims of fact, value or opinion, or policy. Choose three of the statements below and

- identify the kind of claim;
- write thesis statements for the other types; and
- explain how each statement fits in its category.

You may change the wording as long as the topic remains the same. Here is an example:

> Texting offers a wonderful opportunity for staying in touch with friends, but it is distracting to students who are trying to focus in class.

> Claim of value: The statement asserts that texting can distract students from their studies (a bad thing).

> Claim of fact: Recent studies show that 97 per cent of students are distracted by their phones. (The statement asserts that most students are distracted by their phones; data from https://eab.com/insights/daily-briefing/academic-affairs/study-97-of-college-students-are-distracted-by-phones-during-class/.)

> Claim of policy: Use of smartphones should be prohibited during class because texting distracts students from their lessons. (The statement advocates an action based on the value that texting is distracting.)

1. Living through a pandemic teaches people many valuable lessons.
2. Hip hop lyrics are often poetically intricate.
3. Online shopping poses a threat to retailers that rely on in-person contact to sell their products.
4. High school graduates should travel for at least a year before proceeding to college or university.
5. New funding for colleges and universities should be invested in green technology.
6. With the number of sports teams, clubs, and cultural groups on campus, students who do not participate in extracurricular activities do not get good value for their tuition.
7. The government should subsidize organically grown food.
8. Rapid adoption of new technology helped in the sudden switch to online learning.

9. The growing popularity of holistic medicine shows that society is tending toward a more natural approach to health care.

10. While advocates of a shorter work week believe that this measure will help our troubled economy, opponents say this will only weaken the economy and create social problems.

Evidence

A claim will not be accepted without support, or evidence, to back it up. But evidence alone is not enough; you must also demonstrate your credibility (your knowledge of the topic, your reliability, and your fairness.) The effort of gathering and arranging evidence may be wasted if you do not seem credible.

When you are reading and writing an essay, here are some questions you should consider:

- Is the evidence used appropriate for the discipline and does it demonstrate fairness?
- Is the evidence organized logically?
- Are there enough sources?
- Does the evidence pass the CARS test discussed in Chapter 1?

Organization of Evidence

Choose the best evidence gathered from sources such as books, journals, and personal experience to support the main points and subpoints of your claim. These points have the best impact when they are organized appropriately and ordered logically. Some organizational methods include those studied in Chapter 4: definition, classification/division, cause–effect, comparison and contrast, problem–solution, and chronology.

Kinds of Evidence

Your topic, your discipline, and the assignment's instructions will help you decide which type of evidence to use, with some kinds used more than others. Writing in the humanities often relies on primary, or original, sources. If you write an English essay, for instance, your primary sources are literary works. The primary sources commonly used in historical research are biographies, newspapers, letters, and records from the era being studied.

Social sciences writing tends to focus on facts and figures, statistics and other numerical data, case studies, interviews, questionnaires, and personal observation. Scientific studies may use similar kinds of evidence, but they frequently rely on experimental methods. Examples are important in almost every discipline.

> **Support** in an essay is provided by the use of ample and credible evidence. **Evidence**, such as that gathered from books, journals, or personal experience, gives your claim more credibility.

> →9 Chapter 9 discusses fairness in more detail.

> ←4 Chapter 4 discusses organization.

> Original sources are known as **primary sources.**

> **TIP**
> If you are going to conduct interviews, administer questionnaires, or use personal observation, make sure you follow the ethics guidelines of your school and respect the rights of your subjects.

> **EAL**
> If you are asked to participate in research, it is your right to decline or even quit the study. Participation is voluntary.

Hard evidence includes facts, statistics, and statements from authorities (experts).

→11 Chapter 11 discusses paraphrasing and using direct quotations.

TIP

Remember that special interest groups and similar organizations cite data for a specific purpose. Evaluate the facts and statistics with this purpose in mind.

→9 The essays in Chapters 9 and 11 use facts and
→11 statistics effectively.

An authority can be used for support if they are an expert in your subject. An expert is a person who is experienced or well-educated and has published or produced significant work about a subject. An authority who is not an expert carries less weight.

Soft evidence indirectly supports your points and helps the reader understand them.

Using a variety of evidence will produce a stronger essay. However, it is important to find hard evidence—facts, statistics, and statements from authorities or experts—to support your key points. Hard evidence is essential in a factual claim and can be effective in a policy claim. It may be less important in a value or an opinion claim, which appeals to reason, emotion, and ethics. Evidence in the form of examples, analogies, brief narratives, description, or personal experience could produce an effective argument.

The evidence you choose for an essay must be credible and fit in your essay in a way that supports your thesis. When writing, you need to clearly link your paragraph point to your evidence.

Facts and Statistics

Facts can be proven to be true and are the strongest evidence that you can use. Using facts from reliable sources enhances your credibility as a knowledgeable writer. Again, apply the CARS test to your information.

Statistics must come from reliable sources. Look out for possible bias or distortion and use caution with statistics cited by people or organizations promoting a specific cause or viewpoint. Imagine that your student union wants to use student funds to build an indoor pool and the campus newspaper reports that 94 per cent of those asked are in favour of the project. How many students were surveyed? How was the survey conducted? Perhaps only the students using the gym were asked. Reliable sources reveal their information-gathering methods, which you can evaluate.

Be aware that statistics and factual data are used for a specific purpose and that organizations may report on only those studies that agree with their mission or viewpoint. They may also present the statistics in a biased way. For example, the statement that almost 3 per cent of students support banning vending machines on campus is interpreted very differently by an audience than stating that over 97 per cent of students support having vending machines. Evaluate evidence individually with the source's objective in mind. If you are not sure that a source is trustworthy, ask your instructor or librarian.

Authorities and Experts

An authority can be used for support if that person has direct knowledge of your subject. An authority who is not an expert carries less weight. For example, citing Albert Einstein in an essay that argues a mathematical point provides hard evidence. In an essay about vegetarianism, citing Einstein would provide soft evidence, as he is not considered an expert in this area. As you research your topic, you will discover who the experts are. You may also be able to interview an expert, asking questions related to your claim (see "Research" in Chapter 4).

Examples, Illustrations, Case Studies, Precedents

While hard evidence provides direct support, soft evidence provides indirect support for your points and helps the reader understand them. Kinds of indirect support include examples, illustrations, case studies, and precedents.

Examples are used in both speech and writing. Examples should always be relevant and representative. A teenager arguing for his independence might name several friends who live on their own. His parents might refute the argument by pointing out that the friends are not representative—one has a full-time job and another spent the summer travelling in Europe before moving out of her parents' house.

Examples can make a point by making it specific and concrete. They are especially useful if you are writing for a non-specialist reader, as they make it easier to understand a difficult or an abstract point. Illustrations, case studies, and precedents are extended examples that can be used to explain or reinforce important points.

An illustration is a detailed example, which is usually an anecdote or a brief narrative. Student writer Graeme Verhulst uses an illustration to support his point in the following excerpt. Using logic, the reader can draw different conclusions from the premises:

> **Consider the example of the hydroelectric dam that the Urra company constructed in Colombia. The dam provides electricity to industry and profit to the companies and people who invest in it. The area flooded by the dam was inhabited by Indigenous Peoples. The river was a source of fresh water and fish, and on the river's now flooded banks were food plants that sustained them. ... If an analysis of this situation were based on the premise that all people should be treated equally and with respect, then through reason, the conclusion would be that this was a bad thing for the Indigenous Peoples living along the river. If, however, the basic premise was that business interests are primary, then the logical conclusion would be that the hydroelectric dam was a good thing.**

Case studies are often used as support in the social sciences, education, and business; they can also be the focus of research studies. Because case studies are practical, real-life examples, they can support a hypothesis. For example, to test the hypothesis that involving youth in decision-making could produce a safer school environment, a Vancouver school planned a series of student-led initiatives and activities. The results revealed that the students felt safer and had improved their pro-social and conflict resolution skills: the outcome supported the hypothesis.

Case studies are frequently used for marketing and sales support in business. A case study outlines a client's problem and then shows how your company's product or service solved that problem. Case studies include quotes from the satisfied client and information about the product or service. These case studies help influence new clients by showing them specific instances in which your company saved another client time and money.

A precedent is an example that refers to the way a particular situation was handled in the past. Legal judgments establish precedents that influence future court decisions. Once you have established an action as a precedent, you apply it to your argument. The successful use of precedents

An example uses concrete details to translate an abstract claim into something the reader can more easily understand. An example is considered soft evidence.

TIP

Examples are especially useful if you are writing for a non-specialist reader, as they make it easier to understand a difficult or abstract point.

An illustration is a detailed example that usually takes the form of an anecdote or a brief narrative.

A case study is a carefully selected example that is closely analyzed in order to provide a testing ground for the writer's claim.

A hypothesis is a prediction or expected result of an experiment or other research investigation.

A precedent is an example that refers to the way a particular situation was handled in the past.

as evidence depends on your ability to convince the reader that both of the following are true:

1. Similar conditions apply to your topic.
2. Adhering to the precedent will produce a desirable result.

If you were arguing that Canada should offer free post-secondary studies to all academically qualified individuals, you could refer to the precedent of Denmark, one of the first countries to provide universal access to post-secondary schooling. You must make two points clear:

1. The situation in Denmark is comparable to the situation in Canada.
2. Denmark has profited from this system, so Canada will likely benefit from a similar course of action.

Analogies, Description, and Personal Experience

Analogy, description, and personal experience are suggestive and indirect; they cannot prove a claim on their own. You may use them in your essays if your instructor approves.

Analogy (a kind of comparison) and description can help the reader understand and relate to a point. Like narration, description may also play a limited role in argument, perhaps to attract interest in the essay's introduction or to set up a main point.

Personal experience can be either direct experience or observation and can help the reader relate to your topic. Keep your voice objective when using this kind of example, as any bias will affect your credibility. Personal experience can be effective in supporting a value claim. For example, if you have personal experience with homeless people by working in a food bank, you could use it to help support a related policy claim.

Credibility

As previously stated, demonstrating credibility as a writer will strengthen your claim. Knowledge of the topic, reliability/trustworthiness, and fairness create writer credibility. Showing your knowledge isn't enough to make you credible. You must convince the reader that you also are reliable and fair.

Remember, too, that clear and grammatical writing and a well-structured essay also give your work credibility. If the reader sees grammar and spelling errors, they will wonder whether your research and logic are also below standard.

You demonstrate knowledge through the points you make in the essay and the kinds of evidence you use to support them. But you can seem knowledgeable without seeming reliable. You show your reliability or trustworthiness by being able to answer "yes" to such questions as the following:

- Is your essay well structured?
- Are your paragraphs unified, coherent, and well developed?

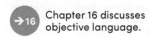

Chapter 3 discusses analogy, description, narration, and personal experience in detail.

Personal experience is a type of example that takes the form of direct experience or observation. It can often be effective in supporting a value claim.

→16 Chapter 16 discusses objective language.

Three factors contribute to credibility: knowledge of the topic, reliability/trustworthiness, and fairness.

- Is your writing clear, your grammar correct, and your style effective?
- Have you used the rules and procedures of your discipline (if applicable)?
- Have you used critical thinking skills effectively? Are your conclusions logical and well founded?

In an expository essay, fairness is demonstrated by using evidence objectively. In an argumentative essay, it is shown by considering opposing views. While presenting a strong case for your views, you can pinpoint the shortcomings and limitations of the other positions. A fair writer is objective in addressing the other side, avoiding slanted language that reveals bias. You can demonstrate reliability by avoiding misuse of reason, and you can demonstrate fairness by using emotional appeals selectively and without prejudice.

EAL

Slanted language means words and phrases are used to deceive the reader or manipulate them. For example, when using statistics, a study may state that 62 per cent of students would prefer later class time, but an unethical writer may use additional words, such as *just* 62 per cent, which changes the emotional reaction in the reader.

EXERCISE 8.2

Taking one of the claims for each statement in Exercise 8.1, determine how you would most effectively support it in the body of an essay. This exercise could take the form of a group discussion that specifically refers to the following elements:

- *Organization of evidence*: Which patterns of organization/development would you likely use? What other patterns could be used? (See Chapter 4.)

- *Kinds of evidence*: Which kinds of evidence would most effectively back up your claim? (See "Kinds of Evidence" earlier in this chapter.)

- *Credibility*: Which of the three categories of credibility seem the most important, and why? What general or specific strategies could you use to ensure your support is credible?

The following essay was posted as a blog (the underlined words indicate hyperlinks to supporting documents, such as journal articles, in the original). As you can see, even writers who use modern technology often follow the basic essay format. The author uses these patterns to help introduce evidence. While reading, think about how each element affects your view of the writer's credibility.

Harnessing the Power of Nature to Fight Climate Change

When it comes to reducing greenhouse gas emissions, habitats themselves can be critical allies

Brian Banks

The writer, Brian Banks, claims that many Canadians have not heard the term "natural climate solutions" in the introduction but then gives a partial definition of this term so that readers will understand the following points.

The author uses the words *rest easy* so that the reader feels more comfortable or relaxed and then supports this comfort with an example to reassure the audience that they are not the only ones who do not know about this way to fight climate change.

The author is supporting the points by including research; however, this research is not cited nor referenced.

The author is quoting an expert in order to support a claim. Again though, Banks has not stated what the source is.

The author is suggesting ways to implement the change he is advocating for. He is giving directions and explaining a process.

[1] The 2019 federal election campaign might have been the first time that many Canadians heard the term "natural climate solutions." It came in a pledge by Prime Minister Justin Trudeau to invest $3 billion in those solutions to "conserve and restore" lands across the country as part of the government's platform to fight climate change.

[2] If you were one of the uninitiated, rest easy. Among policymakers, awareness that land conservation is one of the most powerful and economical tools available for reducing greenhouse gas emissions has only recently caught hold.

[3] An important catalyst was a 2017 study that found natural climate solutions—defined as the practice of avoiding or sequestering carbon emissions by conserving, restoring or better managing forests, grasslands, wetlands, and agricultural lands—can deliver more than one-third of the global reductions needed by 2030 to prevent dangerous levels of global warming.

[4] Three years on, awareness of this potential and momentum to start applying it is building fast. In February [2020], just before COVID-19 hit Canada, more than 400 conservation, government, private sector, and Indigenous leaders held a summit on the topic. Their goal: mobilize government and other actors to move this work forward to help meet the country's climate goals.

[5] "There's huge potential for nature-based climate solutions," says Amanda Reed, director of strategic partnerships at Nature United and one of the summit organizers. She cites three reasons: Canada's boreal forests, West Coast rain forests, northern peatlands, and coastal wetlands store huge quantities of carbon and take in more every year; our existing frameworks and political will to act on climate; and the fact that many areas with the greatest carbon mitigation potential are in the hands of Indigenous communities with a wealth of knowledge in stewarding lands and waters.

[6] The appeal of natural climate solutions doesn't stop at greenhouse gas mitigation, however. That's because they also provide many "co-benefits." Foremost among them: protecting habitat and biodiversity, the second great ecological emergency of our time. Other co-benefits include cleaner air and water and healthier soils; landscapes that are more resilient to climate change and natural disasters; support for sustainable industries and jobs; and enhanced social and recreational amenities.

[7] Where does the work on natural climate solutions in Canada go from here? An important next step is determining Canada's specific mitigation potential. This includes calculating what overall percentage of our carbon reduction budget can be met with natural climate solutions, as well as identifying which actions—such as improved forest management or grassland restoration—in which locations promise the highest, most cost-effective impact.

[8] To help point the way, 16 public, non-profit, and university institutions, including Nature United, just finished a study that is due to publish this fall.

The study isolates around two dozen specific actions, or "pathways," and, according to Reed, "will be the first to aggregate the potential reductions in land-based emissions" from forests, grasslands, wetlands, and agricultural lands across Canada.

[9] The research factors in uncertainties, such as the impact of wildfires, and includes safeguards that rule out carbon initiatives that would have severe negative impacts on biodiversity or local communities. The ultimate goal, says Reed, is "real data" that policymakers can trust and invest in.

Banks, Brian. "Harnessing the Power of Nature to Fight Climate Change." *Canadian Geographic*, June 30, 2020, https://www.canadiangeographic.ca/article/harnessing-power-nature-fight-climate-change.

Post-Reading Questions

1. Is this an expository or argumentative paper? Support your answer with examples from the essay.
2. Identify the thesis statement. Which paragraph is it in? Why do you think it is placed here?
3. What type of claim does Banks make? How would this essay be different if the author had used a different type?
4. How does the author support the claim being made?
5. Do you believe the author is using slanted language in the essay?
6. Does the author use hard or soft evidence? Support your answer.
7. What type of audience is Banks writing for? Support your answer with examples from the essay.
8. Are there any areas where you think the writer loses credibility? Where? Why?
9. Is the conclusion of this essay appropriate? Explain your answer.
10. Could the author have organized this essay in a more logical way? Explain.

Chapter Review Questions

1. What are the two main elements used in all essays?
2. How are factual claims different from other types of claims?
3. What are the advantages to using certain kinds of claims? When would these advantages occur?
4. What kinds of evidence can be used in an essay?
5. What is the difference between hard and soft evidence?
6. Give three examples of primary sources.
7. Why is a writer's credibility important?
8. How does a writer establish credibility?
9. How does incorrect grammar affect the audience's view of the writer?
10. Why is the choice of experts important for supporting your points?

9 The Argumentative Essay

By the end of this chapter, you should be able to

- distinguish between logical and emotional arguments;
- identify and avoid common errors of logic;
- choose appropriate evidence for an argumentative essay;
- acknowledge the opposing point of view in an essay;
- create an outline for an argumentative essay; and
- create and deliver oral presentations.

Argumentative essays rely on logic and reason supported by convincing evidence. Careful planning and critical thinking skills help you avoid errors in logic that can destroy credibility. This chapter will introduce you to some of the most common errors in logic, discuss effective argumentative strategies, and include examples of well-argued essays.

▲ Photo: garagestock/Shutterstock

Expository versus Argumentative Writing

Any essay is either exposition (Chapters 6 and 7) or argument, and these purposes influence how it will be organized. Exposition explains or informs; argument persuades your audience to change its mind or see your point of view (see Table 9.1).

To determine the type of essay, pay attention to the prompts included in an essay assignment. If you are asked to explain the difference between college and high school, you will write an expository essay. If, however, you are asked to explain whether a business diploma is more valuable than a journalism diploma, you will use argument and draw a conclusion based on what you have written. You want readers to understand the validity of your conclusion with argument: you want them to accept your points. Understanding the assignment is crucial for your success.

Here are examples of each type.

Sample topic for an expository essay:

Explain how cycling to school affects students.

The word *explain* is in the prompt, so you will need to inform and explain. Sample topic for an expository essay that might use some argument:

What can students do to improve mental and physical health?

How might argument be involved? What assumption are you making about the topic that the reader would be expected to agree with?

Sample topic for an argumentative essay:

What should people do to improve overall health and wellness?

Verbs like *must* and *should* usually signal an argumentative thesis.

> Exposition informs, explains, describes, or defines a topic. An expository essay uses claims of fact. An argument attempts to persuade your audience to change its mind or to see your point of view through claims of value or policy.

← 7 See Chapter 7 for an expository essay template and Table 9.3 for an argumentative essay template.

TABLE 9.1 Expository versus Argumentative Writing

Expository Writing	Argumentative Writing
Use a fact-based thesis (see "Claim of Fact" in Chapter 8).	Use a value- or policy-based thesis to state the claim that will be supported throughout the essay (see "Claim of Value" and "Claim of Policy" in Chapter 8).
Begin by researching a topic and then refine your thesis to reflect your research.	Consider your view on an issue and brainstorm what arguments your readers may have that differ from yours. Look for supporting material that will counter their objections.
In your body paragraphs, use your researched facts, data, and expert resources to logically explain the points that you are using to support your thesis.	In your body paragraphs, use appeals to reason, emotion, and ethics to logically persuade your reader that the opinion expressed in your thesis is correct.
If you are writing about a controversial topic, do not take sides. You may explain both positions by using objective language.	You can take one side on a topic, but you must acknowledge that the other opinion exists and then rebut that opposing view.

Emotional versus Logical Arguments

Many daily arguments are emotionally based, such as when people argue about a favourite actor. Arguments can also be based on reason and ethics (moral standards). Even résumé writing involves argument—you are convincing an employer to hire you.

An argumentative paper requires the same logical and critical thinking skills that you use every day. Appeals to reason, emotion, and ethics can be used in argument, as the following scenario suggests:

> **You meet with your instructor to discuss a disappointing essay grade. By your effective use of reason, you try to convince her to change your mark, conceding the validity of some of her criticisms (concessions are used in many arguments). Going through the paper systematically, you focus on points that seem arguable, ask for clarification or elaboration, and present your counter-claims. As you do, you come across as a responsible, conscientious student. You make an ethical appeal, telling her that you know her to be fair-minded, reiterating her helpfulness, your interest in the course, and your emotional desire to do well. In this way, you succeed in establishing common ground, as you would try to do with the reader of your essay. If you argue with integrity, you will leave a good impression.**

An appeal calls on reason, ethics, or emotion to persuade a reader that an argument is valid. An argument attempts to persuade your audience to change its mind or to see your point of view through claims of value or policy.

When you make a concession, or concede a point, you acknowledge its validity and show that you are fair and reasonable. Arguers often concede a minor point and follow with a strong point of their own.

TIP
Successful arguments make appeals to reason, ethics, and emotion. Of these, appeals to reason and logic are usually the strongest.

EXERCISE 9.1

There may not always be a firm line between exposition and argument, but you may be asked to write an essay that is either one or the other, and your reader should recognize the type they are reading. Determine whether the statements below are most suited to argument or exposition by labelling them "A" or "E."

1. British Columbia's environmental policy is better than Alberta's policy.

2. Legislators should impose an outright ban on smoking in public places.

3. While neither nuclear power nor solar power is a perfect solution for providing electricity, when used in combination, they provide an effective alternative to the use of oil and gas.

4. Social media has become part of many people's lives; however, inappropriate posts can damage one's professional reputation.

5. Non-organic food receives negative publicity, but without the use of chemicals, farms would not be as productive as they are.

In an argumentative essay, appeals to reason and logic are strongest. Ethical appeals can play a vital secondary role in establishing your credibility for certain topics. Subtle emotional appeals can also be useful, depending on their placement in the essay, your topic, and your audience.

The sole reliance on emotional appeals, however, will affect your credibility.

In the following scenario, Ivannia Herrera summarizes an argument over what might seem a trivial issue; however, the underlying issues are important. In the course of the argument, some values are considered more significant than others. Although informal, the excerpt contains many features of a formal argument, such as a claim and supporting evidence. Rebuttals and concessions are also involved ("Emotional versus Logical Arguments" and "Rebutting the Opposing View" in this chapter). Read the argument carefully to find the appeals to reason, emotion, and ethics.

Tempest in a Teapot

Background: My roommate and I share a kitchen and utensils. Each day I make tea in a small stainless steel pot, which has a glass cover and a pouring spout with tiny holes that serve as a strainer. I pour two cups of water into the pot, let it boil, then add the leaves. When the tea is ready, I strain the tea water from the pot, leaving the tea leaves behind. I leave the pot on the counter until the next time I make tea.

The reason for the argument: My roommate has made it plain she does not enjoy seeing the pot with drenched tea leaves in the bottom.

This table lists the points that Ivannia and her roommate made during the argument. Which points seem the most convincing? Why? Are there any irrelevant points? Are points missing?

My Side	Roommate's Side
If I leave the pot with the tea leaves on the counter, I can reuse them three times. Since I make the same type of tea several times a day, it makes sense that I reuse the leaves rather than throw them out, which will cost me more money in the long run.	The pot is left on the counter for many hours. Though it's okay to reuse the leaves, the kitchen looks messy. I don't like the kitchen looking dirty with an unclean pot sitting there every day. Furthermore, I can't use this pot because it is always filled with tea leaves that I can't throw away.
I bought all the pots and pans in this household, and I am happy to share them; however, if you need a pot like this to use regularly, you should consider buying one yourself.	I also bought utensils for the household—and even the computer. I share these things and understand the concept of sharing. I think that having roommates means having to compromise.
I think of myself as a clean person, and I contribute greatly to the cleanliness of the household. I think that your having to look at a small pot is a small "defect," considering. . . . Drinking tea is part of my daily life, and I enjoy it. As well, it costs me $6 per month; if I were to discard the tea each time, I would be spending $18 per month, and I can think of better ways to spend those extra $12!	I am not saying that you should throw away the tea leaves, but just find a better way to use them so they are not in sight and taking over the pot. I think that the cleanliness of my living space is a reflection on me, which is why I want a clean environment. I do not like seeing a messy pot, and this is my "defect." I also think I should be able to use the pot if I like, and I can't with the leaves in it.
We both agree on the need to compromise. I'm willing to compromise and buy a ball strainer that can hold the tea leaves inside for as long as need be. It is a small ball attached to a chain; the ball divides in half, the tea leaves are put in one half, the ball is closed, and it is placed inside a cup filled with boiling water. I suggest we compromise and each pay half for the ball strainer.	I'm happy to pay for half of it, as long as you keep the ball with the tea leaves in a cup in your own room. That way, you can bring it out anytime you want tea, but it will be out of my sight.

The writer starts by abruptly stating an opinion that not all readers will share.

The author uses a fact and an example.

The writer fails to support this point, which is based simply on moral high ground—they also use flawed reasoning in assuming there are only specific "intended purpose" for these vehicles.

The writer makes broad generalizations that cannot be argued against. Facts or statistics are more effective for showing a claim's validity.

Again, the author uses a generalization and provides no support.

The writer ends using opinion only, which is ineffective.

Argument, Opinion, and Facts

Ivannia's discussion in Exercise 9.2 contains the necessary elements of argument. However, the following sample paragraph is based solely on opinion and cannot be considered an argument. The writer oversimplifies and uses generalizations that are not backed up by evidence.

Canadians in cities do not need to drive pickup trucks.

Pickup trucks are designed for specific uses, such as contracting and landscaping. Just because you see an empty truck does not mean it is not used for these purposes.

If all pickup trucks were used for their intended purpose, then they would be beneficial.

However, most people who purchase them seem to live in towns and cities, and the pickup trucks never seem to be dirty, which shows they are not used for work.

Many of these vehicles are driven on highways with rarely more than one passenger and with empty beds. These overly large vehicles use precious resources and pollute the environment.

Unless people can prove that the pickup truck is going to be used for the purpose for which it was designed, they should not be allowed to purchase one.

As the examples demonstrate, being opinionated is not the same as arguing. The writer of the following paragraph also focuses on opinion instead of reason.

Institutions of higher learning are meant for people hoping to broaden their interests and knowledge in order to contribute to society. I, myself, agree with this principle, and I also agree that a degree can help me acquire a job and be good at it. Along with this, I do not doubt that these institutions facilitate higher cognitive functioning. What I do not agree with is the approach that these institutions have toward the sciences. In fact, I categorically oppose the favouritism that is always shown to the sciences whenever financial matters are considered.

EXERCISE 9.3

Rewrite the paragraph on higher learning, eliminating the references to opinion and changing the pronouns *I*, *me*, etc., to *one* or a suitable noun. Does the revised paragraph sound more forceful? How is the writer's credibility enhanced?

TIP

Many arguments are based on opinion; however, effective arguments are objective and use neutral language.

TIP

In your argumentative essays, always separate fact from opinion. Support your opinions with logic and/or reliable evidence.

Opinions are not the same as facts. Opinions can be challenged, but facts can be verified by observation or research. Effective arguers are always clear about when they are using researched evidence and when they are using opinion. They also include an opposing view to argue against.

When reading, use your critical thinking skills to ask if the writer clearly separates facts from opinion. Some examples will help clarify the difference.

Fact (not challengeable):

Some people feel that self-driving cars are more dangerous than cars humans operate.

Opinion (challengeable):

Self-driving cars are dangerous.

Fact:

There are over a million French-speaking Canadians outside Quebec.

Opinion:

French-speaking Canadians only live in Quebec, so English-speaking Canadians shouldn't worry about learning French.

EXERCISE 9.4

Consider the two pairs of statements above. In groups, discuss the ways that fact differs from opinion in each case. Using your own topics, write two statements for each, one representing a fact and the other an opinion.

Faulty Reasoning

You must create arguable claims and support them with well-reasoned points and specific argumentative strategies. Faulty reasoning can harm your credibility.

> Faulty reasoning can result from an invalid argument, a lack of proof for a claim, or an opinion that is not clearly separated from fact.

Logical, Emotional, and Ethical Fallacies

A fallacy is a misleading or unsound argument. Arguments that use logical, emotional, or ethical fallacies affect your credibility: we do not trust someone who misuses logic or reason. For example, we might mistrust a person who argues that all campus pubs should be closed because a small percentage of students are underage.

> A fallacy is a misleading or unsound argument. Misuse of emotional or ethical appeals is unfair to the other side: emotional fallacies exploit emotions and are thus very different from valid appeals.

People frequently misuse emotion when building their argument. We know that larger vehicles are more harmful to the environment, but that doesn't mean that all drivers of pickup trucks in the city should be condemned, as stated in the excerpt in "Argument, Opinion, and Facts," above. The vehicles have several uses within a city: for example, a landscaper might need a truck for work. By stating that all such drivers do not care about the environment, the writer is guilty of misusing emotional appeals.

Some fallacies are based on faulty inductive reasoning, such as cause–effect fallacies (e.g., "If I wash my car, it will rain"). Other fallacies derive from the faulty use of deductive reasoning, presenting general or universal statements that may not be true, such as "All people who ride bicycles are environmentalists."

Table 9.2 lists common argumentative fallacies that misuse reason, emotion, or ethics. Including them in your essays will weaken your argument. Readers will catch your errors and you will lose credibility.

TABLE 9.2 Argumentative Fallacies

Types	Term	Definition	Example
Irrelevant	Red herring	Attempts to distract the reader, often on an ethical matter. There may be some validity to the point, but it should not form the basis of an argument.	We need to accept higher tuition fees because education is important. (This argument makes a broad comment that distracts from the truth: higher tuition fees bring in more money and are unrelated to the quality of education.)
	Straw man	Misrepresents an opponent's main argument by substituting a false or minor argument in its place. The point is to get the audience to agree.	Thaddeus Tuttle points out that, while women have not achieved wage parity with men, they often take maternity leave, which means they don't work as much as men. (Among its flaws, this argument ignores the basic principle of equal pay for equal work.)
Emotional	Bandwagon	Argues in favour of something because it has become popular.	Everyone is using smart speakers. I have to get one too, even though my Bluetooth one works just fine.
	Dogmatism	Common type of argument that asserts a point based on a firm, perhaps passionate, belief, without supporting evidence.	I believe that everyone should oppose whale hunting. (In argumentative essays, it's best to avoid references to your own opinion; instead, you should let your points talk for you.)
	Either/or	Suggests that there are only two available options.	You are either with me or against me. (These arguments often also lack logic.)
Logical	Circular	An argument that does not move forward or that continues in a circle. The main point is repeated but not expanded.	Applied degrees are now available at some community colleges in Canada. They are only offered there because community colleges teach applied skills.
Evidence	False analogy	Compares two things that are not alike. A true analogy can support a point, but you need to have a real basis for comparison.	How can people complain about circuses that use wild animals in their acts? We keep animals that were once wild, such as cats, in small spaces in our homes.
	False cause	Asserts that, simply because one event preceded another one, there must be a cause–effect relationship between them.	Tamara forgot to wear her lucky watch for the exam; consequently, she failed. (Superstitions can arise when people assume a causal relationship between two events. Of course, there are causal relationships between many events; for example, if Tamara walked in front of a car and was hit, her action obviously resulted in her injury.)
	Hasty generalization	Forms a conclusion based on little or no evidence.	I talked to two people, both of whom said the text was useless, so I will not buy it. (If many people bought the text, two people do not constitute a good sample.)
	Prediction	Denies that an effect arises from a cause because it hasn't happened yet—therefore, it's not going to. The arguer projects into the future without considering probability or other evidence.	I did well on the last test and I didn't study much; therefore, I don't need to study much for the final exam.
	Tradition ("the way we have always done it")	Argues for a course of action because it has been followed before, even if the same conditions no longer apply.	You should not compose your essay on a computer. Handwriting is much better.

You need to be objective when you argue and ensure that your arguments are always based on logic and that your appeals to emotion are always moderate. Being logical will show reliability and trustworthiness; being moderate will show fairness.

TIP
Writers need to look closely and objectively at the way they argue to ensure that their arguments are based on logic and that their emotional appeals are moderate.

=== EXERCISE 9.5

For each of the following statements, indicate the type(s) of faulty reasoning used.

1. In our family, males have always been named "Harold" and females "Gertrude"; therefore, you should name your twins "Harry" and "Gerty."

2. If you don't get a degree in law, medicine, or business these days, you're never going to make any money.

3. When I serve you dinner, it's terrible not to eat all of it when you consider that one-third of the world's population goes to bed hungry.

4. The teacher hasn't called on me to answer a question for three consecutive days; it looks like I don't need to do the reading for tomorrow.

5. I know I went through the red light, officer, but the car in front of me did, too.

Using Slanted Language

When writers show a lack of objectivity by using slanted or loaded language, they lose credibility. Slanted language can vary from extreme direct statements to qualifiers (adjectives or adverbs) that subtly convey a bias. If you use slanted language, readers could easily take offence and question your fairness. Remember that your credibility is at risk if your purpose is to distort the truth. See Chapter 8 for examples of slanted language.

Slanted language reveals the writer's bias, affecting credibility. This language can take direct forms, such as accusation, or can be more indirect.

=== EXERCISE 9.6

The following paragraph uses faulty logic, emotional appeals, and slanted language. Analyze the arguments, determine what makes them ineffective, and suggest improvements. Focus on identifying illogical statements and unfair appeals to emotion.

The legalization of marijuana will destroy society as we know it. The typical Canadian will be exposed to many harsh drugs, such as coke, crack, and heroin, due to the increased acceptance of drugs within the community. Rehabilitation clinics for chronic drug users are going to be a huge drain on the economy. There need to be new laws and screenings implemented to prevent people from working with heavy machinery or operating a motor vehicle while impaired by marijuana. Canadian business owners could be dissatisfied with many of their employees, and then discrimination will rear its ugly head. Firing someone for smoking marijuana and not being productive at work is not discrimination; however, the point would be made that it is. Clearly, our society is sinking to a despicable level since this drug has been legalized.

Strategies for Creating Your Argument

You can use a variety of strategies to create an effective argument, including

- making a claim of value (something is right or wrong);
- making a claim of policy (a policy or practice needs to be changed);
- interpreting facts, such as statistics, to support your claim;
- providing evidence from the experts;
- supporting your points with credible examples, such as case studies;
- supporting your points using soft evidence, such as analogy, description, or personal experience;
- defining a term or concept, especially if the term could be misunderstood; and
- comparing your ideas to others that the audience understands.

 See Chapter 8 for more about claims.

Using these strategies and avoiding fallacies will help you create an essay that builds your credibility. Also, you need to use strategies that your audience understands.

Arguable Claims

The thesis of a reason-based argumentative essay is your claim—your arguable topic. If you and a friend start debating whether Harvey's is better than A&W, who is right? If you use only subjective standards (such as what you think tastes better), neither of you is "right" because the topic is based on opinion, which cannot alone form a reason-based argument. On the other hand, you could base your argument on the respective nutritional values, fat content, or additives and preservatives in each chain's foods. These subtopics can be supported by evidence that will support your claim.

> **TIP**
> A topic that can be argued is based on objective, not just subjective, standards and has an opposing viewpoint.

The topic also needs an opposing viewpoint. You could not write an argumentative essay on the benefits of good health, as there is no opposing view. Obvious claims, such as "Computers have changed a great deal in the last decade," are unarguable.

Specific, Interesting, and Manageable Claims

Like a thesis statement, your claim must be specific, interesting, and manageable (SIM). In this section, we focus on a sample argumentative claim, showing the kinds of questions you can ask to help you develop a strong and effective thesis for an argumentative essay.

See Chapter 7 for more about thesis statements.

Specific Claims

> **TIP**
> A specific claim must not be vague but state clearly and precisely what you will be arguing.

A specific claim states clearly and precisely what you will be arguing. The reader should know whether the claim is one of fact, value, or policy. Consider the following statement:

Parents of children who play hockey would like to see fighting eliminated from the game at all levels.

Although this claim is arguable and has an opposing viewpoint, it is not specific enough. The words *parents*, *would like to see*, and *at all levels* are vague and need further definition. Also, "eliminated from the game at all levels" seems unconnected to the rest of the claim. Do parents want fighting eliminated from professional hockey too or just at the levels where their children participate?

An expanded thesis statement can help make the claim more specific. In the revised thesis statement, the claim is expressed more clearly through specific words as well as the inclusion of main points (using the word *should* clearly reveals a policy claim):

Fighting should be prohibited in hockey, since violent NHL players give young hockey players negative role models, and this reinforces a "win at all costs" mentality.

It is often a good idea to follow the claim by defining concepts central to your argument. In the previous example, the writer might define what they mean by *fighting*. Does a fight start when the gloves are dropped, when there is excessive physical contact, or when a third player joins in? Definition enables you to make the topic more specific.

An "all or none" kind of claim is also non-specific. If your claim is too broad, use qualifiers such as *usually*, *often*, *sometimes*, *in part*, *many*, *some*, *several*, or *a few* to restrict its scope or reword your claim to make it more realistic. Alternatively, you can use verbs and verb phrases that qualify and limit, such as *contribute to*, *may*, *play a role in*, and *seems*.

Interesting Claims

To be interesting, a claim should be written for a specific audience. In the claim about fighting in hockey, the intended audience is hockey parents as well as people who can make changes to hockey rules. Many fans of professional hockey would not be interested in the main point of the argument, as it applies mostly to children. Those who never watch hockey or don't have children playing the sport probably would be even less interested. Similarly, an argument about how best to prevent the growth of single-celled algae in China's lakes and reservoirs might be interesting to biologists but probably not to the average reader.

Along with audience interest, consider your audience's viewpoint. Are most people likely to agree with you, disagree, or be neutral? Will they possess general knowledge of the topic? Will most people have heard of the topic? These kinds of questions are extremely relevant when you write the body of the essay and support your claim. If your audience includes many who disagree with your claim, it may be important to establish common ground and to convince them that you have similar values and goals.

Manageable Claims

Manageable claims are determined partly by whether they are specific and interesting. They also depend on the essay's length, the support available, and the complexity of the issues raised by the claim.

TIP
To be interesting and specific, a claim should be written for a specific audience. Who might be interested in the topic but not share your viewpoint?

Establishing **common ground** is a strategy in argument that shows an opponent that you share similar concerns or basic values.

→ 9 See "Rebutting the Opposing View" just ahead in this chapter for specific audience strategies.

TIP
Factors in manageable claims include essay length, support available, complexity of the topic, and practicality of the claim.

Policy claims, which try to persuade people to take action, need to provide realistic solutions or at least imply that realistic solutions exist. If the change you propose isn't practical, it may be best to reword the claim or change it to one of value. Your thesis statement must be workable and clear to the reader even if your supporting points are complex.

The claim about hockey violence is arguable, specific, and interesting to the intended audience, but is it manageable? Remember that all claims need to focus on one main topic.

It would be too unmanageable to address banning fighting in hockey at both the professional and minor levels. Realistically, would the role model argument motivate NHL executives to ban fighting? To make the statement manageable, the writer could focus either on the idea that NHL players who fight are poor role models or on the consequences of fighting in minor hockey.

Value claim:

Fighting in professional hockey gives young hockey players a negative role model because violence reinforces a "win at all costs" mentality.

Reworded policy claim:

Fighting should be prohibited in minor hockey below the midget level because violence reinforces a "win at all costs" mentality.

Rebutting the Opposing View

The rebuttal is the part of your argument in which you raise the other side's points, usually to strengthen your argument and to appear fair.

When you write an argumentative essay, you should present the opposing viewpoint. Addressing the other side shows the reader that you are aware of it and strengthens your argument by demonstrating that your points are strong enough to counter the opposing point of view. This part of the essay, called a rebuttal, will be determined by the topic, your audience, or your purpose.

Topic-Based Rebuttal

If your reader is familiar with the topic and the major points of opposition, raising and rebutting each one is a good strategy. If your reader knows little about the topic, it may be best to acknowledge only the major counter-argument(s), ensuring that your points are stronger and more numerous. If the main arguments are obvious to everyone, however, there may be little point in giving them space in your essay.

Audience-Based Rebuttal

> **TIP**
>
> Showing how opponents can benefit by agreeing with your thesis is a common argumentative strategy.

Two rebuttal strategies—acknowledgement and point by point—depend on your reader's opinion.

Acknowledgement

If your audience is mildly opposed to your topic or is undecided, you may simply acknowledge the other side and counter it with a strong argument. In such cases, you must decide how much space to devote to acknowledgement. Student writer Laura Benard briefly characterizes the opposing viewpoint by using only a prepositional phrase ("Despite their aesthetic value") ahead of her thesis statement. She presents no real rebuttal but treats the opposing argument, that people use pesticides to make their lawn look attractive, as obvious:

> **Despite their aesthetic value, the negative impacts of maintaining lawns by means of pesticide, lawn mower, and water use are so great that lawn owners should adopt less intensive maintenance practices or consider lawn alternatives.**

A writer will often put the acknowledgement in the form of a dependent clause that contains the less important (opposing) information, followed by their own claim expressed in an independent clause: "Although some may argue [major point of opposition argument], the fact is/I believe that [your thesis]."

It is often necessary to provide background for the reader or a brief summary of the opposing view. In such cases, the writer can begin with this position, then follow with their argument. To decide how much space to spend on the opposing view, consider how objective you want to appear versus the importance of presenting a strong argument of your own.

TIP

A concise method of acknowledging your opponent is to summarize the argument in a phrase or dependent clause and follow with your summarized thesis in an independent clause. When you give background information or summarize the opposing view, make sure you use an objective tone and neutral language. Make your summary as concise as possible.

Point by Point

If your audience strongly opposes your thesis, address their strongest points, stressing the inadequacies and inconsistencies of these points and drawing attention to any fallacies. If your purpose is to arrive at a compromise or find common ground, point out the weaknesses in the form of helpful, constructive criticism. In both cases, raise individual points, usually beginning with the opponent's, and then respond to the weaknesses in this position. Throughout, remain unbiased and objective.

In this excerpt, student writer Spencer Cleave addresses a common argument supporting the US embargo against Cuba. After a concession (italicized), he introduces two counter-claims that attempt to show the weaknesses in the original claim:

> **Many supporters of the maintenance of the trade embargo against Cuba contend that the Cuban government fails to uphold the human rights of its population. *It is true that Cuba has had a number of human rights violations in its past. Thus, it is conceded that Cuba is also morally at fault on certain issues.* However, many reforms have recently been made by the government in an attempt to remedy its human rights problems. These efforts show that the government has a desire to improve the conditions within its own nation. Furthermore, it would be in the best interest of the United States to applaud the Cuban government in any human rights improvements, thus giving the image of a cooperative partner.**

You may choose to address the main points of your opponent's argument systematically, summarizing these points and refuting them with facts and statistics. You can also stress how readers can benefit from considering your view. If your topic is a highly charged one, such as providing safe injection sites for drug users, you may begin by arguing your weakest points and work up to your strongest points. This way, you address all types of

TIP

You do not have to respond to all your opponent's views in a point-by-point rebuttal. In shorter essays, you may not have the space to rebut any more than one. The opposing side might have only one strong argument; you would not need to address weaker ones.

opponents, from the weaker to the stronger. However your reader feels, you should work to establish common ground. Making concessions shows that you're willing to compromise.

Purpose-Based Rebuttal

The primary goal of an argumentative essay is to engage readers who share your concern about the topic or to enable readers to see another side of an issue and view it with greater tolerance. Long-lasting change can often result when the arguer is open and flexible. This approach can be particularly effective with value-based claims.

When reading Suraj Patel's essay, look for any places where the author introduces the opposing view. Try to imagine how you could oppose his points.

Sample Professional Essay

Argumentative Essay

Not Immune: What a Teenager Who Got Vaccinated against His Parents' Will Can Teach Us about Anti-Vaxxers

Suraj Patel

The author is using slanted language, *rebellious youth*, in an unusual way in order to grab the reader's attention and thus makes in interesting claim.

[1] Sometimes it takes rebellious youth to help us see the error of our ways.

EAL

Rebellious youth is a term used by older people to negatively describe teenagers and young adults, especially if the younger people want to change a value or policy that the older people feel is wrong.

[2] Consider Ethan Lindenberger, an 18-year-old from Ohio. His act of rebellion wasn't staying out past curfew or avoiding his homework: It was getting vaccinated on his own, despite his mother's protests.

Using Ethan Lindenberger's quotation shows the author's view about the subject and supports a value-based opinion.

[3] Lindenberger's mother opted her children out of vaccines and fed them messages about the dangers of immunizations. As he posted on Reddit, "My parents think vaccines are some kind of government scheme. It's stupid and I've had countless arguments over the topic."

While Ethan used Reddit for help, there are many other reputable sites to find medical information.

[4] So when he turned 18, he asked Reddit how he could get the shots he had been denied throughout his childhood: flu, pneumonia, chickenpox, hepatitis A, hepatitis B, HPV, meningitis, MMR, tetanus booster, and TDAP (whooping cough).

[5] Redditors gave him guidance, and the thread went viral. The whole episode ended with Lindenberger testifying to Congress earlier this month. In New York, his testimony moved two state lawmakers so much that they're proposing a bill in the state legislature allowing teenagers 14 and up to get vaccinated—even if doing so goes against their parents' wishes.

The author's argument is also supported statistical evidence.

[6] Lindenberger's testimony and this bill couldn't come at a more important time. A measles outbreak recently hit the state of New York, with almost 200 confirmed cases statewide. In Brooklyn alone, there have been 133 reported cases of measles since last October. And around the country in just the first

three months of 2019, 12 states have reported cases of measles—the fastest infection rate on record.

[7] This was not supposed to happen. In 2000, the Centers for Disease Control declared measles eliminated in the United States. So what changed in the two intervening decades?

[8] Simple: a misinformation campaign about vaccines fueled by social media that has led to many more unvaccinated people.

The writer takes the facts that are presented and creates a logical argument.

How people become anti-vaxxers

[9] Lindenberger's mother is a prime case. Her information about vaccines came from "anti-vaxx" groups on Facebook. As her son put it, "She thought vaccines were a conspiracy by the government to kill children."

EAL

> Anti-vaxx means people who are against receiving vaccines, especially for their children. Anti-vaxx is short for anti-vaccine.

[10] She is not alone. On Facebook and elsewhere online, hives of misinformation and pseudoscience push the view that vaccines are dangerous—that they lead to autism, that they are a government plot, or that they cause the diseases they are supposed to prevent.

[11] Researchers and doctors have thoroughly debunked these claims again and again. But in the digital world, myths masquerade as truths. And well-intentioned people like Lindenberger's mother make unsafe decisions as a result.

While the topic of vaccines is a very emotional issue for many people, the author's point of view is supported by providing expert opinion, including from researchers and doctors.

How we can stop anti-vaxxers

[12] What can be done? For one thing, laws can help. In the same way New York state lawmakers took action, we need federal action to allow young people to take their health and safety into their own hands when their parents won't. We also need to strengthen and support legislation that blocks unvaccinated children from attending school. Specifically, lawmakers need to close "religious exemption" loopholes, or severely limit them with the input of medical and public-health professionals, as they allow parents to put other people's children at risk.

The author is clearly arguing using a claim of policy, but in this case, he is arguing for strengthening the policy. However, the author is also making an emotional appeal by introducing the fact that non-vaccinated children put other children at risk.

[13] A federal judge recently supported that view: When parents of unvaccinated children attempted to allow their children to return to a school recently struck by a measles outbreak, the judge blocked their entry. He's not the only one. In Italy, a new law went into effect this month that barred unvaccinated children under six from school and fined parents of children older than six for not vaccinating their kids.

[14] This is not, as some critics would suggest, government overreach. It is common sense, and these proposed measures resemble the many laws on the books that protect the public interest, even when they proscribe individual conduct. For example, driver's license requirements, prohibitions on smoking on airplanes, restrictions on falsely yelling "fire" in a crowded theater—these widely accepted examples put the public interest ahead of private interests. Legislation on vaccines operates in the same spirit.

Here the author is making a claim of value when stating that vaccinating is "common sense."

[15] Laws, however, take time to enact. What we can do right away is take action on sources of misinformation. The public needs to stand up and tell Facebook, Twitter, and other social media platforms that enough is enough. Facebook has begun to take small steps in this direction: They're banning anti-vaccine information from being promoted through ads, and lowering its rank in search results. But they could go further. Pinterest, for example, has blocked searches on vaccinations, and Amazon pulled anti-vaxx documentaries from their catalog altogether. Facebook needs to ban anti-vaccine posts outright, and public pressure could get them to do just that.

[16] Finally, we need to hold our leaders and influencers accountable. No matter how many laws we change or how many platforms we fix, a single stray comment from an authority figure can undo years of work. That goes double for politicians—people whom we entrust to make decisions in the public interest. So when someone like US congressman Mark Green questions the value of vaccines, it isn't enough to move on. Even though he has now flipped his position and insists he vaccinates his kids, it's too late: He gave his credibility—and by extension, Congressional credibility—to those peddling dangerous hoaxes. This isn't a purely partisan issue: Both Democrats and Republicans have questioned vaccines in Congress, sometimes going so far as berating the director of the Centers for Disease Control. There's no place for conspiracy theorists and science deniers in leadership, and they should be voted out of office when the next election comes around.

> While this is a US article, the situation regarding anti-vaxxers in Canada is very similar. Politicians and some in the public believe the misinformation that is spread on social media and distrust government agencies.

[17] Ethan Lindenberger's decision to disobey his mother is a clarion call. We are well past the point of debate on vaccines, and our society runs grave risks by allowing the numbers of unvaccinated children to rise and allowing scientific falsehoods to spread. It is time for society-wide action on this issue—changes to our laws, improvements to our sources of information, and firm resistance to those who peddle pseudoscience. Few acts could be more urgent or more important.

> The author ends by clearly stating an opinion in this debate. Patel has provided evidence to support the argument in the body, and now concludes with suggesting which actions must be taken to combat anti-vaxxers.

Patel, Suraj. "Not Immune: What a Teenager Who Got Vaccinated against His Parents' Will Can Teach Us about Anti-vaxxers." *Quartz*, March 25, 2019, https://qz.com/1579023/how-people-become-anti-vaxxers-and-how-to-stop-them/

Post-Reading Questions

1. Consider your own position toward the issue discussed in the essay. Do you have any knowledge about this or similar issues relating to parental decisions that could affect the children's health?

2. What are the sides of the debate? Which side do you support? How might your prior knowledge and opinions affect your response to this argument?

3. Is there anything that would have made the argument more effective? Be as specific as possible.

4. Are there any questionable appeals to emotion or ethics? Are there any fallacies? If so, give examples.

5. Why does the writer include information from other countries? Is this effective? Why or why not?

Organizing an Outline for Argument

As you now know how to create an argument, you can begin to outline your essay. Make sure your main points are ordered logically to strengthen your argument. You can use the climax, inverted, or mixed order.

Table 9.3 provides a template that you can follow. You do not have to include everything listed; for example, you might not need to include background if the issue is well known to most readers. You can also put the elements in a different order.

If you include a rebuttal, it may not need much space. Depending on the topic and other factors, you might choose to place it before your main points. You could include an acknowledgement in the introduction or background section or begin a point-by-point rebuttal in the first or second body paragraph.

TIP

The order of your points is often vital to argument. In the climax order, the weakest point appears first and the strongest point last. Inverted order does the opposite. The mixed order begins with a moderately strong point, followed by a weaker one, and concludes with the strongest.

 Chapter 2 discusses the methods for ordering points in an essay.

EXERCISE 9.7

Choose one of the following topics and prepare an outline using the template in Table 9.3, narrowing the topic if necessary. Choose a position that you can argue with a value or policy claim; do not create an expository essay with a factual claim.

1. cyber-bullying
2. physical activity during quarantine
3. the influencer culture
4. the gig economy
5. living-wage salaries

TABLE 9.3 Argumentative Essay Template

Introduction	• gain reader's attention and interest • include your claim • suggest the primary developmental method (if there is one) • establish your credibility (knowledge, reliability, and fairness)
Body paragraph 1: Background	• present background information, if relevant
Body paragraph 2: Lines of argument	• present good reasons (logical, emotional, and ethical appeals) in support of your thesis • use all relevant evidence—facts, statistics, examples, and views of experts/authorities • present reasons in specific order related to argument
Body paragraph 3: Rebuttal	• consider opposing points of view • note both advantages and disadvantages of opposing views; may use concessions or common ground • argue that your thesis is stronger than the opposing view and more beneficial to the reader
Conclusion	• summarize your argument • elaborate on the implication of your thesis • make clear what you want the reader to think or do • possibly make a final strong ethical or emotional appeal

As you read the following essay, pay attention to how the author presents and supports her points. For each point, ask yourself whether she convinces you of her view or if you disagree.

Discrimination against Aboriginals in Canada: Bill C-45

Jane Freiburger

[1] Aboriginal people have been discriminated against for centuries. Many Aboriginals feel that land claims, which have been a major issue for well over two centuries, are a good illustration of this discrimination. This is true in many nations, and Canada is a perfect example. Aboriginals feel that obligations under the treaties and the Indian Act are not being met by the Canadian federal government.

[2] On 18 October 2012, the Harper government introduced Bill C-45. This affects the Indian Act, the Navigation Protection Act, and the Environmental Assessment Act. These changes have angered many Aboriginal people as they believe that more laws and legislation will further erode treaty and Indigenous rights and the rights of all Canadians ("9 Questions," 2013). Many Aboriginals feel that this bill discriminates against them by taking the decision-making powers away from them, showing that non-Aboriginals know what was best for them, which is discrimination.

[3] Bill C-45 alters the Indian Act, which includes changes to land management on reserves, making it easier for the federal government to control reserve land (Gotz, 2012). Bill C-45 also alters the Navigable Waters Protection Act. This Act was used to protect 2.5 million rivers and lakes and now only covers 97 lakes and 62 rivers. This leaves rivers, lakes, and oceans vulnerable to exploitation and it leads the way to mining and the controversial Enbridge Northern Gateways pipeline to move forward (Fotheringham, 2013). Again, this alteration is felt to be discrimination, as the people who live on these lands will not be consulted before their lives are disrupted.

[4] In order to protest this loss of rights, many Aboriginals and non-Aboriginals participated in the "Idle No More" campaign in order to bring awareness of the latest issue of discrimination to the Canadian public. Unfortunately, both Prime Minister Stephen Harper and the media added to the discrimination issue. During this protest, Prime Minister Stephen Harper typified Aboriginals as arrogant imperialists and denied that colonization exists. Minorities have always been a focus of the media, particularly framing them as the problem. It is part of the way the news is created rather than it being the people who carry personal prejudices. This type of structural discrimination is not intentional, but it is harmful (Kunz, 2013). In the Idle No More protest, this message was very apparent, supporting the Aboriginal claim of discrimination.

[5] Among the non-Aboriginal population, there is a clear misunderstanding of what the Aboriginals are trying to attain. A recent poll from Ipsos Reid found that about two-thirds of Canadians believe Canada's Aboriginal peoples received too much support from federal taxpayers; they believe that Aboriginal peoples are treated well by the government and most of the problems Native people face are

brought on by themselves. On the other hand the poll also found that two-thirds of Canadians believe the federal government must act now to improve the life of Canada's Aboriginal peoples (Akin, 2013). This poll shows the ignorance on the part of most Canadians and adds to the discrimination that exists.

[6] Discrimination is an ugly aspect of any society, but it is even more disturbing when it is perpetuated by world leaders and the media. Aboriginal people in Canada have suffered through discrimination for far too long, and they have had far too many rights taken away. The Idle No More protest was their way of standing up and fighting back against the "others" in society who believe that they know better than the troublemakers in society. In order to stop this problem in society, people need to stop listening to those in authority and start studying the issues on their own.

References

9 questions about Idle No More. (2013, January 5). CBC News Canada. http://www.cbc.ca/news/canada/story/2013/01/04/f-idlenomore-faq.html

Akin, D. (2013, January 15). Idle no more: Canadian public opinion set against First Nations protesters. *Toronto Sun.* http://www.torontosun.com/2013/01/15/idle-no-more-canadian-public-opinion-set-against-first-nations-protesters

Fotheringham, N. (2013, January 5). *Canada's Bill C-45 reduces protected waterways from 2.5 million to 62 rivers and 97 lakes.* GreenMoxie. http://www.greenmoxie.com/canadas-bill-c-45-reduces-protected-waterways-from-2-5-million-to-62-rivers-and-97-lakes/

Kunz, F. A. (2013). Newscasting: "Problematizing" minorities. In *University of Waterloo, Centre for Extended Learning SOCWK 301 R* (p. 38). The University of Waterloo Book Store and Media.doc.

Post-Reading Questions

1. How does the author of this piece establish credibility?
2. What, if any, fallacies does this essay contain?
3. How does the author gain your attention in this essay?
4. Does the author argue a value claim or a policy claim in this essay? Give evidence to support your answer.
5. Which type of order does the author use for organizing this essay?

Oral Presentations

An oral presentation is often based on argument—you are trying to convince your audience that your point of view is valid. Therefore, you use the organizational patterns of the argumentative essay. You must clearly state your thesis or main idea, use your most convincing supportive points, and discuss your findings. Visuals such as pie charts and graphs can make your evidence stand out and be easily understood by the audience.

Oral presentations are used in the workplace, where proposals or reports are often delivered to a large audience face to face. For example, you may be asked to present a group of directors with a proposal to study a new method for increasing productivity. In this case, you would include your rationale, proposed timeline, and hypothesis. Usually, this information is accompanied by visuals, such as a PowerPoint presentation. Once you have finished your research, you may be asked to present your findings to the group.

Creating a Presentation

Time Limits

For any oral presentation, you must pay attention to the time limit, such as 10 to 30 minutes. Make sure you use this time wisely. If your presentation is too short, your audience will wonder what you have left out or how much you really know about the topic. If the presentation is too long, you risk your audience becoming bored and tuning out before you make all your key points. You may need to allow time at the end for questions, so plan accordingly.

Clarity and Transitions

Oral presentations are unlike written documents. Listeners do not have the readers' luxury of being able to go back over a point that they may have misread or misinterpreted. Therefore, make sure that your points are clear, precise, and logical. To help your audience understand your presentation, be sure to include transitions or markers to draw their attention to a point. When using an illustration, use a marker such as *for example*. When moving to new points, use words such as *additionally* or *on the other hand*. For the most important point, make sure you clearly indicate this to the audience with a marker such as *the most important aspect*. Successful use of these transitions or markers will help the audience clearly understand your movement from point to point.

Less Is More for Research Presentations

When you are making a research-based oral presentation, less is more. Present only your most important information, with illustrations. If you are presenting a report on the rise of multi-tasking, explain the background (i.e., how the concept has evolved since the 1980s and the advent of the personal computer) but do not go into details, such as listing all the articles you reviewed. Move on to discussing some of your methods, such as how you chose a specific group to study. If you are studying students' ability to multi-task, you would give your basic criteria for choosing students—age, years of study, and perhaps their majors—but leave out other criteria such as cultural background or hobbies.

Focus on Findings

Focus most of your time on the findings of your study. Visuals are extremely helpful with this part. You can use charts and graphs to make your findings

TIP

Oral presentations are often used in the workplace to present new ideas to a large audience.

TIP

Good presenters are well organized, and they make sure the audience can clearly follow their ideas.

 Your presentation can be organized using the same methods you use when writing an essay. See "Organizing an Outline for Argument" earlier in this chapter.

TIP

When presenting research, discuss only the most relevant parts.

stand out. For example, you may want to include a pie chart showing the success rates of those who do and do not multi-task. Leave some time at the end to discuss possible ramifications of this study and where research can build on your findings. This is much like including a clincher in your conclusion.

Chapter 7 discusses conclusions and clinchers. ←7

Begin with the Thesis

If you base an oral presentation on an essay, help the audience orient to the topic by beginning with your thesis. State your thesis right away so that the audience knows what it is. Next, present the main points from your essay with brief illustrations. If you have a relevant quotation, put it on a separate slide and pause briefly to give people time to read and absorb it. They are probably seeing it for the first time and will need to reflect on it to understand its importance. End your presentation by stating your conclusion clearly. Unlike essays, presentations can include such markers as *in conclusion*. This helps your audience understand that you are wrapping up. If you don't use a marker, people may not realize the importance of your closing remarks.

Tips for Using Visuals for Maximum Effect

Visuals can add impact but only if they are appropriate and not overwhelming. You want the audience to remember your information, so use graphics for only your most important points and keep the number to a minimum. As a general guideline, do not use more than one visual per minute, as the audience needs time to understand it and what you are saying. Don't overload your audience or cause "death by PowerPoint." In addition, do not use your visuals for your speaking prompts or read from them.

Keep your visuals simple. Each slide or screenshot should contain a minimal amount of information. For example, you can use the "five by five" rule: no more than five lines of text on each slide and no more than five words on each line. If you use graphs or pie charts, include only the most relevant data. Do not create a pie chart that has more than five segments, as the audience will not be able to differentiate the segments (see Figure 9.1 for a sample). Put only one chart or graph on each slide (with relevant documentation if the data are not from your own research).

Use colours that make it easy for the audience to read the slides. Light blue on a white background can be hard to see, as are light letters on a dark background. If you are using a PowerPoint template, use a simple one and avoid using unnecessary animations such as Fly In or transitions such as Blinds. Having points show one at a time is often effective if you want your audience to focus on each separately, but do not using rolling letters or other distracting animations or transitions. These are wonderful for attracting attention, but many available on PowerPoint are not professional enough for the workplace or the classroom.

TIP
When you are creating visuals, less is better.

Delivering a Presentation

Studies have shown that the people who communicate effectively in business are the ones who receive promotions. Use oral presentations as a stage for your abilities.

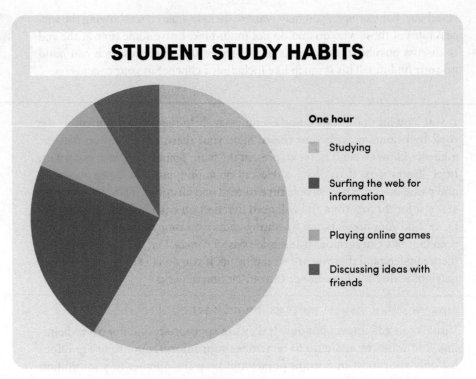

STUDENT STUDY HABITS

One hour

- Studying
- Surfing the web for information
- Playing online games
- Discussing ideas with friends

FIGURE 9.1 Sample slide of a pie chart

Rehearse

It is important to practise before making your presentation. Rehearsing your presentation will help you be more relaxed when standing in front of an audience. Practise speaking slowly. Successful presenters usually speak much more slowly when speaking to an audience. If you find you are speaking too quickly while presenting, pause, take a deep breath, slow down, and articulate your words clearly so that the group can understand the subject. Speaking slowly also helps your audience adjust to factors such as an unfamiliar accent or unknown vocabulary.

When you present in front of a group, you do not want to forget your material, so practise. The more familiar you are with your material, the less likely you are to forget it. Memorize the first few lines of your presentation; you can make a positive first impression by establishing eye contact with your audience, which is vital if you want to keep people engaged. You may want to use prompts as well, by using cue cards, a hard copy of your PowerPoint presentation, or presenter notes in PowerPoint. Make sure you use only key words or phrases to prompt yourself. If you write everything you need to say on your papers, you risk reading those notes and not making eye contact with (and thus not engaging) the audience.

Dress for Success

Your appearance is important. Dress for success. You may not need formal business attire, but you must look professional. You may not appear credible if you wear a rumpled shirt, torn jeans, and old running shoes. Never chew gum. Watch videos of successful presenters to give you an idea.

The success or failure of an oral presentation often lies in the work you do beforehand. Remember that, thanks to YouTube and TED Talks, your audience is used to watching polished presentations and abandoning amateurish or poorly executed ones. Audiences also expect to be entertained. This does not mean you have to tell jokes, but you need to present your material in a relevant, meaningful way. If you do so, and practise beforehand, you are well on your way to creating a presentation that will interest your audience.

TIP
Knowing your material and being able to engage the audience are essential for success.

Important Points to Consider for Making an Oral Presentation

Use the following list to help you prepare and deliver a successful oral presentation.

Preparation

- Know your material and practise a lot beforehand.
- Make notes to help you remember the key points and organizational structure of your topic.
- Create clear, easy-to-see visuals with necessary citations.
- Check your visuals for errors.
- Practise your presentation aloud and time it.
- Decide when you will address any questions. Will you encourage the audience to ask questions as they think of them, or would you prefer them to ask at the end?
- Choose clothes that are appropriate for your audience.

Delivery

- Speak slowly and clearly. Make sure you are loud enough for everyone in the room to hear you.
- Let the audience know when you will address questions.
- Allow your audience time to read your visuals but do not read them yourself.
- Discuss only relevant details.
- Watch your audience for signs of engagement and adjust to them. For example, if they did not seem to understand a point, expand on it. If they look bored, move on to a new point.
- Address all questions from the audience.
- Thank your audience for their time.
- Keep within your time limit.

Chapter Review Questions

1. Why is it important to understand your audience for an argumentative essay?

2. Why is it important to avoid relying on emotional arguments?

3. Why do you need to avoid fallacies when arguing?

4. Why is it important to use objective language in an argument?

5. What are the characteristics of an effective topic for an argumentative essay?

6. Explain why the mixed organization could be useful in an argument.

7. Why is it important to acknowledge the other side of the argument?

8. Once you have acknowledged the opposing side, what are some ways you can write a rebuttal?

9. How do essays and oral presentations differ?

10. Why are good communication skills important?

PART THREE
Research

10 Conducting Research

By the end of this chapter, should be able to

- conduct research for an essay topic;
- determine whether sources are reliable;
- use the internet for research; and
- access other research resources.

Each essay you write needs a strong thesis that is supported by research. By adding relevant, reliable outside information, you prove that you are familiar with the topic and are becoming an expert in that field. This chapter is designed to help you develop your research skills so that you can defend your thesis using what experts, such as scientists and other theorists, have discovered about your topic. We will discuss how to explore what you know about a topic and address how to conduct research and where to find reliable sources. Most of the focus is on expository essay writing, but it can be applied to argumentative essays as well.

▲ Photo: Rawpixel.com/Shutterstock

Developing Research Skills

Great thinkers and writers build on the knowledge of earlier researchers and thinkers. The Wright brothers did not just suddenly know how to build an airplane. They studied previous designs and ideas and built upon ideas, such as Samuel Langley's aerodrome. Before creating his aerodrome, Langley, no doubt, studied gliders and other designs for flying machines. Examples of progress like this can be found in the sciences, the social sciences, and the humanities. Most experts depend on others' findings to help their own explorations; then, their new research adds to the store of knowledge within their chosen field.

Research is an important part of most essays. To use research effectively, you need to explore, check, and recheck what others have written. Once you have all the evidence you need from primary sources (literary texts, historical documents, surveys, questionnaires, and interviews) and secondary sources (authoritative books and journal articles, oral presentations, and conference papers), you synthesize it (i.e., put it together) to create your essay.

A successful expository essay relies on the presentation of your information. As mentioned before, the essay should be interesting and appealing for your audience. Don't just assemble your research, plunk it down in the paper, and add transitions. Examine what someone else has found and then rewrite the points in your own words. For an expository research essay using claims of fact, you need to find reliable information, analyze what has been discovered about the topic and what the conclusions are, and come to a logical conclusion of your own.

Writing a research essay involves drafting an outline, adding and checking citations, and presenting the information in the most effective way. When you draft your essay, you may begin with an outline, but you will probably go back and add research and check citations. You will also need to accurately represent your research and focus on the most relevant and important aspects. The following section will help you proceed with greater confidence.

Research: Finding and Exploring

After you choose your topic, your next step in writing a research paper involves finding possible sources. At this early stage, it is helpful to write a summary of your purpose as well as a tentative list of source material. Your instructor may even ask for a brief proposal, a document that tells them about the topic you want to study. You write the proposal after you have done sufficient background research to ensure there is enough information for you to proceed. You may be asked to provide relevant citations to show that you have completed the preparation.

In the proposal, explain what the focus of your paper will be and perhaps include a working thesis. It may change as you begin to write, but it shows that you have a specific direction in mind. Providing the reason for writing about your topic is important. If the topic is not assigned, make sure to include why it is relevant to you. If the topic is assigned, do not

Researching a topic involves finding out what others, especially experts, have written or said about it. **Primary sources** are original sources; **secondary sources** comment on primary ones. **Synthesis** is putting together ideas from different sources.

→11 ←8 Chapter 11 discusses the differences between quoting, paraphrasing, and summarizing. See Chapter 8 for more discussion of claims of fact.

TIP
When you write an essay, your instructor judges it not only on grammar and mechanics but also on your critical thinking. Therefore, your essay is not just a rewrite of what others have said but a combination of your thoughts and theirs.

TIP
While exposition implies research, research implies synthesis.

TIP
In-text citation requires acknowledging the source of your quotation, paraphrase, or summary. Chapter 12 discusses citations.

A research **proposal** announces the essay's topic, purpose, and research sources.

A **citation** includes the author name, publication date, title, publisher, location, and (in some cases) page numbers.

Table 2.1 shows how the thought process for a research essay can begin.

TIP

By asking yourself key questions about the topic, you will discover what you already know and what you need to find out.

simply state this as the reason but explain why your particular focus is of interest to you. Your proposal should be a few paragraphs in length so that you are able to expand on your topic fully.

The following proposal was created for the student essay "Computer Ergonomics" in Chapter 11.

[1] **When choosing a topic, one of immediate relevance was ergonomics, as the work force is getting older, and this is a relevant topic for both students and workers.**

[2] **Interest in ergonomics is personal, due to my own age, but also seeing a number of students in the hallways who use wheelchairs of various design, and also those who have been provided with special chairs due to various workplace injuries. Also, more desks at the school are being provided that are adjustable.**

[3] **Curiosity about the changes in ergonomics was a driving force for this essay, and also how people can protect themselves from injuries.**

[4] **Being a well-informed worker is important, so this essay will explore various aspects of the ergonomics issue, including prevention of injuries. The essay will be analytical and will include recommendations.**

Writing a proposal helps you in the "finding and exploring" stage of essay writing. Even if you are not asked to submit a proposal, you will have to think about the topic and use the pre-writing strategies you find the most effective. Some key questions can help you get started:

- What am I interested in?
- Do I know enough to explore a topic thoroughly?
- If I don't know very much, how can I obtain background information?
- What am I hoping to contribute to this subject area?
- Who is my audience?
- What kind of sources would be appropriate given my topic and my audience?
- Where will I find my source material?
- Who are the major authors in the field? How can I find them?
- Have I given myself sufficient time to research, synthesize, organize, compose, document, and revise?

Synthesis I: Integrating

→11 →12 Chapters 11 and 12 also discuss the integration stage.

After you have found your sources, you begin to assimilate the information. By taking notes and summarizing where appropriate, you show that you can accurately represent another person's ideas and integrate them with your own. When you have finished taking notes and understand the information, you are ready to begin organizing your essay.

Again, asking specific questions can help:

TIP

To assimilate means to take other people's ideas and incorporate them into your essay.

- Is my research geared toward supporting my points?
- Have I understood the results of the studies I've looked at and the positions of the experts whose works I have read?

- Are all my sources credible? Do they pass the CARS test? Are there many recent ones?
- Have I summarized or quoted all sources adequately and accurately?
- Which sources are the most important?
- How do the different experts' views or conclusions fit together?
- Are there opposing positions? For example, do some findings challenge others?
- How does my research help me explore the topic?
- Has my research changed my view of my topic? If so, how? Do I need to change my thesis?

Organization: Arranging

Every essay needs a structure, which usually takes the form of an outline or template. Ask yourself these questions when you are ready to organize your essay:

- Do I have enough support to begin an outline? If so, what kind of template should I use?
- Is there an organizational method I should use?
- Do my points thoroughly explore the topic?
- Are some points inadequately developed to produce substantial paragraphs?
- Are all areas of my research relevant to the points I want to make?
- What points are most essential and what sources are most relevant?
- Am I off topic anywhere?
- Does the structure I chose reflect my purpose? Does it reflect my audience? Is it logical?

Synthesis II: Composing

During the first draft stage, you use your sources in your essay. How you use your summaries, paraphrases, and direct quotations is important. Whenever possible, it is best to summarize or paraphrase the original document. This shows the audience that you understand the material you have researched.

Questions to ask include the following:

- Am I over- or underusing my sources?
- Which sources should be summarized, which paraphrased, and which quoted directly?
- Am I using my sources effectively? Have I used the best information from them? Have I represented this information correctly?
- Can I use ellipses to omit less important parts of the source?
- Am I providing smooth transitions between my sources and my own writing?
- Is the language level roughly the same throughout? Is it appropriate for my audience?
- Are direct quotations grammatically integrated and easy to read?

TIP

Successful writers create outlines early in the writing process. Even if you don't create an outline before you begin writing, use your first draft to create a working outline to ensure you have organized your information logically for the audience.

←7 ←9 →11 Chapters 7 and 9 discuss outlines for expository and argumentative essays, respectively; Chapter 11 includes an example of a student outline.

←5 →11 Chapter 5 examines summarizing; Chapter 11 discusses paraphrasing and using direct quotations.

TIP

An ellipsis (or three dots) is used at the beginning, middle, or end of a quote when you do not need to use all of the original author's words. This shows the reader that, while you are using the most important information, not all of it is relevant to your essay.

→11 See Chapter 11 for instructions on using ellipses and Chapters 13–15 for help on grammar.

→

TIP

Whether you use MLA or APA, include a source only if you have used information from it in your essay.

→12 See Chapter 12 for instructions on using MLA and APA styles.

TIP

Formal research requires you to analyze, compare, assess, and synthesize the work of experts in your subject area, generally by discussing multiple approaches to a problem.

- Have I double-checked quotations for accuracy?
- Is my own writing clear, grammatical, and effective?

In this stage of the research essay, you must document sources using an appropriate format, such as those of the Modern Language Association (MLA) or the American Psychological Association (APA). Manuals for both styles should be available in your college or university library or bookstore; information is also provided on each organization's website. Chapter 12 discusses both methods.

Use these questions when documenting your sources:

- What documentation style is expected for this essay?
- Where is information on documenting to be found?
- If I am using electronic sources, am I clear on acceptable methods for documenting them? (Has my instructor given me guidance or directed me to specific sites or sources?)
- Do I know what needs to be documented and what does not?
- Could the reader confuse my own ideas or observations with information taken from another source?
- Have I carefully documented other people's words and ideas without cluttering the essay with unnecessary citations?

Researching Your Topic

You already know the basics about research. You probably didn't choose your program randomly. You might have checked websites and talked to people (e.g., current students, graduates, or school counsellors). You likely also relied on factual evidence: programs, prerequisites, tuition fees, housing, and campus size. Perhaps you also consulted objective experts, such as people who have researched the different schools and ranked them according to various criteria.

This process of decision-making based on research is a life skill that includes the critical skills of analysis, judgment, and evaluation. College or university research assignments require similar skills but involve formal research, which involves analyzing, comparing, assessing, and synthesizing the work of experts in your subject area, generally by discussing multiple approaches to a problem. Simply rephrasing these sources or summarizing your own opinions or experiences is not necessarily research.

As discussed before, one common approach to organizing a research paper is to compare and contrast the similarities and differences between two or more ideas. Another method is to evaluate the strengths and/or weaknesses of a point of view based on criteria that you create or borrow from experts. The following example involves both types:

1. Identifying a problem:

   Many people use e-devices to read. Researchers claim that students do not understand material as well when using these devices.

2. Stating a claim or the thesis about this problem (what the writer will explore or prove):

   E-readers affect the way students understand material.

3. Describing the points made by one or more experts concerning the claim:

   Researcher A claims that his study demonstrates that students do not understand material read with an e-device. He presents information gathered from a study comparing the reading comprehension levels between students who used an e-device and students who used paper.

   Researcher B asserts that students comprehend material well regardless of whether they use e-devices or paper. She presents her study showing no significant difference in the reading comprehension levels between students who used e-devices and those who used paper. She goes on to claim that those using e-devices actually gained more knowledge through the use of hyperlinks embedded in the text and the ability to access online dictionaries.

4. Reaching a decision on the merits of these experts' approaches to the thesis:

   Researcher B's arguments are more convincing than those of Researcher A. Researcher B is able to show that students gained a better understanding of the topic because of the additional features available when using e-devices.

5. Concluding with your judgment on the thesis, either by rating the experts' approaches or by suggesting a new way of thinking about the problem:

   Researcher B has provided a strong argument that the use of e-devices for reading actually benefits students. While this is a relatively new field, this researcher created an additional parameter to study, which sheds light on how students use e-devices, rather than just testing reading comprehension, as Researcher A did.

Who Are These Experts—and Where Can You Find Them?

Experts are experienced or well-educated people who have published or produced significant work about a subject. A documentary filmmaker may be an expert; their film may provide information for your essay. A journalist may also be an expert on a particular topic, and a person interviewed on radio or television could be very familiar with a topic through their research, knowledge, or personal experience. Library shelves are filled with the publications of experts, and the internet may be another source of expertise. Since the number of experts on a topic can be enormous, you need standards for screening the quality of their information. In the case of the filmmaker, for example, you could consider the following criteria:

- An important part of research is to select sources whose work has been analyzed by others in the field. Is the film reviewed in any journals or other commentaries? These can show you what other filmmakers think about it.
- Is the film part of your institution's collection or available through a reputable organization such as the National Film Board?

Experts are people who are experienced or well educated and have published or produced significant work about a subject.

TIP

When you conduct research, ask your instructor about publication dates. Is there a limit to how far you can go back? Does an article have to be published after a certain year? Depending on the field, research conducted 10 years ago might be extremely dated or relatively new.

- Since you are writing a research paper in an educational context, you may wish to consider the filmmaker's academic credentials.

Another criterion that measures the usefulness of research material is publication date. Since attitudes and analyses change over time, more recent information gives you the latest developments in your field. A further advantage to beginning with recent material is that the source often will refer to previous studies that might be useful. Sometimes just scanning the works cited or reference section at the end of a recent work will suggest other potential sources.

Exploring Your Topic

The first stage in research is finding the major authors and their research in your subject area. You also need to know where to find this information so that you can document them in your essay.

TIP

A useful first step when conducting research is to use a general work, such as a textbook.

This may be easier if your instructor can recommend them. However, looking for a general work, such as a textbook, in your subject area is a useful first step. These books frequently include bibliographies (alphabetical listings of works used or consulted), which you can scan for relevant titles and authors. Look for information in your library's reference section. Look at encyclopedias, dictionaries, and comprehensive guides in your area. Most reference books can't be taken out of the library, but they help you find sources that can be borrowed. Some may be available electronically, so check with the librarians.

Internet search engines, subject directories, and databases can also provide excellent starting points, providing you with general topics that you can narrow down. If you are having trouble finding information about your topic, use the glossary section of your textbook, which contains words relevant to your chosen topic. You can also ask the librarians for help, as they have a lot of experience helping students do research.

Create a list of useful sources that you plan to look at. When you find a book on the list, scan the index and the table of contents to determine how helpful it will be. If it looks promising, read the introduction, preface, or foreword. The author often summarizes their approach and sometimes provides chapter-by-chapter summaries in the introductory section. With articles, read the abstract. Remember to note the date of the work's publication (in books, found on the copyright page—the other side of the title page).

An abstract is a short summary that precedes most academic journal articles.

Your list of sources may not look much like the final list of works you actually use, but it often leads you to the most relevant sources. Not all your possible sources will be usable, so always look for more sources than required.

Note-Taking

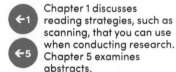

Chapter 1 discusses reading strategies, such as scanning, that you can use when conducting research. Chapter 5 examines abstracts.

Keeping clear records when conducting research allows you to read material efficiently as well as save time (and your sanity) when you write your paper. Make notes as you research your sources, ensuring that you record the following information:

1. A direct quotation, summary, or paraphrase of the writer's idea; if it is a direct quotation, make sure you put quotation marks around it.

2. The complete name(s) of the author(s).
3. The name(s) of editor(s) or translator(s), if applicable.
4. The title of the book, journal, magazine, newspaper, or website affiliation or sponsor.
5. The title of the specific article, chapter, section, or website.
6. Full publication details, including date, edition, or translation; for a journal article, these could be the volume and issue number; for internet sites, the date the site was started or updated.
7. The name and location of the publisher (including province, state, or country) for books.
8. For internet sites, the day you viewed the page and either the uniform resource locator (URL) or the digital object identifier (DOI).
9. The call number of a library book or bound journal for later reference, if needed.
10. The page numbers you consulted, both those where you found specific ideas and the full page range you read (or some other marker for unnumbered online documents, such as paragraph numbers or section headings).

A uniform resource locator (URL) is the address of specific internet content. A digital object identifier (DOI) is a number–letter sequence that begins with the number 10 and is often found on documents obtained electronically through databases. One or the other is used as the last element in a citation for articles found online.

When making notes, don't forget to record your observations, comments, and queries. You need bibliographic details, of course, but you must relate the information to other sources and to your thesis statement. It's important, however, to keep source material separate from your own comments. Write your responses on another piece of paper or in a different colour. Always give yourself clear directions when you take notes and make comments.

Organizing Research Notes

Organizing your notes is an extremely important aspect of research. Being unable to find a key piece of information while working on a research paper is very frustrating. There are many organization methods: write your notes on index cards (remember to number them) or record notes in a journal and use tabs to divide them into particular headings. If you number your journal pages, you can create a table of contents at the beginning of the journal and record the page numbers and a short description of the material recorded. You can also create a computerized record-keeping system, either by using a database program such as MS Access or Excel or by simply creating multiple document files in a folder.

A database is a collection of related data organized for quick access.

A number of software programs can assist you in organizing your research. These include Zotero (www.zotero.org), which helps you organize your research; Mendeley (www.mendeley.com), which helps you organize your research, gives you access to new research, and is cloud based; and others such as EndNote (www.endnote.com) and Nota Bene (www.notabene.com), which are databases. RefWorks (www.refworks.com) creates a references or works cited page based on the information you enter into the system and the documentation style you specify. Just be sure to double-check all your information, as no computer program perfectly creates citations, works cited, or references pages. Again, Chapter 12 provides a useful guide for both MLA and APA.

An electronic document created using any of the above can help you retrieve information if you misplace your notes. However you keep track of your sources, review your final essay to ensure you have eliminated any information and sources you decided not to use.

Learning to use programs such as these takes time, but they generally offer helpful extra features, such as automatic formatting of citations and references or bibliographies. You can also use MS Word to create citations, works cited pages, and references pages. However, when using any of these programs, make sure your in-text citations and references or works cited sections are complete. If you choose to record your notes electronically, back up your work regularly in case of technical failure.

Cross-Referencing

Cross-referencing your notes can make it easier to retrieve your information when you are writing your essay. You can create a list of central words, names, or themes and record where each occurs in your notes. You can cross-reference by writing notes in a margin or by using index cards or computer files. Some students draw a visual aid such as a mind map (graphic organizer) on a large sheet of paper to connect their main words or points. Some word processing programs include a cross-referencing feature for single documents (e.g., in Word in Office 365, this is found under *Insert*). A few of the computer programs we mentioned have keyword-based cross-referencing systems.

Some Useful Research Strategies

Assimilating

- Begin the research by gathering definitions of the important words in your thesis statement.
- Read or view everything with the thesis statement in mind. Resist reading unconnected material, however interesting it might seem, because it will waste time.
- Judge whether a book will be worth your time by checking your cross-referencing words in its index. Read the abstracts of journal articles to determine their usefulness.
- Consider how you can connect the information from different sources by using transitional words and phrases such as *because*, *as a result of*, *on the other hand*, or *in contrast*. This will help you select points that flow logically.
- Try to find an example to support every major statement you wish to make. An example can be a quotation, paraphrase, or larger concept that comments on or proposes a solution to your thesis statement.

Arranging

- When you finish your first round of research, write an outline with paragraphs corresponding to the major elements of your thesis statement. In each paragraph, list the reasoning that supports these points and the examples that support each of them.

TIP

It is important to keep your research notes organized so that you can retrieve information quickly without having to reread material.

- Decide how much space to allot for each section of the paper, taking your instructor's requirements for paper length into serious account.
- Look over your outline. Do you have sufficient examples to support all your major statements? Do you have enough material to meet the required page or word count? If you have neither, perhaps you need to do more research. On the other hand, if you have too many key points and several examples for each, choose only the strongest ones in order to meet length requirements.
- Consider arranging your paper in a word processing program according to the required length.
- Design a timeline for each step in your paper if you haven't done so in a research proposal. This will help ensure that you don't spend too much time on any particular segment.

Using Contradictory Evidence

In the initial research stage, you need to find sources relevant to your topic; however, not all studies on a given topic reach the same conclusion. If your primary purpose is to explain or investigate a problem, assess the contradictory findings and try to discover why they are different, perhaps by analyzing their strengths and weaknesses. This process is a critical thinking skill and a fundamental part of the research process.

In the humanities, your thesis is often based on your interpretation of the findings—you must carefully show how other academics' interpretations differ from your own. An excellent strategy when you discuss conflicting results is to acknowledge another interpretation and use it as a springboard into yours.

Contradictory interpretations should not simply be dismissed without explanation; it is better to acknowledge and qualify them, possibly by briefly discussing their limitations. If you do not address contradictory studies, the reader may assume that you do not know enough about the topic, thus reducing your credibility. For example, many recent studies attempt to show the health benefits of vitamins. If you are investigating the benefits of vitamin E in preventing heart disease and find that credible evidence exists, you still need to acknowledge studies that find no benefit and explain how these findings fit into your claim.

Researching a topic can be a challenging process. If you experience doubts or uncertainties at any stage of the process, talk to your instructor as soon as possible. Don't wait until the day before your paper is due!

Sources of Research Material

Many different kinds of source materials exist. This section discusses most of the important ones.

Primary and Secondary Sources

The distinction between primary and secondary sources is crucial, as essay assignments frequently require that both be identified and referenced. Primary

> **TIP**
> To write a well-researched paper, you must acknowledge findings that contradict your thesis, if any exist. If you ignore them, your instructor may tell you that you didn't research the topic adequately.

TIP

Check with your instructor before using online material as a primary source. Multiple translations/editions of a work are often available, and the online version may not be the most accurate or accepted one.

TIP

CARS stands for credibility, accuracy, reliability or reasonableness, and support. While encyclopedias may seem to pass the CARS test, most of the information is not in-depth, and it is not always supported by sources. Wikipedia is open source, so anyone can change the information, affecting its reliability.

Periodicals are newspapers, magazines, journals, and yearbooks; a yearbook is a book of facts or statistics published every year.

A journal is a periodical that publishes the results of experts' research. Articles in peer-reviewed journals are assessed by other experts before publication.

sources are the original compositions of authors; personal documents, such as letters and diaries; and initial scientific articles reporting on a work. A secondary source is another writer's analysis of and commentary on a primary source. An article that cites someone else's research, a textbook that explains others' theories, and encyclopedia entries are examples of secondary sources.

Start with Secondary Sources

A good way to begin research is to access reference sources such as indexes, almanacs, encyclopedias, dictionaries, and yearbooks. These can provide you with concise summaries of statistics, definitions, and biographies, and a reading list of the principal primary and secondary sources. These books cannot be removed from the library; however, this type of information is widely available on the internet. For instance, an online search of *black hole* and *encyclopedia* returns entries from the *Encyclopaedia Britannica*, *The Canadian Encyclopedia*, and numerous library-based sites offering further links to information on the subject. The *Britannica* entry includes a listing of relevant books, articles, websites, magazine articles, and videos on black holes. Remember that, at the college and university level, citing encyclopedias is not appropriate for research essays. They are a good place to start, but find research that passes the CARS test.

Books

Next, locate books that are relevant to your thesis statement. A book can cover a single topic; it may contain a compilation of articles, essays, or chapters by a number of authors around a topic or it may collect an author's individually pre-published pieces. Books can be located by searching a library's catalogue, the internet, or a database. For instance, Project Gutenberg (http://gutenberg.org) has digitally republished more than 60,000 ebooks, ranging from the contemporary *Human Genome Project, Y Chromosome*, by the Human Genome Project, to the 19th-century novel *The Hunchback of Notre Dame*, by Victor Hugo.

Periodicals

Periodicals are published regularly—for instance, monthly, yearly, or daily. Examples include newspapers, magazines, journals, and yearbooks. Unless you are writing about an extremely current cultural aspect, you will probably concentrate on journals, which publish articles written by academics, scientists, and researchers. The most-respected journals are peer reviewed (other experts in that field have assessed the work prior to its being published).

Researchers publish their findings in scholarly journals in order to share their ideas—and advance their careers. Thousands of scholarly journals publish a wealth of research on just about any topic you can imagine. However, finding these articles online can be a challenge because the journals are generally distributed through expensive subscriptions only. College and university libraries subscribe to those that they consider most valuable and give access to students, faculty, and staff.

To find articles in journals, you can often do a keyword search. This often brings up many journal articles, newspaper and magazine articles, books, and videos, so you may have to include more than one key word. In library database searches you cannot use questions as you can on Google or other internet search engines. If you are looking for a specific journal article in your library's catalogue, you need a citation. Here is an example:

Zigler, E. F., & Gilman, E. (1993). Day care in America: What is needed? *Pediatrics*, 91(1), 175–178.

As you can see, the citation includes the authors' names, publication date, article title, journal title, volume and issue numbers, and page numbers. You might not need the issue number, but record it just in case. If you have the DOI for the article, you can search using that.

If your library has print journals, a "journals only" search in the library's catalogue will lead you to a section where you can look for the journal you want by title. You will be given a call number that you use to find the journal's physical location. If you need help, ask the library staff, who can show you how to search quickly and efficiently.

Internet Searches

College and university libraries subscribe to databases and indexes with many journals, newspapers, magazines, government documents, and trade publications. The databases contain the full texts of many articles; you can save them directly onto your personal computer's hard drive or you can email a link to yourself. Be aware that not all the information you find will be available to you, as your school may not subscribe to journals it feels are not relevant to the school's needs. When you use journal articles, use only full-text articles; never cite from an abstract See Figure 10.1 for an example of a database search page.

Most databases let you search using keywords (including authors' names) and search options. Boolean operators, including the words AND, OR, and NOT, are used to customize your search. If you type AND between two or more search terms, your results will include both terms; if you type NOT between the terms, your results will omit what follows it. If you use OR as a search expander, each result will include at least one of the terms.

Let's say you are considering an essay on either caffeine or alcohol. An EBSCOhost search on "caffeine OR alcohol" turns up 27,388 entries. This is far too many to be useful, so you change it to "caffeine," which yields 1,658 entries. Thinking that you might want to compare caffeine and alcohol, you use the limiter AND, which produces 116 results. To exclude tobacco from your search, you add a second limiter, "NOT tobacco." Using the two limiters ("caffeine AND alcohol NOT tobacco") produces 93 results—a more manageable start.

Some Popular Databases

This section lists several databases that can help you with your research. Some include various disciplines; others are more specific. Each academic discipline has specialized databases and indexes that concentrate on publications that are particularly relevant to the field. You can ask your instructor or librarian to direct you to the most appropriate databases, or you can search your library's website for discipline-related listings.

TIP

Depending on your search engine, you can narrow or expand your search by using specific symbols. Putting words between quotation marks restricts the search to text that contains the words in the order you place them; for example, typing "fair trade coffee" with the quotation marks will return fewer results than if you don't use the marks because you will see only those articles that contain the exact phrase. If you are looking for something that involves children, you can type "child*" and this will give you variations of the word, such as *child*, *child's*, *children*, *children's*, etc. This may help you expand your search if few results appear.

A **keyword** is a word identified by an author or a cataloguer as important in an article. **Boolean operators**, such as AND, OR, and NOT, customize your search.

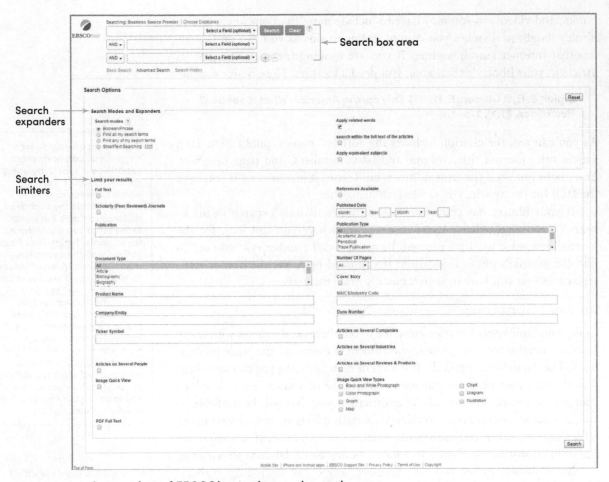

Search box area

Search expanders

Search limiters

FIGURE 10.1 Screenshot of EBSCOhost advanced search page

The screenshot in Figure 10.1 shows how databases typically organize research information. By entering a word or phrase in one or more of the search boxes, you can retrieve any article that contains your keywords in the title or body of the thousands of periodicals available through EBSCOhost.

The list of article results can be enormous and overwhelming. For this reason, EBSCOhost allows you to limit your search to such factors as a specific date range or peer-reviewed journals only.

BioMed Central indexes hundreds of journals offering peer-reviewed research about biology, physical sciences, math, engineering, and medicine. It is an open-access site that is free for everyone.

Business Source Elite is a database assembled for business schools and libraries; it incorporates scholarly journals and business periodicals relating to sales marketing, economics, and accounting.

Statistics Canada is a comprehensive database containing over 18 million government documents.

Criminal Justice Database contains both academic journals and trade magazines. This is for those studying criminology.

EBSCOhost is a database service for more than 9,500 journals on a vast range of discipline areas that allows internet-style (Boolean logic) searching. Widely available through college or university library sites, EBSCOhost is the academic database you should start with, and it might be the only one you need.

Education Resources Information Center (ERIC) is a large database sponsored by the Institute of Education Sciences of the United States Department of Education. It is best known for its expert summaries on educational topics (ERIC Digest Records). The ERIC Social Sciences Citation Index lists more than 3,000 social and behavioural sciences journals published after 1995.

Gale in Context: Canada covers many Canadian topics. You can choose the lexile range (reading level) of the articles to help you do research.

Health Source: Nursing/Academic Edition offers full-text articles from more than 500 health and medical journals and indexes the abstracts of more than 850 publications.

IEEE Xplore contains full-text technical journals, conference proceedings, and active standards in engineering, physics, computer science, and materials sciences. Over 3 million full-text documents are available.

Gartner provides industry-specific information for the IT profession.

Lexis-Nexis Academic Universe contains full-text articles from 17,000 news, business, and legal sources, such as company reports, newspapers, transcripts of broadcasts, wire services, newsletters, journals, case law, government documents, and some valuable reference texts.

Pressreader has articles from 6,000 international newspapers and magazines. Some of the papers are only available for reading while you are on campus.

ProQuest provides access to thousands of current periodicals and newspapers that are updated daily; it contains full-text articles from as early as 1986.

PsycArticles contains academic journals in psychology.

WorldCat, operated by a consortium of more than 10,000 universities, libraries, and colleges, allows users to view or borrow audiovisual materials, books, films, government documents, computer files, and research reports in 400 languages. This "database of databases" has thousands of full-text articles and an interlibrary loan service for non-digitized items.

Libraries often provide an alphabetical listing of the databases and some even organize databases according to areas of study. Most libraries have useful researching tips and resources that can be accessed online. If you need further help, ask your librarians. Their experience in conducting research and helping students can save you valuable time.

Notes about the Internet

When assessing the credibility of a secondary source, you need to understand that anyone with basic computer skills can publish online, which creates both new opportunities and new challenges for researchers. For instance, if you search for essay writing blogs, you will get many results; however, are the authors experts? Are they credible? Again, use the CARS test to assess information.

Searching the internet for laptop prices and using it for academic research require different criteria; for research you need to find trustworthy

TIP
Not all internet sources are of equal value. Make sure you use credible online sources.

authors. To retrieve quality information, you must assess the reputation of a site's creator and check the information in other sources. Even if the author of the site is well respected, it is important to judge their motivation carefully. Ask yourself, "Is the author providing a reasoned argument or just an opinion?" Be aware that personal blogs and listservs are largely designed for conversation and opinion rather than the promotion of academic research; therefore, the information does not pass the CARS test.

Using college or university library websites is best when you are starting to do academic research because they provide a wealth of accurate scholarly information and appropriate online material. The final part of a website's URL indicates these websites. The addresses of degree-granting American educational institutions end with the domain ".edu." Canadian schools' websites generally contain a shortened version of their name, followed by ".ca."

A popular research source is Google Scholar. This site is geared more toward research than other, more commercially focused search engines, including Google and Microsoft Bing. Some of the sources on Google Scholar are peer reviewed, which adds credibility. You can search by keyword and search related articles, giving you a broader view of your topic or providing a new direction for your research. Once again, remember that not all sources are equal. When you have done some research in the field, you will be able to discern which are acceptable and which are not.

Finally, the Directory of Open Source Journals is an open-access directory with many peer-reviewed journals. You can browse by subjects or perform a search. There are over 5 million articles from around the world.

One source to avoid citing is Wikipedia. Much like encyclopedias, this is a good source to start with if you are unsure about your topic and want some basic information. However, like all wikis, it is created by volunteers who add content. Most of the information is accurate, but not all of it is reliable. Sometimes Wikipedia provides links to scholarly papers that can be used in your research essay. However, make sure that the link leads to a credible source and not just further Wikipedia pages.

TIP
While Wikipedia is a place to start, do not cite it in an essay.

You may need to use sources in your essay that are peer reviewed. But if not, you may be able to use blogs, discussion boards, or even personal email correspondence. Credible blogs can provide you with interesting information. Use only those blogs that generally support what your other research has indicated, whether it supports your thesis or not. Avoid blogs that are inflammatory. For example, if you are writing about gaming, don't use a blog stating that gamers are introverts who are unable to function properly in social environments. This type of blog is designed to create discussion based on the writer's opinion but is probably not focused on research.

TIP
Blogs and discussion boards can be useful sources, as the authors can give you an idea about what is considered important in that particular field.

Much like blogs, discussion boards can be a useful research source. The opinions posted can help you understand what others consider important in the area you want to study. These sites can also guide you to relevant, current research for your topic or introduce new areas that you hadn't considered. Again, be aware that anyone can post to discussion boards as long as they belong to that particular group. Not all posts will be an appropriate research source.

Personal email can also be used as a source for many essays. If you know of a person who is well respected in the field you are studying, you may decide to contact them with some questions. Only do this after you have thoroughly researched the topic. By doing the background work ahead of time, you can ask pointed questions that can be integrated into your essay (if the person agrees to participate).

Do not leave contacting a source until the last minute, as it might take some time for your contact to respond, and they may decline to answer your questions. You could provide a deadline for the response, but be reasonable as your contact may be extremely busy.

Notes on Library Research

With so much information available electronically, it may seem unnecessary to go to the library in person. However, libraries continue to be valuable resources, partly because they have books not available online. As well, they are staffed by professionals who understand how information is organized and interrelated. Most librarians can help you save time and direct you to sources you might never come across on your own. Librarians and library technicians have been specially trained and often know of different ways to retrieve information. The help desk staff will answer your questions and assist you with your searches.

Libraries often run courses to familiarize students with the specific systems the college or university uses; it is a good idea to sign up for a session or two. Participating in the same session more than once is often helpful, as the information can be overwhelming, and you can learn things you missed the first time.

Furthermore, libraries hold many important records, which may include

- indexes for many periodicals, images, films, microfiche files, and videos;
- theses and dissertations (book-length documents written by university students as part of their advanced-degree requirements);
- historical documents, including maps and public records;
- collections of textual and graphic material on special subjects, sometimes including original documents;
- clipping files from newspapers and magazines;
- bound volumes of journals; and
- collections of audio and film or video recordings.

In addition, larger libraries store print information that has been gathered but has not been digitized. A great deal of information created before 1985 is available only in paper form at a library. If your college or university library is small or if you are attending a newer school, ask about borrowing privileges at other schools close by. You may be able to access those libraries using only your student card, or you may be able to get special permission to use another school's library if they have information your own does not. Another option is the interlibrary loan. If your school has this service, you can request that documents from another library be delivered to your

TIP
Personal email to a respected member of a particular field can also be used for research essays.

TIP
Librarians and library technicians have been specially trained and often know of different ways to retrieve information. The help desk staff will answer your questions and assist you in your searches.

school's library. However, you do need to plan ahead, as it can take several days or weeks to get the document.

Using electronic sources to access journals that publish paper versions has another frustrating wrinkle: these publications often hold back their latest editions from databases in order to maintain their paid subscriptions. This means that it is still necessary to view the most current issues on paper. As stated earlier, accessing recent studies is vital, especially if your subject is a topical one.

Although the nature of research has changed dramatically with the increasing availability of online resources, it is best to think of the cyber–paper relationship as complementary. Relying on the internet only is inadvisable, and some instructors may specify how much electronic research is allowed.

Alternative Sources

Although this section has emphasized written research information, many disciplines accept evidence from visual or audio media, such as television, film, video, works of art, performances, surveys or questionnaires, interviews, and observations. Using these alternative sources requires the same attention to detail in note-taking as when you use traditional materials, and most citation styles provide instructions for citing and referencing non-textual research information. These approaches are more acceptable in some disciplines than in others—if your essay outline emphasizes alternative information sources, review it with your instructor early in the writing process.

Interviewing can be another source of information. If you have direct access to a noted authority in your field, interviewing can be effective. The main advantage of an interview, whether face to face, by telephone, or by email (as discussed earlier), is that you can ask questions specific to your research rather than searching many potential sources for this particular information. Interview subjects can be treated the same way as other experts; that is, their words can be summarized, paraphrased, or quoted directly. There are also specific methods for documenting interviewees. The college or university community—including, perhaps, one of your instructors—is an ideal place to look for experts.

Chapter Review Questions

1. What is the difference between primary and secondary sources?
2. Why is it important to know the experts in the field you are researching?
3. Why should you not use encyclopedias for your sources?
4. What is the difference between a database and the internet?
5. What sources, other than books, can you find at a college or university library?

6. What is a Boolean operator?
7. What does CARS stand for? Why is using the CARS test important?
8. What does it mean if an article is peer reviewed?
9. How are librarians and library technicians useful?
10. Why should you find more sources for your paper than you actually need?

11 Using Your Research

By the end of this chapter, you should be able to

- create an outline for a research essay;
- recognize and avoid plagiarism;
- integrate summaries and paraphrases;
- use direct quotations in a research essay;
- use a mixture of direct quotation and paraphrase to integrate sources effectively; and
- use signal phrases, ellipses, brackets, and parentheses to integrate sources.

Good writers use primary and/or secondary sources in their writing, but this material is not just inserted into their work. Skilled writers integrate source material seamlessly, making the essay more readable. This chapter discusses several ways to incorporate sources. It also explains plagiarism, a serious academic offence, and outlines the steps for acknowledging others' work properly.

▲ Photo: FatCamera/iStockphoto

Outlines for Research Essays

After you have found your sources, as mentioned in Chapter 10, take notes and summarize the information so that you can accurately represent others' ideas when you begin to combine them with your own. Once you have finished taking notes and understand the information, you are ready to organize your essay.

→12 Chapter 12 also discuss the integration stage.

Again, asking specific questions can help:

- Is my research geared toward supporting my points?
- Have I understood the results of the studies I've researched and the positions of the experts whose works I have read?
- Are all my sources credible? Do they pass the CARS test? Are there many recent ones?
- Have I summarized, paraphrased, or quoted all sources adequately and accurately?
- Which sources are the most important?
- How do the different experts' views or conclusions fit together?
- Are there opposing positions? For example, do some findings challenge others? Have I mentioned those?
- How does my research help me explore the topic?
- Has my research changed my view of my topic? If so, how? Do I need to change my thesis?

Organization: Arranging

Every essay needs a structure, which usually takes the form of an outline or template. Ask yourself these questions when you are ready to organize your essay:

- Do I have enough support to begin an outline? If so, what kind of template should I use?
- Is there an organizational method I should use?
- Do my points thoroughly explore the topic?
- Are some points inadequately developed to produce substantial paragraphs?
- Are all areas of my research relevant to the points I want to make?
- What points are most essential and what sources are most relevant?
- Am I off topic anywhere?
- Does the structure I chose reflect my purpose? Does it reflect my audience? Is it logical?

> **TIP**
> Successful writers create outlines early in the writing process to help them organize their thoughts.

←7 ←9 Chapters 7 and 9 discuss outlines for expository and argumentative essays, respectively.

An outline for a research paper should include the sources you intend to use in the essay. While your instructor may require a specific or minimum number of sources, you should have at least one source (direct quotation, paraphrase, or idea) to support each main point of your body paragraphs.

Whereas an argumentative essay depends on effective reasoning and various kinds of evidence—including examples, illustrations, analogies, anecdotes, and perhaps the findings of secondary sources—an expository essay usually relies heavily on outside support.

Including such sources in your outline will make it easier to write your first draft, when you will focus on integrating the sources with your own words. Moreover, researching your topic before proceeding to the outline can help you determine the topic's viability. Your research may even uncover interesting aspects of the topic you hadn't considered.

The following is student writer Sandy Crashley's outline for an essay on the cost of buying happiness (see the full essay later in this chapter). Although it is brief, the student outline includes enough detail on both the main points and the relevant research for Crashley to elaborate on the former once writing the essay begins. When you read the essay, you'll see that Crashley changed some of sources as the work progressed. Outlines can differ from the final essay, as you will find your ideas may change as you write.

> **TIP**
> Save your research for the body of the essay, where you need to show the audience that the experts support your point of view. Don't waste your material in the introduction, and never place it in the conclusion.

 Chapter 10 examines methods for researching an essay topic.

> **TIP**
> An outline for a research essay should include the sources you will use to support your main points.

Outline for "The Cost of Buying Happiness: Why Less Is More"

Sample Student Essay
Research

Thesis and comment: Reducing the amount one consumes to be happier and healthier—the minimalist movement, the tiny house movement, and the locavore movement.
Topic sentence: Minimalist movement means fewer goods.

A. Home less cluttered (Hancock)
B. Less maintenance, more free time (Kondo)
C. QUALITY VERSUS QUANTITY

Concluding sentence: Fewer goods of better quality will make one happier.
Topic sentence: Tiny houses mean fewer goods and also cost savings.

A. Costs (The tiny life)
B. Cost of house versus income (CMHC)
C. Less cost; more money for other enjoyable activities (Mitchell)

Concluding sentence: Smaller space, fewer goods, more money.
Topic sentence: Locavore movement better for health and environment.

A. Farmer's markets and local income
B. Know where food comes from, so control pesticides and GMOs (Schindler)
C. Savings overall

Concluding sentence: Locavore movement is better for you and cheaper in the long run.
Conclusion: Smaller means less debt and healthier, happier life.

In a small group, select a topic that you are all interested in. Go online or to the library and find some relevant sources. After skimming them, create an outline for a research essay.

Plagiarism

Many people disregard copyright laws. Millions of people download music or movies illegally. Studies have shown a rise in student cheating. File sharing is common, with sites such as YouTube and TikTok making it possible to post videos directly from those sites to Facebook and Twitter. The lines between what can be shared and what cannot are often unclear. However, this sort of "sharing" is not acceptable in academia. It is considered plagiarism. This is a serious academic crime that occurs when a writer uses another's words, ideas, or visuals without stating the source of the information.

All outside sources require parenthetical citations and an alphabetical listing in the paper's works cited or reference section. You must cite secondary sources—whether you quote from them directly, summarize them, paraphrase them, or just refer to them in passing—by using the appropriate style of your discipline.

Plagiarism occurs when a writer

- fails to cite an idea, a paraphrase, or a summary;
- uses the exact language of the source without putting it in quotation marks; or
- uses the identical structure of the original.

Plagiarism can be intentional or unintentional, but both have equally serious consequences, from receiving a zero for that particular paper to failing the course to being expelled from the college or university. Intentional plagiarism includes using sections, sentences, or phrases from a website, book, newspaper article, magazine, etc., without acknowledgement. Buying an essay from the internet or another person, submitting a friend's essay as your own, or reusing a paper you wrote for another class also fall under this crime. Unintentional or inadvertent plagiarism results from careless note-taking, improper documentation, or a lack of knowledge about plagiarism. Therefore, as we have stated throughout this book, it is important to take good notes and to cite all information taken from other sources, both primary or secondary. Take the time to find out what your school's policy is regarding plagiarism.

An instructor can easily detect plagiarism from a shift in tone or word use. Many instructors do an internet search for the questionable material to see if the exact wording appears in another publication. You may be required to provide an electronic copy to a service such as Turnitin before submitting your essay. Such sites compare your paper to

Plagiarism is the intentional or unintentional use of someone else's work as if it were your own.

TIP
Plagiarism does not apply just to the words of the source but also to the idea. You are plagiarizing if you use the language of the source without enclosing it in quotation marks or if you closely imitate the structure of the material cited—even if you change the words.

thousands of documents and post any matching sources for you and your instructor to see.

The following examples demonstrate instances of plagiarism, as well as acceptable paraphrases.

Sample 1

Original:

Anybody who will look at the thing candidly will see that the evolutionary explanation of morals is meaningless and presupposes the existence of the very thing it ought to prove. It starts from a misconception of the biological doctrine. Biology has nothing to say as to what ought to survive and what ought not to survive; it merely speaks of what does survive.

Stephen Leacock, "The Devil and the Deep Sea: A Discussion of Modern Morality." *The Social Criticism of Stephen Leacock*, edited by Alan Bowker, U of Toronto P, 1973, p. 57.

Language of the source unchanged:

A person willing to see *the thing candidly* **would realize that morals cannot be accounted for through evolution.**

Sentence structure unchanged:

Biology does not distinguish between what should and should not survive; it simply tells us "what does survive."

Acceptable paraphrase:

An honest appraisal can tell a person that morals cannot be accounted for through evolution. ... Biology tells us only "what does survive," not what should and should not survive (Leacock 57).

Sample 2

Original:

Previous studies by the American Psychological Association show cheating is relatively infrequent in elementary school, but increases as children become adolescents and progress through grade levels. The increasing incidence of cheating correlates almost perfectly with increasing pressure from teachers to get good grades.

A. Minsky, "Cheating Stats Getting Out of Control: Researcher." *CanWest News*, 9 Aug. 2009. CBCA Current Events.

Language of the source unchanged:

As students progress to higher grades, cheating correlates almost perfectly with increasing pressure.

Language changed, but sentence structure unchanged:

Students cheat more because of mounting pressure to achieve high marks.

TIP

Both intentional and unintentional plagiarism usually lead to the same harsh consequences, such as failing the course or being expelled from school.

→12 Chapter 12 provides detailed information on citing the most common sources used in research essays.

TIP

A good strategy for avoiding plagiarism (and for learning the information) is to study carefully the passage you want to use, close the text, and write out its points from memory completely in your own words. Finally, look at the passage again, ensuring that it is different from what you have written in both its structure and language—and that you have accurately restated the thought behind it.

Acceptable paraphrase:

As students advance from one grade to the next at school, they often feel that they need to perform well, and this pressure seems tied to the frequency of cheating (Minsky).

You may not need to cite all the sources you include in your essay. Anything that can be considered general knowledge or easily obtainable facts usually does not need to be cited, even if you obtained the information from a specific source. If you're writing an essay about the *Titanic*, you don't have to cite a statement that it sank after colliding with an iceberg because this is a well-known fact. You do, however, have to cite a source that states how many people survived, how many did not, and how many lifeboats there were, as many readers do not know these statistics.

General knowledge can vary according to audience. If you are writing for an audience with a knowledge of Canadian history, you may not need to cite the fact that there were four provinces originally. Your readers will either already know this information or can easily obtain it from various sources. If the general knowledge or easily obtainable standards do not apply, make the citation. However, when you are writing about a subject you are studying in your program, make sure you cite information, as it is new to you and you want to show your instructor that you have researched the topic well.

TIP

If a fact is general knowledge for your audience or is easily obtainable by the reader, you usually do not need to provide a citation, unless you are proving to your instructor that you have researched the topic well enough to show that you are becoming an expert in the field.

Integrating Secondary Sources

Using secondary sources enables you to support your argument and to demonstrate your familiarity with source material. Your essay, interwoven with citations in the correct format, reveals your skills as a reader, researcher, and writer. As covered in Chapter 10, you can treat secondary sources in three major ways:

1. Summarize the entire source or the section of it that is most directly relevant to your point.
2. Paraphrase the source.
3. Quote from the source directly.

Summary, Paraphrase, Direct Quotation, Mixed Quotation Format

Using a variety of methods to integrate secondary sources with your own ideas is usually best; however, there are general guidelines to help you choose a style. In all cases, remember that the source must be identified either in a signal phrase or in a parenthetical citation.

Summary

Summarize if you want to use a source's main idea(s) to provide background information, to set up a point of your own (e.g., to show similarity or difference), or to explain a point relevant to your discussion. You can summarize passages of just about any length—from one sentence to several pages.

→11 See "Signal Phrases" later in this chapter for a discussion of signal phrases and parenthetical citations.

←5 For more about summaries and paraphrases, see Chapter 5.

Paraphrase

Paraphrase when you want to cite a relatively small amount of material that is directly relevant to your point. Include all of the original ideas but rephrase them and use an original sentence structure.

Direct Quotation

Direct quotation is used when both the source and the exact wording are important. This could be due to specialized vocabulary in the cited passage or the unique way that the source uses language or expresses the idea. Used selectively, direct quotations are an essential part of most essays.

You can use direct quotations for small or (relatively) large amounts of text. If you choose to quote four or more consecutive lines, use the block quotation format, in which you indent the text one half-inch from the left margin and double-space it but do not use quotation marks at the beginning and end. The usual procedure is to introduce the block quotation by a complete sentence followed by a colon (see the next section). If the original text includes quotation marks, you must retain them. Use double quotation marks first, and then single quotation marks within those if needed, as in this example:

Sarah said, "John told me to just 'walk away,' rather than argue with Peter."

The single quotation marks around *walk away* inform the reader that Sarah is quoting John directly.

Do not use direct quotes if

- the idea in the passage is obvious, well known, or could be easily accessed;
- the material is essentially factual and does not involve a particular interpretation of the facts; or
- the text can be easily paraphrased.

Avoid using large blocks of quoted material, especially as a way of meeting the essay's required length. Some instructors do not include direct quotations in your total word count.

These examples present unnecessary or ineffective direct quotations, followed by preferable alternatives:

Sample 1

"About one-third of infants are breastfed for three months or longer" (Statistics Canada).

Paraphrase:

Approximately 33 per cent of infants receive breast milk for at least three months (Statistics Canada).

Direct quotation is used when the source and the exact wording are important. This could be due to specialized vocabulary in the cited passage or the unique way that the source uses language or expresses the idea.

Block quotation is a method of setting off a large quotation (4 or more lines or 40 or more words) from the rest of the essay's text.

TIP

Use single quotation marks to indicate a word or passage in your source that is in quotation marks; use double quotation marks if these segments appear in a block quotation.

Sample 2

"The greenhouse effect is the result of gases like carbon dioxide, nitrous oxide, and methane being trapped in earth's atmosphere" (Environment Canada).

Paraphrase:

The accumulation of such gases as carbon dioxide, nitrous oxide, and methane in the atmosphere has led to the greenhouse effect (Environment Canada).

The following direct quotations are effective:

Albert Einstein once said, "It always seems to me that man was not born to be a carnivore."

Direct quotation is a good—although not an essential—choice here because Einstein is a well-known person. In the next instance, precise wording matters and gives authority to the passage:

"Neither capital punishment nor life imprisonment without possibility of release shall be imposed for offenses committed by persons below 18 years of age" (UN Convention on the Rights of the Child).

Mixed Quotation Format

A mixed quotation format uses a combination of paraphrase and direct quotation to show a writer's familiarity with a source and confidence in integrating words and ideas smoothly. Here is an example:

In his tribute to Pierre Elliott Trudeau in *The Globe and Mail*, Mark Kingwell finds the "good citizen" behind "the fusion of reason and passion, the virility and playfulness, the daunting arrogance and wit, the politician as rock star."

Compare this statement with the original (the unused text is crossed out).

It's hard to say anything about Trudeau now that has not been said a thousand times before: the fusion of reason and passion, the virility and playfulness, the daunting arrogance and wit, the politician as rock star. All true; all banal. But underneath all that I find a more resonant identity, one which is at once simpler and more profound: the good citizen.

Kingwell, M. "Pierre Elliott Trudeau: 1919–2000." *The Globe and Mail*, 30 Sept. 2000, http://v1.theglobeandmail.com/series/trudeau/mkingwellrefpol_sep30.html.

When you use direct quotations, make sure the quoted material is integrated with the surrounding text grammatically, clearly, and gracefully. When you add or change a word to make it fit your sentence, the changed word must be shown in square brackets. This tells the reader that you made a change to the direct quote.

TIP

Many facts can be paraphrased rather than quoted directly. Avoid quoting long passages of statistical information that can easily distract the reader—paraphrasing the material is usually better.

A mixed quotation format combines significant words of the source (direct quotation) with paraphrasing.

Sample 1
Ungrammatical:

Charles E. Taylor discusses the efforts of scientists "are defining a new area of research termed artificial life" (172).

Grammatical:

Charles E. Taylor discusses the efforts of scientists to "[define] a new area of research termed artificial life" (172).

Sample 2
Unclear:

Art critic John Ruskin believes that the highest art arises from "sensations occurring to them only at particular times" (112).

Clear:

Art critic John Ruskin believes that artists produce the highest art from "sensations occurring to them only at particular times" (112).

Punctuate a direct quotation exactly as it is punctuated in the original, but do not include any punctuation in the original that comes after the quoted material. Note the omission of the original comma after *recklessness*.

Original:

"Any accounting of male–female differences must include the male's superior recklessness, a drive, not, I think, towards death" (Updike 31).

Direct quotation:

In his essay "The Disposable Rocket," John Updike states that "any accounting of male–female differences must include the male's superior recklessness" (31).

TIP
To test whether you've integrated a quotation properly, remove the quotation marks and make sure that the sentence is grammatical. Remember to put the quotation marks back in and to indicate any changes you made to the original with brackets or ellipses.

──────── **EXERCISE 11.2**

Choose five or six passages from a section of one of your textbooks. Using the techniques for integrating sources discussed in this chapter, create direct quotations, summaries, paraphrases, and examples of mixed quotation format for these passages.

Signal Phrases, Ellipses, and Brackets

Signal Phrases

Signal phrases, such as those used in "Using Signal Phrases" in Chapter 5, introduce direct quotations. These phrases contain the source's name (Taylor, Ruskin) and a signal verb (*recalls*, *discusses*, or *believes*). They tell readers exactly where the reference begins and guide them through your process of building your argument. The following paragraph, which uses MLA style, contains two

A **signal phrase** indicates that what follows is taken from another source.

citation formats: the first sentence contains a signal phrase, shown in italics; the second does not:

> **Richard Goldbloom states** that a surveillance video taken in Toronto showed that, in more than 20 per cent of incidents where bullying was involved, peers actively became part of the bullying (2). Furthermore, recent statistics show not only the pervasiveness of the problem but also that outsiders perceive bullying as a problem in schools today (Clifford 4).

The reader would easily be able to separate the two sources at the transition word *furthermore*, so a second signal phrase is unnecessary.

In APA style, the signal phrase, shown in italics, includes the year of the work's publication after the author's name:

> **Asch and Wishart (2004) stated** that the Slavey communities had grade schools by the 1960s, and people left their homes to live in communities so as to retain social benefits (p. 186). As children and parents were reminded, a half-dozen absences from school could result in fines and jail for the parents and the loss of family allowance payments (*The Catholic Voice*, 2000, p. 5).

Ellipses

Using direct quotation doesn't mean that you have to include full paragraphs or sentences from other texts. For example, you may find a passage that discusses two points and you want to discuss only one, so you can leave out the irrelevant part. In fact, keeping it in might confuse the reader. However, make sure that leaving it out would not be misleading or create a bias that does not exist in the original.

Replace any omitted text in a direct quotation with an ellipsis (...). This punctuation mark informs the reader that you aren't quoting the entire sentence or paragraph. If the omitted text includes all the remaining words up to the period at the end of the sentence or you omit one or more complete sentences, add a fourth dot. (Always check with the requirements of your formatting and style guide, as the guides may differ in the use of ellipses.)

Keep the punctuation on either side of the ellipsis only if removing it makes the sentence ungrammatical.

> **"But some damage to the head ... occurs from fighting as a player's head is struck, ... either by a fist or when he falls against the ice."**
>
> Simpson, Jeffrey. Fighting Hockey Violence Will Give You a Concussion." *The Globe and Mail*, 14 Feb. 2009, https://www.theglobeandmail.com/opinion/fighting-hockey-violence-will-give-you-a-concussion/article22733343/.

Brackets

Square brackets or brackets, as opposed to parentheses (round brackets) indicate a change or an addition to a direct quotation, such as a stylistic change (e.g., upper- to lowercase), grammatical change (e.g., verb tense), or clarification (e.g., adding a word to make the context clearer). The

---

An ellipsis (...) indicates the omission of one or more words within a direct quotation. Add a fourth dot if you omit all the words up to and including the final period.

TIP

As a general rule, do not use an ellipsis at the beginning or end of a direct quotation.

Square brackets (or brackets) are punctuation marks that, when used in a direct quotation, indicate a change or addition to the original passage. Parentheses, like dashes, are a form of punctuation that may enclose text that explains or expands on something. Parentheses would be incorrect in the example shown here.

following example illustrates these kinds of changes (although you would probably paraphrase a passage that contained this many brackets and ellipses):

> **The text states that "[a]ll secondary sources require parenthetical citations and an alphabetical listing ... at the end of [the] essay. ... [Students] must cite secondary sources, whether [they] quote from them directly, summarize them, paraphrase them, or just refer to them in passing by using the [MLA or APA] style."**

Original:

> **All secondary sources require parenthetical citations and an alphabetical listing in the works cited section at the end of your essay (MLA) or the references section (APA). You must cite secondary sources, whether you quote from them directly, summarize them, paraphrase them, or just refer to them in passing by using the style preferred by your discipline.**

You may occasionally use brackets to explain an unfamiliar term within a direct quotation:

> **Emergency room nurse Judith McAllen said, "We triage [prioritize by severity of injury] patients if it's a non-emergency, and don't treat them on the basis of their arrival time."**

Avoid using brackets any more than is strictly necessary.

Inserting *sic* (which means "thus") between square brackets tells the reader that what comes before it occurs in the original exactly the way it appears in your quotation. One use is to show an error in the original:

> **As people often say, "Vive le [sic] différence!"**

[Sic] here calls attention to the article error: *le* should be *la*. In APA documentation style, italicize *sic*.

Documentation: In-Text Citations

Understanding where and when to document can also be confusing. If you document too much, your paper will not flow well; however, if you do not properly document your sources, you will be plagiarizing.

Parenthetical citations (the parentheses you see after a quotation, paraphrase, or summary that contain bibliographic information) convey information about the source while helping the reader clearly understand your writing. The general rule is to cite enough to give the reader the information needed while avoiding unnecessary citations.

Do not cite every statement or fact from a source if you use that one source for consecutive references. You can sometimes combine a few references from the same source in one citation. If you use three pages from a work by Jackson, you could refer to a page range: (Jackson 87–89). This

> **TIP**
> Parenthetical citations convey information about the source while interfering as little as possible with the essay's content and readability.

citation tells the reader that you used the source continuously—perhaps one idea came from page 87, two facts from page 88, and a paraphrased passage from page 89. However, if your own or another source's information is inserted in between your references to Jackson's material, you need to cite Jackson more than once. Do not include the citation at the end of the paragraph. Use the citation immediately after you have used another author's words, ideas, or illustrations.

In the essay that follows, Sandy Crashley mainly uses paraphrasing to support her points. She uses the APA style for citation.

→12 For more on APA style, see Chapter 12.

Sample Student Essay

Research

The Cost of Buying Happiness: Why Less Is More

Sandy Crashley

[1] Society assigns status to people according to what they wear, what they own, what they drive, and what they do. This appears to be how to determine if one is successful in North America. A variety of "fads" or "movements" have crept into society recently which rail against this concept that people are defined by their "stuff," and an attempt is being made to redirect people's ever-consuming natures to view success with a less-is-more perspective. The minimalist movement, the tiny house movement, and the locavore movement are all centred on reduction, and the enrichment this reduction will then bring to one's life. The people who participate in these movements believe that money does not buy happiness.

[2] The minimalist movement is all about having fewer goods. The Dalai Lama has said, "If one's life is simple, contentment is sure to come" (Becker, 2014). Following this doctrine, people limit their possessions, which they then believe liberates them and allows them to be happy. This in turn frees people to invest in what they are truly passionate about, such as doing things that make one happy (Hancock, 2014, p. 141). Also, by removing the excess items, a home becomes less cluttered and requires less time to maintain. Also, by de-cluttering and maintaining a minimalist environment, people spend less time purchasing unnecessary goods. This savings in time can instead be spent on quality time with family or friends, or on hobbies that bring pleasure. Furthermore, people who follow the minimalist movement often realize that they don't need all of their belongings, and thus they can save money by not buying the latest gadget. The possessions that those who participate in the minimalist movement do keep or buy will actually come to mean something and be of value to them and make them happy (Kondo, 2014, p. 38). The focus is around need, not want, as well as quality over quantity. The minimalist approach to life is not without its obstacles. As with any habit, it takes conscious effort to adjust from the pursuit of material things to pursuits of a more enriching kind, such as spending time with family and friends. The memories and bonds forged through these times will dwarf the joy of a new iPod. So, while the minimalist movement requires life changes, in the end, the cost of happiness is much cheaper than trying to find happiness in the latest consumer trends.

Crashley paraphrases the source.

In the closing sentence, the writer links this paragraph to the thesis.

[3] All of the benefits of the minimalist movement can also be applied to the tiny house movement. The tiny house campaign continues to gain momentum

198 **PART THREE** Research

through social media, advertising, and television shows, like FYI's *Tiny House Nation* and HGTV's *Tiny House Builders*. This movement advocates for a minimalist culture, as a smaller space means limited room to put things. Therefore, multiple possessions actually become a burden. Cost savings are also enhanced, as the average-sized 186-square foot "tiny house" costs only $23,000 when co-built by the owner (The Tiny Life, 2015; Portland Alternative Dwellings , 2012). The modest expense will put the cost of housing below the 32 per cent of gross monthly income for most people, as is recommended by the Canada Mortgage and Housing Corporation (n.d.). One of the greatest factors of the 2008 recession in Ontario, and the continued risks to the economy, is the inflated housing market. The average home price in Ontario in December 2014 was $437,601, according to the Canadian Real Estate Association ("*Housing sales decline*", 2015). Couple that with current low interest rates that could increase significantly, and many people may find themselves in a position of finding their homes unaffordable. As tiny homes require fewer materials in order to build them and use less energy to heat and cool, there is also a large positive environmental impact to the movement. Those who participate in this movement do not require a burdensome mortgage, and they can, instead, focus on building a career and life that they love, rather than needing a job with high pay and long hours to pay high mortgage fees and utility bills. These people can also enrich their lives with travel and hobbies, and they have the ability to save for a secure retirement. Again, the tiny house movement, like the minimalist movement, is not without its own challenges. Obtaining land is not easy, with the majority of residential land being purchased in bulk by large house-building companies, leaving remnants expensive for the individual to purchase. As a "tiny house" does not provide collateral to secure, bank loans can often be difficult to obtain and many building laws do not support a "tiny house" in their definition of "minimum habitable structure" (Mitchell, 2012, para. 7). There is also the social pressure, as Ryan Mitchell (2012) states, "In our society today, bigger is better, more is better, we are conditioned to want more ...." (para. 8). However, by living with less, these people are not burdened with the societal obsession of acquiring more just for the sake of appearances, and they have more time and energy for the pursuits that help one feel fulfilled.

[4] Owning a trailer-sized house in the closest vacant field or possessing fewer goods are not concepts that some are comfortable with. The minimalist and tiny house movements require some significant commitment. Another option to consider is the locavore movement. This movement, while sometimes more expensive than the other two, can provide happiness as well. Centred on local eating, this campaign aims to source food products from within a 100-mile radius. When people are able to eat whole foods and obtain them from known local farmers, people can attempt to safeguard against GMOs, pesticides, and other chemical enhancements that many do not want in mass-produced, over-processed foods. The nutrient value is preserved in this food, and it usually tastes better, as it is not harvested early to survive long travel. This lack of travel, as well as a limitation on packaging, is also of great value to the preservation of the environment. This often creates a sense of well-being in those following the locavore movement. Additionally, the income to local farmers, vendors, and other businesses promotes sustainable communities and a balanced economy. Following this movement can be as simple as travelling to the local farmer's market on a weekly basis. Those who buy locally believe that what they are doing benefits many, which adds to their sense of satisfaction. They can also develop a close personal bond with the farmers and

Here the author paraphrases from two sources that provide the same information.

Crashley clearly links the two movements so that the reader does not lose sight of what was said in the first body paragraph.

Note that when using an electronic source where there are no page numbers, the author indicates the paragraph from which the information was taken when citing a direct quote.

Notice the use of the ellipsis. The rest of the quotation is not relevant to the point, so Crashley omits it; however, the necessary information is in the essay.

Again, in the concluding sentence, Crashley links the paragraph to the thesis while also wrapping up the paragraph.

The writer links the three main ideas for the reader.

Note that there are no citations in this paragraph. Does this affect the paragraph's credibility when compared to the others?

vendors, which adds to their happiness. However, depending on where people live, year-round local eating can pose a challenge. The solution to this chief obstacle is to plan: buy seasonal foodstuffs in bulk, then freeze or can items for use in the off-season. While the initial cost is high, there is significant savings over time. For some, the locavore movement may require as much commitment as the tiny house and minimalist movement do; however, the locavore movement is easier to moderately integrate into a family's natural rhythm and everyone can enjoy the nutritional, environmental, and social benefits.

The closing paragraph summarizes the body paragraphs.

[5] When it comes to happiness, many North Americans are raised to pursue "the dream." As soon as they are old enough to have a job, they join the consumer culture and often end up pursuing a job that can pay for future life "needs," instead of doing something they really love to do. Through this whole process, life becomes about working to pay for people's lives, instead of actually living them. What is it that people want to define their happiness or success? According to those who follow the above movements, people need not follow the path of others. These people have found that material goods do not buy happiness, but that a life of luxury means less.

Note the rhetorical thought that the author leaves the reader with.

Perhaps money really does buy happiness, as long as one is not defined by possessions.

References

Canadian Mortgage and Housing Corporation. (n.d.). *Step 2: Are you financially ready?* http://www.cmhc-schl.gc.ca/en/co/buho/hostst/hostst _002.cfm

Hancock, M. (2014). Buy less, live more. *Alive: Canada's Natural Health & Wellness Magazine.* http://www.alive.com/lifestyle/buy-less-live-more/

Housing sales decline in December. (2015). CBC News. http://www.cbc.ca/ news2/interactives/housing-canada/

Kondo, M. (2014). *The life-changing magic of tidying up: The Japanese art of decluttering* (C. Hirano, Trans.). Ten Speed Press.

Mitchell, R. (2012). *Top 5 biggest barriers to the tiny house movement.* http:// thetinylife.com/top-5-biggest-barriers-to-the-tiny-house-movement

Portland Alternative Dwellings. (2012). *How much does a tiny house cost?* http:// padtinyhouses.com/how-much-does-a-tiny-house-cost/

The Tiny Life. (2015). *Tiny houses and the people who live in them.* http:// thetinylife.com/what-is-the-tiny-house-movement

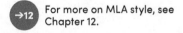

→12 For more on MLA style, see Chapter 12.

Student writer Mike Butler uses some of the different methods we've discussed to integrate sources. He follows the MLA style in his essay.

Computer Ergonomics
Mike Butler

[1] In these technological times, many people are working at jobs that involve long hours sitting in front of a computer. In 1996 a study was done by Hanson that discovered 55 per cent of those studied had enough pain in their upper limbs to force them to get a professional medical opinion (Labeodan 66). As a result, working in an office setting at a computer for long durations can have serious negative effects on the body but fortunately there are many ways to avoid these strains and potential injuries.

Strains and Musculoskeletal Disorders

[2] There are many types of strain and musculoskeletal disorders that can result from prolonged use of a computer. These can be extremely painful and incapacitating and can affect the muscles, tendons, ligaments, joints, and nerves. Spacebar thumb and pop-up pinkie are nicknames given to computer specific strains to the body (Edwards 42). Carpal tunnel syndrome is a very common ailment and can be caused from leaning the wrists on the keyboard while typing (Edwards 42). Tendonitis develops because the pressure blocks the blood supply to the nerves in the hands. It can become such a problem that even small daily tasks like turning door knobs and opening jars are difficult to impossible without assistance (Linden 26). The wrists, back, neck, eyes, and shoulders can all become sore and damaged from improper posture while at the computer. Barbara Headley, an expert in her field of chronic muscle pain treatment, studied more than 700 patients for a period of time in regards to repetitive strain injuries (Taylor para. 4). She found that the body will rely on muscles not designed to do the job when the primary ones get tired. Initially, soreness from computer use will actually start at the back muscles, then move to the neck and only after that to the hands and arms (Taylor, para. 4). Most people won't complain or realize there is a problem until they feel it in their hands, which by then is a far greater problem because it has been going on for so long (Taylor, para. 4). All in all, there are many strains and disorders that can arise from working at a computer.

How to Prevent One's Own Injuries

[3] The cheapest and easiest way to avoid problems is to take matters literally into one's hands. Exercise, stretching, and rest breaks are key to avoiding the physical ailments that come from using a computer excessively. Exercises and stretches that work the pectoral, shoulder, and neck will all help prevent repetitive strain injury (Taylor para. 4). To prevent injury, these exercises should be done daily, even stopping work throughout the day if there is pain (Taylor para. 4). People's bodies are meant for movement, so minibreaks of just a few minutes throughout the day will allow for a good stretch and will aid in the prevention of strain to the body (Edwards 42). It is easy to work this in by standing during phone calls, walking to a colleague's desk instead of emailing, or standing to read long documents. If relief isn't found from stretching, then massage can be helpful to release trigger points to regain normal movement (Linden 26). As important as all of these are, if people's work stations are not set up properly, it is a losing battle (Linden 26). Proper typing posture is obtained by sitting up with the spinal column directly above the pelvis and rolling the pelvis slightly forward.

This uses deep core muscles for maintaining this proper seating position, which are very strong and efficient (Linden 26). By sliding a small rolled up towel under the tail bone, this position is achieved and easily maintained on any type of chair (Linden 26). Feet should be flat on the floor and the monitor directly in front of your body with the top of it at eye level and about an arm's length away. It is much more comfortable to place any work items within your reach zone. Arms should be at a 90-degree angle when on the keyboard and should not rest on the wrist pad when typing. At the very least, change positions and move throughout the day to improve circulation and reduce fatigue.

How to Prevent with Equipment

[4] If people are not able to keep pain at bay through their own means, then many assistive devices are currently on the market to help. Ergonomic chairs come in all shapes and sizes and can be adjusted to fit all different bodies. Split keyboards are basically cracked down the middle and split so that the wrists don't have to bend at odd angles to reach the keys. These can sit on keyboard trays that slide under the desk and are adjustable as to height, angle, and depth. Flat-screen monitors are much easier on the eyes than the older rounded variety (Edwards 42) and wireless mice are both easy to reach and built to conform to the shape of one's hand. Therefore, as this problem of computer ergonomics becomes more prevalent in an office environment, more and more ergonomic devices are developed to aid in this area.

[5] Most importantly, in order to avoid physical injury is to educate users about computer ergonomics and to use what is learned on a daily basis for the rest of one's working life. It is just not enough to have the best chair and office equipment if posture is poor and a workstation improperly set up. Even a basic workstation can be appropriate if arranged well and the user pays attention to their body and takes minibreaks throughout the day (Linden, 26). Prevention is the best way to avoid long-term injury.

Works Cited

Edwards, Albert. "Beating Computer Strain." *Ergowise*, vol. 28, no. 2, 1997, pp. 42–49.

Labeodan, T. "Knowledge of Computer Ergonomics among Secretarial Staff in a Nigerian University Community." *International Journal of Health, Wellness & Society*, vol. 2, no. 3, 2012, pp. 65–74.

Linden, P. "Too Much of a Good Thing: Prevention of Computer-Related Repetitive Strain Injuries among Children." *The Journal*, vol. 26, no. 1, 1998, p. 26, http://eds.b.ebschost.com/eds/detail/detail?vid=5&sid=ae096823-f3d7-4fca-8cba-7bc1068.

Taylor, P. "Keyboard Grief." *The Globe and Mail*, 30 Dec. 1993, http://re.ocls.ca.rap.ocls.ca/ra/login.aspx?url=http://search.proquest.com/docview/385146459?accountid=40483.

Townsend, J. "Ergonomics at the PC: Raising Employee Comfort Levels through Training." *American Society of Safety Engineers*, vol. 43, no. 12, 1998, pp. 20–23, http://ra.ocls.ca.ocls.ca/ra/login.aspx?url=http://search.proquest.com/docview/200423522?ac counted=40483.

Post-Reading Questions

1. Examine both student essays and identify the different ways the writers incorporated their sources. Find examples of direct quotation, paraphrase, summary, and mixed format.
2. Does Butler rely too much on one particular method for integrating his sources? Give evidence to support your answer.
3. How effective is Butler's introductory paragraph? Why do you think he chose to use a quotation?
4. How much background information does Butler give about his topic? What does this tell you about his intended audience?
5. Look at the works cited list. Do you feel that Butler includes enough sources? Do they seem reliable? Give evidence to support your answers.

Chapter Review Questions

1. Why is outlining an important part of essay writing?
2. Why is it crucial to cite your sources?
3. What kind of information does not require a citation?
4. Summarize the section on plagiarism in two or three sentences.
5. What are the three main ways of integrating information from a source? What are their differences?
6. When should you avoid direct quotations in essays? When should you use them?
7. What are signal phrases and why are they important?
8. What is the mixed quotation format method of source integration?
9. How could you indicate a grammatical change to a direct quotation in order to integrate it smoothly with your own writing?
10. What are ellipses and when should you use them?

12 APA and MLA Documentation Styles

By the end of this chapter, you should be able to

- cite sources according to APA and MLA styles;
- create references and works cited lists; and
- incorporate citations into your writing.

As you saw in Chapters 10 and 11, the points in your research essays must be supported with information from outside sources. These sources need to be given proper credit and be documented in a consistent manner. This chapter introduces the American Psychological Association (APA) and Modern Language Association (MLA) styles. You will find common citations and references in print and electronic formats, with examples of each. Sample APA and MLA essays are included to illustrate how to use these styles correctly to format your essay.

▲ Photo: Alberto Masnovo/Shutterstock

Choosing Your Citation Style

Citations, references, and other bibliographic information are important because they

- give appropriate credit to others' work;
- establish your credibility as a researcher;
- show where your own work fits into other work in the field;
- help you avoid plagiarism, a form of theft and the most serious academic crime, and its severe penalties;
- enable readers (such as markers) to trace or verify your sources;
- find the reference if you need it for further research; and
- enlarge on a matter (in a footnote or an endnote) that would be disruptive if placed in the text for MLA.

Most styles require an abbreviated citation—placed in parentheses—in the sentence where the reference appears. Although there are many subtle differences among documentation styles, the main elements of a citation usually include

- the last name(s) of the author(s);
- the year of publication; and
- the page number or a similar locator of the information.

Further details are given in an alphabetized list at the end of the essay under a heading such as "References" or "Works Cited."

Different areas of academia favour distinct styles. Business, education, psychology, social sciences, and some physical sciences use APA; literature, philosophy, and religion use MLA. Other major formats, which we will not discuss in this chapter, include the Council of Science Editors (CSE) and *The Chicago Manual of Style* (*CMS*). Subject areas such as chemistry, engineering, medicine, and music have their own style specifications. Your program or your instructor should be the final guide in your choice of citation style.

Each documentation format has a manual and website. If you are using the print version, which you can probably obtain at your school's library, ensure that it is the most current edition. Your library or resource centre should have online resources to help you correctly format your document. The examples in this chapter are styled according to the following manuals:

American Psychological Association. (2019). *Publication Manual of the American Psychological Association* **(7th ed.).**

Modern Language Association of America. (2016). *MLA Handbook* **(8th ed.).**

The MLA also publishes the MLA *Style Manual and Guide to Scholarly Publishing*.

A **citation** includes the author last name, publication date, and location in the text, using page or paragraph numbers. A **reference** gives complete retrieval information for a source used in an essay.

TIP

If you have another person's information in the body of your essay, then it must be included in the references or works cited section. Conversely, if you have information in the references or works cited section, then you must have an in-text citation. If you did not directly use a paper, do not include it in the references or works cited section.

TIP

APA and MLA are both parenthetical styles, meaning that parentheses are used to enclose brief bibliographical information about the source within the main text.

The following sections in this chapter provide the basic standards for documenting sources in APA and MLA, with examples to illustrate each format. Both APA and MLA update their standards and criteria regularly. Check with your instructor to make sure that this text contains the most recent changes. To look for the most current information, check the associations' respective websites. For APA use https://apastyle.apa.org/instructional-aids/ and their search function to find the information you need. For MLA go to https://style.mla.org/.

If you use other websites for citation and reference help, always double-check the information with at least one other site and take note of when the website was last updated to ensure you are using the latest edition. For hard-to-find formats, ask for help from your instructor or from experts in your college library or writing centre.

APA

APA in-text citations include the author's last name, year of publication, and page number(s).

APA style is parenthetical—whenever you directly quote, paraphrase, or summarize an author in your essay or use an author's idea, you include a citation in parentheses in the sentence. You also provide a more complete description of all your sources that you cited in a reference list, which appears on the final page(s) of your essay.

APA In-Text Citations

── EAL

> Foreign names can be confusing for anyone. If you are not sure of which name is the last name, ask your instructor or a librarian.

Generally, APA in-text citations include the author's last name, and the work's year of publication. Separate the items with commas. For direct quotes, add the relevant page or paragraph number(s) at the end of the sentence and use the abbreviation *p.* or *pp.* for *page* or *pages* or *para.* or *paras.* for *paragraph* or *paragraphs* (do not italicize the abbreviations). In most cases, the end punctuation of the sentence comes after the closing parentheses.

(Ashton, 2019, p. 12).

(Carson, 2020, paras. 5–6).

← 11   Sandy Crashley's essay "The Cost of Buying Happiness: Why Less Is More" (in Chapter 11) uses the APA format.

If the sentence gives the author's name (i.e., uses a signal phrase) and does not include a direct quotation, do not repeat the name in the parenthetical citation. Include the publication year (and page number(s) or paragraph number(s), if necessary) immediately after the author's name.

Author   *Title*   Publication information   **Electronic source**

Ashton (2008) **found that ...**

Carson's (2020) **research showed ...**

Here are more guidelines for APA in-text citations:

Citation after a direct quotation: Give the author's last name, year of publication, and page or paragraph number. If there is no signal phrase (i.e., the author is not named in the sentence), include all the information at the end of the quotation.

> **During both world wars, the Canadian government often employed masseuses because surgery and medical care were insufficient "to restore severely wounded men" (Cleather, 1995, p. ix).**

If the author is named in the signal phrase, follow with the publication year; place the page number at the end of the quotation and before the punctuation.

> **According to Stambouli and Traversa (2002), "each gallon of gasoline produced and used in an internal combustion engine releases roughly 12 kg of CO_2" (p. 299).**

Block quotation: A quotation of 40 words or more begins on a new line and is indented one half-inch from the left margin. Quotation marks are not used, and the text is double spaced. The author's last name, year of publication, and page or paragraph number(s) appear in parentheses at the end of the quotation and *after* the punctuation. If the authors are mentioned in the signal phrase introducing the quotation, follow their name with the year of publication and place the page number only in parentheses at the end of the quotation and after the punctuation.

> **(Ellis & Bochner, 2000, pp. 81–82)**

A paraphrase includes all the content of the source put entirely in your own words. A summary uses your own words to summarize larger sections of the text. See Chapter 5 for paraphrasing and summarizing.

Citation for a paraphrase or summary: State the author's last name and year of publication.

> **Plastic bags were not invented to be single use, but to be used multiple times (Weston, 2019).**

Citation referring to an indirect source: Sometimes it is necessary to refer to a source found in another work, as you may not have access to the original paper. In this case, include the original author's name in the sentence and cite the indirect source, which is the one you found. Include the phrase *as cited in* (not italicized) before the author's last name. In the references section, list the details for your source.

An **indirect source** is one that is cited in another work. Always use original sources whenever possible, but if you have to cite information from an indirect source, include the phrase *as cited in* before the citation.

Author   *Title*   Publication information   **Electronic source**

Francis Bacon (as cited in Lindemann, 2001) observed that language affects our thinking when he said that "words react on the understanding" (p. 93).

Personal communication, including interviews, lectures, conversation, emails, texts, and oral presentations when the work cannot be retrieved by the reader. Give the author's last name and first initial(s), the phrase *personal communication* (not italicized), and the date of the conversation. Note that in previous editions of APA, the type of communication was also included, but this is no longer required in the 7th edition.

(J. Derrida, **personal communication,** September 20, 2000).

Personal communications are cited only in the text of your essay; they are not listed in the references section. This is the only time that something used in your essay is not in the references section.

Multiple sources in one citation: You may include more than one relevant source in a single citation if your point applies to both. Order the sources alphabetically by last name and separate them with a semicolon.

TIP
You may include more than one source in a single citation. Separate the sources with semicolons.

The practices of teaching composition in college have not radically changed in the last few decades (Bishop, 2005; Williams, 2007).

APA In-Text Citations by Format

Number or Kind of Authors

Work by one author: Give the author's last name, year of publication, and page number (if required). A book with both an author and an editor or translator is usually cited by the author.

(Bloom, 2002, p. xviii)

Work by two authors: State the last names of both authors, with an ampersand (&) between them; year of publication; and page number (if required).

TIP
When you refer to a work with two authors in a citation, use an ampersand (&) before the last author's last name. Use *and* when listing the author names in the main text.

(Higgins & Wilson-Baptist, 1999, p. 44).

When naming the authors in the text of your essay, as in a signal phrase, use the word *and* instead of an ampersand.

Higgins and Wilson-Baptist (1999) argue that "a tourist exists outside of experience. A traveller, though, submerges herself in the new" (p. 44).

Works by three or more authors: Use the first author's last name followed by the abbreviation *et al.* (not italicized), which means "and others." Include the publication year and page number (if required) every time, unless the same authors are mentioned more than once in a paragraph.

(Smith et al., 2020, p. 34)

Author   *Title*   Publication information   **Electronic source**

Two or more works by the same author in the same year: Add lowercase letters alphabetically (*a*, *b*, *c*, etc.) to distinguish works published in the same year.

> **(Foucault, 1980a, p. 37)**

The *a* in the example indicates that the writer has used at least two works written by Foucault and published in 1980. This citation must correspond with the entry for 1980a in the references list.

Two authors with the same last name: Include the authors' first initial(s) to distinguish the names.

> **(Sinkinson, S., 2001, p. 225; Sinkinson, B., 2001, p. 237)**

Group or organization as author (corporate author): Documents published by companies, schools, and government departments may not list an author. In this case, use the group or organization's name. If the name is long or is known by an acronym or abbreviation (for example, the United Nations Children's Fund is commonly known as UNICEF), include the full name in the first citation followed by the acronym in square brackets, the year of publication, and page number (if required). Use the abbreviation or acronym with the year throughout the rest of the paper.

> **(American Educational Research Association [AERA], 2001)**
>
> *later citations:* **(AERA, 2001)**

TIP

If no author is given for a source, use the name of the group or organization.

Work with an unknown author (including many dictionary and encyclopedia articles): When the author is unknown and there is no company name, use the first few words of the work's title followed with the year of publication and page number (if required).

> **("Plea to City Hall," 2003)**

Anonymous author: If the author is listed as *Anonymous*, cite in the same way as a named author, using *Anonymous* (not italicized).

> **(Anonymous, 1887, p. 12)**

TIP

Many articles retrieved from a database are viewed as Portable Document Format (PDF) files. In such cases, use the page numbers in the document, which are usually the same as those of the print version (if one exists).

Electronic Sources

Sample in-text internet citation: Include the author's last name, year the site was created or last updated.

> **(Gregoire, 2000)**

Internet site without an author or without a date: Use the full or abbreviated title in quotation marks, the year the site was created or last updated. Use the abbreviation *n.d.* (not italicized) if the site does not include a date.

> **("Muchinfo's Poll," 2002)**
>
> **(Canadian Cancer Society, n.d.)**

Author   *Title*   Publication information   Electronic source

Non-Text Sources

Film, video, audio, tv broadcast, and musical recording: Use the most senior production person's name, such as the film's director, and the year of public release or broadcast. For a TV series, use the name of the executive producer.

(Coppola, 1979**)**

Installation, event, performance, or work of art: Use the format followed by other non-text resources, such as the name of the artist(s) and date of presentation or creation.

(Byrdmore, 2006**)**

APA References

In APA style, the references section contains complete bibliographical information for a work's in-text citations. Follow these guidelines when creating a reference list:

- Begin the references on a new page at the end of the essay and number the section as part of the overall work.
- Centre the title ("References") an inch from the top of the page.
- Double-space the list, with 1-inch margins.
- Begin each entry flush with the left margin; use a hanging indent for subsequent lines. Do not number the entries.
- Alphabetize the list by author last name, usually the first item in each entry.
- Italicize titles of books, journals, plays, films, and other full-length works. Do not set titles of chapters or articles in quotation marks. Capitalize only the first word, the first word after a colon, all proper nouns, and acronyms (e.g., NFB or CBC) regardless of how the original is capitalized.
- Omit words such as *Publishers*, *Inc.*, and *Co.* in publishers' names. Include the full names of associations, corporations, and university presses.
- Use the following abbreviations where appropriate.

    - ed. (edition)
    - Ed. (Editor), Eds. (Editors)
    - No. (Number)
    - p. (page), pp. (pages)
    - para. (paragraph)
    - Pt. (Part)
    - Rev. ed. (Revised edition)
    - Trans. (Translator[s])
    - Vol. (Volume), Vols. (Volumes)

The standard APA reference begins with the author's last name followed by initial(s), not given name(s); publication date; title of work; and publication details. Here are two examples of specific types.

Author   *Title*   Publication information   **Electronic source**

If you are unsure of the author's last name, check with your instructor or librarian.

Sample book entry: Include the author's name, date of publication, title of book, and publisher

> Fries, C. C. **(1962).** *Linguistics and reading*. **Rinehart & Winston.**

Sample journal entry: Provide the author's name, date of publication, title of article, title of journal (italicized), volume number (italicized), issue number (if required), page range, and DOI or URL. Note that the comma after the journal title is also italicized and that there is no end punctuation after a DOI or URL. The abbreviations *p.* or *pp.* are not used in journal entries.

> Valkenburg, P. M., & Jochen, P. **(2007).** **Who visits online dating sites? Exploring some characteristics of online daters.** *CyberPsychology and Behavior, 10,* **849–852.** **https://doi.org/10.1089/cpb.2007.9941**

Number or Kind of Authors

Work by one author: See "Sample book entry."

Work by two authors: Invert both authors' names and separate them with an ampersand (&).

> Luckner, J., & Nadler, R. (1992). *Processing the experience*. Kendall/Hunt.

Work by three or more authors: List all the authors as they appear, up to 20 names. If there are more than 20 authors, list 19 names, then use an ellipsis followed by the final author's name.

> **Terracciano, A., Abdel-Khalek, A. M., Ádám, N., Adamovová, L., Ahn, C. -k., Ahn, H. -n., Alansari, B. M., Alcalay, L., Allik, J., Angleitner, A., Avia, M. D., Ayearst, L. E., Barbaranelli, C., Beer, A., Borg-Cunen, M. A., Bratko, D., Brunner-Sciarra, M., Budzinski, L., Camart, N., ... McCrae, R. R.** (2005). **National Character Does Not Reflect Mean Personality Trait Levels in 49 Cultures.** *Science, 310*(5745), 96–100. **https://doi.org/10.1126/science.1117199**

Two or more works by the same author: Works by the same author are arranged chronologically, earliest to latest. Works with the same author(s) and publication year are arranged alphabetically by the first major word of the title. In the example, the earliest article is listed first; the *h* in *history* precedes the *P* in *Power*, justifying the order of the second and third items.

> Foucault, M. **(1977).** *Discipline and punish: The birth of the prison* **(A. Sheridan, Trans.). Random House.**

> Foucault, M. **(1980a).** *The history of sexuality* (Vol. 1) **(R. Hurley, Trans.). Random House.**

A URL (uniform resource locator) is the address of specific internet content.

TIP
If you are retrieving information from your library's databases, make sure you are using the permanent URL and not your search URL. Your instructor or librarian can help you determine the proper one to use.

TIP
The order for most references is author's last name and initial(s); publication date; title of work; and publication details, which vary depending on whether the work is a book, journal article, or electronic document.

◀10 Chapter 10 discusses DOIs.

TIP
For a work with two to 20 authors, invert all authors' names and use an ampersand (&) between the second-last and the last name.

Author *Title* Publication information Electronic source

Foucault, M. (1980b). *Power/Knowledge: Selected interviews and other writings 1972–1977* (C. Gordon, Ed.). Harvester Press.

Work by two authors with the same last name: The alphabetical order of authors' initials determines the sequence. If two works have the same first authors, the last names of the second authors determine the order.

Jason, L. A., & Klich, M. M. (1982). Use of feedback in reducing television watching. *Psychological Reports, 51,* 812–814.

Jason, L. A., & Rooney-Rebeck, P. (1984). Reducing excessive television viewing. *Child & Family Behavior Therapy, 6,* 61–69.

Group or organization as author (corporate author): Use the full group name in place of the author's name. If the name begins with an article (e.g., *The*), omit it. If the organization is also the publisher, do not repeat the organization's name at the end of the reference. If the reference is to a webpage or DOI, the URL will follow the title of the article.

Education International. (2008). *Guide to universities & colleges in Canada.*

Work with an unknown author (non-electronic source): Alphabetize the entry by the first major word in the title. When an author is listed as "Anonymous," alphabetize by the letter *A*.

Interveners. (1993). *Canadian Encyclopedia* (Vol. 11, pp. 344–348). Smith Press.

No date: Use *n.d.* (not italicized) after the author's name where you would normally put the date.

TIP

When there is no author in a non-electronic source, alphabetize the entry by the first major word in the title. (Do not include words such as *The*.)

Source Type

Edited work: Begin with the editor's name followed by *Ed.* (one editor) or *Eds.* (more than one editor; not italicized) in parentheses.

Corcoran, B., Hayhoe, M., & Pradl, G. M. (Eds.). (1994). *Knowledge in the making: Challenging the text in the classroom.* Boynton/Cook.

Chapter or other type of selection, such as an essay, in an edited volume: Begin with the author's name, year of publication, and chapter (or essay) title. Follow with the name(s) of the book's editor(s), not inverted, preceded by *In* and followed by *Ed.* or *Eds.* (not italicized). The reference concludes with the book title, page range (in parentheses), and publication information.

Williams, N. (1989). Behold the Sun: The politics of musical production. In C. Norris (Ed.), *Music and the politics of culture* (pp. 150–171). Lawrence & Wishart Limited.

Translated work: Place the translator's name and the abbreviation *Trans.* (not italicized) in parentheses after the work's title.

TIP

The usual order for an essay or other selection in an edited book is author name, year, essay title, book editor's name preceded by *In*, the abbreviation *Ed.*, book title, page range, and the publisher's name.

Author   *Title*   Publication information   Electronic source

Lacan, J. **(1977).** *Écrits: A selection* **(A. Sheridan, Trans.). W. W. Norton. (Original work published 1966)**

To cite a translated book in the text of your essay, use both the original and the current publication dates:

(Lacan, 1966/1977)

Volume in a multivolume work: Include the volume number after the title.

Bosworth, A. B. (Ed.). (1995). *A historical commentary on Arrian's history of Alexander* (Vol. 1). Oxford University Press.

TIP

For editions beyond the first, include the edition number in parentheses after the title.

If referring to more than one volume, give the specific volumes or range (e.g., Vols. 1–3).

Second or subsequent edition of a work: Include the edition number after the title.

Suzuki, D. T., Griffiths, A. J., & Lewontin, R. C. (1989). *An introduction to genetic analysis* (4th ed.). W. H. Freeman.

Article in a journal with continuous pagination: If a journal's pagination continues from one issue to the next, include the volume but not the issue number. Page numbers for journal articles are not preceded by *p.* or *pp.*

Garner, R. (2003). **Political ideologies and the moral status of animals.** *Journal of Political Ideologies, 8,* 233–246.

TIP

Whether you include the issue number in a citation depends on whether each issue is numbered separately (include issue number) or the numbering continues from the previous issue (do not include issue number).

Article in a journal that is paginated by issue: If each issue of a journal is numbered separately, include both volume (italicized) and issue number (in parentheses and not italicized).

Trew, J. D. (2002). **Conflicting visions: Don Messier, Liberal nationalism, and the Canadian unity debate.** *International Journal of Canadian Studies, 26*(2), 41–57.

Article in a magazine: Provide the complete date in the year-month-day format. Do not abbreviate month names. Include the volume and issue numbers if available.

Knapp, L. **(2007, September/October).** Licensing music to the film and television industries. *Canadian Musician, 29***(5), 49–56.**

Article in a newspaper: Include the author's name or, if none is given, the title of the article. Include abbreviation *p.* or *pp.* before the page number(s). If the article continues later in the work, give all page numbers and separate them with commas. A letter to the editor or an editorial follows the same format and includes specific information in square brackets after the title (e.g., [Letter to the editor]).

Lawyer seeks mistrial for client accused of illegal midwifery. (2003, April 20). *National Post*, p. A8.

TIP

Unlike journal and magazine articles, newspaper articles require the abbreviation *p.* or *pp.* with all page numbers included. References also include the exact publication date (i.e., year-month-day format).

Author   *Title*   Publication information   Electronic source

Book/movie review: Follow article format with the reviewer's name as author and include *Review of the*, the medium, title, and the author's or director's name in square brackets (e.g., [Review of the film *Avengers End Game*, by Anthony Russo & Joe Russo]) after the title.

> Mihm, S. **(2009).** Swindled: The dark history of food fraud, from poisoned candy to counterfeit coffee **[Review of the book** *Swindled: The dark history of food fraud, from poisoned candy to counterfeit coffee*, **by B. Wilson].** *Business History Review, 83***(2), 379–381.**

Government document: If the author is unknown, begin with the name of the government followed by the agency (e.g., ministry, department, Crown corporation) and the document name.

> British Columbia. Office of the Auditor General. (2005). *Salmon forever: An assessment of the provincial role in sustaining wild salmon.*

In cases or reports, such as government documents, the report number can be placed after the title (e.g., Research Report No. 09.171).

Indirect source: Give the work the citation comes from, not the original text.

Personal communication: Because they cannot be reproduced or verified, personal communications (including emails, phone calls, interviews, lectures, oral presentations, and conversations) are not included in the list of references.

←12 For more on indirect sources, see "APA In-Text Citations" earlier in this chapter.

TIP
Do not include personal communications (including emails, phone calls, interviews, and conversations) in the reference list.

TIP
APA encourages the use of a DOI where available, instead of a URL.

Electronic Sources

The APA manual recommends that electronic sources include the same elements of print sources in the same order, with exact location information added as needed. As we mentioned in "Sample journal entry," include a journal article's DOI if it is available (you'll find it with the other publication information, such as journal title and volume number, and/or on the first page of the article).

Not all publishers use this system. If the DOI is unavailable or your instructor tells you to do so, cite the URL of the journal's or publisher's home page. If the document would be hard to locate from the home page, provide the exact URL or as much as is needed for retrieval. APA does not require your date of access for internet sources, but you should confirm electronic links before including them in your paper. More information on referencing electronic references in APA format is available at https://extras.apa.org/apastyle/DOI-URL/#/

Sample electronic reference: Citation formats follow those of print sources with the title of the website included. There is no period after the DOI or URL.

> Czekaj, L. (2014, May 23). **Promises fulfilled: Looking at the legacy of thousands of black slaves who fled to Canada in the 1800s.** Federation for the Humanities and Social Sciences. http://www.ideas-idees.ca/blog/promises-fulfilled

Author   *Title*   Publication information   **Electronic source**

If it is necessary to break the URL over more than one line, break before punctuation, such as the slash before *blog* in the example; never use a hyphen unless it is part of the URL.

Group or organization (corporate or government) website: If there is no author, use the organization's name.

> Environment Canada. (2009, August 12). 10 things you should know about climate change. http://www.ec.gc.ca/cc/default.asp?lang=En&n=2F049262–1

The complete URL is given here because it would be hard to locate the document from the organization's home page.

Article in an online-only journal: Follow the format for a print article; add the URL at the end. Note the journal name is in italics.

> Rye, B. J., Elmslie, P., & Chalmers, A. (2007). Meeting a transsexual person: Experience within a classroom setting. *Canadian On-Line Journal of Queer Studies in Education, 3*(1). http://jps.library.utoronto.ca/index.php/jqstudies/index

Article from a database (with a DOI): The name of the database is not usually required.

> Martel, M. (2009). "They smell bad, have diseases, and are lazy": RCMP officers reporting on hippies in the late sixties. *Canadian Historical Review, 90*, 215–245. https://doi.org/10.3138/chr.90.2.215

In this example, the quotation marks in the title indicate a direct quotation.

Article from a database (no DOI): The home page of the journal is used; the name of the database is not usually required.

> Barton, S. S. (2008). Discovering the literature on Aboriginal diabetes in Canada: A focus on holistic methodologies. *Canadian Journal of Nursing Research, 40*(4), 26–54. http://cjnr.mcgill.ca/

No date: Place *n.d.* (not italicized) where the date would normally go.

> Merriam-Webster. (n.d.). Hegemony. In *Merriam-Webster.com dictionary*. Retrieved July 30, 2021, from https://www.merriam-webster.com/dictionary/hegemony

E-book: Use *n.d.* (not italicized) for the date and include the URL.

> Radford, B. (n.d.). *Soil to social*. http://on-line-books.ora.com/mod-bin/books.mod/javaref/javanut/index.htm

Electronic version of a print book: Ebooks references are formatted using the same pattern as print book: author, year, title, publisher, URL or DOI if available.

> Frederick Douglass (1881). *My escape from slavery*. University of Virginia Library. http://xtf.lib.virginia.edu/xtf/view?docId=modern_english/uvaGenText/tei/DouEsca.xml

TIP

The name of the database is not usually required in a reference, even if there is no DOI.

Author   *Title*   Publication information   Electronic source

Message posted to an online forum, discussion group, or blog post: Use the following format: Last name or user name (year, month, date). Comment title or the first 20 words of the comment. [Comment on the blog post "Title of Blog Post"]. *Title of Blog.* URL

> Carrick. (2009, November 15). I especially love your observation that we are many things—in fact more than the sum of these parts. I too [Comment on the blog post "Success is not measured by word count"]. *WrightingWords.* http://www.wrightingwords.com/2009/11/15/success-is-not-measured-by-word-count/

Non-Text Sources

Film or video: Use the following order: producer, director, year, and title of film followed by *Film* (not italicized) in square brackets. Conclude by giving the studio.

> Coppola, F. F. (Producer & Director). (1979). *Apocalypse now* [Film]. Zoetrope Studios.

Episode from a television series: Use the following order: writer, & director, year and date of first broadcast, title of episode, (series/season number, episode number) [TV series episode]. Then give the producer's name and the title of the series in italics. Conclude by giving the broadcasting company.

> Lindelof, D. (Writer), & Bender, J. (Director). (2005, September 21). Man of science, man of faith (Season 1, Episode 1) [TV series episode]. In J. J. Abrams (Executive Producer), *Lost.* American Broadcasting.

Music: For song lyrics, use the following order: writer, (copyright year), title of song [Song]. On *title of album.* Record label. Add the URL at the end if the material can be retrieved from services such as SoundCloud or from the artist's site. If the lyrics are taken from a YouTube video, sheet music, or web page use the recommended strategies for those media.

> Morrison, V. (1993). Gloria. [Song] On *Too long in exile.* Polydor.

The following student essay uses the APA documentation style.

Polar Bears: Bright Outlook or Grim Future
Adam Cook

Introduction

[1] The population of the polar bear (*Ursus maritimus*) species has been alarmingly decreasing throughout the years. The polar bear is classified as a vulnerable species, with approximately 8 of the 19 polar bear subspecies in decline. Polar bears have to continuously fight the extreme odds of man, machine, and the global

Author   *Title*   Publication information   Electronic source

environment just to keep their place on this planet. Everything from the human race overhunting and encroaching evermore on their territory, to the garbage and toxic pollution that is sweeping and growing over the Arctic, to the drastically changing weather and temperature fluctuations is unquestionably haunting and harming the future of the polar bear species, if indeed they even have one.

Impacts

[2] Humans: The human race is the number one cause for the dwindling population of the polar bear species. Every year, humans intrude further and further onto the polar bears' natural territory. Humans have almost pushed them right off of their land directly into the water with nowhere to go. Humans have so little regard for this species that we have intensely overhunted them for years to make carpets, coats, good luck charms, medicinal uses, head-trophies, etc. It is well known that the commercial hunting of polar bears almost drove them to extinction. Humans regularly disturb their breeding cycles, hibernation timeframes, and birthing den procedures, which causes immense stress to the mother polar bear. She can even lose her cubs if being disturbed during the developmental stages of the fetus in the mother's womb. American zoologist Dr Steven C. Amstrup conducted an 11-year study that proves the negative impacts that humans have on hibernating and prenatal polar bears. On top of that, humans have negative effects on the polar bears' food chain. Humans have hunted and also overhunted many of their own food sources to the point of depletion, which thus leave polar bears undernourished, stressed, and incredibly desperate for food (Amstrup, 1993). If polar bears are to survive, humans need to respect and maintain the natural habitat of these creatures.

[3] Garbage and Pollution: A major factor affecting the polar bear species is the ever-growing rate of garbage and pollution hitting their homeland. Every year, scientists are noticing the increasing trend of various amounts of garbage from all parts of the world making its way to the Arctic regions. Air and water pollution are negatively impacting the polar bears' natural territory and their species as a whole as time goes on. Over 80 per cent of marine pollution expels from land-based activities (WWF, n.d.). Everything from numerous types of deadly oils, varieties of virulent fertilizers, mounds and mounds of garbage, masses of sewage disposal, slews of toxic chemicals, and other contaminates affect the natural habitat of polar bears. Oil spills cause a great deal of damage to the marine environment. Fertilizer runoff has had severe negative impacts for coastal areas around the world. This runoff has some nutrients that can lead to eutrophication. Eutrophication is when algal blooms increase so significantly that it drains the water's dissolved oxygen, which horribly leads to the suffocation of the marine life (Walsh et al., 2011). Eutrophication has resulted in large "dead-zones" in many parts of the world such as the Bering Strait. Mounds of garbage also float their way throughout the oceans, containing copious amounts of plastic and non-decomposable garbage, glass items, packaging material, lumber, and toxic canisters. If people do not dispose of garbage correctly, just about every single item tossed incorrectly can orbit and grow in the seas and oceans. In many areas of the globe, man-made sewage typically flows substantially or completely untreated straight into the seas and oceans. Extensive research has shown that much of the urban sewage drained into the Atlantic Ocean from South America is completely untreated. This sewage can lead to eutrophication as well. Unfortunately, almost every single marine creature is contaminated by or with man-made chemicals. The human race once truly believed that the ocean was so vast that every single chemical, toxin, or bit of garbage would eventually dilute throughout the oceans and break down to the point that it vanished. The truth

Note that many of the points in this paragraph are deemed general knowledge, so they do not need to be cited. See Chapter 11 for more on general knowledge.

Author   *Title*   Publication information   Electronic source

of the matter is that these dumped items have not simply disappeared. On top of that, certain dumped toxins and chemicals that have found their way into the food chain have become more concentrated and found at higher levels compared to years past (WWF, n.d.). In order to protect polar bears from these toxins and the contaminants in their food sources, humans have to become responsible caretakers of the planet.

[4] Climate Change: The environment in which polar bears live in is extremely sensitive and can be easily disturbed. They typically live throughout the Arctic region, which is comprised of ice and snow. These natural elements that make up the Arctic are what the polar bears undeniably depend on for survival. Nowadays, such reductions in the thickness and length of the ice and extreme changes in the ice dynamics all negatively alter the condition and success of the polar bears' survival. Examples of this include Hudson Bay and James Bay in Canada. The ice is melting earlier in the spring and being formed later in the fall. The time polar bears spend on the ice is precious for hunting their prey. This is the time when they get to restore their body fat and fitness levels. Unfortunately, this crucial time for storing up fat and energy for the time when there is less ice and sparse food reserves is becoming dangerously finite. As the timeframe without food lengthens, their bodies start to decline quickly. This is certainly critical for mothers that are pregnant or nursing. Scientists have pointed to either lack of fat from the mother or lack of food to be number one causes for death in cubs. With such significant reductions in the ice length and thickness throughout the summer months, the open window for the polar bears' hunting time is ever more decreasing (Castro de la Guardia et al., 2013). Will this cause alone be the ultimate destruction of the polar bears' future?

Cook assumes that people agree with the climate change evidence often spoken about in the media and with the fact that climate change exists. Would his argument be better with citations from outside sources?

Conclusion

[5] The polar bears are indeed an incredibly intelligent, strong, resourceful species that are truly the king of the food chain in the Arctic, but these admirable qualities are not enough for them to continue battling these ever-growing, negative effects moving forward into the future. Polar bears are directly threatened from how very little regard the human race has for them, other species, for the environment, and for the Earth as a whole. From years and years of gathered, factual research, scientists have estimated that two-thirds of the polar bear population could become extinct by 2050 (WWF, 2012). The way the human race continues to use and abuse the planet, undoubtedly the climate change supporting scientists will be correct about the polar bears' extinction unless immediate and corrective actions are engaged by people united. Can the human race pull it together, or are the polar bears' days truly numbered? Only time will tell.

APA requires that the references begin on a new page at the end of the essay.

References

Amstrup, A. C. (1993, April). Human disturbances of denning polar bears in Alaska. *Arctic Institute of North America, 46*(3), 246–250. http://arctic.journalhosting.ucalgary.ca/arctic/index.php/arctic/article/view/1349/1374

Castro de la Guardia, L., Derocher, A. E., Myers, P. G., Terwisscha van Scheltinga, A. D., & Lunn, N. J. (2013, September). Future sea ice conditions in Western Hudson Bay and consequences for polar bears in the 21st century. *Global Change Biology, 19*(9), 2675–2687. doi:10.111/gcb.12272

Author   *Title*   Publication information   Electronic source

Walsh, J. J., Dieterle, D. A., Chen, F. R., Lenes, J. M., Maslowski, W., Cassano, J. J. Whitledge, T. E., Stockwell, D., Flint, M., Sukhanova, I. N., & Christensen, J. (2011). Trophic cascades and future harmful algal blooms within ice-free Arctic Seas north of Bering Strait: A simulation analysis. *Progress in Oceanography, 91*(3), 312–344.

World Wildlife Fund. (n.d.). *Marine problems: Pollution.* http://wwf.panda.org/about_our_earth/blue_planet/problems/pollution/

World Wildlife Fund. (2012). *Effects of climate change on polar bears.* http://assets.worldwildlife.org/publications/398/files/original/Effects_of_Climate_Change_on_Polar_Bears_fact_sheet.pdf

MLA

Like APA, MLA style is parenthetical, meaning that it includes in-text citations. However, the reference list is called "Works Cited," and the information is presented differently.

MLA In-Text Citations

MLA in-text citations include the author's last name(s) and page number(s) in parentheses. Separate the items with a single space; do not use a comma unless you need to include both an author's name and title or separate the author's name from the paragraph number in an electronic source. Do not use the abbreviation *p.* or *pp.* before the page number. When including a page range, omit the repeated numbers over 100 (e.g., 212–47, not 212–247; but 34–37). In most cases, the end punctuation comes after the closing parentheses.

> **(Ashton 12)**

If the author is named in a signal phrase, only the page number appears in parentheses.

> Ashton **found that ...** (12).

Here are more guidelines for MLA in-text citations:

Citation for a direct quotation, paraphrase, or summary: Give the author's last name and page number. The first example has no signal phrase; the second has one. When you use a signal phrase, place the citation at the end of the quotation, not after the author's name.

> **During both world wars, the Canadian government often employed masseuses because surgery and medical care were insufficient "to restore severely wounded men"** (Cleather ix).

> **According to** Stambouli and Traversa, **"each gallon of gasoline produced and used in an internal combustion engine releases roughly 12 kg of CO_2"** (299).

Author   *Title*   Publication information   **Electronic source**

MLA in-text citations include the author's last name and page or paragraph number(s).

Block quotation: Begin any quotation longer than four typed lines on a new line; indent it half an inch from the left margin and set it double spaced. Do not use quotation marks. Include the author's last name and page number after the final punctuation mark.

> **(Ellis and Bochner** 81–82**)**

Citation referring to an indirect source: Sometimes it is necessary to refer to a source found in another work because you can't access the original source. In this case, include the original author in the sentence but use the indirect (your) source in the citation. Use the abbreviation *qtd. in* (not italicized) at the beginning of the citation.

> **Francis Bacon observed that language affects our thinking when he said, "words react on the understanding" (qtd. in Lindemann 93).**

In the works cited list, give the details for the indirect source (in this example, for Lindemann).

Personal communication, including interviews: Give the person's last name only.

> **(McWhirter)**

Multiple sources in one citation: You may include more than one relevant source in a single citation if your point applies to both. Alphabetize the sources by last name and separate them with a semicolon.

> **The practices of teaching composition in college have not radically changed in the last few decades (Bishop** 65**; Williams** 6**).**

However, if the citation is lengthy, consider moving the entire citation to a note.

MLA In-Text Citations by Format

Number or Kind of Authors

Work by one author: Give the author's last name and page number. A book with an author and an editor will typically be cited by author.

> **(Bloom** 112**)**

Work by two authors: Give the last names of both authors, with the word *and* before the second name, and the page number:

> **(Higgins and Wilson-Baptist** 44**)**

Work by three or more authors: Include the last name of the first author followed by the abbreviation *et al.* and page number.

> **(Terracciano et al.** 96**)**

Two or more works by the same author: Give the author's last name, a shortened version of the work's title, and a page number. Separate the first two items with a comma.

> **(Foucault,** *Power/Knowledge* 37**)**

TIP

If you have to cite information from an indirect source, include the phrase *qtd. in* (not italicized; *qtd.* is an abbreviation for *quoted*) before the citation.

 →12 The section "MLA Notes" later in this chapter discusses MLA notes.

TIP

If you cite two sources in the same sentence, placing the citation after each one may help with clarity: "One study looked for correlations between GPA and listening to music (Cox and Stevens 757) while another related academic performance to three types of music (Roy 6)."

Author   *Title*   Publication information   **Electronic source**

Two authors with the same last name: Include the authors' first initials along with the page number. If the authors have the same initial, include their full names instead.

> **(S. Sinkinson 225; B. Sinkinson 237)**

Group or organization as author (corporate author): If a document does not have an individual as an author, use the group's or company's name. If possible, include the full name in the sentence to avoid long citations. It is also acceptable to shorten the organization's name and place it in parentheses, accompanied by the page number, in the same manner as a standard author citation.

> **The United Nations Children's Fund reports that Indigenous children are at exceptional risk of becoming refugees (204).**

or

> **Some child protection advocates suggest that Indigenous children are at exceptional risk of becoming refugees (UNICEF 204).**

TIP
If no author is given, use the name of the group or organization—as a signal phrase, if possible.

Work by an unknown author (including many dictionary and encyclopedia entries): Give the title and the page number. Use the full title if it is short; condense long titles. Distinguish articles from complete works by placing the former in quotation marks.

> **("Plea to City Hall" 22).**

Electronic Sources

The most challenging aspect of citing online documents is that they often lack page numbers. Use the following guidelines to determine how to cite this material.

Citation of an entire website: Give the author's last name or website name within the sentence and do not include a parenthetical citation.

> **In his article, Dillon compares reading practices for print media to those for electronic media.**

TIP
If you are referring to a website as a whole rather than a specific part, include the author's name within the sentence and do not include a parenthetical citation.

Citation from a specific passage: Give the specific location of the material. If there are no page numbers, include the relevant paragraph or section numbers preceded by the appropriate abbreviation (*par./pars.* or *sec./secs.*; none are italicized). Insert a comma between the author's last name and the abbreviation. If the reference is specific but nothing in the document is numbered, cite it without a page, paragraph, or section reference.

> **One firmly entrenched belief is that reading screens will never replace reading books and other print media (Dillon, sec. 1).**

TIP
For electronic documents without page numbers, use paragraph or section numbers if either is given. Insert a comma to separate the author's name from the number and use the abbreviation *par.* or *sec.* (not italicized), respectively.

Website without an author: Use the site's title (set in italics) to direct readers to the source of any information.

> **(*LHC Machine Outreach*)**

Author *Title* Publication information Electronic source

Film, video, audio, tv broadcast, musical recording, and other non-textual media: Give the name of the individual(s) most relevant to your discussion in the text. In the case of a film, this person could be the director, performer, screenwriter, or other contributor. If your focus is on the whole work, use the title. Do not include a parenthetical citation.

> Francis Ford Coppola's **film** *The Conversation* **explores the psychology of surveillance.**

In the works cited section, the entry would be alphabetized under *C* for *Coppola*, the film's producer.

MLA Works Cited

In MLA style, the works cited section contains complete bibliographical information for a work's in-text citations. Follow these guidelines when creating a works cited list:

- Begin the list on a new page at the end of the essay and number the section as part of the overall work.
- Centre the title ("Works Cited") an inch from the top of the page. Do not underline or bold it.
- Double-space the list, with 1-inch margins.
- Begin each entry flush with the left margin; indent subsequent lines half an inch.
- Alphabetize the list by the first item in each entry, usually the author's last name.
- Capitalize the first letters of all major words in a work's title, even if the source does not.
- Omit words such as *Inc.* and *Co.* after the publisher's name and the articles (*The* or *A*) before it. Abbreviate *University Press* to *UP* (not italicized). Spell out *Press* (not italicized) for publishers other than university presses.
- Abbreviate months with more than four letters. Use the following abbreviations where appropriate.
  - assn. (association)
  - ch. (chapter)
  - ed. (edition)
  - P (Press)
  - par. (paragraph), pars. (paragraphs)
  - pt. (part)
  - rev. (revised)
  - rpt. (reprint)
  - sec. (section)
  - U (University)
  - vol. (volume)

Author   *Title*   Publication information   Electronic source

The standard works cited entry begins with the author's last name followed by their complete first name (unless the author has published only initial[s]). Italicize titles of complete works, such as book and journal titles, websites, plays, films, and artistic performances; place quotation marks around titles of articles, essays, book chapters, short stories, poems, web pages, and TV episodes.

Sample book entry: List the book (pamphlet or brochure) information in the following sequence: author, title (italicized), publisher, and year of publication.

> Fries, Charles C. *Linguistics and Reading*. Holt, Rinehart and Winston, 1962.

Sample journal entry: List the information in this order: author, title of article (in quotation marks), title of journal (italicized), volume number, issue number, year of publication, and page range.

> Valkenburg, Patti M., and Peter Jochen. "Who Visits Online Dating Sites? Exploring Some Characteristics of Online Daters." *CyberPsychology and Behavior*, vol. 15, no. 1, 1996, pp. 41–50.

Number or Kind of Authors

Work by one author: See "Sample book entry."

Work by two authors: Invert only the first author's name. Insert a comma before *and*.

> Luckner, John, and Reldan Nadler. *Processing the Experience*. Kendall/Hunt, 1992.

Work by three or more authors: Give only the first author's name followed by *et al.* (not italicized).

> Festial, Lawrence, et al. *When Economics Fails*. U of Minnesota P, 1956.

Two or more works by the same author: Arrange the works chronologically from earliest to most recent publication. The author's name appears in the first listing only, with three hyphens substituted for it in the additional citation(s).

> Foucault, Michel. *Discipline and Punish: The Birth of the Prison*. Translated by Alan Sheridan, Random House, 1977.
>
> ———. *The History of Sexuality*. Translated by Robert Hurley, 3 vols., Random House, 1978.

Work by two authors with the same last name: Alphabetize by the authors' first names. If two works have the same first author, use the second authors' last names.

> Srivastava, Sarita, and Margot Francis. "The Problem of 'Authentic Experience.'" *Critical Sociology*, vol. 32, no. 2–3, 2006, pp. 275–307.
>
> Srivastava, Sarita, and Mary-Jo Nadeau. "From the Inside: Anti-Racism in Social Movements." *New Socialist*, vol. 42, 2003.

TIP

The order for most works cited entries is the author's full name, title of work, and publication details, which vary depending on whether the work is a book, journal article, or electronic document.

TIP

In a work by two authors, include all names with only the first author's inverted. Use a comma between the first author's first name and the word *and*. With three or more authors, include only the first author's name and use the abbreviation *et al.* to indicate that there are at least three more.

Author   *Title*   Publication information   Electronic source

TIP

When a work has a group rather than an individual as an author, use the group name.

Group or organization as author (corporate author): Use the full group name in place of the author's name. If the organization name begins with an article (e.g., *The*), omit it. When the group is both the author and publisher, begin with the document's title and include the organization's name only as the publisher.

> *Guide to Universities & Colleges in Canada*. 2000 ed., Education International, 2000.

Work without an author, publisher, or date (non-electronic): If the work does not provide an author's name, begin with the title. Use the following abbreviations for missing publication details: *n.p.* means "no publisher"; *n.d.* means "no date" (do not italicize the abbreviations in your citations). Use square brackets to identify any information that isn't from the source and add a question mark if the information may be unreliable.

> No author name (unsigned encyclopedia entry):
>
> "Interveners." *Canadian Encyclopedia.*, **1985 ed.**

> No publisher:
>
> Webb, Noah. *The Great Haileybury Forest Fire*. n.p. [1971?].

> No publishing date:
>
> Case, Michael. *Opus Dei*. Slipshod Press, n.d.

Source Type

Work by an author with an editor or a translator: Begin with the author's name unless you refer primarily to the editor's work (e.g., their introduction or notes), as shown in the second example. The original publication date can be included after the title.

> Hawthorne, Nathaniel. *The Scarlet Letter*. 1850. **Edited by John Stephen Martin, Broadview, 1995.**

> Martin, John Stephen, editor. *The Scarlet Letter*, **by Nathaniel Hawthorne**, 1850, Broadview, 1995.

Follow the same format for a translated work.

> Calvino, Italo. *Why Read the Classics?* **Translated by Martin McLaughlin, Pantheon, 1999.**

TIP

The usual order for an essay or other selection in an edited book is author's name, essay title, book title, book editor's name preceded by *edited by*, publication details, and page range.

Chapter or other type of selection, such as an essay, in an edited volume: Begin with the author's name and chapter (or essay) title. Follow with the book title and book editor's name, not inverted and preceded by *edited by* (not italicized), the publication information, and the page range.

> Sanders, Douglas E. "Some Current Issues Affecting Indian Government." *Pathways to Self-Determination: Canadian Indians and the Indian State*, **edited by Leroy Little Bear, Menno Boldt, and J. Anthony Long, U of Toronto P, 1984, pp. 113–21.**

Author   *Title*   Publication information   Electronic source

If you use more than one work from the same collection, you can economize by creating one entry for the work as a whole and abbreviated entries for specific works.

Main entry:

Little Bear, Leroy, Menno Boldt, and J. Anthony Long, editors. *Pathways to Self-Determination: Canadian Indians and the Indian State*. U of Toronto P, 1984.

Specific entry:

Sanders, Douglas E. "Some Current Issues Affecting Indian Government." Little Bear, Boldt, and Long, pp. 113–21.

Introduction, preface, foreword, or afterword: Give the author of the part being cited followed by the section name (not in quotation marks). The title of the complete work comes next, then the work's author preceded by *by* (not italicized).

Scholes, Robert. Foreword. *The Fantastic: A Structural Approach to a Literary Genre*, by Tzvetan Todorov, translated by Richard Howard, Cornell UP, 1975, pp. v–xi.

Volume in a multivolume work: State the volume number if you use one work; give the number of volumes used if you refer to more than one.

Bosworth, A. B., ed. *A Historical Commentary on Arrian's History of Alexander*. Vol. 1, Oxford UP, 1980.

If you used two volumes, *2 vols.* would replace *Vol. 1* in the example. In your essay, the parenthetical reference includes the volume number after the author's name; separate the volume number from the page number with a colon. **Second or subsequent edition of a work:** Include the edition number after the title (or editor, translator, etc.).

Suzuki, David, Aaron Griffiths, and Rebecca Lewontin. *An Introduction to Genetic Analysis*. 4th ed, Freeman, 1989.

Book published before 1900: The publisher's name can be omitted.

Baring Gould, S. *Old Country Life*. 5th ed, 1895.

Article in a journal: Whether the numbering of the journal continues with each succeeding issue (continuous pagination) or restarts with every new issue, include both the volume and issue numbers if they are available.

Trew, Johanne Devlin. "Conflicting Visions: Don Messier, Liberal Nationalism, and the Canadian Unity Debate." *International Journal of Canadian Studies*, vol. 26, no. 2, 2002, pp. 41–57.

Article in a magazine: Cite the complete date (in day-month-year format) if the magazine is issued every week or every two weeks; include the month and year for magazines published monthly or every two months.

TIP
Always include the journal's volume and issue numbers in your citation if they are available.

Author   *Title*   Publication information   Electronic source

If the article breaks off and continues later in the work, give the first page number followed by a plus sign, not the whole page range (e.g., 12+ indicates that the article begins on page 12 and continues somewhere after page 12).

> Knapp, Lonny. "Licensing Music to the Film and Television Industries." *Canadian Musician*, Sept/Oct. 2007, pp. 49–56.

Article in a newspaper: Cite the author if given; if not, begin with the title. Give the day, month, and year and then the page number. Precede the page number with the section number or letter if the article is in more than one section. If the article breaks off and continues later in the work, cite the first page number followed by a plus sign, as for a magazine article. A letter to the editor follows the same format and includes *Letter* (not italicized) after the title.

> "Lawyer Seeks Mistrial for Client Accused of Illegal Midwifery." *National Post*, 20 Apr. 2003, p. A8.

Book/movie review: Follow the reviewer's name by the review's title; if there is no title, continue with *Review of* and book/movie title followed by *by* and the author's (director's) name (do not italicize these terms). Conclude with the publication information.

> Mihm, Stephen. Review of *Swindled: The Dark History of Food Fraud, from Poisoned Candy to Counterfeit Coffee*, by Bee Wilson. *Business History Review*, vol. 83, no. 2, 2006, pp. 379–81.

Government document: If the author is unknown, begin with the name of the government followed by the agency (e.g., ministry, department, Crown corporation) and document name.

> British Columbia, Office of the Auditor General. *Salmon Forever: An Assessment of the Provincial Role in Sustaining Wild Salmon*. Office of the Auditor General of British Columbia, 2005.

Indirect source: Cite the work where you found the citation rather than the original text.

> Lindemann, Erika. *A Rhetoric for Writing Teachers*. 4th ed., Oxford UP, 2001.

Personal communication, including interview: Include a description of the communication.

> Carr, Emily. Letter to Lawren Harris. 12 December 1940.

Electronic Sources

As online sources often change or even disappear, the MLA recommends that you download or print research material that may become inaccessible. In cases where some relevant information is unavailable (such as page or paragraph numbers), cite what you can so that the reader is able to access the source. Note that a URL is used only if the source would be otherwise

Author   *Title*   Publication information   **Electronic source**

hard to locate. (If you need to divide the URL between two lines, break it after single or double slashes.) Including the date of access is optional but can be helpful to your reader.

Sample electronic citation: Include the title of the website after the work's title and then provide the site's publisher or sponsor (use *n.p.* if that name is unavailable). Give the date the website was created or last updated.

> Czekaj, Laura. **"Promises Fulfilled: Looking at the Legacy of Thousands of Black Slaves Who Fled to Canada in the 1800s."** *Federation for the Humanities and Social Sciences*, 23 May 2014, **www.ideas-idees.ca/ blog/promises-fulfilled.**

Group or organization (e.g., corporate or government) website: If there is no author, use the organization's name.

> Environment Canada. **"10 Things You Should Know about Climate Change."** 12 Aug. 2009, **www.ec.gc.ca/cc/default.asp?lang=En&n= 2F049262-1.**

The URL is included because the page would be hard to locate otherwise.

Article in an online-only journal: Online-only journals are cited in the same manner as print journals, except with a DOI or URL. The DOI is preferable if it is available; if using the URL, omit *http://* or *https://*.

> Rye, B. J., Pamela Elmslie, and Amanda Chalmers. **"Meeting a Transsexual Person: Experience within a Classroom Setting."** *Canadian On-Line Journal of Queer Studies in Education*, vol. 3, no. 1, 2007, **jqstudies.library.utoronto.ca/index.php/jqstudies/ article/view/3269/1444.**

Internet article based on a print source and retrieved from a database: In addition to the information required for the print version of a journal article, include the name of the database.

> Barton, Sylvia S. **"Discovering the Literature on Aboriginal Diabetes in Canada: A Focus on Holistic Methodologies."** *Canadian Journal of Nursing Research*, vol. 40, no. 4, 2008, pp. 26–54. *Ingenta*, **www.ingentaconnect.com/content/mcgill/ cjnr/2008/00000040/00000004/art00003?crawler=true.**

Work online that first appeared in print: Include details of the print source and follow with the title of the website and date of access.

> Douglass, Frederick. "My Escape from Slavery." *The Century Illustrated Magazine,* **Nov. 1881, pp. 125–31. Electronic Text Center, University of Virginia Library,** xroads.virginia.edu/~drbr/douglas. html.

Letter or email: If the letter is published, cite it as you would a work in an edited volume, adding the date of the letter. If it is a personal letter or

TIP

Make sure that none of the URLs in your essay, including the references or works cited page, are hyperlinked. They must be in plain text, not underlined or in a different colour.

TIP

In addition to the information included in the print version, journal articles retrieved from a database require the database's name.

Author   *Title*   Publication information   Electronic source

email, include a description, such as *Received by the author* (if you received it; not italicized) and date.

> Barrett, Anthony. *"Re: Lives of the Caesars."* **Received by the author, 15 Aug. 2008.**

Message posted to an online forum, discussion group, or blog post: Follow the guidelines for "Sample electronic citation." If no title is given, include a generic label after the author's name.

> Koolvedge. *Comment on "Massacre in Peru." Adbusters.org,* 8 Aug. 2009, 9:28 a.m., **www.adbusters.org/blogs/dispatches/-massacre-peru.html#comments.**

Non-Text Sources

The general rule for citations of non-text sources is to feature the person(s) most relevant to your discussion, along with a description of their role. For example, if your paper is about actors, you can cite their contribution in a film either alongside or instead of naming the director.

Lecture or other oral presentation: Give the name of the speaker, the title of the presentation, the meeting and/or sponsor (if applicable), date, and location detail. Conclude with *Lecture*, *Reading*, etc. (not italicized).

> Armstrong, Nancy. "Darwin's Paradox." **Department of English, David Strong Building, 2 Apr. 2009, University of Victoria, Victoria. Lecture.**

Film or video: Begin with the work's title unless you are referring mainly to one person's contribution (for example, a performer or writer). Follow with the name(s) of the most relevant individuals and conclude with the distributor's name and year of release.

Citing the film:

> *Apocalypse Now.* **Directed by Francis Ford Coppola, United Artists, 1979.**

Citing a specific individual:

> **Brando, Marlon, performer.** *Apocalypse Now.* United Artists, 1979.

Performance (e.g., play, concert): Begin with the title of the performance and follow with the relevant information, usually the writer, director, and main performers. Conclude with the company name, theatre, city, and date of performance.

> *Macbeth.* **By William Shakespeare. Directed by Des McAnuff, Performances by Colm Feore and Yanna McIntosh, Stratford Shakespeare Festival Company. Festival Theatre, Stratford, ON. 1 June 2009.**

If you are citing one individual's contribution, begin with that person's name (see "Film or video").

Author   *Title*   Publication information   Electronic source

Episode from a television or radio series: For a broadcasted episode, use the following order: title of episode (in quotation marks), title of program (italicized), network, call letters of local station, city, and date of broadcast.

> "Man of Science, Man of Faith." *Lost*. CTV, CFTO, Toronto, 21 Sept. 2005.

If you watched the episode online, include the season and episode numbers, the site name, and URL.

> "Smoke Gets in Your Eyes." *Mad Men*, season 1, episode 1, AMC, 19 July 2007. *Netflix,* www.netflix.com/watch/70143379?trackId=15036065& tctx=0%2C0%2Cefd6765f-0b19-42d1-9e97-f1e33c888817-16461049.

Information relevant to the episode (e.g., the writer or director) follows the episode title; information relevant to the series follows the series title. If you are citing one individual's contribution, begin with that person's name (see "Film or video").

Music: Use the following order: performer (or other most relevant individual), recording title, label, and year of issue.

> Morrison, Van. *Too Long in Exile*. Polydor, 1993.

If you are citing a specific song, place its name in quotation marks after the performer's name; use a period before and after the song's name.

Work of visual art: Use the following order: artist, title (italicized), date of composition (or *n.d.* if this is unavailable), name of institution that contains the work, and city.

> Escher, M. C. *Drawing Hands*. 1948, Cornelius Collection, National Gallery of Art, Washington.

Interview: Begin with the name of the interviewee and follow with *Interview by* (not italicized) and the interviewer's name. Conclude with the publication details.

> Murakami, Haruki. Interview by Maik Grossekathöfer. *Spiegel Online International*, 20 Feb. 2008.

If you are the interviewer, begin with the interviewee, followed by the type of interview (e.g., *Telephone Interview*; not italicized) and date of interview.

MLA Notes

MLA permits either footnotes (at the bottom of the page) or endnotes (at the end of the document) as a way of including information you feel is valuable but does not fit well within the text. You may use notes to explain a point further, to cite multiple sources or related points of interest, or to suggest additional reading. However, use notes sparingly; do not overwhelm or

---

Author   *Title*   Publication information   Electronic source

distract the reader from your main text. These notes are indicated by a superscript (raised) number directly to the right and above the word most related to the note or at the end of a phrase; they are numbered consecutively throughout the paper. Format the notes to match the rest of the document by double-spacing and indenting each note.

This exercise tests your ability to use summary, paraphrase, direct quotation, mixed quotation format, block format, signal phrases, ellipses, brackets, and APA and MLA in-text citations.

I

The following is from a paragraph in the document "The Gender Wage Gap in Canada: 1998–2018," written by Rachelle Pelletier, Martha Patterson, and Melissa Moyser and published on the Statistics Canada website on 11 October 2019. The URL is https://www150.statcan.gc.ca/n1/pub/75-004-m/75-004-m2019004-eng.htm. This is the 18th paragraph in the paper.

> Changes in job attributes also contributed to the decrease in the gender wage gap that occurred over the 20 years. Particularly important in this regard was union coverage. While the proportion of men covered by a union or collective agreement decreased by 8.6 percentage points between 1998 and 2018 (from 38.2 per cent to 29.5 per cent), the equivalent proportion for women held steady at a little less than 36 per cent. These differing trends largely reflected the fact that men with union coverage were concentrated in manufacturing—a declining sector through the first half of the period—whereas women in unionized jobs have been concentrated in health care and social assistance, and educational services. Since union coverage is associated with higher average wages, the decrease in the proportion of men with union coverage led this variable to account for 9.3 per cent of the decrease in the gender wage gap that occurred between 1998 and 2018.

1. Paraphrase the first two sentences. Do not use a signal phrase or any direct quotations. Use either APA or MLA style for the parenthetical citation.
2. Paraphrase the third and fourth sentences but include one direct quotation that is no more than eight words (choose the most appropriate words for the quotation). Use a signal phrase to set up the paraphrase. Use either APA or MLA style for the parenthetical citation.
3. For the final sentence, use brackets and grammatically integrate the direct quotation into the complete sentence. Do not use a signal phrase.

II

The following passage is from Steven J. Vaughan-Nichols's article "iPhone vs. Android: Which Is Better for You?" which was published on 1 May 2018 on the website of *ComputerWorld*. The URL is https://www

.computerworld.com/article/2468474/iphone-vs-android-which-is-better-for-you.html. The paragraph is the third in the article. Integrate the text into a paragraph of your own as if you planned to use it in an essay. In APA or MLA style, use a signal phrase and followed by a direct quotation of the passage.

> And make no mistake: The fight is between these two mobile operating systems. All the alternatives are pretty much dead and buried. Microsoft, for example, recently admitted, "We had no material Phone revenue this quarter." Canonical, Ubuntu Linux's parent company, has given up on smartphones. BlackBerry exists only as a brand name, and the manufacturer making "BlackBerry" phones is now using Android.

III

1. Paraphrase the above passage using either APA or MLA style. Include one direct quotation no longer than three words; do not use a signal phrase.
2. Summarize the passage in one sentence of no more than 20 words (there are 62 words in the original); begin with a signal phrase and use APA or MLA style. Do not use any direct quotations.

The following academic article is annotated to show some of the similarities and differences between academic essays and the kind of essays you will write. Academic essays, which usually appear in academic journals and can be accessed electronically through your school's databases, are longer and more complex than most student essays. Many of the challenges they present, however, can be overcome by knowing where to look for information. Following these steps will make the reading process easier:

1. Read the title and abstract to get an idea of the essay's purpose, topic, and results or findings. If the essay includes specific headings, they may also give useful information.
2. Read the introduction, especially the last paragraphs, where important information is placed.
3. Read the conclusion or discussion section (or, if it is not labelled as such, the last few paragraphs) in which the findings are summarized and made relevant, applying the reading strategies discussed in "Reading Strategies" in Chapter 1.
4. If you know the essay will be crucial to your own research, go back and read the other sections closely.
5. Before reading the essay, review the five questions in "Reading Strategies" in Chapter 1.

Sample Student Essay

MLA

The Historical Influences on Québec's Traditional Desserts

Melissa Donnelly

[1] Québec was one of the earliest parts of Canada to be inhabited by French explorers and colonizers. The explorers brought recipes and traditions with them from France. However, the ingredients needed to recreate the dishes weren't readily available, so people planted fruit trees such as apple, pear, and plum, providing them access to familiar fruits. Grains and cereals were also quickly introduced for creating flour for baking and cooking. While this solved some problems, most people could not afford many ingredients, such as sugar, which were commonly available in France. The lack of ingredients meant that traditional recipes had to be adapted using accessible goods, which lead to uniquely traditional Québec desserts. This report investigates the influences that have helped to create traditional Québec desserts, including the early French settlers, their subsequent contact with Indigenous Peoples, and the natural ingredients available from the land.

[2] Traditional Québec desserts began with the recipes French colonizers brought with them to North America. These people brought the recipes for traditional desserts common in France (Neilly 2). One such recipe was for sugar pie (tarte au sucre), which was a quintessential dessert in France (Libman 1). Brad Dunne states in the Canadian Encyclopedia that the original sugar pie recipe was "a single-crust pie with a filling made from flour, butter, salt, vanilla, and cream ..." (1). Dunne states that the recipe for sugar pie is "a likely precursor to the butter tart" (Dunne 1), one of Québec's most well known desserts. The possible connection between sugar pie and butter tarts illustrates how influential the original French desserts were in Québec.

[3] Contact between the French and Indigenous Peoples influenced the flavours of traditional desserts in Québec. The early exposure to these peoples heavily influenced what are considered traditional Québec desserts today (Libman 1). This influence can be seen by the fact that early desserts in Québec were often flavoured with ingredients introduced to the French by Indigenous people such as wild berries and herbs (Salloum 7). Thus, traditional French recipes were further adapted.

[4] However, it was not just ingredients which were introduced by the Indigenous Peoples, it was also cooking techniques (Schalk 2). Many of the wild ingredients introduced to the French required Indigenous cooking techniques to process them properly (Schalk 2). For example, the sugar from maple sap was produced using a method taught to the French by the local Indigenous population (Daily life 1–3). As the demand for sugar started to rise, the use of maple sugar increased. Boiling maple sap for sugar became more widespread (Daily life 1). The use of maple syrup further changed the flavours of traditional desserts, making them unique to Québec.

[5] Locally available ingredients had a major impact on the traditional desserts of Québec, at times modifying original French recipes into something quintessentially Québecois. For example, the original recipe for sugar pie called for brown sugar (Libman 1); however, maple syrup soon became the sweetener of

---

Note that the introduction has no research in it. The writer saved the research to support her body paragraph ideas.

How easy is it to visualize the pie based on this description? Writers often use a description like this so that the reader can visualize something and it becomes real.

By using information from other sources, the author supports her arguments and adds to the credibility of the essay.

As today's readers were not alive at the time of colonization, Donnelly includes professional research to support her points and, again, increase her credibility.

choice because it was locally available (Libman 1). Furthermore, the availability of maple syrup also played a major role in flavouring one of Québec's most iconic desserts, Pouding chômeur (Elton 3). Pouding chômeur, also known as maple pudding, began as a dessert flavoured with brown sugar (Elton 3). This dessert changed over time much in the same way that sugar pie was modified. By using local ingredients, the original French recipes began to acquire a unique flavour.

[6] Other local food was also used in traditional recipes. In-season wild fruit, such as berries, played a major role in influencing desserts (Parks Canada 1). In the journal *Americas* Habeeb Salloum discusses how wild berries were eaten fresh or were used in the preparation of in "jams, jellies, and relishes [which] were prepared to last …" (Salloum 7). Raspberry compote and raspberries with milk and sugar both became very popular after-dinner treats because wild raspberries were so widely available (Parks Canada 1). Blueberries were also a popular choice for pies (Salloum 9). Salloum explains that blueberries were particularly important in "the Saguenay-Lac-Saint-Jean region [which] became known for its blueberry pies" (9). The inhabitants took full advantage of the ingredients locally available to them.

[7] The unique desserts in Québec have been influenced by many variables. Most importantly, the French colonization, the influence of Indigenous Peoples, and the locally available ingredients have shaped the traditional desserts known in Québec today. Those who arrived to colonize Québec had to find ways to adapt to their new surroundings and to what was commonly available. Salloum rightly noted that while many of the dessert recipes had their origins in "France, they evolved in Québec to become that province's unique culinary art" (2). Without the influence of even one of these factors, Quebec's dessert landscape would be very different. It was this unique combination of influences working in early Québec that led to the desserts known and enjoyed today.

Note that the author relies on repetition to help her readers understand her thesis. For example, sugar pie is mentioned more than once, but the reader's increased familiarity with the dessert helps in the understanding of how the dessert has changed.

Here the author is showing how some desserts became popular because of ingredient availability.

The author has used research to support her thesis that desserts in Quebec have changed because of a variety of factors. Do you feel her sources were appropriate?

Works Cited

Canadian History Museum. *Daily Life*. https://www.historymuseum.ca/virtual-museum-of-new-france/daily-life/foodways/.

Dunne, Brad. "Butter Tart." *The Canadian Encyclopedia*, 2016, https://thecanadianencyclopedia.ca/en/article/butter-tarts.

Elton, Sarah. "Pouding Chomeur." *The Canadian Encyclopedia*, 2014, https://www.thecanadianencyclopedia.ca/en/article/pouding-chomeur.

Libman, Max. "So What Is Quebec Cuisine, Anyway? The History Of Quebec's Most Popular Dishes." 14 Mar. 2017, *Medium*, https://medium.com/@brockbradley/so-what-is-quebec-cuisine-anyway-the-history-of-quebecs-most-popular-dishes-7ccf7ffd5723.

Parks Canada Heritage Gourmet Recipes. "Iced Cheese à La Bourgeoise." 2017, https://www.pc.gc.ca/en/culture/gourmand-gourmet/recette-recipe78.

Parks Canada Heritage Gourmet Recipes. "Raspberry Compote." 2017, https://www.pc.gc.ca/en/culture/gourmand-gourmet/recette-recipe43.

Salloum, Habeeb. "The Taste Of Tradition In Quebec." *Americas*, vol. 53, no. 2, 2001, pp. 58–59, https://web-a-ebscohost-com.eztest.ocls.ca/ehost/detail/detail?vid=3&sid=12f1cfc4-29d1-494f-a567-76e09cb365a3%40session mgr4006&bdata=JnNpdGU9ZWhvc3QtbGl2ZSZzY29wZT1zaXRl#AN=4120367&db=rch.

Schalk, Danielle. "La Belle Cuisine: Examining Quebec's Rich Food Culture." *Foodservice and Hospitality*, 28 Apr 2017, https://www.foodserviceandhospitality.com/la-belle-cuisine-examining-quebecs-rich-food-culture/.

Chapter Review Questions

1. Why are citations needed in an essay?
2. What citation styles are commonly used by writers?
3. Can you combine different citation styles? Why or why not?
4. Why is it important to use the most current style guide when documenting your sources?
5. What is the difference between an in-text citation and a references/works cited entry?
6. What order is used in the references/works cited to list the sources used in your essay?
7. What are the basic elements of APA in-text citations? How does the use of a signal phrase affect this list?
8. What are the basic elements of MLA in-text citations? How does the use of a signal phrase affect this list?
9. When adding information to a references/works cited page, why do you need all the relevant information?
10. How can documentation add to the credibility of your essay?

PART FOUR
Grammar

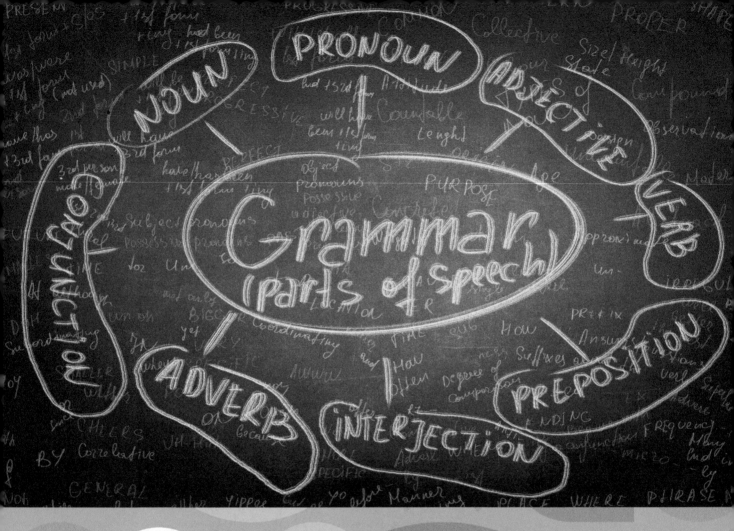

13 Sentence Essentials

By the end of this chapter, you should be able to

- use correct grammar;
- identify parts of speech;
- create proper sentence structure;
- use phrases and clauses correctly in a sentence;
- avoid sentence fragments; and
- detect sentence errors and know the correct methods for joining sentences.

This chapter and the next two introduce the basic concepts for understanding and using English grammar and punctuation. We begin with the parts of speech and then sentences, phrases, and clauses. Chapter 14 offers guidelines for using certain punctuation marks, and Chapter 15 discusses how to craft grammatically correct sentences.

▲ Photo: StunningArt/Shutterstock

Grammatical Groundwork

Using correct grammar adds to your credibility as a writer. Your reader will understand what you are saying, and your message will be clearly communicated. Grammar errors, on the other hand, give the reader the impression that you are either careless or unknowledgeable about the basic rules of communication. Many people love nothing more than to find grammatical errors in other people's work and feel the need to correct them. Most college and university instructors do not want to see grammar mistakes, so avoiding the most common ones leaves a very good impression.

In order to improve your writing and, hence, your credibility (and decrease your reader's frustration), you need to know the building blocks used to create any written document. To learn the more complex rules of grammar, we need to begin with the parts of speech.

> **TIP**
> It is not always necessary to remember the grammatical terms, and there are many, but it is important to write grammatically correct sentences.

Parts of Speech

Nouns

Nouns are people (*Brad*), places (*Saint John, New Brunswick*), and things (*desk*), but nouns also include qualities (*honour*), and concepts or ideas (*terabytes*). They can be divided into the categories shown in Table 13.1.

> A noun is the name of a person, a place, a thing, or an idea.

TABLE 13.1 Noun Types and Functions

Type	Function	Example
Proper	A name; usually begins with a capital letter	*Bob; Lambton College*
Common	Refers to a general group; is not capitalized	*dog; orange; air*
Concrete	A physical object or something experienced with the senses	*house; cement; lamp*
Abstract	Concept, idea, or abstraction	*Wi-Fi; terabyte; charitable*
Count	Items that can be counted; often written with an *–s* or *–es*	*boat/boats; cat/cats person/people; child/children*
	Sometimes the word forms change.	
	Sometimes require a number to indicate the amount because the form does not change	*one shrimp/five shrimp; one moose/10 moose*
Non-count	Items that can't be counted, such as liquids	*air (molecules of air, not airs);*
	Can be singular or plural	*water (drops/bottles/glasses of water, not waters)*
		scissors; mail
Collective	Groups that can be identified as either singular or plural; if the individuals in the group are acting as one unit, use the singular verb; if they are acting separately, use a plural verb.	*jury; staff; team*

Add your own examples for each type of noun in Table 13.1. If you are unsure what type your example is, look it up in a dictionary.

Some nouns can be proper or common. For example, *dad* is a common noun when it is not used as a person's name:

My dad is an engineer.

However, it is a proper noun (as is *Clair*) in the following sentence:

Dad, I would like to introduce you to Clair.

Subject–verb agreement with collective nouns can be challenging. Consider these sentences (the verb is underlined):

The jury <u>is</u> unanimous.

The jury members have decided one verdict and are acting together, so *is* is used.

The jury <u>are</u> divided in their opinions.

Because the members cannot agree, they are treated as individuals; therefore, *are* is used.

> Subject–verb agreement means that a sentence's verb must match its subject in number (i.e., a singular subject requires a singular verb, and a plural subject requires a plural verb).

> 13 For more on subject–verb agreement with collective nouns, see the section "Rules for Subject–Verb Agreement" later in this chapter.

Identify the nouns and noun types in the following sentences.

1. The children built a large snow fort.
2. The doors were slammed closed by the wind.
3. The women present were all wearing hats.
4. I would like five glasses of water, please.
5. I bought a hard drive that has five terabytes of memory.
6. I went to Niagara Falls yesterday.
7. I graduated from Red River College last summer.
8. My job as assistant manager is very challenging.
9. Legends say that King Arthur's Knights of the Round Table were loyal and chivalrous.
10. Learning a new language is difficult. For example, my mom is fluent in Dutch, but I can't understand it at all.

Pronouns

Using too many nouns in a sentence can be repetitive. Consider this sentence:

Tom said that Tom was going to Tom's mother's house to give Tom's mother a present.

There are so many *Tom*s that the reader may wonder how many people are involved. Pronouns, which replace nouns, make the sentence much clearer (the pronouns are underlined):

> **Tom said that <u>he</u> was going to <u>his</u> mother's house to give <u>her</u> a present.**

Make sure your use of pronouns does not baffle the reader. Here is an unclear pronoun reference:

> **Sarah told Jill that <u>she</u> failed the exam.**

Who failed the exam, Sarah or Jill? In this case, you need to use a name rather than a pronoun:

> **Sarah told Jill that <u>Sarah</u> failed the exam.**

Pronouns can be found at the beginning of sentences (subject pronouns) or near the end of a sentence (object pronouns). They can indicate ownership (possessive pronouns) or refer to the person already discussed (reflexive pronouns; see Table 13.2). Here are some examples:

> **Yuko and <u>I</u> went to the store.**
>
> **This is <u>her</u> book. This book is <u>hers</u>.**
>
> **Sam, himself, wrote the music for Yukon Blonde's song.**
>
> **Carlos gave the notes to Emma and <u>me</u>.**

(Notice there is no apostrophe with possessive pronouns.)

To determine whether to use *I* or *me* in the last sentence, ignore *Emma and*. You will then see that *me* is the correct pronoun here.

Indefinite Pronouns

Indefinite pronouns, such as *everybody*, *someone*, and *each*, are often used to indicate people in general. As Table 13.3 shows, some are always singular, some are always plural, and some can be both.

A pronoun is a word that takes the place of a noun (in this case, also called the antecedent) in a sentence.

A reflexive pronoun ends with –*self* (e.g., *himself*). This type of pronoun can be used only if the person has been referred to earlier in the sentence.

An indefinite pronoun (i.e., *each, either, one, everyone*) refers to an unspecified individual or group. Most are considered singular and therefore take a singular verb.

TABLE 13.2 Types of Pronouns

Subject	Object	Possessive	Reflexive
I	*me*	*my, mine*	*myself*
you	*you*	*your, yours*	*yourself*
he	*him*	*his*	*himself*
she	*her*	*her, hers*	*herself*
it	*it*	*its*	*itself*
we	*us*	*our, ours*	*ourselves*
you	*you*	*your, yours*	*yourselves*
they	*them*	*their, theirs*	*themselves*

TABLE 13.3 Common Indefinite Pronouns

Singular	Plural	Both
everyone	all	none (not one or not any)
everybody	more	
someone	most	
each	some	
anyone	any	
anybody		
no one		
nobody		
either		
neither		

EAL

If the pronoun is singular, use a singular verb. If the pronoun is plural, use a plural verb. If the pronoun can be either singular or plural, examine the whole sentence to decide whether to use a singular or plural verb.

EXERCISE 13.3

Determine whether the underlined pronoun is correct or incorrect in the following sentences.

1. Abiha and <u>me</u> are going to the movies tonight.
2. Greg and <u>myself</u> believe that the test results are inaccurate.
3. Can you deliver this to Lara and <u>her</u>?
4. We need to buy the dog <u>it's</u> own water dish.
5. This car belongs to <u>ourselves</u>.
6. Between you and <u>me</u>, George drives poorly.
7. Microsoft is a giant in the computer industry. Some say <u>it</u> is the only reliable company.
8. Jill is as tall as <u>I</u>.
9. Travis fixed the engine <u>himself</u>.
10. Go get <u>yourself</u> an ice cream.

When you write sentences using nouns and pronouns, you must make sure that the pronouns agree in number and gender with the nouns that are being replaced (the antecedents). However, the person's name may not indicate the gender pronoun that the person prefers, so it is important to choose gender-inclusive pronouns (*they, them, their*) to respect their preference even though it means that a plural pronoun is used to replace a singular noun.

The antecedent in a sentence is the noun that the pronoun replaces.

When the noun's gender is unclear (*teacher* or *doctor*), the correct choice is the gender-inclusive personal pronoun. Today, many people add their gender pronoun preference to their signature in their emails and other correspondence.

A student left <u>their</u> textbook in the classroom. [This sentence is gender inclusive.]

Verbs

As children, we learn that verbs are action words. These include *run, jump, drive, eat, feel* (physically), and *sing*. Some verbs are still actions, but they can't be seen, such as *think, imagine,* and *suggest*. However, some verbs are states of being (e.g., *hope, love,* and *feel* [emotionally]). The verbs in the examples are underlined:

I <u>ran</u> down the hill.

The texture of this fabric <u>feels</u> rough.

May I <u>suggest</u> the poutine as a starter?

She <u>feels</u> sad because the concert <u>was</u> cancelled.

Verbs also link the subject of a sentence to a description of it. These linking verbs include all forms of the *to be* verb (*is, are, was, were,* etc.) and words such as *look* and *seems*.

Phillipe <u>is</u> very articulate.

Sometimes verbs are composed of more than one word; the additional words are called helping or auxiliary verbs. The most common helping verbs are forms of *to be* (*am, are, is, was, were, will be,* etc.) and *to have* (*have, has, had,* etc.).

Sukhdeep <u>will be</u> going home for the holidays.

You <u>have had</u> ample time to complete the assignment.

A modal verb is placed before the main verb to express necessity, obligation, possibility, or probability. These modal verbs are *can, could, may, might, ought to, shall, should, will,* and *would*.

You <u>should</u> wash your car before winter comes.

> The pronouns *they, them,* or *their* are used to make language gender inclusive.
> **TIP**

A verb is a word that conveys an action, a state of being, or a condition.

A linking verb joins (links) a subject to a noun or an adjective that follows the verb.

 Appendix A lists the various tenses of English verbs.

A helping, or auxiliary, verb combines with a main verb to form a different tense

A modal verb appears before the main verb to express necessity, obligation, possibility, or probability.

EXERCISE 13.4

Read the following sentences and determine whether the verb (which is underlined) is an action word, state of being, or linking verb.

1. She <u>is</u> sad.
2. The music <u>sounds</u> wonderful.
3. He <u>drives</u> to the beach every weekend.

4. It <u>seemed</u> as if he were floating on air.
5. She <u>ran</u> the race in record time.
6. He <u>ate</u> all the cake.
7. Some musicians say they <u>feel</u> the music as they play.
8. Terrence <u>was</u> upset.
9. She <u>speaks</u> quickly.
10. They <u>are</u> members of the top band.

Modifiers: Adjectives and Adverbs

Adjectives, Articles, and Determiners

An adjective modifies, or describes, a noun or a pronoun. It can come before or after the noun or pronoun and be more than one word. Articles (*a*, *an*, and *the*) and determiners (such as *this* and *her*) also act as adjectives. An adjective answers the following questions: Which? What kind? How many?

Let's look at a few examples.

The tall woman is happy.

The, *tall*, and *happy* tell us about the woman.

The dusty, old sports car sat in the broken-down barn.

The, *dusty*, *old*, and *sports* describe the noun *car*; *the* and *broken-down* describe the noun *barn*.

He is an expert.

The adjectives *an* and *expert* describe the pronoun *he*.

Nouns can also become adjectives when they are used to modify other nouns.

The CN Tower was the world's highest free-standing structure for many years.

CN is normally a noun—as in *CN is a prosperous company*—but is an adjective in this sentence because it tells us which tower. *World's* modifies the noun *structure* and is thus also an adjective here.

Adverbs

An adverb describes verbs, adjectives, other adverbs, and even complete sentences. Adverbs often end in *–ly*, such as *really*, *quickly*, and *sharply*. They answer these questions: When? Where? Why? How? To what degree? How much?

Usain Bolt runs quickly.

The adverb *quickly* modifies the verb *runs*.

An **adjective** describes a noun or pronoun and usually comes before the word it modifies, but it can also follow a linking verb, where it modifies the subject. An **article** (*a*, *an*, or *the*) precedes and modifies a noun

An **adverb** modifies a verb, an adjective, an adverb, or a sentence.

TIP

Many people drop the *–ly* from adverbs, so you may see or hear sentences such as *That was real short*. When writing for school, do not make this mistake.

Usain Bolt runs <u>very quickly</u>.

In this sentence, both *very* and *quickly* are adverbs. *Quickly* modifies the verb *runs*, and *very* modifies the adverb *quickly*.

Some actors look <u>very</u> tall on film.

In this sentence, *very* modifies the adjective *tall*.

Some adverbs can also act as conjunctions to connect two independent clauses or two complete thoughts. These are most commonly called conjunctive adverbs.

Richard was hired on Monday; <u>however</u>, he was fired on Tuesday.

Note the semicolon separating the clauses and the comma after *however*.

Be careful not to confuse conjunctive adverbs with regular conjunctions (such as *and*, *or*, and *but*), which join words, phrases, and clauses. A conjunctive adverb joins two independent clauses.

Joiners: Prepositions and Conjunctions

Prepositions

A preposition is a small word or short phrase that often refers to place or time, such as *before*, *after*, *between*, *in front*, *except*, and *over*. It joins the noun or pronoun that follows to the rest of the sentence. Table 13.4 contains common prepositions.

Prepositions introduce prepositional phrases, which function as adjectives or adverbs depending on what part of speech they modify. A prepositional phrase never contains the simple subject of the sentence. In the

 See the next section for more information on conjunctions.

An independent clause is a group of words that has a subject and a predicate and can therefore stand alone as a complete sentence. A conjunctive adverb (e.g., *however*, *therefore*, or *thus*) joins two independent clauses. It is preceded by a semicolon and usually followed by a comma.

A clause is a group of words containing both a subject and a predicate. A clause may be independent or dependent.

A preposition joins a noun or pronoun to the rest of the sentence, adding information.

TABLE 13.4 Common Prepositions

about	*beside(s)*	*like*	*since*
above	*between*	*near*	*than*
across	*beyond*	*next (to)*	*through*
after	*by*	*of*	*throughout*
against	*despite*	*off*	*to*
along	*down*	*on*	*toward(s)*
among	*during*	*onto*	*under*
around	*except*	*opposite*	*until*
as	*for*	*out*	*up*
at	*from*	*outside (of)*	*upon*
before	*in*	*over*	*with*
behind	*inside*	*past*	*within*
below	*into*	*regarding*	*without*

following examples, the preposition is italicized and the rest of the prepositional phrase is underlined:

The letters are *in* <u>the attic</u>.

***During* <u>the summer vacation</u>, she planted trees.**

They laughed *at* <u>him</u>.

Conjunctions

A conjunction is a word or phrase that connects words, phrases, and clauses of equal or unequal weight or importance. In other words, conjunctions can join two complete thoughts, an incomplete thought and a complete thought, or groups of words.

A coordinating conjunction joins equal units—word to word, phrase to phrase, clause to clause. An important use of these words is to join independent clauses in compound sentences. *For*, *and*, *nor*, *but*, *or*, *yet*, and *so* (collectively known as FANBOYS) are coordinating conjunctions.

Bob is planning to go skiing this weekend, <u>but</u> Susie is going to a hockey game.

In this compound sentence, there are two complete thoughts: *Bob is planning to go skiing this weekend* and *Susie is going to a hockey game*. The coordinating conjunction we use depends on whether we are adding ideas (*and*), contrasting them (*but*, *yet*), or showing a cause and effect relationship (*so*). Note the comma before the conjunction.

A subordinating conjunction joins unequal units. You can join a dependent clause (meaning that the thought is unclear unless you join it to a complete one) to an independent clause (a complete thought). In the following examples, the subordinating conjunction is italicized and the dependent clause is underlined. When a dependent clause is placed before an independent clause, as in the second example, a comma needs to separate the two:

I went to the store *because* <u>I needed milk</u>.

***Because* <u>I needed milk</u>, I went to the store.**

Unlike what many have been taught, as long as you complete your thought, you can begin a sentence with *because*, *while*, *since*, or *although*. However, if you don't include an independent clause, your reader will wonder what the rest of the idea is.

Correlative conjunctions occur in pairs and require parallel structure.

She will <u>either</u> go to college <u>or</u> take a year off to travel.

<u>Both</u> Nicola and Dimitri enjoy opera.

 →13 See "Prepositional Phrases" later in the chapter for more on prepositional phrases.

A **conjunction** is a word that joins words, phrases, or clauses.

A **coordinating conjunction** joins equal units, such as two independent clauses.

 →13 See "Sentence Patterns" later in the chapter for a discussion of compound sentences.

A **subordinating conjunction** joins a dependent clause, which contains less important information, to an independent clause, which contains more important information

A **dependent clause** is a group of words that contains a subject and a predicate but expresses an incomplete thought. It needs more information to form a complete sentence.

→13 For a list of common subordinating conjunctions, see Table 13.6.

A **correlative conjunction** is a two-part grammatical unit that joins parts of a sentence; both must be used to complete the sentence.

This exercise is a take on the game Mad Libs. Your instructor divides the class into four or eight groups and assigns each a part of speech (noun, verb, adjective, or adverb). Each group comes up with 10 examples of its respective part. Try to think of unusual or funny words. Keeping your textbook closed, decide the order you will use your words. Choose one member of the class to read the following sentences. As the blanks come up, one member of the part of speech group will read the group's chosen word. For example, in the first sentence, the "verb group" provides its chosen word at the first blank, then the "adjective group" at the second, and so on until the sentence is complete. The idea isn't to try to make sense but to create strange sentences that are grammatical.

1. If you do not _____ your _____ _____, someone might _____ _____ your _____.
                    verb   adj noun   adv verb   noun

2. We all occasionally _____ _____, but some _____ _____ _____ their _____ every day.
                          verb adv   noun (pl) adv verb   noun

3. The _____ _____ looked ready to _____ _____ into the _____ _____.
            adj noun   verb adv   adj noun

4. Before you _____ your _____ _____, it's best to _____ your _____ _____.
                verb   adj noun   verb   noun adv

5. The _____ _____ that _____ on the _____ _____ _____.
            adj noun   verb   noun verb adv

In the following article, identify

five nouns

two pronouns

six verbs

three adjectives

two adverbs

four prepositions

two conjunctions

Justin Trudeau, Canada's newly elected prime minister, must be the only 43-year-old who is ecstatic to be returning to the house he grew up in.

Canada's new premier has had to shake off his privileged background. The son of the country's iconic 16-year PM Pierre Trudeau, Justin was born in the Canadian prime minister's residence at 24 Sussex Drive. However, there are some aspects of his evolving personality, after a lifetime in the media spotlight, that are just now coming to the fore.

As ever, ahead of the zeitgeist, British comedian John Oliver lampooned Trudeau's changing image on the eve of Canada's federal election.

"If you do a Google image search on him you can find every poor fashion choice that he has ever made. From a 90s boyband member one week before entering rehab, to an LL Bean sweater model who just underwent a lobotomy to Johnny Depp's evil twin," Oliver said on his late-night comedy show *Last Week Tonight*.

In March 2012, Trudeau entered the Canadian psyche not as the son of a much-loved former prime minister but as a fighter, literally. He beat Conservative senator Patrick Brazeau in a charity boxing match, giving his opponent a bloody nose in the final round.

Paton, Callum. "Justin Trudeau: Boxer, Practical Joker, 'Evil Johnny Depp' and Now Liberal Canadian Prime Minister." *International Business Times*, October 21, 2015, http://www.ibtimes.co.uk/justin-trudeau-boxer-practical-joker-evil-johnny-depp-now-liberal-canadian-prime-minister-1525057.

Sentences

In academic writing, you must always use full sentences. Knowing the parts of speech is necessary, as sentences are built from them, but you must also know the elements of sentences (see Table 13.5). For example, one way to examine a sentence is to identify the complete subject and the complete predicate. *I ran* has the subject *I* and the predicate *ran*. Therefore, it is a complete sentence. It is also an example of a simple sentence, as it contains one subject and one predicate. (Note that nouns and pronouns can be the subject of a sentence or part of the predicate.) Your instructor may also ask you to identify direct objects (DO), indirect objects (IO), and subject complements (SC). Understanding these will help you identify errors in your sentence structure.

> A complete subject is the subject of a sentence plus its modifiers. A complete sentence contains at least one subject and one predicate and expresses a complete thought.
>
> A direct object (DO) receives the action of the verb; an indirect object (IO) is part of a prepositional phrase and usually tells for whom the action in the sentence is done. A subject complement (SC) is a noun or an adjective following the verb that gives more information about the subject.

TABLE 13.5 Definitions of Sentence Components

Element	Definition	Example
Simple subject (SS)	The noun or pronoun that performs the action of the verb (the "doer" of the action)	The hungry <u>twins</u> ate all the sandwiches. (The noun *twins* <u>is</u> the simple subject. We ignore the adjectives *the* and *hungry*.)
Complete subject (S)	The simple subject of the sentence, plus its modifiers. It answers the reader's question, Who or what is this about?	<u>The hungry twins</u> ate all the sandwiches. (For the complete subject, we include both the adjectives and the noun.)
Simple predicate (SP)	The complete verb of the sentence.	The hungry twins <u>ate</u> all the sandwiches. (The verb *ate* is the simple predicate. Everything else is left out.)

Element	Definition	Example
Complete predicate (P)	The complete verb of the sentence, plus its modifiers, objects, etc. It tells us something the subject is doing or what is being observed about it.	The hungry twins <u>ate all the sandwiches</u>. (For the complete predicate, we include the verb *ate* and all the modifiers.)
Direct object (DO)	It receives the action of the verb.	I gave the <u>ball</u> to him. (The noun *ball* receives the action, so it is the direct object.)
Indirect object (IO)	It is usually preceded by a preposition (such as *in, between, with*); it is also called the object of the preposition.	I gave the ball to <u>him</u>. (Note that *him* follows a preposition, so it is the indirect object.)
Subject complement (SC)	It follows a linking verb (often a form of *to be*, such as *is, are, was, were*) and can be linked to the subject.	Shelley is <u>happy</u>. (The adjective *happy* describes Shelley, so it is a subject complement.)

EXERCISE 13.7

For the following sentences, identify the parts of speech and sentence elements.

1. I slept.
2. Henry bought a ball.
3. Mr. Safi gave the test to Joshua.
4. Stacey is homesick.
5. The bright red car drove quickly around the block.

→13 The next section in this chapter explains sentence patterns.

EXERCISE 13.8

For each of the following sentences, identify the complete subject and the complete predicate.

1. Bob and his roommate Yan went to the movies.
2. Bob and Yan, who are big horror fans, really enjoyed the new super-hero movie.
3. The hungry pair ate too much popcorn and drank too much pop.
4. Both Bob and Yan spent too much money.
5. Bob and Yan are now poor.

EXERCISE 13.9

Identify the simple subject and simple predicate in the sentences in Exercise 13.8.

A complete sentence contains at least one subject and one predicate. Grammatically, it needs nothing else to complete the thought, although more detail might be required for clarity. For example, the following sentence is complete because it has both a subject (*Peter*) and a predicate (*drove*):

Peter drove.

However, you could add more information so that the reader doesn't wonder where to or whom:

Peter drove Alice to the train station.

The subject and predicate are the same, but we have added a direct object (the noun *Alice*) and a prepositional phrase (*to the station*). The phrase contains a preposition (*to*), two adjectives (*the* and *train*), and a noun (*station*).

Sentence Patterns

Complete sentences come in four basic patterns: simple, compound, complex, and compound-complex. In each of the following examples, the subject is underlined and the predicate is italicized:

Simple sentence: Subject + Predicate

<u>Peter</u> *drove*.

<u>Peter and Gill</u> *drove*.

Compound sentence: Subject + Predicate, + coordinating conjunction (FANBOYS) + Subject + Predicate

<u>Peter</u> went sailing, and **<u>Layla</u>** went horseback riding.

<u>Peter and Gill</u> *went on a picnic*, but **<u>Alice and Layla</u>** *went sightseeing*.

Put another way, a compound sentence is two simple sentences joined by one of the FANBOYS words.

Complex sentence: Subject + Predicate + Subordinating Conjunction + Subject + Predicate

or

Subordinating Conjunction + Subject + Predicate + Subject + Predicate

This type of sentence uses a subordinating conjunction to join an independent and a dependent clause. In the following examples, the independent clause is italicized, and the dependent clause is underlined:

Spring is often muddy in Canada <u>while summer is not</u>.

A simple sentence contains one subject and one predicate. Two or more independent clauses joined by a coordinating conjunction make a compound sentence; an independent clause joined to a dependent clause by a subordinating conjunction creates a complex sentence. A compound-complex sentence is a compound sentence joined with a complex one.

While summer is not always muddy in Canada, *April showers can make a muddy spring.*

Compound-complex sentence: Subject + Predicate + coordinating conjunction (FANBOYS) + Subject + Predicate + Subordinating Conjunction + Subject + Predicate

***Spring is my favourite season,* and *summer is my second favourite* because I love warm temperatures.**

Prepositional Phrases

A phrase is a grammatical unit that often acts as a part of speech and lacks a subject, predicate, or both. A prepositional phrase acts as either an adverb or an adjective. As you've seen earlier in this chapter, a group of words that includes more than one part of speech can modify a verb. In this case, it functions as an adverbial phrase.

Noun and Verb Phrases

In the following example, the combination of the indefinite pronoun *some* and its modifier, *of the injured*, makes a noun phrase. The entire phrase, *some of the injured passengers*, is the sentence's subject because it tells us who had to be hospitalized:

Some of the injured passengers had to be hospitalized.

A phrase, then, can function as a noun subject or object.

Finally, consider the next example, in which the verb phrase *we will be looking* acts as a unit in the sentence, conveying the action of the subject *we*:

We will be looking carefully for the person with a red flag on their backpack.

Verb phrases are very common because you will often need helping verbs to create different tenses beyond the one-word simple tenses (verb phrases are underlined):

Simple present: **I think, you say, she takes**

Simple past: **I thought, you said, she took**

Present progressive: **I am thinking, you are saying, she is taking**

Past perfect: **I had thought, you had said, she had taken**

In addition to forms of *to be* and *to have*, verb phrases occur when modals combine with main verbs to convey ability (*can, could*), possibility (*may, might*), necessity (*must, have*), and other meanings.

A **phrase** is a group of grammatically linked words that lacks a subject, predicate, or both. It functions as a single part of speech.

A **prepositional phrase** consists of a preposition and a noun or pronoun (the object of the preposition). The phrase can act as an adverb to modify a verb (an adverbial phrase) or as an adjective to modify a noun or pronoun (adjectival phrase).

A **noun phrase** is a group of words that acts as a noun in a sentence and can be either the subject or an object.

A **verb phrase** is a group of words that acts as the verb in a sentence.

Appendix A contains more information about verb tenses.

Identify the word groups in parentheses as adverbial, adjectival, noun, or verb phrases and then indicate the subject of each sentence.

1. Tomorrow, (the class time) will be changed (for the rest) (of the semester).
2. (Some of the food) (in the fridge) (has spoiled).
3. The store (in the mall) (with the latest fashions) (has closed).
4. A search (of the abandoned house) (turned up) several cartons (of stolen goods).
5. (The 2022 hockey season) (will belong) (to the Leafs).

Identify the different clauses in each of the following sentences.

1. I will meet you at the airport before the flight.
2. Because Stan likes ginger ale, I bought two flats of it.
3. Yesterday, while I was reviewing my finances, I noticed that I forgot to pay my electric bill.
4. I had to pay the bill with my credit card, and I am now at my credit limit.
5. I need to go to the bank to apply for a loan, and I need to visit my parents because I need more money this month.

Identify the phrases in the sentences of Exercise 13.11.

Imperative Sentences

An imperative sentence, or a command, does not require a subject in the sentence. This silent subject is always the pronoun *you*, and the reader understands the subject from the context of the sentence.

> **Close the door!**
>
> **Put your pencils down.**
>
> **Go to your room.**

In each of these sentences, we can imagine the word *you* at the beginning.

An imperative sentence issues a command. Its subject, *you*, is always understood even though it is not expressed.

TIP

In writing, context is the text surrounding a word or an idea that clarifies its meaning.

Indicate which of the following are complete sentences. Mark with an *S* those that contain only a subject and a *P* those that contain only a predicate. Use an *N* if there is neither subject nor predicate.

1. The empty cup on the bench.
2. Signed his name to the bottom of the petition.
3. Faith heals.
4. Can grammar rules be bent?
5. Eat your Brussels sprouts!

Sentence Errors

Sentence Fragments

There are four types of sentence fragments: missing subject or predicate, add-on, –*ing*, and dependent clause.

A **sentence fragment** is a major grammatical error that consists of an incomplete clause or a dependent clause on its own.

Missing Subject or Predicate

In this type of fragment, either a subject or a predicate is missing. The following sentence is incomplete because it consists only of a subject and a phrase that expands on it; the subject isn't doing anything:

A driver who never stops at red lights.

Who never stops at red lights tells us what kind of driver they are but goes no further. The sentence needs a predicate, such as *is dangerous*, to be complete:

A driver who never stops at red lights is dangerous.

Similarly, *thousands of tourists around the world* is a fragment. Something essential is missing: What about the tourists? Do they exist? Are the tourists doing something? What do they look like? Who saw them? To answer any of these questions is to complete a thought—and the sentence:

Thousands of tourists around the world experience jet lag.

The Taj Mahal is seen by thousands of tourists from around the world.

The first example adds a predicate (*experience jet lag*); the second adds a subject (*the Taj Mahal*), introduces a verb (*is seen*), adds a preposition (*from*), and turns the fragment into part of the predicate.

EXERCISE 13.14

Complete the fragment *thousands of tourists around the world* in two ways other than those discussed. Then, complete the following fragments by adding predicates.

1. The store that opened on the weekend
2. The brilliant idea that came to me in the middle of the night
3. A song that can get everyone dancing

4. The kind of doughnut that doesn't have a hole in the middle

5. The beach towel that was on the ground

Add-On Fragment

TIP

Add-on fragments lack a subject and a predicate. They may begin with a word (e.g., *especially*), a phrase (e.g., *such as*), a transition word or phrase (*also, as well as, besides, especially, except (for), for example, including, like*), or a preposition (*on, in, to*).

Add-on fragments contain neither a complete subject nor a complete predicate. Writers can mistake them for complete sentences because there is usually a pause between them and the preceding sentence in speech; you may mistakenly associate a pause or drawn breath with a new sentence. The easiest way to fix these kinds of fragments is to make them part of the previous sentence or to supply the missing essentials. Punctuation may not be needed; at other times, you can use a comma or a dash.

FRAGMENT **Exaggerated images of fitness are everywhere. Especially in teen-oriented media.**

CORRECT **Exaggerated images of fitness are everywhere, especially in teen-oriented media.**

or

Exaggerated images of fitness are everywhere—especially in teen-oriented media.

FRAGMENT **Sewage contains more than 200 toxic chemicals that are flushed down sinks or toilets. Not to mention the runoff from roads.**

CORRECT **Sewage contains more than 200 toxic chemicals that are flushed down sinks or toilets, not to mention the runoff from roads.**

When you begin a sentence with a preposition, check that the sentence expresses a complete thought and includes both a subject and a predicate.

FRAGMENT **On top of the biggest sundae.**

Who or what is there and what is taking place?

CORRECT **The cherry was on top of the biggest sundae.**

–ing Fragment

An *-ing* fragment occurs when an incomplete verb form (or base verb form) is mistaken for a complete verb.

A third kind of fragment occurs when an incomplete verb form, or base verb form—usually the present participle ending in *–ing*—is mistaken for a complete verb. Other incomplete verb forms that can cause this error include past participles and infinitives. To avoid sentence fragments, always ensure you write a complete verb form.

Here are some examples of incomplete verb forms:

- *listening, studying, thinking, being* (present participle form of verb)
- *given, thought, written, taken* (past participle form of verb)
- *to begin, to tell, to be, to look* (infinitive form of verb)

While complete verb forms can be joined to a subject by adding a helping verb, incomplete verb forms can't.

INCOMPLETE **She listening. They given.**
COMPLETE **She was listening. They are given.**

The following are examples of fragments with incomplete verb forms:

FRAGMENT **Dogs running around the fenced-in play area.**

What are the dogs doing? If you said "They are running," you have changed the fragment into a complete sentence by adding the helping verb *are*:

CORRECT **Dogs <u>are running</u> around the fenced-in play area.**
FRAGMENT **As a new doctor fascinated by innovative surgery procedures.**
CORRECT **As a new doctor, he was fascinated by innovative surgery procedures.**

> **TIP**
> Learn how to recognize incomplete verb forms in your writing. Doing so will help you avoid this kind of sentence fragment.

The first three fragment types can act as nouns, adjectives, and adverbs in a sentence but not as verbs.

Incomplete verb form as noun: **Eating sensibly is the best way to lose weight.**

Eating is the noun subject of this sentence.

Incomplete verb form as adjective: **My growling stomach told me it was time to eat.**

Growling is an adjective modifying *stomach*, the noun subject. Note that there is another incomplete verb form in this sentence—*to eat*—which acts as an adjective modifying *time*.

EXERCISE 13.15

> Add a subject, a predicate, or both to the fragments in Exercise 13.13, making them complete sentences.

Dependent Clause Fragment

A dependent clause fragment is the most common type of fragment because, at first glance, a dependent clause looks a lot like a grammatical sentence. You can identify a dependent clause by the word it begins with—a subordinating conjunction or a relative pronoun (see Table 13.6).

TABLE 13.6 Common Subordinating Conjunctions and Relative Pronouns

after	ever since	unless	which
although	if	until	whichever
as	if only	what	while
as if	in case	whatever	who
as long as	in order that	when	whoever
as soon as	once	whenever	whom
as though	since	where	whose
because	so that	whereas	why
before	that	wherever	
even though	though	whether	

A dependent clause fragment sounds incomplete and leaves us wondering about the missing part. Consider this fragment:

Because he was late.

You can think of a dependent clause as searching for an answer to a question—in this case, What happened because he was late? When you provide that information in an independent clause, you will have a complete sentence. You can also test a sentence for completeness by asking whether it is true or false. You can't tell whether the fragment *Because he was late* is true or false because you are missing information:

Because he was late for work, he lost some pay.

The subordinating conjunction that introduces the dependent clause indicates the relationship between the dependent and independent clauses, such as one of cause–effect (*as*, *because*), time (*before*, *since*, *when*, *while*), or contrast (*although*, *though*, *whereas*). If you take away the subordinating conjunction, you are left with a subject and a predicate and a sentence that expresses a complete thought. Another way to fix a dependent clause fragment, then, is to remove the subordinating conjunction; you will have a simple sentence expressing one idea. However, it may not be the idea you intended to convey:

He was late for work.

This is a complete sentence, but it does not explain the consequences of his being late.

→13 See "Conjunctions" for more information about subordinating conjunctions.

The following may or may not be complete sentences. For each one that is a fragment, identify the type and make it into a complete sentence.

1. Completing the test on time.
2. Huge tears rolled down his cheeks.
3. Being that she worked late.
4. He promised to call her tomorrow. To see if she was still all right.
5. A murder of crows, along with a flock of sheep.
6. He must be guilty. Since he's already confessed.
7. Walking beside the tracks, he eventually reached the town.
8. Introducing our next prime minister.
9. For example, the reboot of the famous TV show *The X-Files*.
10. Swimming on her back.

Check your answers in Appendix D and then do questions 11–20.

11. Because trips create memories.
12. Stress can make us victims of illnesses. Including mild to life-threatening ones.
13. Which is an example of a dependent clause.
14. The objection was overruled. As the judge felt that the jury needs to hear the statement.
15. Learning about people from different ethnic groups.
16. Painting is a good hobby and helps people see the world more clearly. Such as the increased perception of shadows.
17. Golf courses always include obstacles. These are water hazards and sand traps.
18. Although there are options in today's schools for Indigenous students to learn about their culture.
19. Sounds and textures are common features of dreams. While smell and taste are usually absent.
20. The horse is my favourite animal. Which is a Chinese Zodiac symbol.

To test whether you have written a dependent clause fragment, answer these questions: 1) Does the idea sound complete? 2) Can you answer "true" or "false" to it? 3) Does it begin with one of the words in Table 13.6? If the answer to question 1 or 2 is "no," it is probably a fragment.

Find the four sentence fragments in the following passage; correct them by joining them to complete sentences or by adding information.

When considering college or university. Many students must decide where to live. If they are going to school close to home, they may decide to continue living with their families. Listening to their parent's advice. However, if the school is far away and commuting is not possible, students must decide whether to live in the school residence or in an apartment. Residences are convenient. Especially if there is a meal plan available. Meal plans that are nutritious. Apartments might be a better idea though, especially if students need to work. Not all residences are close to where jobs are. Privacy might be an issue in residence. Not all students can get their own rooms. Apartments may provide privacy, but only if there is no need for roommates. Many factors need to be considered when choosing where to live.

EXERCISE 13.18

Construct compound, complex, and compound-complex sentences from these independent clauses (simple sentences). After you have joined the clauses in the most logical way, identify the sentence type, ensuring that you have at least one example of each. You can make small changes to the clauses and sentence order.

1. They intended to eat at Benny's Bistro.

   They saw a long line-up outside Benny's.

   They went to Kenny's Kitchen instead.

2. There may be nearly 2 million kinds of plants in the world.

   There are likely at least as many different kinds of animals.

   No one can know how many species have evolved, flourished, and become extinct.

3. Timothy Findley's story "Stones" takes place in Toronto.

   Norman Levine's "Something Happened Here" takes place in northern France.

   Both stories describe the tragic assault by Canadian troops on Dieppe during the Second World War.

4. We may suspect that Earth is not unique as a life-bearing planet.

   We do not as yet have any compelling evidence that life exists anywhere else.

   We must restrict our discussion of the presence of life to our own planet.

5. Cooking has become a popular hobby.

   Many celebrities have cooking shows.

   These celebrities have written cookbooks that promote their shows.

Run-On Sentence

A run-on sentence isn't just a long sentence: it's a major grammatical error in which two sentences are not properly separated.

A sentence may contain one or more subject–predicate clauses, but they must be joined correctly with commas and conjunctions so that the reader can distinguish the ideas. Otherwise, they must be separated by a period to form separate sentences. A run-on sentence occurs when a writer joins two sentences without including any punctuation between them. The writer charges through the end of the first complete thought and into the second one, like a driver running a stop sign. However, a run-on sentence is not the same as a long sentence with FANBOYS words or other conjunctions.

INCORRECT   **The cruise to Alaska was full Tom and Yumi decided to fly to Jamaica instead.**
The Dene peoples live in northern Canada they speak different languages.

Once you determine where the first clause ends and the second one begins, make them into two simple sentences or use a comma and the appropriate coordinating conjunction to join them.

CORRECT   **The cruise to Alaska was full. Tom and Yumi decided to fly to Jamaica instead.**
The cruise to Alaska was full, <u>so</u> Tom and Yumi decided to fly to Jamaica instead.
The Dene peoples live in northern Canada. They speak different languages.
The Dene peoples live in northern Canada, <u>and</u> they speak different languages.

The following run-on sentences contain two complete thoughts or two main ideas. Lines indicate the division between subject and predicate; diagonal lines show where the first sentence ends and the second begins and where a period or a comma and coordinating conjunction should be placed:

INCORRECT   **Many people | have smartphones // smartphones | are very practical devices.**
The poverty line | is very low in Canada // many people | live below the poverty line.
CORRECT   **Many people have smartphones. Smartphones are practical devices.**
Many people have smartphones, <u>as</u> they are practical devices.
The poverty line is very low in Canada. Many people live below the poverty line.
The poverty line is very low in Canada, <u>but</u> many people live below it.

Comma Splice

An error more common than the run-on sentence is the comma splice, which is the joining of two complete sentences by only a comma. This error is like slowing down at a stop sign before charging through. The comma has many uses within the sentence, but it alone cannot connect two sentences.

A comma splice isn't just a problem in comma usage; it's a major grammatical error in which a comma alone is used to separate two complete thoughts.

Comma splices sometimes occur when two clauses are very closely related, or the second clause seems a continuation of the first one. It's important to be able to separate two independent clauses. The simplest way to avoid comma splices is to find where one complete thought (independent clause) ends and the next begins and place either a period or a comma and a coordinating conjunction between them.

Chapter 14 discusses how to use commas properly.

INCORRECT	**Models today are very thin, they look ill.**
	The population is rising, some think the Earth cannot sustain itself.

Although the second clauses in these sentences are closely related in meaning to the first, they are not part of those clauses and must be separated from them by something stronger than just a comma. A "stop" form of punctuation, such as a semicolon or colon, may be a good choice in these cases:

CORRECT	**Models today are very thin. They look ill.**
	Models today are very thin; they look ill.
	The population is rising. Some think the Earth cannot sustain itself.
	The population is rising; therefore, some think the Earth cannot sustain itself.

Chapter 14 contains instructions on using stop punctuation.

Remember that a pronoun generally replaces a noun that comes before it in a sentence. Like a noun, a pronoun can act as the subject of a clause. In the following sentences, a pronoun is the subject of the second clause. Lines indicate the division between subject and predicate; diagonal lines show where the first sentence ends and the second begins and where a period or a comma and coordinating conjunction should be placed:

INCORRECT	**Working in a busy office environment | was completely new to her, // she | had always worked at home.**
	Censorship | does not just mean getting rid of swearing and nudity, // it | can also mean blocking an idea or a viewpoint.
CORRECT	**Working in a busy office environment was completely new to her. She had always worked at home.**
	Working in a busy office environment was completely new to her, <u>for</u> she had always worked at home.
	She had always worked at home, <u>so</u> working in a busy office environment was completely new to her.
	Censorship does not just mean getting rid of swearing and nudity. It can also mean blocking an idea or a viewpoint.
	Censorship does not just mean getting rid of swearing and nudity, <u>but</u> it can also mean blocking an idea or a viewpoint.

If you wish to use a comma to connect two independent clauses, you must also use one of the seven coordinating conjunctions (FANBOYS). Use a semicolon before words such as *however*, *therefore*, or *thus* to join two independent clauses.

Indicate whether each sentence is run-on or contains a comma splice. Fix the errors by using a period to make two separate sentences or, if you already know the rules for using them, other forms of punctuation to join independent clauses.

1. I read two books in two days I did nothing else but read.

2. I couldn't use my laptop today, I forgot to plug it in before the battery was dead.

3. I was frightened during my first driving lesson the instructor yelled at me.

4. It's easy to punctuate sentences, just put a comma whenever you pause.

5. It was late when she finished watching the movie she took a taxi home.

6. Magazines are available for digital download, this is better for the environment.

7. Technology continues to evolve, but we can't always predict whether this is good or bad.

8. Humans are imitators, conforming is something they are good at.

9. Many immigrants want to learn about Canadian culture they take courses about it.

10. Binge drinking is a serious problem, many students engage in this behaviour.

Correct the errors in the following sentences.

1. He managed to pass the year though he seldom did his homework, what will happen to him next year is anyone's guess.

2. The opening ceremonies were delayed. On account of rain.

3. She has decided to work at a fast-food restaurant. Not a great place for tips.

4. Movies provide entertainment for people, different people prefer different genres such as horror.

5. Since she bought the new tablet.

6. The only way a person can learn. To pay attention to what is going on in class.

7. He wished he could excel at sports. Happy cheering his team from the sidelines.

8. The concept that "bigger is better" is part of our culture, it is promoted by both advertisers and the media these days.

9. Understanding the theory of relativity and its impact on our daily lives.

10. Justin Trudeau was the second-youngest person to become Prime Minister of Canada, Joe Clark was the youngest.

Check Appendix D for the correct answers before doing questions 11–25.

11. The Romans were willing to change their religious beliefs quite easily, the Greeks, however, were less willing to do this.

12. Although video games can eat up your time if you are not careful.

13. The computer is not the only way to access email today, telephones, tablets, and even watches are equipped with email capability.

14. It seems that the North American mass media prescribes two roles for women, they can be sex objects or passive housewives.

15. Martial arts are attracting more people than ever before. Especially those who want to gain self-control and self-awareness.

16. We can no longer turn our backs to what is happening in the north it is time to take action.

17. Google has an office in Kitchener, Ontario, it employs people from around the world.

18. Her message about crime was lost on the audience, they wanted to hear about terrorism.

19. Part of a long line of police officers.

20. Speaking in public is distressing for some, the most common fear is that people will laugh even if the presentation is serious.

21. During noisy debates, the Speaker in the House of Commons needs to speak loudly, their message will not be heard otherwise.

22. One of the most tragic events of the twentieth century. The detonation of the atomic bomb over Hiroshima.

23. Podcasts are current, up to date, and appear automatically, thus they can be enjoyed anywhere at any time.

24. I have been to London and Paris both cities have world-class art galleries.

25. Many factors contribute to poverty. Including geographic factors, disease, and lack of education or health care.

EXERCISE 13.21

Identify and correct the sentence errors in the following paragraph.

The "Freshmen 15" is not a recent phenomenon this refers to the weight students typically gain during their first year at college or university. What concerns doctors now is the amount of weight gained during this time. In the 1970s and 1980s, students typically gained 5 pounds, now it is up to 15. This is a very unhealthy weight gain. Once the weight is gained. It is very hard to lose. Because of this. Cafeterias are starting to offer more nutritional meals with fewer calories. Student councils are beginning to be proactive and inform students of the dangers of excess weight gain. School gyms are offering more classes to help students battle this weight gain. In the future, many hope that the "Freshman 15" becomes non-existent.

Chapter Review Questions

1. What is a noun? A noun phrase?
2. What is a verb? A verb phrase?
3. What is an adjective?
4. What is an adverb?
5. What is a preposition? Prepositional phrase?
6. What is the difference between a coordinating and a subordinating conjunction?
7. What are the different types of sentence patterns?
8. What are the two essential parts of a sentence?
9. What are the different types of sentence fragments?
10. What is the difference between a run-on sentence and a comma splice?

14 Punctuation

By the end of this chapter, you should be able to

- use commas;
- use semicolons;
- use colons;
- use dashes and parentheses;
- use apostrophes; and
- avoid common punctuation errors.

This chapter will introduce you to the current standards for properly using punctuation and ways to avoid some common errors. Once you have studied the rules, you may notice other people's mistakes in using commas, semicolons, colons, dashes, parentheses, and apostrophes. That means your writing is at a professional standard, so don't let others influence you. Various exercises will help reinforce the punctuation rules you need to know in order to write error-free documents.

You will notice that there are many grammatical terms that you need to remember in order to understand proper punctuation. As a quick recap, an independent clause acts as a complete sentence and a complete thought, while a dependent clause has a complete sentence structure, but it cannot be used on its own, as it is an incomplete thought. Recognizing the difference is key to avoiding some of the most common punctuation errors.

Do Commas Matter?

Proper comma use does matter because readers look for commas in specific places to help them read. When a comma is missing or misplaced, the reader might have to reread the sentence in order to understand its meaning. This can get in the way of communicating your message. Comma errors also result in loss of credibility. The following examples labelled as incorrect are missing commas and could confuse a reader. The correct versions are much easier to follow.

INCORRECT	**The year before a deadly forest fire ravaged much of the countryside.**
CORRECT	**The year before, a deadly forest fire ravaged much of the countryside.**
INCORRECT	**Although dating services may ask you for a photo appearance is less important than personality.**
CORRECT	**Although dating services may ask you for a photo, appearance is less important than personality.**

Correct comma use guides the reader through the sentence, clarifying the relationships among its parts.

Myths about comma use abound. For example, the "one-breath rule" states that you should insert a comma wherever you naturally pause. This rule is simply too vague to be of use in formal writing; it can even lead you astray.

In general, commas separate the smaller or less important units in a sentence. When used with coordinating conjunctions, they also separate independent clauses. In a sentence, commas separate

 See Chapter 13 for more on independent clauses.

- items in a series;
- independent clauses;
- parenthetical (types of non-essential) information; and
- adjectives, dates, addresses, titles, and the like.

> **TIP**
> Commas separate the smaller or less important units in a sentence. When used with coordinating conjunctions, they also separate independent clauses.

Rule Category 1: Items in a Series

This rule category applies to three or more grammatically parallel items. These can be single words, phrases, or clauses. Here are some examples.

A series of three nouns:

It doesn't matter whether the items in the series are words, phrases, or clauses.

> **TIP**
> Commas separate three or more items (words, phrases, or clauses) in a series.

A series of three predicates:

Every Saturday, Davina gets up, drinks a large coffee, and stumbles to the door before she realizes what day it is.

A series of three clauses:

Flowering plants produce seeds, ferns produce spores, and coniferous trees produce cones.

The comma before the last item in a series, referred to as the serial (or Oxford) comma, is often omitted in informal writing.

INFORMAL **My three favourite months are May, June and September.**
FORMAL **My three favourite months are May, June, and September.**

However, the serial comma often makes a sentence much easier to understand. Be sure to use it if the last element or the one before it contains two items. In this example, the last item in the list is a compound (*toast and jam* is a single thing consisting of two elements):

She ordered orange juice, an omelette with cheese, and toast and jam.

The serial comma is especially helpful to the reader when the second-last or the last item is significantly longer than the other items.

The two-year specialization includes 10 half-courses, 2 full courses that involve internships in health-care facilities, and a research paper.

Rule Category 2: Independent Clauses

2a: Use a comma to separate two independent clauses with a coordinating conjunction between them. In other words, use a comma before the coordinating conjunction in a compound sentence.

The course was supposed to be offered in the fall, <u>but</u> it was cancelled.

The grocery store is two kilometres away, <u>so</u> he never walks.

Dyana was the best dancer on the cruise ship, <u>and</u> she won an award to prove it.

Exceptions to this rule may be made if the second clause is very short or if the clauses are so closely related that they could be considered compounds (i.e., the ideas are hard to separate). In the following sentence, there is no comma between *dress* and *and* because the clauses are short:

"She wore the dress and I stayed home," sang Danny Kaye in the movie *White Christmas*.

2b: Use a comma after an introductory word, phrase, or clause when an independent clause follows it.

After six years as committee chair, it was time for her to retire.

To get the maximum enjoyment from his sound system, Curtis put it in a room where the acoustics were excellent.

If you have an introductory word that modifies the complete sentence, use a comma after that word.

TIP
A list or series contains three items separated by commas. Do not use a comma to separate two items unless they are two independent clauses with one of the FANBOYS words between them. FANBOYS words are conjunctions used to join two equal elements. The FANBOYS words are *for, and, nor, but, or, yet,* and *so.*

TIP
Always include the serial comma in a list of three or more items unless your instructor tells you otherwise.

TIP
Use a comma before the coordinating conjunction in a compound sentence.

←13 See Chapter 13 for descriptions and examples of sentence patterns.

TIP
Use a comma after an introductory word, phrase, or clause when an independent clause follows it.

Unfortunately, we have run out of mineral water.

Today, we will study the use of commas.

If your sentence begins with a dependent clause that introduces a complete thought (or an independent clause), use a comma after the introduction. The dependent clauses are underlined in these examples.

While <u>the drinking age is 19 in most provinces</u>, it is only 18 in Alberta.

When <u>she first encountered the Canadian education system</u>, she was surprised by the many differences between the North American and Japanese systems.

2c: In general, use a comma before a concluding word or phrase when an independent clause precedes it.

W.J. Prince wrote to his client Larry Drucker, asking direction in the case.

This rule applies when a statement is followed by a reference to the person or group that made the statement.

"We still think of a powerful man as a born leader and a powerful woman as an anomaly," Margaret Atwood once said.

Students who participate in sports or social activities are more likely to consider themselves satisfied with their lives than those who do not, according to a recent study.

Rule 2c does not usually apply when an independent clause is followed by a dependent clause. If you begin with a dependent clause and follow it with an independent one, follow rule 2b. If you begin with an independent clause and conclude with a dependent one, you do not generally use a comma. However, a dependent clause that begins with *although*, *though*, *even though*, or *whereas* suggests a contrast with the independent clause and should usually be preceded by a comma.

No comma required: The sleek Siamese cat lay on the sofa <u>where it was sunny</u>.

Comma required (use of *whereas* suggests contrast): The sleek Siamese cat lay on the sofa, <u>whereas the old Labrador retriever curled up by the fire</u>.

Rule Category 3: Parenthetical Information

When you place information in parentheses (or round brackets), you signal to the reader that it is less important than the other parts of the sentence. Commas are used in a similar way, showing whether a clause adds additional or non-essential information (non-restrictive) or essential information (restrictive). Both types modify and follow nouns and often begin with the relative pronouns *who*, *whom*, *which*, or *that*. Three rules help you decide on the importance of a clause and thus punctuate accordingly.

> **TIP**
> Combining rules: The following sentence illustrates rules 2a and 2b.
>
> In America, [2b] **20 per cent of homeless children repeat a grade in school, [2a] and another 16 per cent of these children are enrolled in special education classes.**

> **TIP**
> In general, use a comma before a concluding word or phrase when an independent clause precedes it.

> **TIP**
> Combining rules: The following sentence illustrates rules 2b and 2c.
>
> By banning the use of cellphones, [2b] **Newfoundland and Labrador encouraged its drivers to focus on the road, [2c] reducing the number of collisions.**

> **TIP**
> In general, use a comma when you begin a sentence with a dependent clause and follow it with an independent clause, but do not use a comma if you begin with an independent clause and follow with a dependent clause.

> **TIP**
> In grammar, *parentheses* means round brackets.

A non-restrictive clause contains information that can be left out of the sentence without affecting the meaning. A restrictive clause contains information that is necessary for the reader to understand the sentence.

Relative pronouns introduce dependent clauses.

3a: Use commas before and after non-restrictive phrases or clauses. Although the information may be important, it can be left out without changing the main point of the sentence. A restrictive clause is essential to the meaning of the sentence. If you left it out, the sentence would mean something different or would be ungrammatical.

> **Tony, who often wears a leather jacket, was identified as one of the rescue team.**

> **A man who wore a leather jacket was identified as one of the rescue team.**

The main idea in the first sentence is that Tony was identified as part of the rescue team. Tony's leather jacket may be important elsewhere in a larger narrative, but it is not part of the main idea here; therefore, this information is enclosed by commas. Note that two commas are required, just as two parentheses would be.

In the second sentence, the information about the jacket is essential to the person's identification. Without the clause *who wore a leather jacket*, the sentence would mean simply that a man, not a woman, was on the rescue team. This is how you can test whether information in clauses beginning with *who*, *which*, or *that* is restrictive: if you omit the clause and the sentence says something different, the information is essential. Try omitting the *who* clause in this example:

> **Many students, who take out loans, have a heavy debt burden after graduation.**

Removing the clause leaves you with a sentence that says simply *Many students have a heavy debt burden on graduation*. That's different from the more specific statement about those students with loans. Therefore, *who take out loans* is a restrictive clause and no commas should be used.

> **Many students who take out loans have a heavy debt burden after graduation.**

When writing clauses, whether non-restrictive or restrictive, use *who* to refer to people. Use *which* to refer to non-humans in non-restrictive clauses and *that* to refer to non-humans in restrictive clauses.

> **The actor <u>who</u> appeared in the movie <u>that</u> we saw last night also starred in *The Avengers*.**

3b: Use commas to set off appositives—nouns or phrases that are grammatically parallel to a noun or phrase before it. Appositives name, rephrase, specify, or explain the noun or noun phrase that comes just before. The appositives in the following sentences are underlined.

> **Her first work, <u>a short story collection called *Drying the Bones*</u>, received outstanding reviews.**

TIP
Use two commas around a non-restrictive clause to separate it from the rest of the sentence, just as you would use parentheses.

TIP
Use *who* to refer to people in restrictive and non-restrictive clauses. Use *which* to refer to non-humans in non-restrictive clauses and *that* to refer to non-humans in restrictive clauses.

Seal hunting, <u>a traditional means of livelihood among Inuit</u>, has been criticized by some environmentalists.

TIP
Use commas around nouns that (re)name the previous noun and are grammatically parallel with it.

Use commas around true appositives. Sometimes, however, the second noun completes the first, giving essential information. In this case, do not set off the second noun with a comma. If in doubt, remove the second noun or noun phrase and see if the sentence is still complete and makes grammatical sense.

The lion, king of the beasts, is the subject of many fables by the ancient Greek writer Aesop.

Why are there commas around *king of the beasts* but not before *Aesop*? Which is the true appositive?

TIP
Combining rules: The following sentence illustrates appositive rule 3b and independent clause rule 2a.
His first purchase, [3b] the painting of the Northern Ontario landscape by Tom Thomson, [3b] is now worth thousands of dollars, [2a] but he says he will never sell it.

3c: If a word or phrase interrupts the flow of the sentence, use commas. Such words or phrases—including *after all, for example, however, in fact, indeed, needless to say,* and *therefore*—often emphasize or qualify a thought.

I believe, however, that there are only two seasons in Canada. They are, I feel, winter and construction.

TIP
Use commas around words and phrases that interrupt the flow of the sentence.

←13 See "Prepositional Phrases" for more examples of adverbs and adverbial phrases.

Rule Category 4: Conventional and "Comma Sense" Uses

In addition to those given above, a number of other comma rules must be followed.

4a: Use commas to set off the name of the person being addressed directly.

I can tell, Naomi, that you really do understand the math concepts taught last week.

4b: Coordinate adjectives are used to describe the same noun and are interchangeable. If you can use *and* between them, add commas.

The tall, gangly baby giraffe was born yesterday.

4c: Use a comma to separate a quotation from the rest of the sentence, as in attributions (i.e., where a source is named).

The sign says, "Trespassers will be prosecuted."

"I am not a crook," said Richard Nixon.

TIP
Use commas between coordinate adjectives before a noun; with dates, addresses, and titles; and before and after direct quotations.

4d: Use a comma to distinguish names and locations in addresses.

The Prime Minister of Canada, 24 Sussex Drive, Ottawa, Ontario, Canada

Convention also dictates that you place a comma after the name of a province, territory, state, or country if the sentence continues.

I lived in Calgary, Alberta, until I moved back to Quebec.

4e: Use a comma to separate the day and year in a date. Do not use a comma in day-month-year or month-year format.

October 7, 1951

but

7 October 1951; October 1951

4f: Use commas to separate degrees, titles, and similar designations.

Sabrina Yao, MD, PhD, FRCPS

4g: Use commas to separate groups of three digits in non-metric numbers.

The output of chemical waste was 13,890,457 tons per day for that factory.

In 2016, the population of Nunavut was 35,944, according to Statistics Canada.

In 2019, the daily circulation of the print edition of *The Globe and Mail* averaged 899,000 Canadians.

In the metric system, insert a space rather than a comma between every three digits in a number of more than four digits (the space is optional with four-digit numbers).

13 890 457; 29 474; 2356

4h: Place commas and periods inside quotation marks and most other punctuation outside. (In the UK, the convention is to place commas and periods outside quotation marks).

The new topic, "Where Ecological Ends Meet," has been posted.

We have been told that our meals "are not gratis"; however, the company has paid for our transportation.

4i: In some cases, you will have to apply "comma sense." If a sentence seems confusing when you read it, you might need to insert a comma to clarify it. Commas in the following sentences ensure the sense intended.

In 1971, 773 people were killed in an earthquake in Peru.

He asked his team to meet in his office now, and again the following week.

---TIP

Your instructor can tell you whether to use metric style when writing. Otherwise, use the industry standard for your profession.

Commas are used between some elements in addresses, dates, degrees, and numbers and between quotations and their source.

---TIP

Place commas and periods inside quotation marks and most other punctuation outside.

Combining rules: The following sentence illustrates the rule for comma use with quotations (4h) and the independent clause rule 2c.

"You should always put periods and commas inside quotation marks," [4h] said Professor LeGuin, [2c] "though this system is predominant in North America and may not apply in other countries."

Note that because the second half of the quotation is a continuation of the speaker's sentence, there is no capital letter on *though*.

Add commas to the following sentences where required and name the rule category you use (each sentence may reflect either one or two rules).

1. While he was waiting for the bus he read his graphic novel.

2. Because he was hungry he ordered hash browns two eggs bacon and toast.

3. I would like to buy an electric car and a new bicycle after I graduate.

4. Lions tigers and bears are not all found in the North American wilderness.

5. While most of the class wants to leave early John however does not.

6. The CN Tower was the world's tallest free-standing structure until the 1990s.

7. My white cocker spaniel Trixie is very spoiled.

8. The dusty pans in the damp broken cupboard need to be replaced.

9. "Stop" she yelled.

10. I wanted to buy his portrait but it wasn't for sale.

After you've checked your answers in Appendix D, complete questions 11–20.

11. As well as rare hybrid roses the nursery carries a wide range of orchids.

12. It feels hotter than the actual temperature because of the humidity.

13. Ryan Reynolds a Canadian actor is famous for his kindness to fans.

14. Even though most people are aware of global warming and climate change fewer understand how to calculate their *carbon footprint*.

15. *YouTube has been a popular video channel but now TikTok is favoured by young people.*

16. Trust is important in any relationship and it always takes time to develop.

17. People have immigrated to Canada from countries in Asia Europe the Middle East and Central and South America.

18. Caffeine which is a stimulant is unregulated and completely legal.

19. Understanding grammar is important yet very few people study it.

20. "Although we all should vote" stated Niko "not enough people do."

Add commas to the following sentences where required. More than one comma rule applies in most sentences.

1. Even though I had planned my trip for months I had forgotten to pack essentials so I had to buy them on my trip.

2. My trip included stops in Moscow St. Petersburg and Vladivostok before I returned home to Saint John New Brunswick.

3. My sister Tamara came with me despite being afraid of flying.

4. Her first flight was on May 30 2001 but she never flew after that.

5. The flight attendant who was fluent in English and Russian was very kind to my sister on this trip.

6. Julie the flight attendant had worked for Air Canada for 15 years but now she worked for KLM.

7. Julie said that while Air Canada was a good company to work for she wanted to live in Amsterdam.

8. My trip to Russia while planned in detail was full of surprises.

9. I did not expect such hot humid weather in St. Petersburg.

10. Before I go to Russia again I will study the language so that I can communicate with more people.

After you've checked your answers in Appendix D, complete questions 11–20.

11. The Model T the first mass-produced automobile was available in any colour as long as you wanted black.

12. Timira completed her biology exam her English oral exam and her math quiz all in one day following two weeks of little sleep few meals and a lot of studying.

13. Steven had to go into the city to buy paints and palettes canvasses brushes and primer in order to complete his mammoth costly project.

14. Canadian artists such as Keanu Reeves often do not achieve fame unless they move to the USA namely Hollywood.

15. After visiting her ancestral homeland China and meeting her sisters from her mother's first marriage Amy Tan wrote the novel *The Joy Luck Club*.

16. The woman in the red hat is in charge of ticket sales.

17. On August 1 2011 the CN Tower introduced a new feature known as the EdgeWalk.

18. Unless something is done quickly many children will become obese because they get little daily exercise.

19. Donald Sutherland is known to many generations of Canadians because of his decades of screen work but many young people know him as President Snow the despised leader in the movie *The Hunger Games*.

20. Jeff Deffenbacher PhD a specialist in anger management thinks that some people have a low tolerance for everyday annoyances.

When Commas Are Not Required

Do not use a comma to separate simple compounds (two words, or phrases joined by a conjunction such as *and*). Only a series of three or more items requires commas.

INCORRECT	**Some of the heaviest damage from steroid use occurs to the heart, and the liver. [two nouns]**
	Logging reduces the number of old-growth forests, and destroys these habitats. [two predicates: *reduces . . .* and *destroys . . .*]
CORRECT	**Some of the heaviest damage from steroid use occurs to the heart and the liver.**
	Logging reduces the number of old-growth forests and destroys these habitats.

Do not use a comma to separate the subject and the predicate. This error is probably the result of writers mistakenly applying the "pause" non-rule.

INCORRECT	**The only way our society is going to be fixed, is if we change our laws.**
	One advantage in using helicopters to fight fires, is the accuracy of their drops over the scene of the fire.
CORRECT	**The only way our society is going to be fixed is if we change our laws.**
	One advantage in using helicopters to fight fires is the accuracy of their drops over the scene of the fire.

It is easy to be distracted by parentheses (or round brackets) and mistakenly insert a comma between a subject and a predicate. In the following example, another option is to add a comma after *Medicine* and after *sports* and remove the parentheses:

| INCORRECT | **The American College of Sports Medicine (a body that advances research into exercise and sports), considers all physically active females at risk for developing eating disorders.** |
| CORRECT | **The American College of Sports Medicine, a body that advances research into exercise and sports, considers all physically active females at risk for developing eating disorders.** |

→14 "Dashes and Parentheses" later in this chapter discusses parentheses.

Do not use a comma alone to join independent clauses or with a word other than a coordinating conjunction (one of the FANBOYS words). This produces a comma splice, which is a serious grammatical error.

INCORRECT	**Football is one of the most popular sports in North America, it is also one of the most brutal of all sports.**
	You must use the buttons provided at the bottom of the pages to navigate through the application, otherwise, you could lose your connection.
CORRECT	**Football is one of the most popular sports in North America. It is also one of the most brutal of all sports.**
	You must use the buttons provided at the bottom of the pages to navigate through the application; otherwise, you could lose your connection.

TIP

In the second sentence, a semicolon is used after the independent clause. Semicolons will be discussed in the section on semicolons under "Other Forms of Punctuation" later in this chapter.

Chapter 13 provides more information on comma splices.

Add commas in these paragraphs, following the rule categories discussed in this chapter and avoiding comma splices. A few commas have been included to help with comprehension, but they may be incorrect.

1. Since the Peloton was introduced in February 2012 many people have decided to stop going to the gym and they are exercising at home with the use of modern equipment and online classes. In addition, to the Peloton there are now smart exercise mirrors online classes and virtual running cycling swimming or walking challenges. These tools seem to be an improvement over the older exercise equipment that people bought but didn't use. There are numerous stories of treadmills being used for storing clothing on, exercise bikes collecting dust in the corner and exercise DVDs that are in an unused dusty drawer. Because of the price of the newer equipment and the instant availability of classes online experts say that people will exercise more than in the past. However all of the above ignores the problem of staying motivated enough to continue an exercise program in order to get fit. If someone could invent a bottle of motivation and sell it at a reasonable price Canadians might become fitter.

2. Autism is a much misunderstood problem, often children with autism are viewed as a "handful" and "hyperactive." Very little is known of its causes and characteristics can vary making a diagnosis difficult. In children it is even harder because other children can exhibit some of the characteristics associated with autism. Although autism can cause many behavioural difficulties autistic children can still live near-normal lives if they are surrounded by understanding caregivers. Working with autistic children can change a person and make one realize the need for better understanding and education. Treating autism can be difficult because often there is no feedback from the patient. Over the years there have been many ideas of how to treat autism but not all were correct and have at times made treatment problematic.

Other Forms of Punctuation

The careful use of semicolons, colons, dashes, and parentheses gives your writing polish and precision. The semicolon and colon are stronger, more emphatic marks of punctuation than the comparatively mild-mannered comma. Learn how to use these marks to implement stronger breaks, longer pauses, and emphasis in your writing.

Semicolons

As discussed, one of the major functions of commas is to separate independent clauses in a compound sentence. Two rules for semicolons also involve independent clauses; the third rule is to separate items in a series that contains commas.

1. To join independent clauses: You may use a semicolon rather than a comma and a coordinating conjunction (FANBOYS) to join independent clauses if there is a close relationship between them. A semicolon alerts the reader to this connection. Consider the following examples:

> **My family went camping for the weekend, and my cousins went to their cottage.**

> **My family went camping for the weekend; my cousins went to their cottage.**

> **Yesterday, I took my car in for repair, and I picked up my new computer.**

In the first set of sentences, the second clause is related to the preceding one. They both involve family, so they have a shared focus. Therefore, a semicolon can be used. However, in the third sentence, there is not a shared focus, so a semicolon cannot be used.

Additionally, a semicolon is often used if you want to stress a contrast between two independent clauses, as in these examples:

> **Scott was impatient to get married; Salome wanted to wait until they were financially secure.**

> **Japanese food is generally good for you; fast food is not healthy.**

Note that the semicolons in both sentences could be replaced by a comma and the coordinating conjunction *but*—they could not be replaced by a comma alone.

Here are other examples where a semicolon stresses the close relationship between independent clauses:

> **Gymnastics is not just any sport; it's one of the most challenging and physically taxing of all sports.**

> **Some children may have lost a parent due to illness or divorce; others may have been cared for by grandparents or other relatives.**

2. To join independent clauses by using a conjunctive adverb: The second rule involves using a semicolon with a conjunctive adverb or a transitional phrase followed by an independent clause. Table 14.1 lists the most common conjunctive adverbs and transitional phrases. In the following examples, these terms are underlined.

> **My roommate lacks charm, friendliness, and humour; <u>still</u>, he is an excellent cook.**

> **I like my courses this semester; <u>however</u>, I dislike having three 8:00 a.m. classes.**

TIP
Use a semicolon to replace a comma + a coordinating conjunction in closely related independent clauses.

TIP
Do not use a semicolon to separate an independent clause from a dependent clause.

→ 14 The section "Rule Category 2: Independent Clauses" provides the rules for punctuating independent and dependent clauses.

TIP
A conjunctive adverb acts as a conjunction. They often indicate a more complex relationship between independent clauses.

TABLE 14.1 Common Conjunctive Adverbs/Transitional Phrases

accordingly	likewise
afterward	meanwhile
also	moreover
as a result	namely
besides	nevertheless
certainly	next
consequently	nonetheless
finally	on the contrary
for example	on the other hand
further(more)	otherwise
hence	similarly
however	still
if not	subsequently
in addition	that is
indeed	then
in fact	therefore
instead	thus
in the meantime	undoubtedly
later	

Adverbs such as *however* and *therefore* can act as ordinary adverbs (interrupters) or as conjunctive adverbs (joiners). A common error is to confuse these uses. The following sentences illustrate this distinction. The first requires commas because the adverb occurs in the clause as an interruption between the subject *he* and most of its predicate. In the second, a semicolon is required before the conjunctive adverb because *however* is joining two independent clauses:

> **Dr Suzuki will not be in his office this week; he will, <u>however</u>, be making his rounds at the hospital.**

> **Dr Suzuki will not be in his office this week; <u>however</u>, he will be making his rounds at the hospital.**

In the following sentences, *therefore* changes its function from interrupter to joiner:

> **The CEO has been called away for an emergency briefing; her secretary, <u>therefore</u>, will have to cancel her appointments.**

> **The CEO has been called away for an emergency briefing; <u>therefore</u>, her secretary will have to cancel her appointments.**

← 13 See Chapter 13 for more about conjunctions.

TIP

Use a semicolon before words such as *however* and *therefore* if they are joining independent clauses. Follow the joining word/phrase by a comma.

At first, it seems that the only difference between these sentences is *therefore*'s placement. If you look closely, though, you can see that changing the word's position can change its function. In the second sentence, an independent clause precedes and follows *therefore*, requiring the semicolon before and the comma after. (The comma is required because *therefore* introduces an independent clause.)

Be careful not to confuse the words and phrases in Table 14.1 with subordinating conjunctions, another large group of joiners that connect dependent to independent clauses. *Although* and *whereas* are sometimes mistaken for conjunctive adverbs, but they are subordinating conjunctions and cannot be used to join two independent clauses.

Examples:

Conjunctive adverb:

The tests will be held in class every two weeks; on the other hand, the exams will only be held twice.

Subordinating conjunction:

Although we have tests every other week, we only have two exams.

3. **To separate items in a series (the serial semicolon):** A semicolon can be used between items in a series if one or more of the elements contain commas. Without semicolons, these sentences would be confusing:

Her whirlwind tour included stops in London, England; Paris, France; Einhoven, The Netherlands; and Berlin, Germany.

In order to form the club, we have Amy, the president; Sam, the vice-president; Samira, the treasurer; and Emi, the secretary.

You may also use semicolons to separate items in a list where each piece is a long phrase or clause, especially if there is internal punctuation. Using semicolons to separate the items makes this sentence easier to read:

The role of the vice-president will be to enhance the school's external relations; strengthen its relationship with alumni, donors, and business and community leaders; implement a fundraising program; and increase the school's involvement in the community.

> **TIP**
> Subordinating conjunctions make an independent clause dependent, so the dependent clause must then be joined to an independent clause.

 See "Joiners: Prepositions and Conjunctions" for more on dependent and independent clauses.

> **TIP**
> Don't put a semicolon before or a comma after subordinating conjunctions (e.g., *although* or *whereas*). They do not join independent clauses but introduce dependent ones.

> **TIP**
> A semicolon can be used between items in a series if one or more of the elements contain commas or if one of the elements is much longer than the others.

EXERCISE 14.4

Read the following sentences and insert the correct punctuation. You may need to move some words within a sentence to make it correct.

1. One of my roommates rode her bicycle to school most of the time therefore she is more physically fit than I am.

2. SPCA officers work for but are not paid by the government it is donations in fact that provide their salary.

3. If homelessness continues to increase it will be costly for taxpayers moreover homelessness affects downtown businesses.

4. Although sailing is a popular sport among older people younger adults cannot afford the price of boats.

5. Many young people however enjoy kayaking or paddle boarding.

TIP

A semicolon should be preceded and followed by an independent clause unless it is being used to separate items in a series.

Do not use a semicolon if what follows it is a fragment. In the first example below, an incomplete verb form (an *–ing*) follows the punctuation. In the second sentence, a prepositional phrase (*such as* and two nouns) follows. In both cases, a comma should replace the incorrect semicolon to separate the independent clause from the concluding phrase.

> INCORRECT **Valuable land is destroyed when it is cleared for grazing; reducing habitats for other animals.**
> **For many years, Canada has been a leader in multiculturalism, along with a few other countries; such as the United States and England.**

Do not use a semicolon to introduce a list or series; a colon is correct.

> INCORRECT **Shakespeare's last plays are sometimes called romances and include the following; *Cymbeline*, *A Winter's Tale*, and *The Tempest*.**

Colons

It is often said that a semicolon brings the reader to a brief stop, but the colon leads the reader on. The colon has three main uses: to set up a quotation, to set up or introduce a list or series, and to separate an independent clause from a word, phrase, or clause that answers, completes, or expands on what precedes it.

TIP

You may use a colon to set up a direct quotation if the preceding thought is complete and fully expressed.

1. To set up a quotation: When you use direct quotations in your essays, you can set them up formally with a colon.

> The *Oxford English Dictionary* defines the word *rhetoric* this way: "The art of using language so as to persuade or influence others."

> Health Canada has made the following recommendation for dentists: "Non-mercury filling materials should be considered for restoring the primary teeth of children where the mechanical properties of the material are safe."

Direct quotations can also be set up less formally with a comma or no punctuation. To determine which is appropriate, treat the complete sentence as if it contained no quotation and see if one of the rules for using commas applies.

> According to the American Academy of Dermatology, "a tan is the skin's response to an injury, and every time you tan, you accumulate damage to the skin."

> **The most general definition of evolution is "any non-miraculous process by which new forms of life are produced" (Bowler 2).**

In the first sentence, a comma rule dictates the use of a comma before the quotation; in the second, there is no rule that necessitates a comma. A comma after *is* would be incorrect.

2. To set up or introduce a list or series: The most formal way to set up a list or series is to make a complete statement followed by a colon and the list of items.

> **Before going camping, you need to prepare many items: a tent, food, water, clothing, and lighting.**

Do not insert a colon before you start the list unless you write a complete sentence first. Normally, you would not use a colon after *including* or *such as* or right after a linking verb (e.g., *is* or *are*), though these words are often used to set up a list or series.

INCORRECT   **Caffeine withdrawal can have many negative effects, such as: severe headaches, drowsiness, irritability, and poor concentration.**
One of the questions the committee will attempt to answer is: Does our current public-health system work?

CORRECT   **Caffeine withdrawal can have many negative effects, such as severe headaches, drowsiness, irritability, and poor concentration.**
One of the questions the committee will attempt to answer is, Does our current public-health system work?

3. To separate an independent clause from a word, phrase, or clause that answers, completes, or expands on what comes before it: What follows a colon may answer, complete, or expand on what is asked or implied in the preceding independent clause. This could be as little as a word or as much as an independent clause. Like the comma and semicolon, then, the colon can be used to separate independent clauses; however, what follows the colon must answer the question asked in the previous clause.

> **There is only one quality you omitted from the list of my most endearing characteristics: my modesty.** [answers, What quality?]

> **David's driving test was a memorable experience: he backed over a curb, sailed through two stop signs, and forgot to signal a left turn.** [answers, Why was the test memorable?]

> **The New Testament of the Bible gives the ultimate rule for Christians: to treat others the way you want them to treat you.** [answers, What rule?]

If what follows the colon is at least the equivalent of an independent clause, it may begin with a capital letter. It is perfectly acceptable to begin with a lowercase letter, however, as in the examples.

> **TIP**
> You may use a colon to separate an independent clause from a word, phrase, or clause that answers or completes what precedes it.
> What precedes a colon must be an independent clause that makes a complete statement.

Dashes and Parentheses

Although some people use em dashes (named because they are the width of the letter *m*) and parentheses interchangeably, their functions are different. Imagine that you are in a crowded room where everyone is talking. Somebody takes you aside and begins speaking in an unnaturally loud voice about the latest rumour; other people are listening, which is the design of the person talking. A couple of minutes later, somebody else approaches and very discreetly whispers the same information in your ear. Using em dashes is like giving information that is meant to be overheard, to be stressed. But information in parentheses is more like an aside. Parentheses enclose additional information that is not important enough to be included in the main part of the sentence.

Em dashes, then, emphasize a word or phrase or convey a break in thought. You can find em dashes in Microsoft Word by choosing *Insert*, then *Symbol*, *More Symbols*, and *Special Characters*. Another option is to use the shortcut key: Ctrl Alt – (minus on the number pad).

Don't use one hyphen if you want to set off a word or phrase. Hyphens are a mark of spelling—not punctuation.

Where dashes emphasize, parentheses de-emphasize. Use them sparingly to include a word or phrase, or occasionally a sentence, that isn't important enough to be included as part of the main text. You may also use parentheses to refer to a source in a research essay.

"Crayolas plus imagination (the ability to create images) make for happiness if you are a child" (Robert Fulghum).

Punctuating parenthetical insertions depends on whether the statement in parentheses is complete or part of the larger sentence. If it is complete, place the end punctuation inside the closing parenthesis, as the punctuation pertains only to what is between the parentheses. (For example, the period in this sentence goes inside.)

If the parentheses enclose part of the larger sentence, punctuate the sentence just as you would if there were no parentheses. The following sentence illustrates punctuation that has nothing to do with the parenthetical insertion but is required to separate independent clauses. Notice the lower-casing of *both*:

Cassandra wanted to be an actor (both her parents were actors), but she always trembled violently as soon as she stepped on a stage.

Use dashes and parentheses sparingly in your writing.

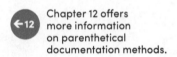

Chapter 12 offers more information on parenthetical documentation methods.

TIP

You may use em dashes occasionally to set off words from the rest of the sentence.

TIP

You may use parentheses to include less important information of the sentence.

Using the rule categories discussed, place the proper punctuation.

1. May flowers bring on my asthma October leaf mould affects my allergies.

2. Every essay needs three parts an introduction a body and a conclusion.

3. He travelled to the honeymoon capital of the world Niagara Falls.

4. Mayumi tended to look on the good side of things Glenn usually saw the bad side.

5. The following is not a rule for comma use put a comma wherever you pause.

6. While I agree that studying math is important I can't understand the use for algebra.

7. Marselina who has a fine ear for music can't sing a note.

8. Whenever I order designer clothing for my boutique, I shop in Toronto, Ontario, Buffalo, New York, and London, England.

9. The Online Dictionary defines animal cruelty this way "treatment or standards of care that cause unwarranted or unnecessary suffering or harm to animals."

10. The tuition increase has affected many lower income families therefore there is an even greater demand for student loans.

After you've checked your answers in Appendix D, complete questions 11–20.

11. In order to calculate the area needed you must use geometry.

12. Gerald preferred large trucks his wife liked small cars.

13. Sam a bit player in our theatre group is an accountant.

14. His plans for the new development included the following an apartment complex single-family residences a 60-store mall and a multi-use recreation centre.

15. Oil electricity and solar power are popular sources for heating homes however the most popular is natural gas.

16. The tour includes visits to the following museums the Prado in Madrid Spain the Louvre in Paris France and the Rijksmuseum in Amsterdam the Netherlands.

17. I thought planting trees was the ideal summer job Benjamin however did not.

18. School cafeterias often offer unhealthy options, such as hot dogs, which have virtually no nutritional value, hamburgers, which have a high fat content, and poutine, known as "heart attack in a bowl."

19. The zero emissions of a battery-electric vehicle come with a drawback, the emissions are only as clean as the means used to generate the power.

20. As rainwater especially that coming off the lake travels downward through the soil it may collect a number of pollutants furthermore an extended period of time may elapse before this pollution is discovered.

Correct or add commas in the following passage. Among your changes and additions, include at least one semicolon.

1. Swimming in the lake is one of the joys of a Canadian summer. In the winter those who live close to a lake dream of warm days picnics on the beach the smell of suntan lotion and the sound of waves rolling into shore. Swimming however is a skill that needs to be learned one cannot simply go to the lake swim and be safe. Not knowing how to swim can lead to needless drownings. There are many Canadians who believe that the basic swimming skills need to be taught to all children especially if they are going to spend any time near water. Because of this organizations are trying to raise money to send children to swimming classes. Organizations fundraise so that parents have access to funds to pay for their children's swimming lessons. Some people feel that as many refugees and immigrants come from areas where swimming was not possible these children really need to learn the skills required to understand respect and swim in the water. With more children learning how to swim through this funding, the summer dream of spending the day in the lake safely is becoming attainable.

Apostrophes

> The apostrophe is a mark of spelling that indicates the possessive or shows where letters have been omitted in a contraction.

Technically, the apostrophe isn't a mark of punctuation; it is a mark of spelling that indicates the possessive case of nouns and some indefinite pronouns. It is also used in contractions, to show the omission of one or more letters.

Apostrophes for Possession in Nouns

> The possessive case indicates relationships such as ownership.

The possessive case indicates ownership and similar relationships between nouns and pronouns, such as association, authorship, duration, description, and source of origin. The possessive indicates that the second noun belongs to or is associated with the first. When an apostrophe and *s* are added to a noun to show the possessive, the noun functions as an adjective and can be replaced by the corresponding possessive adjective. Most pronouns, however, do not show the possessive through an apostrophe.

> **the hard drive of the computer/the computer's hard drive/its hard drive [ownership]**
>
> **the landlady's apartment/her apartment [ownership]**
>
> **the tenants' rights/their rights [association]**
>
> **Dvorak's *New World Symphony*/his symphony [authorship]**

Singular Nouns

> **TIP**
> Singular nouns take an apostrophe + *s* to indicate the possessive.

The usual rule with a singular noun, including proper nouns ending in *s*, *ss*, or the *s* sound, is to add *'s* to make it possessive.

> **the attorney's portfolio; Mr Price's car; the week's lesson**

Because it may look and sound awkward to add an apostrophe + *s* to a singular proper noun ending in *s*, some authorities add only the apostrophe (e.g., *Tracy Jarvis' book*, meaning *the book of Tracy Jarvis*). Others follow the rule for singular nouns (*Tracy Jarvis's book*). Either treatment is acceptable. When you are writing your essay, choose one or ask your instructor which to use and apply it consistently.

Plural Nouns

With a plural noun, an apostrophe is added after the *s* to make it possessive.

> **the islands' inhabitants; the Hansons' children; the Gibbses' marriage certificate; two weeks' lessons; the readers' perceptions**

Make sure you carefully distinguish between singular and plural nouns when applying the rules for possessives.

company + 's	→	**the company's profits** [one company]
companies + '	→	**the companies' profits** [more than one company]
society + 's	→	**our society's attitude toward war** [one society]
societies + '	→	**past societies' attitudes toward war** [many societies]

A few plural nouns do not end in *s*: *children, women, men, people*. They are treated as singular nouns for the possessive.

> **the popular children's book; the women's group**

Joint Ownership

In the case of joint ownership, where both nouns share or are equal parties in something, only the last noun shows the possessive. Decide from the context of the sentence if both nouns reflect a truly equal, shared relationship. In the following sentences, the assumption is that Salem and Sheena shared hosting duties at one party but that the general manager and the district manager received separate wages:

> **I attended Salem and Sheena's party.**
>
> **Morana raised the general manager's and the district manager's wages.**

Piaget and Montessori did not share the same belief or theory:

INCORRECT	**Piaget and Montessori's beliefs about how children learn were similar in many ways.**
CORRECT	**Piaget's and Montessori's beliefs about how children learn were similar in many ways.**

Apostrophes are sometimes misused with plural nouns. Avoid the following incorrect uses:

INCORRECT	**I have 6 CD's.**
	TV's are on sale this week.

The 1990's were a decade of extravagant spending.
The lemon's are on sale this week.

Exception: Apostrophes can be used for clarity with numbers, letters, or symbols to indicate the plural.

Adrian got two A's and three B's this semester.

Apostrophes with Indefinite Pronouns

Like nouns, but unlike other kinds of pronouns, many indefinite pronouns take an apostrophe + s to show the possessive.

In times of stress, it is not in *one's* best interest to act quickly or reflexively. [i.e., the best interest of one]

Contractions

The second main use of the apostrophe is to show missing letters. People often confuse the contraction *it's* (*it is*) with the possessive form *its* (as in *I gave the dog its bone*). The contraction *who's* (*who is*) is sometimes confused with the possessive form *whose* (*the man whose house I'm renting*). Contractions are not generally used in formal writing. You should check with your instructor to see if they are acceptable in your assignment.

> Indefinite pronouns, unlike personal pronouns, take an apostrophe + s to indicate the possessive (e.g., *one's beliefs*).

> **TIP**
> Don't confuse *its*, the possessive pronoun, with *it's*, the contraction for *it is*.

EXERCISE 14.7

For the following sentences, add apostrophes and make any other necessary changes to the nouns requiring the possessive.

1. Societys rules do not always correspond to behaviour.
2. My aunt and uncles cottage is for sale; its list price is $450,000.
3. Ones education should not depend on the financial resources of ones parents.
4. The schools biggest draw for new students was the brand-new recreation complex.
5. The citys buses run on natural gas its more cost-effective.
6. Johns biggest complaint is about the schools expensive cafeterias.
7. Ryans and Jessicas birthday is on the same day.
8. Apples, oranges, mangoes, and tomatoes are the stores specials today.
9. Its a shame that Lennys parents werent able to attend their sons graduation ceremonies. (Lenny is an only child.)
10. I dont know whether this etching is theirs, but theres no doubt its worth a lot in todays market.

The following passage concerns responses to the article "Spin Doctors," posted on the Canoe website. Punctuate the text for correctness and effectiveness, ensuring that all punctuation is used properly. Minimal punctuation has been provided in places to aid in understanding; however, some may be incorrect.

Reader reaction was swift and impassioned. The sites traffic which averages 65 to 70 million views each month experienced an additional 50,000 page views within the first 10 days of the posting. The investigation drew more than 400 letters to the editor hundred's of emails to the message boards and more than 16,000 responses to an online poll.

The intensity of the response surprised veteran investigative journalist Wayne MacPhail the articles author. Although the sheer volume of letters was unexpected it proved to him that there was an audience for online journalism in Canada. MacPhail has experimented with hypertext reporting since the late 1980s but outside of "Spin Doctors" he believes that by and large newspapers have done a "woeful job" of building an audience for Web-based investigative reporting. . . .

Unlike it's media rivals Canoe has never made journalism it's only or even its most important focus. A headline announcing the top story of the day appears underneath the Canoe banner but there are so many other things to do, shopping email contests Web utilities and lifestyle tips all compete with the news.

The CNEWS section isnt necessarily the first place people are expected to go on the network though it is usually at the top of the highlighted sections. It is also part of the site that changes the most during daylight hours. In other words when CNEWS changes the entire home page changes. A "This Just In" feature was recently added but theres no set schedule for posting stories. Despite this expansion of the news section Canoes promotional material drives home the message that the site is about much more than current events. One recent ad reads, "shop chat email read, in that order."

Stevens, Tara. "Paddling into Cyberspace." *Review of Journalism*, Spring 2000, https://rrj.ca/1075/.

Chapter Review Questions

1. What are the comma rules?
2. When should you not use a comma?
3. Identify at least one comma use that you did not already know or that you had previously learned incorrectly.
4. When do you use semicolons?
5. When should you not use a semicolon?
6. When do you use colons?
7. When should you not use a colon?
8. Why do you use dashes or parentheses?
9. What are the rules for apostrophe use?
10. Provide examples of incorrect apostrophe use that you have seen outside the classroom.

15 Agreement, Pronoun, and Sentence Structure Errors

By the end of this chapter, you should be able to

- ensure subject–verb agreement;
- fix pronoun errors;
- edit for gender bias;
- use modifiers for clarity; and
- use parallelism to create clear sentences.

The grammar rules discussed in this chapter are easily missed when you are writing an essay draft. Your credibility as a writer will be improved and your documents will be easy to understand when you avoid these relatively common errors.

▲ Photo: Lamai Prasitsuwan/Shutterstock

Agreement

If the subject of a sentence is singular, such as *the student*, then the verb must be singular as well, as in *The student has an online class this semester*. If the subject is plural, such as *the students*, the verb must be plural, as in *The students have an online class this semester*. If you are replacing a noun with a pronoun, both must also match in number, person, and gender, as in *Thomas bought his mother a present*. When the gender is unknown, then a gender-inclusive pronoun (*them*, *they*, *their*) should be used. These forms of agreement reinforce the close connection between a subject and the verb, and the close connection between a noun and the pronoun that replaces it.

Subject–Verb Agreement

Deciding whether a subject is singular or plural is not always straightforward. The specific rules explained here help you apply the important principle of subject–verb agreement.

Usually, the subject of a sentence or clause is the noun or pronoun that performs the action of the verb (or that exists in the state expressed by the subject complement). In most cases, the subject is before the verb and is easy to find.

<u>Kevin and Nigel</u> *are* happy that they passed the exam.

Sometimes the subject is harder to spot for one of the following reasons.

1. The sentence begins with *Here is/are*, *There is/are*, *There has/have been*, etc. Because the subject follows the verb, you have to look for the first noun/pronoun to determine whether the subject is singular or plural. In the following examples the noun is underlined and the verb is italicized:

There *are* many <u>reasons</u> to support the legalization of marijuana.

Here *is* one <u>person</u> who supports raising the drinking age.

2. The sentence is phrased as a question. You may need to look for the number of the subject.

What *is* the main <u>reason</u> for legalizing marijuana?

Where *are* all the <u>people</u> who are in favour of raising the drinking age?

3. The subject is delayed. Because the sentence begins with a prepositional phrase, the noun(s) may seem to form the subject, which is actually later in the sentence. You can always rearrange these kinds of sentences to confirm that they use a delayed subject construction.

After the long drive to the city, finding a place to park *was* <u>our first goal</u>.

Agreement means that a verb must agree with its subject and a pronoun must agree with its antecedent, or the noun it replaces.

 Chapter 13 discusses pronouns and antecedents.

Subject–verb agreement means that a verb must agree with (i.e., match) its subject in number—that is, a singular subject requires a singular verb, and a plural subject requires a plural verb.

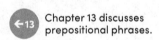
TIP
If a sentence begins with a phrase such as *Here/There is*, is a question, or uses a delayed subject construction, look ahead to find the subject.

 Chapter 13 discusses prepositional phrases.

A **delayed subject** appears after a prepositional phrase and the verb.

Sentence rearranged with subject first:

<u>Our first goal</u> *was* finding a place to park after the long drive to the city.

Among Graham's favourites *was* <u>the latest album</u> by Yukon Blonde.

Sentence rearranged:

<u>The latest album</u> by Yukon Blonde *was* among Graham's favourites.

4. For linking verbs, always examine the subject closely. Don't be distracted by what follows the verb; the subject alone determines whether the verb is singular or plural.

Tanning <u>salons</u> *are* not the safest way to get a tan.

The <u>topic</u> for discussion tomorrow *is* the pros and cons of indoor tanning.

5. A noun or pronoun that directly follows a preposition (e.g., *of*) cannot act as a subject; it is the object of the preposition. If there are several nouns before the verb, backtrack carefully to find the noun or pronoun that is the subject of the sentence. You can put parentheses around the distracting words:

> **TIP**
>
> If several nouns come before the verb, identify the true noun/pronoun subject before deciding whether the verb should be singular or plural.

A long <u>list</u> (of items, including vegetables, fruits, meats, and several kinds of bread) *was* handed to Tao.

The <u>roots</u> (of his dissatisfaction)(with the course) *go* very deep.

A related problem occurs when a writer mistakes a prepositional phrase or even a dependent clause for a subject. The following sentences can be fixed by omitting the preposition and beginning the sentence with the noun subject:

← 13 Chapter 13 discusses dependent clauses.

INCORRECT **By choosing to take a few correspondence courses may afford a student athlete greater flexibility in meeting academic requirements.**

By choosing has been mistaken for the subject.

CORRECT **<u>Choosing</u> *to take* a few correspondence courses may afford a student athlete greater flexibility.**

INCORRECT **With the development of the computer led to automated robots on the production line.**

With the development of the computer has been mistaken for the subject.

CORRECT **The <u>development</u> of the computer *led* to automated robots on the production line.**

INCORRECT **Although Edna thinks of her children at the last moment before her death does not change the fact she still *is willing* to leave them.**

Although Edna thinks of her children at the last moment before her death, a dependent clause, has been mistaken for the subject. A dependent clause contains its own subject.

CORRECT **Although Edna thinks of her children at the last moment before her death, <u>she</u> still *is willing* to leave them.**
Edna thinks of her children at the last moment before her death, though this does not change the fact that <u>she</u> still *is willing* to leave them.

Rules for Subject–Verb Agreement

 The section "Precision and Logic" in Chapter 16 also discusses subject–verb agreement.

1. A compound subject joined by the conjunction *and* usually requires a plural verb form.

    Thanh <u>and</u> his friend *are* visiting Ottawa.

A compound subject contains two nouns, two pronouns, or a noun and a pronoun acting as one subject.

Occasionally, a compound subject expresses a single idea.

<u>Rhythm and blues</u> *was* always popular with younger audiences.

<u>To compare and contrast</u> the roles of setting in the novels *is* sure to be a question on the exam.

In both examples, the compound subject can be treated as a singular subject since the elements are so closely connected that separating them changes their meaning.

2. When the nouns or pronouns in a compound subject are linked by a correlative conjunction (*either . . . or* or *neither . . . nor*), the noun or pronoun nearest the verb determines its form. These conjunctions suggest a choice between one thing or the other much more than *and*.

    The chairs <u>or the table</u> *is* going to auction.

    The table <u>or the chairs</u> *are* going to auction.

    Neither famine <u>nor floods</u> *are* going to force the people to leave their homes.

    Neither floods <u>nor famine</u> *is* going to force the people to leave their homes.

Note that when you change the order of the nouns making up the compound subject in these sentences, you need to change the number of the verb as well.

TIP
When using a compound subject, look at the joining word(s) to determine whether the subject is singular or plural.

3. A prepositional phrase can also be used to join two nouns in a compound subject. *As well as*, *along with*, *in addition to*, *together with*, and *combined with* are examples of such phrases, which do not have the strength of *and*. When you use one of these joiners,

you stress the first element more than the second one. Logically, then, the verb form agrees with the first element.

> The <u>instructor, as well as her students</u>, *is* going to attend the symposium on the environment.

> The Australian <u>prime minister</u>, along with his ministers for education and foreign affairs, *is* set to arrive tomorrow.

As you can see, the prepositional phrase is set off with commas. If it makes it easier, you can ignore the elements within the commas, which then may help you determine the correct verb form.

> The <u>instructor</u>, (as well as her students), *is* going to attend the symposium on the environment.

> The Australian <u>prime minister</u>, (along with his ministers for education and foreign affairs), *is* set to arrive tomorrow.

To stress equality, the sentences would be changed:

> The <u>instructor and her students</u> *are* going to attend the symposium on the environment.

> The Australian <u>prime minister, minister for education, and minister for foreign affairs</u> *are* set to arrive tomorrow.

4. A collective noun refers to a group. The noun appears singular but may be either singular or plural, depending on context. If the context suggests singular, the verb form is singular; if plural, the verb is plural. Examples of collective nouns include *audience*, *band*, *class*, *committee*, *congregation*, *family*, *gang*, *group*, *jury*, *staff*, and *team*.

A collective noun may be singular or plural, depending on context. If in doubt, consider it singular.

Whenever the context suggests that the members of the group are considered *one unit*, all doing the same thing or acting together, the verb form is *singular*; when the members are considered *individuals acting independently*, the corresponding verb form is *plural*.

← 13 See Chapter 13 for a discussion of nouns.

> The <u>jury</u> *is* out to consider the evidence.

> After the lecture, the <u>class</u> *are* going to be able to ask questions.

Most often, a collective noun is considered singular; if in doubt, choose this form. If a plural verb with a collective noun sounds odd, rephrase the subject so that the collective noun acts as an adjective before an appropriate plural noun.

> After the lecture, <u>class members</u> *are* going to be able to ask questions.

5. With these phrases, the verb form is singular, even though the noun or pronoun that follows is plural: *each of*, *either/neither of*, *every one of*, *one of*, *the only one of*, and *which one of*. Again, if it makes

it easier, ignore the nouns or pronouns after these phrases.

One of (our 115 students) *has* written an A+ essay.

Alec **is the only one** (of those attending) who *has* **difficulty speaking before a large group.**

6. An indefinite pronoun refers to non-specific individuals or objects. Most indefinite pronouns are considered singular and take a singular verb in agreement. *Anybody, anyone, anything, each, either, everybody, everyone, everything, neither, nobody, no one, nothing, one, somebody,* and *someone* are singular indefinite pronouns.

Everybody *is* **welcome.**

Some experts believe that when context clearly indicates the use of plural agreement with the antecedents *everyone* and *everybody,* as in the next example, you may use the plural pronoun.

When the pepper was spilled, everyone rubbed their noses.

7. There is a separate rule for phrases involving portions and fractions + *of,* such as *all, any, a lot, a variety, a number, (one-)half, more, most, much, none, part, plenty, some,* and *the majority/minority.* The form of the verb depends on whether the noun or pronoun following *of* is singular or plural.

In these examples, the verb agrees with the double-underlined word:

None of the missing pieces *have* **been found yet.**

Some of the losses incurred with the companies' merger *are* **being absorbed by the shareholders.**

Half of the pie *is* **gone.**

One-third of the employees *are* **out on strike.**

8. Subjects referring to distance, time, money, weight, or mass are usually *singular.* When the subject is *the number of,* the verb is *singular* (in contrast with rule 7).

Twenty kilometres *is* **not a great distance to an experienced hiker.**

A number of cars **were stolen last night.**

The number of people attending the courses *has* **dropped in the last two years.**

9. Some nouns ending in *s* are singular; therefore, they require a singular verb. Examples include *athletics, billiards, darts, economics, gymnastics, mathematics, measles, mumps, news, physics, poli-*

An indefinite pronoun is a pronoun that can be used in place of a noun for an unspecified individual or group. Most indefinite pronouns (e.g., *anything, each, everyone*) are considered singular even though they may refer broadly to many people, objects, etc.

TIP

When the subject is *a number of,* the verb form agrees with the noun/pronoun following *of;* when the subject is *the number of,* the verb is singular.

TIP

Most errors in subject–verb agreement occur in one of three situations: 1) the use of a compound subject, 2) the use of an indefinite pronoun as the subject, or 3) the use of intervening words between the subject and the verb.

tics, and *statistics*.

Statistics *is* **an inexact science.**

No news *is* **good news.**

Depending on their context, however, many of these nouns can be considered plural and should take a plural verb form. For example, *statistics* could refer to facts rather than to one subject:

The statistics on global warming *are* **alerting politicians to the need for worldwide action.**

Whether the titles of artistic works or the names of companies are singular or plural does not affect the verb. A singular verb needs to agree with the subject.

"Voices Lost in Snow" *is* **a story in *Montreal Stories*, a collection of Mavis Gallant's fiction; McClelland & Stewart** *is* **the publisher.**

10. The following terms are plural and require the plural form of the verb: *both, few, many, parts of, several*.

A well-educated few *seem* **to care about correct grammar and punctuation these days, but both** *are* **essential parts of the writing process.**

Pronouns at Work

Pronoun–Antecedent Agreement

Most problems in pronoun–antecedent agreement apply to personal pronouns, such as *she, he, they*, and *them*, as well as to the possessive form of pronouns, *his, hers*, and *their*. A pronoun must agree with its antecedent or preceding noun in number. If you have difficulty finding the antecedent, see which noun in the sentence can be substituted for the pronoun.

The first thing that usually strikes us about a person is their physical appearance. [Since the gender of the person is not known, the gender-inclusive pronoun should be used.]

Dieters should realize that a diet only works when they [dieters] **restrict their** [dieters'] **caloric intake.**

Most of the rules for subject–verb agreement also apply to pronoun–antecedent agreement. For example, a compound noun before the pronoun requires the plural form of the pronoun or possessive pronoun.

Connie and Steve *have* **invited me to their cottage.**

If the compound subject includes the word *each* or *every*, the singular form should be used. Again, if it is easier, ignore the words after *each*. This will help you decide which pronoun to use.

Each book and magazine in the library *has* **its own entry.**

The rule for **pronoun–antecedent agreement** also applies to possessive adjectives, such as *their*, which are formed from pronouns. A pronoun's antecedent is the noun it replaces, and a pronoun must agree with its antecedent in number.

See Chapter 13 for more on pronouns and antecedents. "Pronoun Case" later in this chapter discusses personal pronouns in more detail.

When two nouns are joined by *or* or *nor*, the pronoun agrees with the closest noun.

> **Neither the prime minister <u>nor his advisors</u> *were* certain how to implement <u>their</u> proposal.**

> **Neither his advisors nor <u>the prime minister</u> was certain how to implement <u>his</u> proposal.**

As with subject–verb agreement, a collective noun requires the singular pronoun replacement if it is thought of as a unit; however, if individuals are being referred to, the pronoun takes a plural form.

> **Our hockey <u>team</u> *will play* <u>its</u> final game on Saturday. [The team will be playing as a unit.]**

> **The <u>team</u> *will be receiving* <u>their</u> new jerseys Friday. [Each individual team member will be given a jersey.]**

With a pronoun referring to a portion or fraction, agreement depends on whether the noun following *of* is singular or plural.

> **Studies show that a significant <u>number of college and university students</u> *are* cheating on <u>their</u> exams and essays; however, a much larger number are not.**

If the pronoun follows an indefinite pronoun such as *anybody*, *one*, or *someone*, then you should choose a gender-inclusive pronoun.

> **<u>One</u> should be careful about pronoun agreement, or <u>one's</u> teacher will certainly point out the error to <u>one</u>.**

Although grammatically correct, this sentence could be improved for clarity by replacing the indefinite pronoun *one* with a personal pronoun. In this case, gender-inclusive pronouns are appropriate.

> **<u>One</u> should be careful about pronoun agreement, or <u>their</u> teacher will certainly point out the error to <u>them</u>.**

For clarity, a better option would be to write the sentence as follows:

> **<u>Student writers should be careful about pronoun</u> agreement, or <u>their</u> teachers will certainly point out the error to <u>them</u>.**

In the next example, a singular pronoun replaces the singular *one*—but the sentence is incorrect because the possessive adjective *his* and the personal pronoun *him* refer to only one gender.

INCORRECT	**<u>One</u> should be careful about pronoun agreement, or <u>his</u> teacher will certainly point out the error to <u>him</u>.**
CORRECT	**A <u>student</u> forgot <u>their</u> textbook in the classroom.** **A student's textbook was left in the classroom.**

Professional and academic writing is expected to be **gender inclusive**, respecting all genders. Sentences can be rewritten or the plural pronouns *they*, *them*, and *their* should be used instead of *he or she*, *him or her*, or *his or hers* so that sentences are shorter and are inclusive of all genders.

Gender-inclusive language is the careful use of terms and grammatical forms that include all genders. When an antecedent is either a generic singular noun or an indefinite pronoun, the personal pronoun that follows must be gender inclusive.

The problem of agreement is especially common when the first noun is either an indefinite pronoun or a singular noun that is not gender specific and is a generic noun such as *reader*, *writer*, *student*, *teacher*, *individual*, *character*, or *person*. Here are three options to consider in this situation.

1. Use a gender-inclusive pronoun.

    <u>Anybody</u> not willing to put in long hours for little pay should give up <u>their</u> idea of becoming a writer.

2. Change the singular *anybody* to a plural noun.

    <u>People not willing</u> to put in long hours for little pay should give up <u>their</u> idea of becoming a writer.

3. Revise the sentence to use the gender-neutral pronoun *you*. This option is not always possible and may occasionally sound too informal for academic writing.

    If <u>you</u> are not willing to put in long hours for little pay, <u>you</u> should give up <u>the idea</u> of becoming a writer.

EXERCISE 15.1

Using all the options presented in the last section, fix the pronoun–antecedent agreement errors in the following paragraph.

Gardening is becoming a popular hobby, as many people want fresh, organic vegetables and bright flowers he or she can appreciate throughout the summer. There is also a movement to create a more natural habitat for wildlife. However, before pulling out a lawn, a gardener must first make sure they know what to plant. Gardeners must consider things like whether plants are drought resistant or it needs a lot of shade. A gardener must also plan their garden with care so that they can achieve the effect they dream of.

EXERCISE 15.2

Choose the correct form of the verb and/or pronoun for these sentences and make any other necessary changes in agreement. Rewrite the sentence where required.

1. Neither the film's director nor its producers (was/were) on hand to receive (his/her/their) prestigious award.
2. The child, as well as (his/her/their) parents, (thinks/think) the room is too small. [The child identifies as female.]

3. The student must study for (his/her/their) exam. [The student identifies as male.]
4. One should never expect to succeed in a career unless (one/they) (is/are) willing to work hard.
5. Everyone who works during the year (is/are) obliged to file (his/her/their) income tax return.
6. Her set of baby teeth (was/were) complete when she was only 18 months old.
7. None of the company's products (requires/require) testing on animals.
8. Lining the side of the highway (is/are) a lot of billboards advertising fast-food restaurants.
9. Every specimen of the horned grebe (has/have) a distinctive tuft on each side of (its/their) head.
10. The maximum number of people allowed on this elevator (is/are) 30.

EXERCISE 15.3

Correct the subject–verb agreement and/or pronoun–antecedent agreement errors in the following sentences. Some contain no errors; others contain more than one.

1. Every person in the community should have the right to attend university and create new opportunities for themselves.
2. Especially unique to adolescent depression are physical symptoms, such as headaches.
3. The taste of Bob's burgers are excellent, but they could be better.
4. There has been a number of sales because it is "back to school" time.
5. Better public transportation and more bike lanes means less pollution.
6. An unusual story by Neil Gaiman leave the reader wanting to read more.
7. Use of rechargeable batteries are not as high as many would expect.
8. A group of students, parents, and teachers are forming as they disagree with the government's planned changes.
9. Everyone who has purchased tickets is eligible for the grand prize, but they must be residents of Canada to claim their prize.
10. If children are denied the opportunity to play, how can they develop emotionally and physically?

Other Problems with Pronouns

Errors in *pronoun reference*, *pronoun case*, and *pronoun consistency* also cause writers problems.

Pronoun Reference

Consider life without pronouns.

A Lost Loonie Leads to a Lesson Learned

Alex and Alex's lawyer, Alan, left in Alex's limousine for Loonies Unlimited to buy Alex's landlady, Alice, a litre of light lemonade. Alice

told Alex and Alan to also buy a litre of light lemonade for Alice's long-time lodger, Alison. When Alex and Alan alighted at Loonies Unlimited, Alex and Alan were alarmed that Alex had left Alex's loonie in Alex's loft. So Alphonse, of Loonies Unlimited, allowed Alex and Alan only one litre of lemonade, along with a length of limp licorice, and Alphonse loudly lamented Alex's and Alan's laxness.

EXERCISE 15.4

Rewrite "A Lost Loonie Leads to a Lesson Learned," replacing as many nouns as possible with pronouns and ensuring that the antecedents are clear. If in doubt about the clarity of antecedents, refer to the section on pronoun reference.

As discussed earlier, the relationship between pronoun and antecedent must always be clear—this principle is called pronoun reference. You can test for pronoun reference errors by seeing whether you can replace a pronoun with a specific noun that appears earlier in the sentence (i.e., its antecedent).

> **As reality shows have become more popular, they** [reality shows] **have become more and more bizarre.**

The principle for pronoun reference is simple: each pronoun should refer clearly to a specific antecedent or preceding noun.

In the next example, the antecedent is unclear:

> **Reality shows have become more popular while their participants have become more and more bizarre; consequently, they** [reality shows? participants?] **can no longer be believed.**

There are four kinds of pronoun reference errors, which can be repaired in different ways.

1. **No reference (missing antecedent):** This error occurs when the pronoun has no apparent noun antecedent. Consider this sentence:

    > **Following the prime minister's speech, he took several questions from reporters.**

The personal pronoun *he* apparently replaces *prime minister's*, which is a possessive adjective. Pronouns replace nouns, not adjectives. In the following sentence, the noun antecedent is implied but not actually stated; grammatically, the reference is missing.

> **One thing that Canadians are especially proud of is its national health-care system.**

TIP

If the antecedent is missing, revise the sentence by adding an antecedent that agrees with the pronoun.

Where there is no antecedent, one must be provided or the pronoun replaced with an appropriate noun.

> **After the prime minister spoke, he took several questions from reporters.**

or

After speaking, the <u>prime minister</u> took several questions from reporters.

One thing that <u>Canadians</u> are especially proud of is <u>their</u> national health-care system.

Speakers and writers tend to use the impersonal third-person pronoun *it* or *they* to refer vaguely to some unmentioned authority. Avoid this habit in your formal writing.

> **<u>It is said</u> that most people do not like public speaking.**
>
> BETTER   **Most people do not like public speaking.**
>
> **<u>They say</u> that adults need at least eight hours of sleep a night.**
>
> BETTER   **Adults need at least eight hours of sleep a night.**

If a sentence begins with a prepositional phrase, the noun in that phrase cannot be the antecedent. These examples illustrate this problem and its solutions:

> INCORRECT   **With the new pots and pans, <u>it</u> makes cooking more enjoyable for the chef.**
>
> CORRECT   **The new pots and pans make cooking more enjoyable for the chef.**
>   or
>   **With the new pots and pans, the chef finds cooking more enjoyable.**

Again, if you are not sure what the main noun is, ignore the prepositional phrase.

> **(With broom in hand,) the <u>janitor</u> began <u>her</u> daily cleanup of the lab.**

2. **Remote reference:** A reader should not be expected to connect a pronoun to a noun when they are separated by more than one sentence.

> **In George Orwell's prophetic book *1984*, people's lives were watched over by television screens. These screens, along with brainwashing techniques, enabled people to be kept under firm control. <u>It</u> is an example of dystopian fiction.**

The pronoun *it* is used too late. Many nouns have intervened, so the reader has to spend time trying to understand what *it* is referring to. Repeating the noun instead of using a pronoun is often the best solution when the antecedent is far away.

3. **Ambiguous (squinting) reference:** This error occurs when the pronoun seems to refer to two or more nouns, either of which could be the antecedent.

> **When <u>Peter</u> gave <u>his</u> driver's licence to <u>Paul,</u> <u>he</u> was surprised to see that it had expired.**

Who was surprised in this sentence? The pronoun *he* could refer to either *Peter* or *Paul*.

> **The problem for readers aspiring to look like the models in women's magazines is that <u>their</u> photos have been airbrushed.** [*Their* has two grammatical antecedents: *readers* and *models*.]

> **In 1916, a member of the Russian parliament denounced Rasputin before <u>his</u> colleagues.** [Does *his* refer to the member's colleagues or to Rasputin's?]

Sometimes it is possible to correct an ambiguous reference by repeating the noun, but the result is not always pleasing:

> **When <u>Peter</u> gave his driver's licence to <u>Paul,</u> <u>Peter</u> was surprised to see that it had expired.**

Rewriting may be the better solution:

> **On giving his driver's licence to Paul, <u>Peter</u> was surprised to see that it had expired.**

> **The problem for readers aspiring to look like the models in women's magazines is that <u>the models'</u> photographs have been airbrushed.**

> **In 1916, a member of the Russian parliament denounced Rasputin before <u>the House</u>.**

4. **Broad reference (vague reference):** A reference is broad or vague when the pronoun (often *this*, *that*, or *which*) refers to a group of words, an idea, or a concept rather than to *one specific noun*.

> INCORRECT   **Children these days are too prone to lazy habits, such as watching YouTube and TikTok. <u>This</u> shows we have become too permissive.**

TIP

If the antecedent appears to be an idea rather than a specific noun, add a noun that sums up the idea to the part of the sentence where the error occurs.

This replaces the whole preceding clause, which is too much. The next example is acceptable in informal writing, even though the pronoun *which* replaces *received top marks* rather than a specific noun. The meaning of the sentence, however, is clear:

> **She received top marks for her final dive, <u>which</u> gave her the gold medal in that competition.**

In the following sentence, the pronoun *this* refers to an idea rather than a specific noun, making the meaning of the second independent clause unclear:

> INCORRECT   **Many older drivers are retested if they have had medical problems, but <u>this</u> needs to go further.**

To correct a broad reference, you often need to rewrite the sentence. Sometimes, the easiest way is to add a noun and change the pronoun into an adjective. (A pronoun that acts as an adjective has the same form as a pronoun—*this*, *that*, *these*, *those*—but it comes before a noun and is a modifier instead of taking the place of a noun.) Examples include *this book* or *that book*.

| CORRECT | **Children these days are too prone to lazy habits, such as watching YouTube or TikTok. <u>This tendency</u> shows that we have become too permissive.** |
| CORRECT | **Many older drivers are retested if they have had medical problems, but <u>this retesting</u> needs to go further.** |

Finally, *it* is a personal pronoun and, like all personal pronouns, should always have a clear noun referent. In some cases, you may need to use a noun instead.

| POOR | **We try not to mention specific businesses by name in our article; however, <u>it</u> can't be avoided in some situations.** |
| BETTER | **We try not to mention specific businesses by name in our article; however, we can't avoid <u>names</u> in all situations.** |

EXERCISE 15.5

Fix the broad pronoun references in the following paragraph.

Genetically modified foods have been engineered to flourish in harsh environments. *This* will help alleviate the need for usable farmland as *this* will enable farming to occur on lands once considered unsuitable for growing crops. *This* will be a major benefit to many nations in Africa, Asia, and South America where there is a shortage of food and available land.

EXERCISE 15.6

Correct the errors in pronoun agreement in the following sentences.

1. She had long, brown hair down to her waist, but her mother said that she had to cut it.
2. While sleeping soundly on the kitchen floor, Jim walked around him.
3. They lived as if nobody else mattered but themselves. That is a problem.
4. This will be her chance to prove whether she is good enough to make the team.
5. They have a responsibility to educate the public.
6. His attorney decided on a not-guilty plea. It was the wrong decision.
7. Josh gave Alan his car keys and told him to drive carefully.
8. The Taylors and the Smiths make delightfully odd couples and their friends agree.
9. The cat will eat only the most expensive kind of deluxe cat food. It is spoiled.
10. After hearing their protests for a long time, he finally agreed to take them along.

Make the necessary revisions to the pronoun errors in the following sentences.

1. *It* says you must keep your seatbelt fastened when you are on a flight.
2. Whenever a meeting is called, *they* are required to attend.
3. *They* say that all good things must end.
4. Pesticides are used on crops, and *this* is our major ground water pollutant.
5. During Roosevelt's Pearl Harbor speech, *he* identified the United States as a peaceful and tolerant nation.
6. I know *it* said "No Parking," but I went ahead and parked there anyway. *They* gave me a $20 fine.
7. Her first cat was a Russian Blue and her second cat was a Bengal. *It* was spoiled.
8. Despite being told that the deadline was May 23, it was missed by Tom.
9. Some psychologists and researchers believe in the "innate" theory of prejudice. According to this theory, ingrained prejudice is cross-cultural and awareness of race is one of the earliest social characteristics to develop in children. *This* finding may help account for its popularity.
10. During the industrial age, with expanding factories and growing cities, they lived in a rapidly changing work environment.

Pronoun Case

Some pronouns change their form to reflect their function in the sentence. You must be aware of pronoun case in order to use the correct form.

Personal Pronouns

Personal pronouns refer to persons. The first person refers to the one doing the speaking or writing; the second person refers to the one spoken to; and the third person refers to the one spoken about. Most nouns can be considered third person and can be replaced by third-person pronouns. Table 15.1 lists the different groups. These distinctions are important because the personal pronoun's role in a sentence determines whether the pronoun is subjective or objective. (Notice that the second-person pronoun *you* doesn't change its case.)

Consider the pronoun forms under "Subjective–Singular" and "Subjective–Plural" in Table 15.1 for this example:

He was swimming in the pool.

He, the third-person singular masculine form of the pronoun, is the subject of this clause/sentence; therefore, it is in the subjective case.

Pronoun case is the principle that a pronoun changes its form depending on its function in the sentence (e.g., *I/me*, *she/her*, *they/them*).

Personal pronouns refer to persons. The *first person* refers to the one *doing* the speaking or writing; *second person* refers to the one *spoken to*; *third person* refers to the one *spoken about*.

TIP

Subjective just means that the word is the subject in the sentence, and *objective* means that it is the object in the sentence. In the table, we will use these terms, but afterward, for simplicity, the pronouns will be referred to as subject or object pronouns.

TABLE 15.1 Personal Pronouns

Pronoun Person	Subjective–Singular	Subjective–Plural	Objective–Singular	Objective–Plural
First	*I*	*we*	*me*	*us*
Second	*you*	*you*	*you*	*you*
Third	*he, she, it*	*they*	*him, her, it*	*them*

> **TIP**
>
> The first- and third-person forms of the personal pronoun and the pronouns *who* and *whom* change case (i.e., *form*) to express their grammatical function in the sentence.

 Chapter 13 has more on pronoun categories.

<u>I</u> was swimming in the pool with <u>her</u>.

The subject *I* is first-person singular, but *her* acts as the object. When a personal pronoun acts as the object of a verb or of a preposition, it is in the objective case.

<u>She</u> spoke so softly that it was difficult to understand <u>her</u>.

She is the subject of the sentence and *her* is the object of *to understand*. Notice the different pronouns in these two sentences:

Anna, the king, and <u>I</u> are going out for Chinese food tonight. [*I* is part of the subject.]

Anna arrived late for her dinner with the king and <u>me</u>. [*Me* is part of a prepositional phrase and it is an object.]

There are two steps to deciding which form to use:

1. Determine if the pronoun is the subject of a clause/sentence or the object.
2. Choose the appropriate form (subjective or objective). Until the forms become familiar, you can refer to Table 15.1.

Pronoun case can be tricky with compounds.

Tina and [*I*? *me*?] plan to attend Mavis's wedding on 15 May.

Ignore the noun in a compound to determine the correct pronoun.

(Tina and) I plan to attend Mavis's wedding on 15 May.

Mavis's wedding will be a joyous occasion for (Tina and) me.

We (students) believe firmly that our rights should be given back to us.

Our rights should be given back to us (students).

Possessive Pronouns

Possessive pronouns, which act as adjectives, also change their case (e.g., my pet alligator; the alligator is *mine*).

The book doesn't belong to Anthony but to Kristy; it is <u>her</u> book.

In this sentence, *her* is acting as an adjective, modifying the noun *book*.

The book doesn't belong to Anthony but to Kristy; it is <u>hers</u>.

In this sentence, *hers* is a possessive pronoun acting as the object of the verb.

Table 15.2 lists the possessive forms of pronouns and the noun (complement) forms.

Relative Pronouns

A relative pronoun *relates* the dependent clause it introduces to the noun that it follows. A relative clause, then, usually functions as an adjective, modifying the preceding noun. Of the major relative pronouns (*who, whoever, which, whichever, that*), only *who* and *whoever* change their form depending on whether they are the subject of the clause or the object of either the verb or a preposition in the clause.

A relative pronoun introduces a dependent clause that usually functions as an adjective, modifying the preceding noun. A clause that begins with a relative pronoun is called a relative clause.

Stephen, <u>who is our valet</u>, is parking the car right now.

You may choose the colour <u>that suits your mood</u>.

To determine the case of a relative pronoun, look at the role the relative pronoun plays within the clause. Is it the subject (*who/whoever*)? Is it the object (*whom/whomever*)?

TABLE 15.2 Possessive Pronouns with Adjectival and Noun Forms

Pronoun Person	Adjectival–Singular	Adjectival–Plural	Subject Complements–Singular	Subject Complements–Plural
First	*my*	*our*	*mine*	*ours*
Second	*your*	*your*	*yours*	*yours*
Third	*his, her, its*	*their*	*his, hers, its*	*theirs*

The old man shouted at <u>whoever happened to be within listening distance</u>.

The old man should be free to shout at <u>whomever he chooses</u>.

In the first sentence, *whoever* is the subject of the clause it introduces. In the second, *he* is the subject of the clause, and the relative pronoun *whomever* is in the objective case.

Another way to determine whether to use *who/whoever* or *whom/whomever* is to replace the relative pronoun with a pronoun such as *he* or *him*. *Whoever* (relative pronoun) *happened to be within listening distance* becomes *he/she* (personal pronoun) *happened to be within listening distance*. In the second sentence, the wording can be changed to *he chooses whomever*. Here *whomever* would correctly be replaced with *him*, not *he*.

> **Jeong-Gyu is someone who will go far.**
>
> **Jeong-Gyu is someone whom will go far.**

The first example is correct. *Who* is the subject of the relative clause *who will go far*.

Interrogative Pronouns

The interrogative pronouns (*who, whom, which, what*) always ask questions. When choosing between the relative pronouns *who* or *whom*, you first need to establish their function (subject or object) to ensure that you are using the correct case.

> **With <u>whom</u> did you go out on Saturday night?** [object]
>
> **<u>Who</u> says you should never reveal your feelings?** [subject]
>
> **<u>Whom</u> would you recommend for the new opening?** [object]

EXERCISE 15.8

Choose the correct form of the pronoun.

1. (Us/We) students need to fight for better public transportation.
2. With (who/whom) did you go to the dance?
3. Shia and (I/me) went surfing for the first time last week.
4. Shia fell off his board and knocked (I/me) off (my/mine).
5. The gift card was for Maya and (I/me).
6. As she entered the room, a mysterious feeling came over (she/her).
7. Jeff Dunham, (who/whom) is a famous ventriloquist, has many odd characters.
8. I can choose (whoever/whomever) I want to be in my group.
9. Between you and (I/me), Professor Singh is a hard marker.
10. To (who/whom) are you texting?

Pronoun Consistency

A pronoun must agree in number, gender, and person with its antecedent—this rule is called pronoun consistency. Referring to different people in the same sentence is acceptable as long as the change isn't arbitrary. If you want to replace a preceding noun with a pronoun, the latter should be the same *person* as its antecedent.

> INCORRECT **During final exams, if <u>students</u> must go to the washroom, raise <u>your</u> hand so <u>you</u> can be escorted there.** [*Students* is third person; *your* and *you* are second person.]

The interrogative pronouns—who, whom, which, and *what—introduce questions.*

TIP

The function of the interrogative pronoun in a sentence determines whether *who* (subject) or *whom* (object) is used.

Pronoun consistency means that a pronoun must agree in number, gender, and person with its antecedent. Do not needlessly switch from one person of pronoun to another. If an antecedent is a noun, use the third-person form to replace it.

CORRECT	**During final exams, if <u>students</u> must go to the washroom, <u>they</u> should raise <u>their</u> hands so <u>they</u> can be escorted there.**

Or, more informally:

During final exams, if <u>you</u> need to go to the washroom, raise <u>your</u> hand so <u>you</u> can be escorted there.

INCORRECT	**It is possible that <u>our</u> desire to make life easier for <u>ourselves</u> will, in fact, make <u>humans</u> redundant.** [*Our* and *ourselves* are first person; *humans* is third person.]
CORRECT	**It is possible that <u>our</u> desire to make life easier for <u>ourselves</u> will, in fact, make <u>us</u> redundant.**

or

It is possible that the desire to make life easier for <u>humans</u> will, in fact, make <u>them</u> redundant.

INCORRECT	**Educators today should teach <u>students</u> learning skills, such as how to manage <u>your</u> money.**
CORRECT	**Educators today should teach <u>students</u> learning skills, such as how to manage <u>their</u> money.**

EXERCISE 15.9

The following paragraph contains errors in pronoun consistency, along with some awkward use of third-person pronouns. Rewrite the paragraph, striving for correctness and effectiveness. Decide which person you want to refer to consistently: this decision might be based on the level of formality you want to use (first- and second-person pronouns, such as *I/me* and *you*, are considered more informal than third-person pronouns, such as *he/him*, *she/her*, *they/them*, and *one*).

You can definitely learn a lot from educational TV; we can learn things that we cannot learn from written texts. If one is a major in commerce, for example, and if he or she watches the business news, he or she can understand the commerce textbook better by applying what he or she learns from the news. Similarly, I think that watching sports programs can provide people with excitement. Watching sports can also give us a better understanding of the game. On the other hand, if one chooses to watch comedy all the time, people are not going to gain any real benefits. I feel comedies are generally meaningless.

Sentence Construction Errors

Sentence construction errors occur when a modifier is not placed as close as possible to the word it is intended to modify, and when coordinate or equal elements in a sentence are not grammatically parallel and complete.

Misplaced and dangling modifiers are examples of errors that result when writers do not follow the first principle. Faulty parallelism and comparisons occur when the second principle is not followed.

Misplaced Modifiers

The main function of adjectives is to modify nouns, while the main function of adverbs is to modify verbs. Prepositional phrases can also function as adjectives or adverbs. A misplaced modifier, then, can be an adjective, adjectival phrase, adverb, or adverbial phrase. It is mistakenly placed next to a part of speech that it is not intended to modify.

The meaning of a sentence in English heavily depends on word order, or syntax; it is partly through syntax that writers communicate their meaning and that the reader understands the message.

Adjectival Modifiers

A one-word adjective usually appears immediately before the noun it is intended to modify, but an adjectival phrase or clause usually follows the noun it modifies. Most misplaced adjectival modifiers are phrases or clauses. Consider the following examples of misplaced modifiers (the modifiers are underlined):

> INCORRECT **I want a <u>hot</u> cup of coffee.**
> INCORRECT **They headed for a child in the front row <u>wearing a long overcoat</u>.**

In the first example, *hot* is modifying *cup*, not *coffee*. The adjective should be placed before the noun *coffee*. In the second example, the child, not the front row, is wearing the long overcoat. The adjectival phrase should follow the noun *child*.

> CORRECT **I want a cup of <u>hot</u> coffee.**
> CORRECT **They headed for a child <u>wearing a long overcoat</u> in the front row.**
> INCORRECT **The furnace thermostat is located upstairs, <u>which displays the temperature settings</u>.**

In this sentence, the adjectival (relative) clause, *which displays the temperature settings*, is placed next to the adverb *upstairs* instead of the noun *thermostat*.

> CORRECT **The furnace thermostat, <u>which displays the temperature settings</u>, is located upstairs.**

Adverbial Modifiers

Misplaced adverbs and adverbial phrases are more common than their adjective counterparts because adverbs can often be moved in a

A **misplaced modifier** is an adjective, adjectival phrase, adverb, or adverbial phrase that is too far away in the sentence from the word it should modify, possibly giving the sentence an unintended meaning.

Syntax means the way words are put together into sentences in a language.

An **adjectival modifier** is a word or phrase that functions as an adjective.

→13 Chapter 13 discusses adjectives and adverbs.

sentence without affecting meaning. However, it is safest to place adverbial modifiers right before or after the word or phrase they are supposed to modify.

An adverbial modifier is a word or phrase that functions as an adverb.

The meaning of the following sentence could be misconstrued:

INCORRECT Students should buy this book because it will give them all the information they need to know about writing <u>in a convenient form</u>.

Presumably, the writer did not mean "convenience in writing" but that the book "will give them . . . information . . . in a convenient form."

CORRECT Students should buy this book because it will give them, <u>in a convenient form</u>, all the information they will need to know about writing.

INCORRECT The conviction carries a penalty of 8 to 10 years in <u>two provinces</u>.

Because of the misplaced prepositional phrase, the writer seems to be saying that, on being convicted, the criminal will have to serve time in two provinces. Either of the following rephrased sentences is correct:

<u>In two provinces</u>, the conviction carries a penalty of 8 to 10 years.

The conviction carries a penalty <u>in two provinces</u> of 8 to 10 years.

Fixing Misplaced Modifiers

The solution to misplaced modifiers, whether an entire clause, phrase, or single word, is simple: move them. The following misplaced modifier makes the sentence awkward or misleading:

INCORRECT The instructor marked the essay I wrote <u>unfairly</u>.
CORRECT The instructor <u>unfairly</u> marked the essay I wrote.

or
I thought the instructor marked my essay <u>unfairly</u>.

Misplaced modifiers can occur anywhere in a sentence; however, they often occur at the end, almost as an afterthought.

INCORRECT Cars today produce large amounts of toxic chemicals that can damage human cells <u>if inhaled</u>.
CORRECT Cars today produce large amounts of toxic chemicals that, <u>if inhaled</u>, can damage human cells.

> **TIP**
> A misplaced modifier should be placed as close as possible to the word(s) it is intended to modify.

One-Word Modifiers

You need to be especially careful in placing one-word modifiers in a sentence, especially with limiting adverbs such as *only*, *almost*, *just*, *even*, *nearly*, *barely*, and *merely*.

One little word out of place can affect the meaning of the sentence. The meaning of the following statement changes depending on where *only* appears.

Only Jared didn't do his homework yesterday.

Everyone but Jared did his or her homework; *only* is an adjective modifying *Jared*.

Jared only didn't do his homework.

The meaning of this sentence is unclear. It could mean the same as the first sentence, that Jared did other things but not his homework, or that the fact Jared didn't do his homework isn't important.

Jared didn't only do his homework yesterday.

Now *only* is an adverb modifying the verb *do* and suggests that Jared did his homework and other things.

Jared didn't do only his homework yesterday.

Placing *only* before *his homework* means that Jared definitely did his homework and other things as well. It might also mean that Jared was involved in doing someone else's homework in addition to his own.

Jared didn't do his only homework yesterday.

Placing *only* between *his* and *homework* implies that Jared didn't have much homework, but he didn't do it.

Jared didn't do his homework only yesterday.

Perhaps Jared is not such a lazy student after all: the only day he didn't do his homework was yesterday!

Dangling Modifiers

Grammatically, a dangling modifier modifies the closest noun, often giving the sentence an unintended meaning.

Misplaced and dangling modifiers can give the communication a quite different, sometimes humorous, meaning from the intended one. The next example seems to refer to precocious parents:

INCORRECT **When only seven years old, my parents decided to enroll me in a Highland dancing course.**

In this sentence, the noun that *When only seven years old* should modify is absent, so it seems that the parents were only seven years old when they decided to enroll their child in dancing.

Consider the following sentence from a résumé, which doesn't mention the applicant:

INCORRECT **When not working or attending classes, my hobbies are gardening, doing macramé, and bungee jumping.**

As dangling modifiers are often *–ing* participle (adjectival) phrases, they are sometimes called dangling participles. These adjectival phrases are dangling because the noun or noun phrase they are intended to modify is not in the sentence. That's why it doesn't help to move the modifier.

Correct dangling modifiers by 1) providing the noun or noun phrase in the independent clause to give the modifier something to modify or 2) turning the dangling phrase into a dependent clause with a subject.

A dangling participle modifies nothing in the sentence, as the noun or noun phrase it should modify is absent.

CORRECT   **When only seven years old, I was enrolled by my parents in a Highland dancing course.** [method 1]

CORRECT   **When I was only seven years old, my parents decided to enroll me in a Highland dancing course.** [method 2]

CORRECT   **When not working or attending classes, I enjoy several hobbies, including gardening, doing macramé, and bungee jumping.** [method 1]

CORRECT   **When I am not working or attending classes, my hobbies include gardening, doing macramé, and bungee jumping.** [method 2]

While a misplaced modifier frequently appears at the end of a sentence, a dangling modifier usually is found at the beginning of a sentence, though occasionally in the middle or at the end. These examples show you how to identify dangling modifiers by asking the appropriate questions.

INCORRECT   **When arriving in Calgary, the clouds had scattered, and the sky was aglow with bands of pink and red.**

INCORRECT   **Though a well-known writer, his latest book failed to make the bestseller's list.**

Who is arriving in Calgary? Who is the well-known writer? The answers are not in the sentences; therefore, the modifiers are dangling. In each case, the missing information needs to be provided in the independent clause, or the dangling phrase needs to be turned into a dependent clause that can modify the independent one that follows.

CORRECT   **When arriving in Calgary, I saw that the clouds had scattered, and the sky was aglow with bands of pink and red.** [method 1]

When I arrived in Calgary, the clouds had scattered, and the sky was aglow with bands of pink and red. [method 2]

CORRECT   **Though a well-known writer, he failed to make the bestseller's list with his latest book.** [method 1]

Though he was a well-known writer, his latest book failed to make the bestseller's list. [method 2]

In the following example, the dangling modifier is at the end of the sentence:

INCORRECT   **Verbal and non-verbal skills are greatly enhanced when living in a foreign country.**

Who is living in a foreign country? This information is missing, so the participial phrase *when living* is dangling. To correct it, add information:

CORRECT
When living in a foreign country, you are able to enhance your verbal and non-verbal skills. [method 1]
Verbal and non-verbal skills are greatly enhanced when you live in a foreign country. [method 2]

EXERCISE 15.10

Working in groups, identify the misplaced or dangling modifiers in the following sentences. Determine whether the meaning is incorrect or ambiguous and then fix the problem using one of the methods discussed in the previous sections.

1. A striped hat was on his head that came to a point.
2. As we were leaving, he promised to visit us with tears in his eyes.
3. Although unambitious and downright lazy, I have never known Sam to break his word.
4. His ego was further inflated by being awarded first prize in the Ben Affleck look-alike contest.
5. Every character has a purpose in Shakespeare's play, big or small.
6. When asked what my favourite sport is, I usually say that it is running without any hesitation.
7. Stepping out of the airplane, the fresh air was most invigorating.
8. Gabriel Kolko describes peace in Vietnam after the war in his book.
9. Opening the door unexpectedly, his eyes fell upon two of his employees sleeping in front of their computers.
10. Teacher Laurie McNamara posed for the photographer with Principal Dan Saunders, who gave her a kidney last month, in the Cloverdale Elementary School hallway.

EXERCISE 15.11

Correct the following sentences, each of which contains a modifier error. In some instances, you will need to reword the sentence for clarity and correctness.

1. As a serious snowboarder, it is exciting to observe the growth of this sport.
2. Over the years, several world-class cyclists have had spectacular careers, such as Eddy Merckx and Greg LeMond.
3. Running down the street without a care in the world, two pedestrians had to quickly move out of his way.
4. Being a member of the Sikh community, my paper will be given a strong personal focus.
5. Built in mere minutes, you will have a fully interactive website for your business or for your personal use.

6. A mother and her daughter were recently reunited after 18 years in a checkout line.
7. Germany has built an extensive network of highways through its countryside, known as the Autobahn.
8. Trying to find a job today, employers are stressing verbal and written communication skills more than ever before.
9. Adolescents essentially experience the same depressive symptoms as adults do.
10. This species of snake will eat frogs, mice, and small pieces of meat in captivity.

The Parallelism Principle

Balanced constructions give a sentence grace and strength, and such a sentence must be constructed so that coordinate words and phrases are treated the same grammatically. Parallelism ensures that the elements in a sentence that have the *same grammatical function* are expressed in parallel structures. Learning the fundamentals of parallelism will help you make your writing grammatically correct and easy to read.

Student writer Allison McClymont was able to use parallel structures to create a dramatic opening for her essay on school uniforms.

> **In the hallways of today's high school, students congregate in various cliques, using their dress as an indicator of their conformity: there are the "jocks" in their letterman jackets, the "nerds" in their high pants and suspenders, the "cheerleaders" in their short skirts and sweaters, and the "arties" in their paint-covered hippie clothes. Other easily identifiable cliques include the "gangsters," the "preppies," the "mods," the "punks," the "weirdos," and "the band geeks."**

Identifying and Fixing Parallelism Problems

Use a two-stage approach to identify and fix non-parallel structures in your writing.

In the first stage, identify structures that should be parallel: *lists, compounds, correlative conjunctions,* and *comparisons*. For example, the following sentence contains a compound object of the verb *prefer*:

> **Ian would prefer <u>to snack</u> on some chips rather than <u>eating</u> a regular dinner.**

In the second stage, make the identified parts parallel. Using our example, the two objects of the verb *prefer*, *to snack* and *eating*, must be expressed in parallel form. Either of these changes is correct:

> CORRECT   **Ian would prefer <u>to snack</u> on some chips than <u>to eat</u> a regular dinner.**
> or
> **Ian would prefer <u>snacking</u> on chips to <u>eating</u> a regular dinner.**

Parallelism is the principle that the elements in a sentence that have the *same grammatical function* are expressed in parallel structures.

 Chapter 3 contains more information on using repetition and creating balanced structures.

Chapter 3 contains more information on using repetition and creating balanced structures.

TIP

You should check to see whether all the elements are parallel whenever you use a list (three or more items), a compound (two items), correlative (paired) conjunctions, or a comparison (two parts).

The next example needs four nouns to make it grammatically parallel:

INCORRECT **The basic human needs are <u>food, clothes, shelter</u>, and <u>having</u> a good job.**

CORRECT **The basic human needs are <u>food, clothes, shelter</u>, and <u>a good job</u>.**

Three predicate adjectives or three independent clauses in the following sentence make the list parallel:

INCORRECT **After her 10-kilometre run, she felt <u>weak</u>, <u>tired</u>, and she <u>badly needed water</u>.**

CORRECT **After her 10-kilometre run, she felt <u>weak</u>, <u>tired</u>, and <u>very thirsty</u>.**
or
After her 10-kilometre run, <u>she felt weak</u>, <u>she was tired</u>, and <u>she badly needed water</u>.

There are also two options for the following sentence: change the infinitive *to sleep* to a gerund (an *–ing* verb acting as a noun) or change *watching* and *looking* to infinitives:

INCORRECT **Our cat enjoys <u>watching</u> TV, <u>looking</u> out the window, and to <u>sleep</u> at the foot of our bed.**

CORRECT **Our cat enjoys <u>watching</u> TV, <u>looking</u> out the window, and <u>sleeping</u> at the foot of our bed.**
or
Our cat likes <u>to watch</u> TV, <u>to look</u> out the window, and <u>to sleep</u> at the foot of our bed.

Finally, this sentence is fixed by using two verbs with the correlative conjunction *neither . . . nor*:

INCORRECT **Neither a <u>borrower</u> be, nor <u>lend</u> to others.**
CORRECT **Neither <u>borrow</u> from nor <u>lend</u> to others.**

You could also follow Shakespeare's example in his play *Hamlet* and use a noun after each part of the conjunction:

CORRECT **Neither a <u>borrower</u> nor a <u>lender</u> be.**

When checking for parallel structure, consider first the structurally essential words, such as nouns and verbs (not their modifiers). If adjectives or adverbs appear in a list without words to modify, ensure they are in parallel form. Look at any larger grammatical units, such as prepositional phrases, which should be parallel to each other. Similarly, dependent clauses should be parallel with other dependent clauses, and independent with other independent.

As seen earlier, the items in a list or series must be parallel. For example, if you use an expanded thesis statement that lists your essay's main points, you need to ensure that all the elements are grammatically parallel.

INCORRECT   **Research into cloning should be encouraged as it could lead to <u>cures</u> for diseases, successful organ <u>transplants</u>, and <u>put an end to infertility problems</u>.**

CORRECT   **Research into cloning should be legalized as it could lead to <u>cures</u> for diseases, successful organ <u>transplants</u>, and <u>solutions</u> to infertility problems.**

The elements are now parallel. Notice that to avoid repeating the word *cures*, a word with a similar meaning, *solutions*, has been used.

Length is not necessarily a factor in parallelism. For example, a simple noun is normally considered parallel with a noun phrase (but not with a prepositional phrase) because they have the same grammatical function.

The following sentence contains two nouns preceded by adjectives and a noun followed by an adjectival (prepositional) phrase. The important words here are the nouns:

Discipline in single-sex schools has been shown to directly affect regular <u>attendance</u>, good <u>grades</u>, and <u>standards</u> for dress and behaviour.

The incorrect versions of the following thesis statements include un-parallel lists:

INCORRECT   **The major forms of eating disorders involve the compulsion <u>to count calories</u>, <u>to constantly exercise</u>, and <u>the need to alter one's appearance</u>.**

CORRECT   **The major forms of eating disorders involve the compulsion <u>to count</u> calories, <u>to</u> constantly <u>exercise</u>, and <u>to alter</u> one's appearance.**

INCORRECT   **Buddhism teaches that one's karma can be affected by many things: <u>your generosity</u> to those less fortunate, <u>your behaviour to</u> strangers, and <u>if you treat</u> even your enemies with respect.**

CORRECT   **Buddhism teaches that one's karma can be affected by many things: <u>your generosity</u> to those less fortunate, <u>your behaviour to</u> strangers, and <u>your respect</u> even <u>for</u> your enemies.**

You also need to be careful that items in a list are *logically* parallel. The following list contains five nouns/noun phrases, but not all of the items are logically parallel.

INCORRECT   **Common injuries in the meat-packing industry include <u>chemical burns</u>, <u>broken bones</u>, <u>lacerations</u>, <u>amputations</u>, and <u>even death</u>.**

CORRECT   **Common injuries in the meat-packing industry include <u>chemical burns</u>, <u>broken bones</u>, <u>lacerations</u>, and <u>amputations</u>. Some accidents even result in <u>death</u>.**

More informal lists that use bullets or numbers also require parallel structure. Choose a starting point; then, ensure that each item has the same grammatical function and, if necessary, form.

INCORRECT

Before choosing a graduate program, a student should investigate

- **the number of graduate students who receive financial support;**
- **the expertise of faculty in the student's desired specialty;**
- **course work required; and**
- <u>**do research opportunities exist for graduate students**</u>**?**

Starting all items in the list with a noun or noun phrase makes the list grammatically parallel:

CORRECT

Before choosing a graduate program, a student should investigate

- **the number of graduate students who receive financial support;**
- **the expertise of faculty in the student's desired specialty;**
- <u>**the**</u> **course work required; and**
- <u>**the research opportunities available**</u>**.**

Compounds

A compound consists of two of the same parts of speech acting as a grammatical unit.

You must apply the principle of parallel structure to compounds. A coordinating conjunction, such as *or*, *and*, or *but*, can signal a compound, as can a prepositional phrase joiner such as *as well as*; in a comparison, *than* or *as* may join the two elements of a comparison.

Once you've identified a compound, look at the important word or phrase in the first element and ensure that the second, which follows the joiner, uses the parallel grammatical structure. Here are several examples of compounds:

INCORRECT	**It is actually cheaper <u>to convert</u> a used vehicle into an electric vehicle than <u>buying</u> a new gas-powered model.**
CORRECT	**It is actually cheaper <u>to convert</u> a used vehicle into an electric vehicle than <u>to buy</u> a new gas-powered model.**

Some compounds with helping verbs cause trouble. In these cases, it may be helpful to draw a line where the first element begins and another where the second begins (after the conjunction). Then, see if both parts line up with the main verb that follows; you can draw a line there too. The main verb in the sentence below is *worked*:

INCORRECT	**The prohibition of marijuana and the laws in place for it | <u>do not</u> and | <u>have never</u> | worked.**
TEST	**The prohibition of marijuana and the laws in place for it | <u>do not</u> . . . worked and <u>have never</u> worked.**
CORRECT	**The prohibition of marijuana and the laws in place for it <u>do not work</u> and <u>have never worked</u>.**

Sometimes a compound phrase ending in a preposition doesn't line up with what follows. Here are examples of a compound in which the words following the verbs don't fit with the object. Again, the presence of a coordinating conjunction can alert you to these tricky kinds of compounds:

INCORRECT   **Most people under 30 <u>are familiar or have heard of</u> the rapper Eminem.**

CORRECT   **Most people under 30 | <u>are familiar with or</u> | <u>have heard of</u> | the rapper Eminem.**

INCORRECT   **"We have to change our production methods to make sure the products we sell are <u>as good</u> or <u>better as</u> any in the world," said the minister of agriculture.**

CORRECT   **"We have to change our production methods to make sure the products we sell are | <u>as good as</u> | or <u>better than</u> | any in the world," said the minister of agriculture.**

Correlative Conjunctions

A specific kind of compound involves correlative conjunctions, joiners that work in pairs (*either . . . or, neither . . . nor, both . . . and, not . . . but, not only . . . but also*). Logically, the part of speech that follows the first half of the compound should also follow the second half. It might be helpful to draw a line after each conjunction:

INCORRECT   **A college diploma today is an investment <u>not only</u> | in students' financial resources but also | their time.**

What follows *not only* is a prepositional phrase that begins with *in*; therefore, a prepositional phrase, not just a noun (*time*), must follow the second member of the pair:

CORRECT   **A college diploma today is an investment <u>not only in</u> students' financial resources <u>but also in</u> their time.**

INCORRECT   **The lack of classroom availability means <u>either</u> constructing new buildings <u>or</u> lower the number of students accepted into programs.**

CORRECT   **The lack of classroom availability means <u>either</u> <u>constructing</u> new buildings <u>or lowering</u> the number of students accepted into programs.**

Comparisons

Faulty comparisons sometimes have to do with logic. Because comparisons are always made between two things, both elements must be fully expressed for the comparison to be complete. Often either the comparison is left incomplete or the terms being compared are incompatible; that is, they cannot be compared because there is no basis for comparison.

You need to ask if the two parts of a comparison are grammatically parallel, if both parts of the comparison are fully expressed, and if the two

> **TIP**
> *Than* is the word for comparisons, not the adverb related to time, *then*. Other words and phrases can also signal comparisons: *compared to, similar (to), different (from), as, like,* etc.

objects of the comparison can logically be compared. In the next sentence, the reader is left to assume whom males are being compared to:

INCOMPLETE **An unfortunate stereotype is that males are more scientific and less intuitive.**

COMPLETE **An unfortunate stereotype is that males are more scientific and less intuitive <u>than females</u>.**

INCOMPATIBLE **I have found that students are less judgmental at university compared to high school.**

You can ask what precisely is being compared and if the comparison is logical; grammatically, the writer is comparing a perceived trait of *students* at university to high school. People must be compared to people.

CORRECT **I have found that <u>people</u> are less judgmental at university <u>than they are</u> in high school.**

The two sides of the comparison are now complete and compatible.

INCOMPATIBLE **In the study, men's running times were recorded for 30 more years than women.**

What is being compared here? Are the terms comparable? The writer is comparing running times (for men) to women.

COMPATIBLE **In the study, men's running times were recorded for 30 more years than <u>women's times</u>.**

EXERCISE 15.12

Each of the following word groups contains three or four main points related to a topic. Using these lists, write a thesis statement for each topic, making sure that the sentences are parallel. Put the points in whatever order you like.

1. Why I like toe socks:
   - warm and comfortable
   - they are the latest fashion in socks
   - come in many colours and designs

2. The advantages of yoga:
   - to relax and reduce stress
   - to exercise
   - also can meet people in yoga classes

3. The importance of computers to students:
   - they provide entertainment
   - cutting down on homework time is important
   - you can obtain a wealth of information quickly

4. Living with roommates:

- they can create a lot of mess
- invade your personal space
- you can talk to them about your problems

5. The benefits of coffee:

- coffee helps you wake up
- it improves your mood
- it improves your concentration

After you've checked your answers in Appendix D, complete questions 6–10.

6. The comparison of two recreational drugs:

- their possible dangerous side effects
- who uses them
- the effects they produce in the user

7. The facts about organically grown food:

- the way organically grown food is farmed
- the cost of these kinds of foods
- their nutritional value

8. The advantages of home birthing:

- allows the parents to maintain control over their surroundings
- a positive and friendly place for the child to be born
- is as safe as a hospital birth if common sense is used

9. School uniforms are beneficial:

- promote school identity and school pride
- they save parents money and hassle
- reduce the pressure of students to conform to the latest fashions
- to make it easier for school authorities to enforce discipline

10. The legalization of marijuana:

- it is less addictive than some other illegal drugs
- the Canadian government has already made it legal under certain circumstances
- governments could increase their revenue by selling it
- making it legal would reduce crime since people wouldn't have to obtain it illegally

EXERCISE 15.13

These sentences contain parallelism errors. Identify the kind of error (series, compounds, correlative conjunctions, or comparisons) and fix it.

1. A good journalist is inquisitive, persistent, and must be a good listener.

2. Music can directly affect your thoughts, emotions, and how you feel.
3. In this essay, I will be looking and writing about the role of women in the military.
4. Tiddlywinks is not only a game of considerable skill but also strategy.
5. Television can affect children in a variety of negative ways since children often lack judgment, are naturally curious, and easily influenced.
6. When Jim has the choice of either jumping or to stay on the doomed ship, he chooses to jump.
7. Aman never has and never will be good at golf.
8. She was not only the best teacher I have ever had, but also I was impressed by her modesty.
9. Physical education teaches children not only to work well together but also patience and discipline.
10. Although two very different American writers, Nathaniel Hawthorne's and Mark Twain's works are nevertheless similar in many ways.

Passive Constructions: The Lazy Subject

Ordinarily, the subject of a sentence is acting, as in this example:

Ezra placed the book on the table.

In a passive construction the subject of the sentence is not doing the action:

The book was placed on the table by Ezra.

The direct object, *book*, has become the subject, and the original subject, *Ezra*, is now the object of the preposition *by*. The verb form has also changed. This sentence has a subject that is acted on rather than acting. Further, the passive construction requires more words than the active to provide the same information. Effective, direct English is geared toward the *active voice*.

> In a passive construction, the subject of the sentence does not perform the action. Instead, the noun that receives the action is the subject and is placed at the beginning of the sentence.

EXERCISE 15.14

Use your school's database to find some newspaper articles. Search the documents for examples of passive voice constructions.

The passive voice uses a form of the verb *to be* followed by a past participle. If the actor is named, it follows the preposition *by*. In the following sentence, the subjects are clearly the actors; you can't add the preposition *by* after *determined* or after *pleased*. This sentence uses an active construction:

Dana <u>was determined</u> to succeed at any cost; I <u>am pleased</u> to see him succeed.

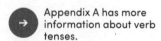 Appendix A has more information about verb tenses.

The following sentence contains three indicators of a passive construction:

The <u>door was opened</u> <u>by</u> a tall, sinister <u>man</u>.

The subject (*door*) is not doing the opening; the preposition *by* precedes the actor (*man*); and the simple past of *to be (was)* combines with the past participle of the main verb *(opened)* to form the passive voice of the verb.

Here's how to change a passive to an active construction:

1. Move the subject so that it follows the verb as the direct object.
2. Move the object of the preposition *by*, the actor, to the beginning of the sentence/clause to replace the passive subject.
3. Remove the identifying passive forms of the verb and the preposition *by*.

A tall, sinister man ~~was~~ opened the door ~~by~~.

Here's a slightly more complicated example:

PASSIVE	**The special commission <u>was informed</u> of its mandate <u>by</u> a superior court judge last Monday.**
ACTIVE	**A superior court judge informed the special commission of its mandate last Monday.**

In its active form, the sentence contains fewer words, and the thought is expressed more directly.

As a general rule, *don't use the passive voice if the active will serve.* However, there are times when the passive is acceptable or is even the better choice:

1. When the subject is unknown or is so well known it doesn't matter.

   Pierre Trudeau <u>was first elected</u> prime minister in 1968.

It is unnecessary to mention that the voters or the electorate elected him.

2. When passivity is implied or if the context makes it seem natural to stress the receiver of the action.

   When a cyclist completes a hard workout, massages <u>are usually performed</u> on the affected muscles.

In this sentence, the massages are more important than the person giving them.

ACCEPTABLE PASSIVE	**The woman <u>was kidnapped and held</u> hostage by a band of thugs.**
QUESTIONABLE PASSIVE	**Several of the thugs <u>were picked out</u> of a line-up <u>by</u> the woman.**

> **TIP**
> A fast way to change a passive into an active construction is to move the noun or pronoun that follows *by* to the beginning of the sentence. Then, the other required changes will be easier to see.

In the first sentence, the woman obviously is the passive recipient of the thugs' action. In the second sentence, she is doing the action; therefore, the active voice is preferred:

ACTIVE   **The woman <u>picked</u> several of the thugs out of a line-up.**

3. When the rhythm of the sentence requires it or because it is rhetorically effective.

    The books obviously <u>had been arranged</u> by a near-sighted librarian.

In this sentence, the librarian's near-sightedness is important; the placement of the adjective near the end of the sentence gives it emphasis.

4. When, in academic writing, it is unnecessary to mention the author of a study or the researcher, the passive may be used to stress the object of the study or the method of research.

    Through case studies, a comparison of two common methods for treating depression <u>will be made</u>.

In the following examples from academic writing, the passive is preferred either because the actor doesn't matter or because the writer wants to stress the receiver of the action:

In 1891 the science of embryology <u>was shaken</u> <u>by</u> the work of the cosmopolitan German biologist and vitalist philosopher Hans Driesch (Bowring 401).

The emergence of second-hand smoke (SHS) [as a cancer hazard] <u>has been offered</u> as a viable explanation for the increased enactment of local smoking restrictions (Asbridge 13).

— EXERCISE 15.15

The following sentences use passive constructions. Change unnecessary uses of the passive voice to form active constructions. You may have to add the actor, or "active" subject (see the example). Be prepared to justify your decision to keep any passive constructions.

Example:

PASSIVE

The suspect's behaviour had been watched for more than one month.

The suspect's behaviour had been watched [by the police] for more than one month.

> TIP
> Don't use the passive unless you want to de-emphasize the actor (active subject).

ACTIVE

The police had watched the suspect's behaviour for more than one month.

DECISION

Leave as passive because *suspect's behaviour* **is more important to the meaning than** *the police.*

1. I was given two choices by my landlord: pay up or get out.
2. It was reported that more than a thousand people were left homeless by recent flooding.
3. The dog was let out by her owner.
4. The concert was performed by the band in April.
5. Beethoven's Third Symphony, *The Eroica*, originally was dedicated to Napoleon.
6. Education needs to be seen by the government as the number one priority.
7. The library books were returned by Marc.
8. After the snowstorm, the streets were plowed by the city trucks.
9. Poverty in First Nations communities must be addressed by the federal, provincial, and First Nations' governments.
10. The book written by Ian Rankin became an instant bestseller.

EXERCISE 15.16

The following five paragraphs contain various errors discussed in Chapters 13–15.

1. Identify and correct the following:

   a. comma splice
   b. comma error
   c. pronoun case error
   d. broad pronoun reference
   e. missing pronoun antecedent
   f. two pronoun–antecedent agreement errors
   g. omitted apostrophe
   h. ambiguous pronoun reference
   i. failure to use gender-neutral language

   In my family, my father and sister play video games as much as me. They have become very complex, and can even improve problem-solving in children. By progressing through increasing difficulty levels, it can help childrens thought processes. On the one hand, if the child goes straight to the hardest setting, it may feel discouraged, on the other, if the child tries to systematically progress through increasing levels, he can learn the mechanics of the game step by step. This can help in the study of math, as the child may learn to persevere until he finds the solution.

2. Identify and correct the following:

    a. comma error
    b. subject–verb agreement error
    c. sentence fragment
    d. two parallelism errors
    e. misplaced modifier
    f. dangling modifier
    g. pronoun inconsistency
    h. comma splice

    Having a job and earning one's livelihood is a necessary goal in life, it is one of the reasons you acquire an education. At the place where I work however, many people come in expecting to find a job lacking presentation skills. Many are poorly dressed, do not know how to behave, and they may not speak grammatically. Untidy, disorganized, and unprepared, I still have to match them with a prospective employer. They lack the skills to present themselves to others and knowing what to do in public. Although they may be highly intelligent people.

After you've checked your answers in Appendix D, complete questions 3–5.

3. Identify and correct the following:
    a. comma splice
    b. misplaced comma
    c. parallelism error
    d. two omitted apostrophes
    e. sentence fragment
    f. two pronoun–antecedent agreement errors

    Logic can be defined as "the science of the formation and application of a general notion." Meaning that logic is apt to vary according to ones way of seeing certain things as important. A vegetarians logic, asserts that it is completely unnecessary—not to mention cruel—to eat animals in our day and age. Today's meat eater also has his logic. For him, meat is to be enjoyed, the taste of the food and the social interaction involved is to be cherished. We need to allow time in our busy lives to eat more and feeling guilty about it less.

4. Identify and correct the following:
    a. four comma errors
    b. semicolon error
    c. comma splice
    d. pronoun case error
    e. apostrophe error
    f. dangling modifier

The Myers–Briggs personality test is based on the work of Swiss psychologist, Carl Jung, and two Americans; Isabel Briggs Myers, and her mother Katharine C. Briggs. Myers developed the tests, and tried them out on thousands of schoolchildren; she wanted to see how the test results would correlate with vocation. Consisting of a series of questions requiring a yes or no response, she tested a group of medical students, who she followed up on 12 years later and who confirmed the test's validity. Variations of Myer's test are sometimes given by employers today, however, the results should not be the sole means for a hiring decision.

5. Identify and correct the following:

   a. comma splice
   b. comma error
   c. punctuation error other than comma
   d. parallelism error
   e. two apostrophe errors
   f. subject–verb agreement error
   g. pronoun–antecedent agreement error
   h. broad pronoun reference

   According to the principle's of Buddhism, neither sensual pleasures nor self-mortification bring about enlightenment, instead, the "Middle Way" is the path between these extremes; this can be understood through the "Four Noble Truths." These truths are: the truths of suffering, of the origins of suffering, of the cessation of suffering, and finding the path to end suffering. The Buddhas teaching asks each individual to examine her own conscience, and to come to a conclusion about the nature of truth.

EXERCISE 15.17

Identify and then correct the error(s) in each sentence.

1. Written through the eyes of a young boy, one can see the perspective of the Indigenous Peoples.

   a. dangling modifier
   b. misplaced modifier
   c. pronoun–antecedent agreement error
   d. comma error

2. The daily stresses of students, such as project or assignment due dates, teaches you to manage your time wisely.

   a. subject–verb agreement error
   b. pronoun inconsistency
   c. more than one error
   d. parallelism error

3. Parents sometimes push their children so hard to excel that they lose interest altogether.

   a. colon error
   b. pronoun reference error
   c. more than one error
   d. subject–verb agreement error

4. My roommate thinks it would be better for society, if all drugs were decriminalized.

   a. dangling modifier
   b. comma error
   c. subject–verb agreement error
   d. none of the above

5. Contributors to homelessness include the lack of well-paying jobs, increasingly large families and, probably the most important factor, which is the cost of living in a large city.

   a. dangling modifier
   b. more than one error
   c. comma error
   d. parallelism error

6. One of the most tragic events of the twentieth century. The detonation of the atomic bomb over Hiroshima.

   a. sentence fragment
   b. comma splice
   c. pronoun reference error
   d. none of the above

7. With the increasing media focus in the 1980s on the plight of home-less women, came the need for more research, unfortunately, this re-search was not comprehensive.

   a. comma splice
   b. more than one error
   c. pronoun–antecedent agreement error
   d. parallelism error

8. Optometrists have been reshaping the cornea in order to correct vi-sion for 50 years.

   a. parallelism error
   b. comma error
   c. misplaced modifier
   d. subject–verb agreement error

9. Information on airlines, currency exchange, and other passenger ser-vices are available on this website.

   a. subject–verb agreement error
   b. comma error
   c. more than one error
   d. run-on sentence

10. Many people are intrigued by the lives movie and TV heroes seem to live; these viewers tending to be teenagers.

   a. more than one error
   b. semicolon error
   c. parallelism error
   d. sentence fragment

EXERCISE 15.18

Identify the error (a, b, c, or d) and correct it in the sentence (there is one error in each sentence).

1. Anorexia <u>starts</u> when <u>a person</u> decides to take control over <u>his</u> <u>body</u>
        a   b   c d
   weight.

2. There <u>are</u> three types of turbine engines used in aircraft<u>;</u> the <u>turbojet,</u>
      a   b   c
   the turbofan<u>,</u> and the turboprop.
        d

3. Work <u>songs</u> and street <u>vendors</u> <u>cries</u> <u>are</u> examples of traditional
       a   b c d
   African American music styles.

4. <u>Reforms</u> of the UN Security Council <u>include</u> abolishing the veto or
     a   b
   <u>to extend</u> the Council beyond the <u>current five</u> members.
     c   d

5. Results from a recent study <u>showed that</u> patients <u>suffering from</u>
                 a   b
   osteoarthritis, <u>who listened to music for 20 minutes each day</u>, reported
                c
   <u>a 66 per cent</u> reduction in their perception of pain.
     d

After you've checked your answers in Appendix D, complete questions 6–10.

6. As a <u>known</u> anarchist<u>,</u> <u>Chomsky's views</u> <u>have been</u> much debated.
      a   b c   d

7. The brain of <u>a drug addict</u> <u>is</u> physically <u>different from</u> <u>a non-addict</u>.
         a b   c   d

8. The tobacco in cigarettes is not <u>the only</u> problem<u>,</u> <u>cigarettes</u> contain
                                              a   b   c

   many dangerous chemicals <u>as well</u>.
                                        d

9. By teaching <u>today's</u> youth safe and healthy approaches to sexuality<u>, it</u>
                          a   bc

   will elevate <u>their</u> self-esteem.
                        d

10. Holly Hunter, the actress <u>who</u> <u>I</u> most admire<u>,</u> appeared in several
                                           a   b   c

    <u>award-winning</u> movies.
            d

Chapter Review Questions

1. How do you find the subject of a sentence?
2. Does a prepositional phrase that follows a subject affect the verb form? If so, how?
3. What is a compound subject? How is a verb form affected by a compound subject?
4. When is a collective noun followed by a plural verb form?
5. Are most indefinite pronouns considered singular or plural? Why?
6. What are the three situations that cause most subject–verb agreement errors?
7. Why is the sentence *Every student should always finish his homework* incorrect?
8. How can you check for pronoun–antecedent errors?
9. What are the four kinds of pronoun reference errors?
10. When is it correct to use *who* in a sentence or clause? When would the use of *whom* be correct?
11. What are misplaced modifiers? Give an example.
12. What are dangling modifiers? Give an example.
13. What is parallelism and why is it important?
14. What is a compound?
15. When should you use passive sentence constructions?

16 Achieving Clarity and Depth in Your Writing

By the end of this chapter, you should be able to

- achieve clarity in writing;
- cut unneeded words and phrases;
- avoid weak sentence constructions;
- use direct and forceful language;
- distinguish between formal and informal diction;
- recognize confusing words;
- achieve variety and emphasis;
- proofread; and
- format an essay.

Many beginning writers believe that their essay is ready to submit once the first draft is done. Unfortunately, they miss a crucial stage of essay writing—revision. Papers can always be revised for clarity, precision, and conciseness. This chapter will help you create clear, direct, and reader-focused essays.

▲ Photo: Akos Szabo/iStockphoto

Effective Style: Clarity

Style is the way that one writes.

Clear writing, or clarity, is grammatical, concise, direct, precise, and specific.

 Chapter 12 addresses MLA and APA styles.

> **TIP**
>
> Clear writing is the result of hard work and attention to detail. Few writers—experienced or inexperienced—write clearly without making several revisions to ensure that their writing clearly expresses their thoughts.

Revising involves editing to achieve a polished final version.

> **TIP**
>
> When you write for an audience, it does not matter that you understand your ideas; your readers must understand them. Revise with your audience in mind.

> **TIP**
>
> Jargon is words or phrases that are used by certain professions, but these words are not always understood by others.

 Chapters 13–15 provide most of the information you need to write grammatically correct sentences. See "Prepackaged Goods: Clichés" later in this chapter for a discussion of clichés.

If you have written a research essay, you know that style is applied to documentation formats, such as MLA or APA. Style is also a term applied to ways in which people write, as in a dense, sophisticated style or a spare, terse style. No matter what a writer's style, clarity, or clear writing, must be the priority when they write with a specific purpose for a specific audience.

Clarity depends on various factors. One factor is audience. If you write about a specialized topic for a general audience and use words unfamiliar to them, you would not be writing clearly, though a specialist might understand you. Word choice and level of language are other important factors in clear and effective writing.

Writing clearly is the result of hard work and attention to detail. Few writers—experienced or inexperienced—write clearly the first time. They always make several revisions. Much of the revising process focuses on making the language clearly express the thought behind it.

Experienced writers know that their first drafts need several revisions. They look at their writing and ask, "Can this be clearer?" Student writers should also ask themselves this question. If the answer is "yes" or "maybe," try paraphrasing the content. Can you do so easily? Does your paraphrase express the point more clearly? Rewording a phrase or sentence often brings you closer to your intended meaning. However, what is most important is that your readers understand your ideas as you meant them. Revise your work with this thought in mind.

Ask yourself the following questions when revising your work:

- *Is it grammatical?* Do your sentences and paragraphs use proper grammar? Have you checked for errors?
- *Is it concise?* Do you use only as many words as you need? Have you used basic words and simple constructions that reflect what you want to say? Do not use slang, clichés, or jargon, as they are not concise.
- *Is it direct?* Have you used straightforward language? Are your sentence structures as simple as possible given the complexity of your points? Are you using the active voice?
- *Is it precise?* Does it say exactly what you want it to say? Remember, "almost" or "close enough" is not sufficient. Would another word or phrase more accurately reflect your thought?
- *Is it specific?* Is it as detailed as it needs to be? Is it definitive and concrete, not vague or abstract? Do not use adjectives such as *big* or *huge*. Use concrete numbers, if possible, or other words to help the reader understand your point. For example, say "Many people believe this is a problem" instead of "It is a huge problem."

Writers who carefully work to make their writing more grammatical, concise, direct, precise, and specific will likely produce a clear essay. However, experienced writers aim for forceful writing as well by introducing variety and emphasis in their writing.

TIP
Do not use more words than necessary to express an idea.

EXERCISE 16.1

The following paragraph is from an argumentative essay. Find examples that illustrate the stylistic problems discussed to this point. How could the paragraph be clearer?

> Foie gras is considered a delicious delicacy by some, yet it is viewed with disdain by others. Foie gras is duck or goose liver pâté, which is very fatty. It is created by force-feeding the ducks or geese with a corn-based food. Tubes are forced down the animal's throat and then it is forced to consume more food than it would normally, either in the wild or in captivity. Many organizations in both Europe and North America are calling for a ban on the sale of foie gras in order to encourage the immediate cessation of this form of animal cruelty. In some states, such as the glorious state of California, this force-feeding has been outlawed by the courts. Some chefs, including celebrity chefs, refuse to use foie gras, as they firmly believe that the force-feeding practice is unnecessarily cruel and a terrible thing. If more people were aware of the cruel and inhumane treatment of the poor ducks and geese, then maybe they would stop supporting this cruel and inhumane industry. It is our necessary duty to inform the uninformed population.

EXERCISE 16.2

Choose one of the student essays in this textbook. Find examples of how the writer addresses the audience and note any places where using variety in the sentences or paragraphs makes the essay more interesting and the points more forceful.

Why should so much effort be devoted to concise and direct writing? The reason is that such work is easy to follow and keeps the reader's interest. Unnecessary repetition and other clutter dull a writer's points.

Have you ever read a novel filled with pointless details? How interested were you in the book? If you are like most readers, you probably stopped reading. Redundancy and excessive detail create the same reaction in your readers.

Just as concise and direct writing makes you seem reliable, indirect writing may give the sense that you

- lack confidence in what you're saying,
- are trying to impress the reader, or
- are using unnecessary words to reach a word count.

TIP
When you use unnecessary words or express yourself in a meandering way, you increase the odds of making grammatical and mechanical errors.

16 Achieving Clarity and Depth in Your Writing   327

When you use more words than you have to or express yourself in a roundabout way, you also increase the odds of making grammatical and mechanical errors.

Cutting for Conciseness

To achieve conciseness, cut what is inessential. The simplest way to determine if something is unnecessary is to remove it and see if the meaning and effectiveness of the statement changes. If not, you don't need it. Your instructor may indicate problems with conciseness by putting parentheses around what is unneeded or by writing *wordy* or *verbose* in the margin. Don't think of it as criticism but as advice on how to be a better writer.

The following sections describe many common stylistic patterns that student writers adopt, especially in their early drafts. Consider the strategies to avoid them as you revise your essay.

Doubling Up: The Noah's Ark Syndrome

Writers sometimes suffer from "double vision," where two words sometimes automatically pop up: two verbs, two nouns, two adjectives, or two adverbs. Experienced editors offer this formula: one + one = one-half. Put another way, using two words when one is enough halves the impact of the one word.

> **The administrative officer came up with an <u>original</u>, innovative suggestion for cost-cutting.** [Anything innovative is bound to be original.]
>
> **The event will be held at <u>various</u> different venues.** [*Various* and *different* mean the same thing.]
>
> **The accident was a <u>terrible</u> tragedy.** [How can you quantify a tragedy?]

┌─TIP
If a second noun, verb, adjective, or adverb doesn't make your meaning clearer, delete it.

Although it is not always wrong to use two of the same parts of speech consecutively, the terms must not convey the same thing. Be especially wary of verb–adverb combinations; ensure that the adverb is necessary.

> **The airport was <u>intentionally</u> designed for larger aircraft.** [Can a design be unintentional?]
>
> **She <u>successfully</u> accomplished what she had set out to do.** [The word *accomplished* implies success.]

Here are some common verb–adverb pairings and other combinations that are usually redundant. The unneeded words are in parentheses.

(anxiously) fear	(completely) surround
(better/further) enhance	descend (down)
(carefully) consider	dominate (over)
(clearly) articulate	drawl (lazily)
climb (up)	dwindle (down)
combine/join (together)	emphasize/stress (strongly)

estimate/approximate (roughly)
(eventually) evolve (over time)
examine (closely)
fill (completely)
finish (entirely)
gather/assemble (together)
gaze (steadily)
(harshly) condemn
hurry (quickly)
plan (ahead)
ponder (thoughtfully)
praise (in favour of)

progress (forward/onward)
protest (against)
refer/return/revert/reply (back) to
rely/depend (heavily) on
sob (uncontrollably)
(strictly) forbid
(successfully) prove
(suddenly) interrupt
(symbolically) represent
(totally) eradicate/devastate
unite (as one)
vanish (without a trace)

Be wary of repetitive adjective–noun pairings such as the following:

(advance) warning
(brief) encapsulation
(dead) carcass
(fiery) blaze
(future) plan
(knowledgeable) specialist
(mutual) agreement
(new) beginning

(past) memory
(positive) benefits
(powerful) blast
(sharp) needle
(terrible) tragedy
(timeless) classic
(total) abstinence

Redundancies are also evident in such familiar phrases as *consensus of opinion, end result, end product, in actual fact, this point in time, time frame, time period, time span, years of age,* etc. Finally, unnecessary nouns are redundant. These words steal the thunder from other parts of speech, including other nouns and verbs.

The <u>world</u> of politics demands that you kowtow to the ineptitude of others.

The efforts of conservationists in the <u>fields of</u> ecology and biodiversity are leading to renewed efforts to save old-growth forests.

In each of these examples, a weaker noun displaces the most important noun. In the first sentence, we are not talking about a world, but about politics. In the second, the noun *fields* is redundant because ecology and biodiversity are fields of study.

EXERCISE 16.3

Listen to your favourite radio station or podcast or watch one of your favourite TV shows. Pay attention to the language used by the advertisers, announcers, and actors. Write down some of the most frequent examples of doubling up and be prepared to share them with the class.

Phony Phrases

Phony phrases are wordy prepositional phrases. Look for them after verbs and nouns.

UNNECESSARY	**For now, the patient's kidneys are functioning <u>at a normal level</u>.**
BETTER	**For now, the patient's kidneys are functioning <u>normally</u>.**

Here, the preposition *for* introduces the phony phrase:

UNNECESSARY	**The bill was legislated in 1995 <u>for a brief period of time</u>.**
BETTER	**The bill was <u>briefly</u> legislated in 1995.**

A cluster of non-specific nouns, such as *level*, *scale*, *basis*, *degree*, and *extent*, are connected to phony phrases beginning with *on*, *to*, or other prepositions. Watch for these prepositional phrases: *on/at the international level*, *on a regular basis*, *on the larger scale*, *to a great/considerable degree/extent*. Such phrases can likely be replaced by an appropriate adverb.

UNNECESSARY	**Jindra checks her voicemail <u>on a regular basis</u>.**
BETTER	**Jindra checks her voicemail <u>regularly</u>.**

A relative clause is adjectival and may sometimes be replaced by a corresponding adjective preceding the noun. In the following sentence, the relative clause *that is high in protein* modifies *diet*:

UNNECESSARY	**Most bodybuilders follow a strict diet <u>that is high in protein</u>.**
BETTER	**Most bodybuilders follow a strict, <u>high-protein</u> diet.**

The Small but Not-So-Beautiful

Writers may think that small words, such as prepositions and articles, make an ordinary phrase sound more impressive. But these terms can be omitted from many sentences. In these examples, parentheses indicate words that can be omitted:

He was (the) last out (of) the door.

(The) taking (of) life can never be condoned.

The word *that* can be used as a pronoun (demonstrative or relative), adjective, or subordinating conjunction. It can often be omitted if the subject of the second clause is different from the subject of the preceding clause. By methodically checking your first draft for unnecessary *that*s, you can often improve sentence flow. Use the search function in your word processing software to find these problem words quickly.

I thought (that) Silas was going to attend the same school (that) his brother went to.

> **TIP**
> If you can sum up a prepositional phrase with a one-word adverb or adjective, use the one-word modifier.

> **TIP**
> If possible, delete "clutter words" such as *of* or *that*.

Unravel the meaning of the following statement:

It's certain that that *that* that that person used was wrong.

Unintensives

An intensive is a word or phrase that emphasizes the word or expression it modifies but has little meaning on its own. Intensives should be avoided in all levels of formal writing unless they truly add emphasis. The intensives in the following sentence are unneeded:

She is <u>certainly</u> a <u>very</u> impressive speaker.

Words such as *certainly* and *very* are overused and may add nothing to the sentence.

 Many intensives are adverbs modifying verbs or adjectives. In some instances, you can simply replace a weak verb and an intensive with a stronger verb or use a stronger adjective instead of an intensive plus a weak adjective. A better option may be to get rid of the intensive.

> **TIP**
> Instead of using an adverb such as *very, highly, really,* or *extremely* before an adjective, use a stronger adjective or simply delete the adverb.

UNNECESSARY	**He was <u>very grateful</u> for his warm reception.**
BETTER	**He was <u>gratified by</u> his warm reception.**
or	
	He <u>appreciated</u> his warm reception.

Overused intensives:

absolutely	indeed
actually	inevitably
assuredly	in fact
certainly	interestingly
clearly	markedly
completely	naturally
considerably	of course
definitely	particularly
effectively	significantly
extremely	surely
fundamentally	totally
highly	utterly
incredibly	very

Other overused qualifiers:

apparently	hopefully
arguably	in effect
basically	in general
essentially	kind of
generally	overall

perhaps	seemingly
quite	somewhat
rather	sort of
relatively	virtually

Here are some intensives that may clutter your sentences:

aforementioned	in regard(s) to
amidst	in terms of
amongst	in the final analysis
analogous to	in view of the fact that
as a result of	irregardless
as to	notwithstanding the fact that
at this point in time	oftentimes
cognizant of	pertaining to
consequent to	so as to
despite the fact that	subsequent to
due to the fact that	that
each and every	the majority of
in accordance with	thusly
in as much as	whether or not
in comparison to	whilst
in conjunction with	with regard(s) to
in connection with	with respect to
in reference to	

Writing Directly

Writing should get straight to the point. Indirect writing stresses the less important parts of the sentence.

Black Hole Constructions

Banishing all passive constructions would unreasonably limit writers. However, inappropriately passive constructions not only use too many words but also place the stress where it doesn't belong, weakening the entire sentence. Other indirect constructions can also weaken a sentence. Think of them as the black holes of writing: they swallow up the substance of the sentence.

> **TIP**
> Whenever possible, avoid starting sentences with *it is* or *there are* constructions. Using these weak beginnings may make your reader lose interest.

1. *It was*

   It was Mary Shelley who wrote *Frankenstein* in 1816.

As simple as this sentence is, it begins weakly by displacing the logical subject, *Mary Shelley*, and substituting *it was*. The sentence is stronger and more direct when the most important noun is the subject:

Mary Shelley wrote *Frankenstein* in 1816.

If a relative pronoun (*who*, *which*, or *that*) follows the displaced subject, consider getting rid of it and the "empty" subject (*it was*, *there is*, *here is*) to make the statement more direct and concise.

Occasionally, you may want to use *it was* and similar constructions for rhetorical effect. In such cases, emphasis, rather than directness, may determine your choice.

TIP

Notice how many sentences in the sample paragraph in Exercise 16.1 contain weak openings. They affect the entire paragraph, making it hard to read.

UNNECESSARY	**There are a variety of strategies that you can use to reduce excess verbiage in your writing.**
BETTER	**You can use various strategies to reduce verbiage in your writing.**

2. *One of*

Avoid the phrase *one of* in your sentences.

POOR	**The path you have chosen is one of danger and uncertainty.**
BETTER	**The path you have chosen is dangerous and uncertain.**
	or
	You have chosen a dangerous, uncertain path.

3. *The reason . . . is because*

This construction is both illogical and redundant:

INCORRECT	**The reason Jessica is lucky is because she has a horseshoe on her door.**
CORRECT	**Jessica is lucky because she has a horseshoe on her door.**

Numbing Nouns

Writers sometimes fall into the habit of using a weak verb and a corresponding noun rather than a verb that directly expresses the meaning. In each of these cases in the following list, a direct verb replaces a weak verb phrase.

TIP

Weak verb + noun constructions begin with common verbs such as *have*, *make*, or *take* and follow with a noun object, which can usually be made into a strong verb.

Weak Constructions	Strong Constructions
I *had a meeting* with my staff, and I am now asking you to *provide a list of* all your clients.	I met with my staff and now ask you *to list* all your clients.
Inexperienced writers *have a tendency* to be wordy.	Inexperienced writers *tend* to be wordy.
She *made changes* to the document, *making clear* what was ambiguous.	She *changed* the document, *clarifying* ambiguities.
Sam *offered comfort* to Amanda, who *received a failing grade* on her essay.	Sam *comforted* Amanda, who *had failed* her essay.
Canada *made a significant contribution* to the war effort in France and Belgium.	Canada *contributed significantly* to the war effort in France and Belgium.

TABLE 16.1 Nominals

Verb	Nominal	Example
accumulate	*accumulation*	Nominal: The accumulation of evidence is overwhelming. The nominal *accumulation of* can be deleted: The evidence is overwhelming.
classify	*classification*	We will now proceed with the classification of Vertebrata.
		Verb: We will now classify Vertebrata.
intend; install	*intention; installation*	Nominal: Our intention is to complete the installation of the new system this month. Verb: We intend to finish installing the new system this month.

For the weak phrase *has an effect on*, where *has* is the verb and *effect* is the noun, *affect* is the corresponding verb form.

> **Global warming has an <u>effect</u> on major weather patterns. Its <u>effects</u> are widely felt around the globe.**

> **Global warming <u>affects</u> major weather patterns. Its <u>effects</u> are widely felt around the globe.**

┌──────────────────────────────┐TIP
│ Avoid a succession of long   │
│ words if shorter, basic words │
│ are just as effective.   │
└──────────────────────────────┘

Nouns that pile up in a sentence can create a numbing effect. This situation is common with nominals, nouns formed from verbs (see Table 16.1). You can use a polysyllabic noun formed from a verb unless a more concise and direct alternative exists.

> **The conflict between Billy and Claggart ultimately serves as a device in the interruption of the reader's attempts at a coherent interpretation of the novel as an ideological message. In addition to problematizing definitive interpretations, this technique effectively secures a lasting relevance for the novel.**

The thought in these sentences can be expressed more directly and clearly by omitting words and reducing the number of nominals.

> **The conflict between Billy and Claggart challenges a coherent ideological reading of the novel, making definitive readings difficult and ensuring the novel's relevance.**

Euphemisms

A euphemism is a word or phrase substituted for the actual name of something, usually to make it more acceptable or to give it dignity. It is an example of indirect writing.

The term *euphemism* comes from the Greek word that means "to use words for good omen." Many ancient cultures used euphemisms to avoid naming their enemies directly, thereby refusing to give power to those they feared. Today, we use such words out of kindness to those who may be suffering, as a way of speaking about taboo subjects and objects, or as a form of satire or irony. For example, *to pass away* or *pass on* are the most common euphemisms for *die*.

A taboo subject is one that society has decided should not be talked about, unless you use special words. For example, in Canada, people do not go to the *toilet*. Instead, they go to the *bathroom*. Some taboo subjects can be discussed using humour, as long as you know your audience. Again, some people do not say that someone died. They use the phrases *passed away* or *passed on*, but a humorous phrase is *kicked the bucket*.

Along with protecting us from the unpleasant, euphemisms give us false assurance. For example, *urban renewal* avoids the implications of *slum clearance*, *revenue enhancement* has a more positive ring than *tax increase*, and *collateral losses* attempts to sidestep the fact that civilians have been killed during military action. We also sometimes use euphemisms to give something more dignity or a sense of importance: *pre-owned automobile* for *used car* and *job action* for *strike*. The Plain English Campaign once gave a Golden Bull Award to writers who described the act of laying bricks as "install[ing] a component into the structural fabric."

The following classified ad uses some wordy and euphemistic language:

We are seeking an individual who possesses demonstrated skills and abilities, a sound knowledge base coupled with the experience to provide service to mentally challenged teenagers with "unique" and significant challenging behaviours.

The position's requirements can be expressed with half the words:

Applicants need proven skills, knowledge, and experience to serve mentally challenged teenagers with challenging behaviours.

A special category of "acceptable euphemisms" are those that society agrees should be substituted for expressions that have acquired inappropriate or offensive connotations. For example, to refer to someone in a wheelchair as a *cripple* inappropriately stresses the disability and its limitations. A more sensitive and accurate description is *a person with a physical disability* (or *a physical challenge*). The person is not the disability. When you are writing about persons with disabilities, refer to the following resource to ensure lack of bias in your wording: https://apastyle.apa.org/style-grammar-guidelines/bias-free-language/disability.

EXERCISE 16.4

In groups, think of or make up 10 euphemisms. Read the list to your other classmates and have them guess what each describes.

The following sentences can be revised for conciseness and directness. Make the necessary changes and be prepared to justify them.

1. Tanya has been invited to provide us with a summary of the significant main points of her findings.

2. The totally unexpected tsunami turned the fields into either a large waste land or a large junk yard.

3. Gretta was decidedly overjoyed after being the unexpected recipient of an income tax refund in excess of $1,000.

4. The protagonist of *Life of Pi* is confronted with the necessity of making the decision about whether he wanted to continue on living or not.

5. It was because of her clear, beautiful voice that she was made the winner of the singing contest.

6. The disappearance of even one single species at the lower end of the food chain can have dire adverse effects in many instances on the survival of various other species.

7. Although Copernicus's radical idea that the Earth made revolutions around the sun was once considered an extreme heresy and was ridiculed mercilessly by his peers, the idea eventually gained gradual acceptance.

8. The fact is that for many students of above-average intelligence, school can seem tedious and dull, so they begin to act up in class and cause other students who are not as smart to miss the important and salient points of the lesson in question.

9. Perhaps in the heat of emotion the act of capital punishment would seem to be a feasible idea, but when you come to think of it rationally, this act would accomplish virtually next to nothing at all.

10. In protest of their salary freeze, all of the teachers who teach at the high school in Oak Bay have made the unanimous decision not to undertake any tasks of a supervisory nature until the school board has conducted a fair and impartial salary review.

11. Vehicles that have the four-way drive feature option are an extremely practical and pragmatic form of transportation for the majority of the Canadian population in this day and age.

12. There are many people in our society today who have serious drug addictions that take complete and utter control over their lives.

13. From the beginning of its conception, Canada has been a country concerned with promoting an active multicultural society, although the reality of unity within the country is still a large, unanswered question in the minds of most of the people of Canada.

14. A French scientist by the name of Louis Pasteur was the first individual to make the discovery that microbes were harmful menaces to the well-being and healthy functioning of the human body.

15. The reason yoga allows us to live a healthy lifestyle is due to the fact that it provides a strong basis for the efficient functioning of the body's endocrine system.

Rewrite the following passage, aiming for concise, direct writing.

Dear Employers,

The Youth Resource Centre, in conjunction with the Federal Human Resource Department of Canada, has opened the Hire-a-Student office once again this summer, staffing summer employment officers working toward finding the best possible student employees for any jobs that you may have available to post with us at the centre.

Our service, conveniently situated at 147 High Street, is a totally free service to both employers posting jobs in the centre and to students and youths trying to secure employment opportunities throughout the community. The service is a means for you the employer to help advertise any positions you may have available, and is additionally a way to assist students who are showing initiative in finding possible long-term or limited-term seasonal employment.

We are not a solicitation firm, and this is the point that we need to emphasize to the greatest extent. Our service is absolutely free of charge, and our intention is first and foremost to try and find employment for students who seem serious about working, as well as to offer a free alternative to posting jobs in newspapers and ad agencies that could end up costing you an excessive amount of money through advertising ventures.

Working toward Precision: Wise Word Choices

As we have indicated throughout this text, most college and university writing assignments require formal writing, also known as formal diction. You may be more familiar with informal writing, which you probably use in social media and even used in your high school English courses. In informal writing,

- language may be close to speech or be chatty, with colloquialisms, idioms, or even slang;
- contractions are acceptable (e.g., *don't, can't, shouldn't, it's*);
- the first-person (*I, me*) and second-person (*you*) voice may be used;
- sentence fragments may be used occasionally for dramatic effect;
- short paragraphs are the rule rather than the exception; and
- citations for research sources are not given.

Formal writing follows the rules of formal usage and grammar. Therefore, unless you are quoting someone or your instructor tells you otherwise, avoid contractions, colloquialisms, slang, and jargon. For example, do not use any of the following in a formal essay:

catch the bus/catch a ride   downside
do drugs   fall for

Formal writing features the rules of formal usage and correct grammar. **Diction** is related to word choices and level of language; formal and informal writing are examples of different kinds of diction. **Colloquialisms** are words and expressions acceptable in conversation but not in formal writing. An **idiom** is a phrase whose meaning is understood only within the context of the phrase. For example, *his bark is worse than his bite* can be understood only by looking at the overall meaning and not by the meanings of the individual words

give the green light	put a positive spin (on something)
go overboard	put on hold
go to great lengths	put (someone) down
grab the reader's attention	quick fix
mindset	stressed (out)
no way	the way to go
obsess (about something)	tune out
okay	upfront
opt for	way more (of something—*a lot* is
pan out	also colloquial)
price tag	

TIP

Avoid using informal verbs such as *saw*, *has seen*, etc., when you mean *resulted in* or *occurred* (e.g., "The policy that was implemented two years ago *has seen* a 40 per cent drop in violent crime." Revised: "The policy that was implemented two years ago *has resulted in* a 40 per cent drop in violent crime.").

Avoid non-specific and merely qualitative words and phrases, such as *great*, *incredible*, *beautiful*, *terrible*, and the like. You also should refrain from using words and expressions that might suggest a gender, sexual, racial, cultural, or other kind of bias.

Of course, your word choices involve much more than thinking about the level of formality. Effective writers choose their words and phrases carefully. The following example from a student essay demonstrates poor word choice:

The mass production of plastics and ready-to-use products is growing at a <u>staggering</u> rate.

Staggering is informal; the writer could have used *rapid*, *rapidly increasing*, or *exponential* or a specific rate, such as *doubling every five years*.

EXERCISE 16.7

Find uses of informal language in the following excerpt and then provide more concise wording.

There was an article about a campaign that a group called Respect for Animals is waging to convince consumers to boycott Canadian seafood products. The magazine also carried two huge advertisements from the same organization.

The Newfoundland seal hunt is transparently and demonstrably sustainable and humane. There are roughly half a million people in Newfoundland and Labrador, and nearly six million harp seals, which is almost three times as many seals as when I was a kid.

Here's one of those obligatory disclosures: over the years, several environmental organizations—the Sierra Club, the David Suzuki Foundation, Greenpeace, etc.—have subsidized my preoccupation with things that move in the water by having me do research projects for them and so on. With that out of the way, I can now say, if it isn't obvious already, that it's the seal hunt's opponents who turn my stomach.

Glavin, Terry. "An Enviro's Case for Seal Hunt." *The Tyee*, 2007, http://thetyee.ca/Views/2007/03/07/SealHunt/.

Writers usually don't make extreme blunders but choose a word that doesn't quite suit their purpose. These "near misses" can distract or confuse the reader. You should not let the search for the exact word prevent you from fully expressing your ideas in a first DRAFT. But when revising, look up the meanings of all words you're in doubt about—even if you're only a little unsure. You can use a thesaurus to look for words similar in meaning to avoid repeating a word too often. Make sure you use a reliable dictionary to check these new words as well; a thesaurus usually does not provide word connotations.

TIP
Writers often use words that have specific associations or implications. A word's connotation includes its possible meanings in its given context.

Some dictionaries help you to be precise not only by defining the main entry but also by providing distinctions among similar words. For example, the *Gage Canadian Dictionary*, which lists more than six meanings for the adjective *effective*, also defines two words similar in meaning but different in connotation:

Syn. adj. 1. Effective, effectual, efficient = producing an effect. Effective, usually describing things, emphasizes producing a wanted or expected effect: *several new drugs are effective in treating serious diseases*. Effectual, describing people or things, emphasizes having produced or having the power to produce the exact effect or result intended: *his efforts are more energetic than effectual*. Efficient, often describing people, emphasizes being able to produce the effect wanted or intended without wasting energy, time, etc.: *A skilled surgeon is highly efficient*.

Similarly, the *Student's Oxford Canadian Dictionary*, which lists seven meanings for the adjective *nice*, offers the following examples of words that may be more appropriate or more forceful in certain contexts:

we had a delightful/splendid/enjoyable time

a satisfying/delicious/exquisite meal

a fashionable/stylish/elegant/chic outfit

this is a cozy/comfortable/attractive room

she is kind/friendly/likeable/amiable

our advisor is compassionate/understanding/sympathetic

a thoughtful/considerate/caring gesture

Precision and Logic

Imprecision sometimes results from illogical thinking or from writing down an idea quickly. To confirm that what you've written makes sense, you need to look carefully at the relationship among the parts of the sentence, especially at the relationship between the subject and predicate. A weak or non-existent relationship creates a logical error. For example, faulty predication occurs if a verb cannot be logically connected to its subject. In general, avoid *is when* and *is where* after a subject in sentences that

Faulty predication occurs where a verb cannot be logically linked to its subject.

define something. In the following sentence, *faulty predication* is illogically referred to as a time:

INCORRECT	**Faulty predication is when a verb cannot be logically connected to its subject.**
CORRECT	**Faulty predication occurs where [i.e., in a sentence] a verb is not logically connected to its subject.**
	or
	Faulty predication is an illogical juxtaposing of a subject and a verb.

Consider this comment on the setting of Joseph Conrad's *Heart of Darkness*:

The Congo represents an inward journey for the character Marlow.

The Congo is the name of a country and a river. How can either represent a journey? Of course, a *trip through [a country]* or *on [a river]* would be a more logical phrase.

In one kind of faulty predication, an inanimate object is falsely linked to a human action:

Some opponents claim that <u>phys. ed. programs</u> are unwilling to accommodate the needs of all students.

The programs aren't "unwilling," since this implies a will; teachers or administrators may be unwilling.

Some opponents claim that <u>the administrators of phys. ed. programs</u> are unwilling to accommodate the needs of all students.

Sound should also play a role in word choice. You should avoid placing words with similar sounds in close proximity (e.g., *the echo effect*).

Endorphins enable the body to heal itself and <u>gain pain</u> relief.

You should also be wary of unintentional puns in a work of scholarship:

The first experiments in music therapy were <u>noted</u> during the First World War.

An objective voice is the hallmark of both expository and argumentative writing. Though you may be tempted to write ironically or sarcastically, keep the tone objective. Remember, your reader may not share your attitude or may not understand your meaning.

Inappropriate tone: It is well known that college students under stress need to exercise their livers on the occasional Friday night.

Tone shows the writer's attitude toward the subject.

EXERCISE 16.8

Rewrite the following paragraph, replacing informal diction with formal. Note that a word or phrase might be colloquial but necessary due to context or not easily rephrased.

Hosting the Olympic Games is a once-in-a-lifetime opportunity, and it seems like a great idea. It would create world recognition for a world-class city, helping to really put it on the map. On top of that, it would be a fun and exciting time for the citizens of the surrounding area. However, after sober second thought, it is clear that while the Games might pay for themselves, who will pay for the upgrades necessary to get the city in good shape for the Games? Even with the government chipping in for a fair amount of the costs, because that city would be dealing in billions of dollars, even a small chunk of that cost is a lot of money. These small chunks would come from the pockets of the taxpayer, some of whom are not big fans of the Games at all. But although these direct costs are bound to be steep, it is the hidden costs of the Games that will be the real killer.

Verbs with Vitality

Look at the verbs in your sentences. Could you replace them with stronger, more descriptive ones? Could you replace *be* and *have*, which convey a state or condition, with verbs of action? Common verbs, such as *do*, *make*, *go*, and *get*, are not specific. Could you replace them with more precise or emphatic verbs?

 Chapter 13 discusses verbs at length.

The most common verb in English, *to be*, takes many different forms as an irregular verb—*am*, *is*, *are*, *was*, *were*, *will be*, etc.—and appears frequently as a helping verb. Your writing will be more concise if you omit these forms whenever they are unnecessary.

> **The results of the study can be interpreted as ~~being~~ credible.**
>
> **She dreamed of a carriage ~~being~~ pulled by two fine horses.**
>
> **Hypnosis has been proven ~~to be~~ an effective therapy for some people.**
>
> **In 313 BCE, Christianity was declared ~~to be~~ the official religion of Rome.**

TIP

When checking whether a subject fits with its predicate, ensure that the subject can perform the action that the verb describes.

Verbs and nouns are the two most important parts of speech. The verbs you use can weaken or strengthen your writing. Choose them carefully, preferring active to static verbs and deleting forms such as *being* and *to be* when they are unneeded.

As people put on the spot by journalists and the public, politicians sometimes choose vague language to avoid committing themselves to statements they may regret later. A more cynical view suggests that abstract, indefinite language enables them to say little while appearing informed and in control. Notice the lack of specificity in the following comments by Prime Minister Justin Trudeau, made in his testimony to the House of Commons. The comments were aired on *Sunday Scrum* on August 2, 2020:

> There was never any direction by or attempt to influence from me or my staff that the public service recommend WE charity. Getting young people to serve has been a goal of mine well before I ever got into politics. So, I deeply regret how this has unfolded. None of this program was in any way going to benefit any members of my family and that was something I was very comfortable with.

"Sunday Scrum: WE Controversy Continues as Trudeau Testifies." CBC News, 2 Aug. 2020, https://www.cbc.ca/news/politics/sunday-scrum-videos-august-2-1.5672221.

Indicate which verbs in the following paragraph should be made more descriptive.

By the 1800s, inventions were beginning to put people out of work. One of the first inventions that resulted in rebellion was in the craft guild. In 1801, Joseph Jacquard became known as the inventor of the Jacquard loom. This loom was capable of being programmed by pre-punched cards, which made it possible to create clothing design patterns. This invention led to the creation of the Luddites, who were a group made up from the craft guild. These people were against any type of manufacturing technology and went about burning down several factories that were using this new technology. The Luddites were around only for a couple of years, but the name Luddite is still used to describe people who are resistant to new technologies. The Jacquard loom was, in effect, an invention that replaced people. It could do great designs quickly and without making any errors. The replacement of people by machines was beginning.

Suggest how the following passage could be improved by using more specific language and by omitting unnecessary words and phrases.

The time period between 1985 and 1989 was a difficult one for graffiti artists in New York City. This was a time when graffiti barely stayed alive because of the harsh laws and efforts of the Metropolitan Transit Authority, which is known as the MTA. This period was called the period of the "Die Hards" because of the small number of die-hard artists who were able to keep graffiti from dying out completely. As a result of the measures of the MTA against graffiti art and artists, there was a lack of paint available for use and the level of enforcement was extremely high. The only important thing that was happening during these years was the use of markers for tagging. These tags were usually small, of poor artistic quality, and were finished quickly by the artists. These tags can be seen today at some bus stops and in some washrooms throughout the city.

Prepackaged Goods: Clichés

A cliché is a word or phrase that, though often true, has become overused, such as *weak as a kitten*.

Expressions considered clichés today were a veritable breath of fresh air in their prime. (Did you spot the clichés in the previous sentence?) If commentary on the cliché were to be made in clichés, the prose would be wordy and confusing:

However, with the passage of time (more years than you can shake a stick at), they became the stuff of idle minds until after time immemorial they assumed the mantle of respectability and were accepted verbatim as par for the course. Writers worth their salt should avoid clichés like the plague or they will stop all readers with a good head on their shoulders dead in their tracks (to call a spade a spade and to give the devil his due).

EXERCISE 16.11

Although newspaper features use informal writing, it should still be descriptive and concrete. How could you make this passage more interesting?

Steven won the lottery and was now in the money. He decided to buy himself a yacht, even though he didn't have a clue how to sail. When he went to the boat show, he was like a kid in a candy store. He looked at boats that were luxury liners, but they were smaller than cruise ships. He spied cruisers that had everything, including the kitchen sink. As he viewed all the sailing crafts, he wanted to feel the wind in his face and the water splashing over the decks. However, Steven's wife threw cold water on his dream when she pointed out that neither of them could sail and that they got sick as dogs when they were on a friend's boat the previous summer.

Clichés are overworked and unoriginal phrases, dead metaphors that have been drained of their novelty through overuse. Inexperienced writers may reach for them in a vain attempt to "spice up" their writing. Although they may appear in some informal writing, they are poor substitutes for informative, imaginative words.

Common Words That Confuse

English has many word pairs that are confusing because the two words look similar (for example, *affect* and *effect*) or because they have similar, but not identical, uses (for example, *amount* and *number*)—or both. In most cases, the dictionary is the best resource for problems related to meaning and spelling (don't rely on a spell-checker), but usage can be more complicated. We will discuss the top 25 words that give student writers the most trouble. Hints and examples are provided.

Usage is the customary and accepted way that a word is used.

1. **accept, except:** *Accept* is a verb meaning "to receive, to take what is offered." *Except* is a preposition meaning "other than" or "leaving out."

   HINT Think of the "crossing out" connotation of *x* in *except* to remind you that the word means "leaving out." Think of the letter *a* at the beginning of *accept* to remind you that it describes an action.

   EXAMPLE **The bargaining committee accepted all the terms except the last one.**

2. **affect, effect:** *Affect* is a verb meaning "to influence or have an effect on." *Effect*, a noun, means "a result." As a verb, *effect* is used less often; it means "to bring about" or "to cause"—not "to have an effect on."

> HINT   Try substituting *influence* in the sentence; if it fits your intended meaning, *affect* is the word you want. Again, you can also think of the letter *a* at the beginning of *affect* to remind you that it describes an action.
>
> EXAMPLE   **The news of Michael Jordan's return to basketball greatly affected his fans. The effect was also felt at the box office; an immediate hike in ticket prices was effected.**

3. **allot, a lot:** *Allot*, a verb, means "to portion out"; *a lot* can be an adverb ("I sleep a lot") or a noun ("I need a lot of sleep") meaning "a great deal." *A lot* is too informal for most academic writing; you should use the more formal *a great deal*, *much*, *many*, or similar substitutes. The one-word spelling, *alot*, is incorrect.

> EXAMPLE   **My parents allotted me $500 spending money for the term, which was not a lot considering my shopping habit. [informal]**

4. **all right, alright:** *All right* can be an adjective meaning "satisfactory, acceptable, or permissible" or an adverb meaning "satisfactory" or "definitely." *Alright* is not a word.

> EXAMPLES   **The movie was *all right*.**
> **She was *all right* to drive.**
> **It was them *all right*.**

5. **allude, elude:** Both are verbs, but they mean different things. *Allude (to)* means "to refer to something briefly or indirectly"; *elude* means "to avoid or escape, usually through a clever manoeuvre or strategy." *Allude* should be followed by *to*: "In the poem, Hardy alluded to the end of the century."

> HINT   *Allude* is the verb from which the noun *allusion* [a kind of reference, see *allusion*] is formed; you can associate the *e* in *elude* with the *e* in *escape*.
>
> EXAMPLE   **In his prison memoirs, the bank robber alluded to the time in the desert when he eluded capture by disguising himself as a cactus.**

6. **allusion, illusion:** You may have come across the literary use of *allusion*, a historical, religious, mythic, literary, or other kind of outside reference used to reveal character or theme in a work. An

illusion is something apparently seen that is not real or that gives a false impression.

> **HINT** Since the most common mistake is misspelling *allusion* as *illusion*, remember that *allusion*, meaning an outside reference, always begins with *al*. *Illusion* begins with an *i*, which might remind you of the word *eye* and that an illusion is something that is seen.
>
> **EXAMPLES** **The title of Nathanael West's novel *The Day of the Locust* is an allusion to the book of Exodus in the Bible. Optical illusions often use graphics to fool our senses.**

7. **among, between:** The simple distinction is that *between* refers to two persons or things and *among* to more than two.

    > **EXAMPLES** **The senator found himself between a rock and a hard place.**
    > **Ms O'Grady stood among her adoring students for the school picture.**

    Between may be the obvious choice even if more than two things are involved. For example, "Interlibrary loans are permitted between campuses." Even though a number of campuses may be part of the interlibrary loan system, any exchange takes place between two campuses.

8. **amount, number:** Use *amount* to refer to things that can't be counted; *number* refers to countable objects.

    > **HINT** Think of using numbers when you count.
    >
    > **EXAMPLE** **The number of errors in this essay reveals the amount of care you took in writing it.**

9. **beside, besides:** *Beside* is a preposition meaning "next to or adjoining"; *besides* has several meanings as a preposition; as an adverb, it means "in addition (to)."

    > **HINT** Think of the extra *s* in *besides* as an additional letter to remind you of "in addition to."
    >
    > **EXAMPLE** **Jeff stopped beside the display of discounted DVDs. He walked away because he couldn't decide which one to buy; besides which, he was late for a meeting.**

10. **bias, biased:** *Bias* is a noun that refers to a "tendency to judge unfairly"; *biased* is an adjective that means "having or showing a preferential attitude." A person can have a bias (a thing); be a biased person (adjective modifying *person*); or can be biased (predicate adjective after a linking verb). A person cannot be bias.

Also, a person is biased or has a bias against (not to or for) something or someone.

EXAMPLE **His bias against the Rastafarian lifestyle caused him to overlook some of its ideals.**

11. **cite, sight, site:** *To cite,* a verb, is "to refer to an outside source." (The complete naming of the source itself is a citation.) *Sight* (noun or verb) refers to seeing, one of the five senses. *Site,* when used as a noun, is a location or place (usually of some importance). A common error in essays is the use of *site* when *cite* is meant.

HINT Remember that *cite* is a verb referring to "the act of giving a citation"; *site* is "where something is situated or sits."

EXAMPLE **She said the ruins were excavated in 1926, citing as proof the historical plaque that commemorated the site.**

12. **e.g., i.e.:** *E.g.* is an abbreviation for the Latin *exempli gratia,* meaning "for the sake of example"; *i.e.* is an abbreviation for the Latin *id est,* meaning "that is." Use *e.g.* before one or more examples; use *i.e.* if you want to elaborate on or clarify a preceding statement. In both cases, use a period after each letter and a comma after the abbreviation. Because they are abbreviations, they should be avoided in formal writing.

HINT The first letter in *example* tells you that examples should follow *e.g.*

EXAMPLE **J.K. Rowling defied the common formula for success in the children's book market by writing long novels (e.g., *Harry Potter and the Goblet of Fire* and *Harry Potter and the Order of the Phoenix*). Some of Rowling's novels have episodic plots that contain many well-developed characters (i.e., they tend to be long).**

13. **fewer, less:** *Fewer* is the quantitative adjective of comparison and refers to things that can be counted; *less* is the qualitative adjective of comparison, referring to amount and things that can be measured.

EXAMPLES **Don't believe the notice on the mayonnaise jar: "Contains 40 per cent less calories." Calories can be counted.**
There were fewer than a dozen people at the nomination meeting.
The less said about his defection, the better.

14. **good, well:** *Good* may be an adjective, noun, or adverb. When used as an adjective, it should clearly modify a noun (e.g., *a good story*) or be used as a subject complement (predicate adjective, e.g., *The child was good until bedtime*). It cannot be used as a

predicate adjective after verbs that express an action, although it is frequently heard in speech, especially in sports (*I was hitting the ball good*).

> INCORRECT   **She beat the batter good.**
> CORRECT   **She is a good cook and beat the batter well.**

As an adjective, *well* means "in good health" or "satisfactory." As an adverb, it has several meanings, including "thoroughly" and "satisfactorily."

> HINT   Do not use *good* as a predicate adjective after an action verb; you may use it before a noun or right after an intransitive (linking) verb.
>
> EXAMPLES   **Making a good donation to the Children's Hospital made the corporation look good.** [i.e., "appear altruistic," not "appear good-looking"]
> **Although just having come out of the hospital, she looked well and continued to feel well during her recovery.** [*Well* is used as an adjective after linking verbs and means "healthy."]

15. **its, it's:** *Its* is a possessive adjective meaning "belonging to it" and is formed from the personal pronoun *it*. Remember that personal pronouns are never spelled with an apostrophe. *It's* is the contraction for *it is*, the apostrophe indicating that the second letter *i* is left out.

> HINT   Try substituting *it is* if you're having problems identifying the correct form; if it fits, use *it's*; if it doesn't, use *its*. (*Its* is usually followed by a noun.)
>
> EXAMPLE   **It's foolish to judge a book by its cover.**

16. **lay, lie:** Both are verbs. *Lay* is a transitive verb, which must always be followed by a direct object (either a noun or a pronoun). It is incorrect to say, "I'm going to lay down to rest." *Lie* is an intransitive verb; it is not followed by an object.

> HINT   You always lay something down, as a hen does an egg. Then it lies there.
>
> EXAMPLES   **He lay the baby in the crib before going to lie down.**
> **He had lain on the ground for 20 minutes before someone noticed him.** [*Lain* is the past participle of *lie*.]
> **Kim Campbell laid to rest the notion that a woman couldn't be prime minister.** [*Laid* is the past participle of *lay*.]

17. **led, lead:** *Led* and *lead* are forms of the irregular verb *to lead* (rhymes with *weed*); the present tense is also *lead*. However, the past tense and the past participle are *led*. Writers may become confused by the

noun *lead*, the metal, which looks like *to lead* but is pronounced like *led*. Therefore, when they come to write the past tense *led*, they may wrongly substitute the noun *lead* rather than the verb.

HINT   Don't be led astray by thinking there is an *a* in *led*.

EXAMPLE   **Although she led in the polls by a 2:1 margin three months ago, today she leads by only a slight margin.**

18. **loose, lose:** *Loose* is an adjective meaning "not tight"; *lose* is a verb meaning "not able to find" or "to be defeated."

HINT   When you lose something, it is lost. *Lost* is spelled with one *o*.

EXAMPLE   **If you don't tighten that loose button, you're going to lose it.**

19. **onset, outset:** Both are nouns that mean a "beginning." *Outset* means "setting out," for example, on a journey or to do something; you can also use the phrase *at the outset* to refer to the early events of a narrative or play. *Onset* refers to a force or condition that comes upon one.

EXAMPLE   **At the outset of my fourth decade, I experienced the onset of mild osteoarthritis.**

20. **than, then:** *Than* is a conjunction used in comparisons (*He's happier than he knows*). *Then* is an adverb with temporal connotations meaning "consequently," "at that time," "after that," etc.

HINT   If you're comparing one thing to another, use *than*. *Then* "tells when."

EXAMPLE   **Warren said he was better at darts than Mark, and then he challenged him to a game to prove it.**

21. **their, there, they're:** *Their* is a possessive adjective meaning "belonging to them"; *there* is an adverb meaning "in that place"; *they're* is the contraction of *they are*, the apostrophe indicating that the letter *a* is left out.

HINT   If you're uncertain about *they're*, substitute *they are*; *there* (meaning "in that place") is spelled the same as *here* ("in this place") with the letter *t* added.

EXAMPLE   **There is no excuse for the rowdy behaviour in there; they're supposed to be in their rooms.**

22. **to, too:** *To* is a preposition indicating "direction toward"; *too* is an adverb meaning "also."

HINT   *To* is usually followed by a noun or pronoun as part of a prepositional phrase; substitute *also* for *too*.

EXAMPLE   **The next time you go to the store, may I come along, too?**

23. **usage, use:** Many writers overuse *usage*, which refers to "a customary or habitual pattern or practice." It applies to conventions of groups of people, such as "language usage of the English." Usage shouldn't be used simply to mean a repeated action.

INCORRECT   **The usage of email has allowed businesses to increase their efficiency.**
EXAMPLE   **I have no use for people who are always correcting my usage of *whom*.**

24. **who's, whose:** *Who's* is the contraction of *who is*, the apostrophe indicating the omission of the letter *i*. *Whose* is the possessive adjective meaning "belonging to whom."

HINT   Try substituting *who is*. If it fits, *who's* is the correct form.
EXAMPLES   **Whose turn is it to do the dishes?**
            Who's going to do the dishes tonight?

25. **you're, your:** *You're* is the contraction of *you are*; *your* is a possessive adjective that means "belonging to you."

HINT   Try substituting *you are*. If it fits, *you're* is the correct form.
EXAMPLE   **You're going to be sorry if you don't take your turn and do the dishes tonight.**

Here is a list of 50 additional words that often give students trouble:

Don't say...	When you mean...
adolescents	adolescence (the time one is an adolescent)
aforementioned	this/previously stated
around	about (in reference to numbers)
associated to	associated with
attribute to	contribute to
avoid	prevent
base off/around	base on
conscience	conscious
continuous	continual
council	counsel
could of/would of	could have/would have
different than	different from
downfall	disadvantage

Don't say . . .	When you mean . . .
downside	disadvantage
entirety of	all
farther	further (*farther* applies to physical distance)
half to	have to
imply	infer
insure	ensure
irregardless	regardless
lifestyle	life
like	as
locality/location	place
majority of	most
man	human/humanity
manpower	resources
mindset	belief
misfortunate	unfortunate
multiple	many
none the less	nonetheless
obsess about	to be obsessed about
obtain	attain
overexaggerate	exaggerate
passed	past
popular	common
principal	principle
prior/prior to	before
references	refers to (references is a plural noun)
reoccur	recur
seize	cease
so	very
thanks to	due to
that	who/whom/where, etc.
thru	through
till	until
to transition	to change
upon	on
weather	whether
were	where
which	who/whom

As you progress through your course, you may have problems with other words. Add them, along with definitions and correct usage, to this list.

EXERCISE 16.12

From the lists provided in the previous sections, choose 10 words that give you trouble. Find their definitions and then write sentences using the words correctly.

Example:

Amount: the quantity of something; used for non-count nouns

The amount of rain that fell in June this year is equal to all the rain that fell last year.

Number: the quantity of something; used for count nouns

It is hard to count the number of raindrops that fall into a cup.

Providing Depth: Variety and Emphasis

When you revise an early draft to improve clarity, you will likely find opportunities to make your prose more interesting. Variety and emphasis in your writing make a competent piece of writing compelling. Thus, they are worthwhile goals in all forms of essays: personal, literary, argumentative, and expository.

Sentence Variety

Length

You can vary the lengths of sentences for rhetorical effect. Just as short paragraphs suggest underdeveloped points, short, choppy sentences could suggest a lack of content. On the other hand, several long sentences in a row could confuse a reader. That doesn't mean you should write only sentences that are between 15 and 20 words. Although sentence length alone is no measure of readability, consider revision if you find you have written more than two very short or very long sentences in a row.

You can use appropriate conjunctions to connect short sentences. Join simple sentences with one of the seven coordinating conjunctions (FANBOYS). If the idea in one sentence is less important than the idea in the sentence before or after it, use the subordinating conjunction that best expresses the relationship between them. Join independent clauses with a semicolon or a colon.

TIP

Avoid writing too many overly short or overly long sentences. Using proper grammar, combine short sentences or break longer sentences into shorter ones.

 "Conjunctions" in Chapter 13 introduces coordinating conjunctions and subordinating conjunctions. See also "Joiners: Prepositions and Conjunctions" in Chapter 13 for information on joining sentences and clauses. See "Other Forms of Punctuation" for more information on semicolons and colons.

EXERCISE 16.13

The following paragraph has too many short sentences. Using the strategies mentioned in this section, revise the paragraph to make it more effective.

During the Earth's long history, there have been various periods of glaciation. This fact is well known. There is also evidence of one great glacial event. It is possible that the

> Earth was once completely covered by ice and snow. Skeptics argue this is impossible. They say that the Earth could never have become this cold. The idea of the tropics being frozen over is unlikely, they believe.

You can also join independent clauses with a conjunctive adverb or transitional phrase, but make sure that a semicolon precedes the connecting word or phrase. You may be able to connect phrases or clauses grammatically through a parallel relationship, such as apposition. The second phrase or clause could also modify the preceding word, phrase, or clause—for example, a relative (adjectival) clause could give information about a preceding noun clause.

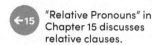 "Rule Category 3: Parenthetical Information," rule 3b, in Chapter 14 offers information on punctuating appositives.

EXERCISE 16.14

> The following paragraph consists of sentences that are too long. Using joining strategies, revise the paragraph to make it more effective.
>
> Finding a definition for "the homeless" is difficult, but the most common definition, which is used both in the media and in current research, defines the homeless as those who lack visible shelter or use public shelters. Literature about homelessness is sparse, and it was not until the 1980s that the incidence of homelessness began to be reported in the media, but homelessness has existed for centuries, and literature on the subject dates back to the feudal period in Europe.

Generally speaking, you waste space when you begin a new sentence by repeating part of the previous sentence or begin a new paragraph by recapitulating part of the previous one. Although repetition can be used to build coherence, it should not create redundancy.

In 1970, Gordon O. Gallup created the mirror test. This test was designed to determine whether or not animals are self-aware.

Revised: In 1970, Gordon O. Gallup created the mirror test, designed to determine whether animals are self-aware.

When checking your work for overly long sentences, consider breaking up sentences with more than two independent clauses or one independent clause and more than two dependent clauses. See if the relationships between the clauses are clear. If they are not, divide the sentences where clauses are joined by conjunctions, transitional words and phrases, or relative pronouns.

"Relative Pronouns" in Chapter 15 discusses relative clauses.

Structural Variety

You can also experiment with phrasal openings to sentences. Consider beginning the occasional sentence with a prepositional, participial, infinitive, or absolute phrase instead of the subject. A prepositional phrase begins with a preposition followed by a noun or pronoun; it is adjectival or adverbial and modifies the closest noun (adjectival) or verb (adverbial). A participial phrase, which ends in *–ing*, *–ed*, or *–en*, is a verbal phrase acting as an adjective. An infinitive phrase, which is preceded by *to*, can act adjectivally or adverbially. An absolute phrase, consisting of a noun/pronoun and a partial verb form, modifies the entire sentence.

In this short excerpt from an essay about the death of a moth, Virginia Woolf uses the different types of phrases:

> **After a time, tired by his dancing apparently, he settled on the window ledge in the sun, and the queer spectacle being at an end, I forgot about him. Then, looking up, my eye was caught by him. He was trying to resume his dancing, but seemed either so stiff or so awkward that he could only flutter to the bottom of the window-pane; and when he tried to fly across it, he failed.**

Woolf, Virginia. *The Death of the Moth, and Other Essays*. Harcourt, 1942.

Note the types of modifiers: the prepositional phrase *After a time*; the participial phrases *tired by his dancing* and *looking up*; and the absolute phrase *the queer spectacle being at an end*.

Creating Emphasis

Writers can create emphasis by presenting main points or details in a particular order. Two kinds of sentences vary in the presentation of the main idea: periodic and cumulative sentences. Periodic sentences begin with modifiers before the independent clause. Cumulative sentences work the other way: they begin with an independent clause and are followed by modifying or parallel words, phrases, or clauses. While periodic sentences create anticipation by delaying the main idea, cumulative sentences develop the main idea by drawing it out. Many sentences are slightly or moderately periodic or cumulative, depending on whether the writer began or ended with modifiers. However, a writer can employ either type to create a specific effect. In the following examples, the independent clauses are underlined.

Periodic:

> **Unlike novelists and playwrights, who lurk behind the scenes while distracting our attention with the puppet show of imaginary characters—and unlike the scholars and journalists, who quote the opinions of others and take cover behind the hedges of neutrality—<u>the essayist has nowhere to hide</u>.**

Sanders, Scott Russell. "The Singular First Person." *The Sewanee Review*, vol. 96, no. 4, 1988, pp. 658–672.

 "Prepositions" in Chapter 13 explains prepositional phrases.

> **TIP**
> Make sure that when you use a participial phrase at the beginning of a sentence you include the word it is intended to modify so that it does not dangle. See "Dangling Modifiers" in Chapter 15 for information on dangling modifiers.

Emphasis is the importance or stress that you place on an idea. A word or phrase has greater or less emphasis depending on where it appears in the sentence. You can begin a sentence with detail and follow with the main idea or begin with the main idea and follow with detail. These orders will produce contrastive effects.

Cumulative:

<u>The root of all evil is that we all want this spiritual gratification</u>, this flow, this apparent heightening of life, this knowledge, this valley of many-colored grass, even grass and light prismatically decomposed, giving ecstasy.

Lawrence, David Herbert. *Studies in Classic American Literature.* Penguin, 1990.

A writer can also delay the main idea and generate tension by beginning with a prepositional phrase:

Behind the deconstructionists' dazzling cloud of language lie certain more or less indisputable facts.

Gardner, John. *The Art of Fiction.* Vintage, 1991.

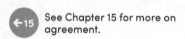 See Chapter 15 for more on agreement.

When the subject follows the verb and is thus delayed in this kind of construction, ensure that the verb agrees with the subject.

Other ways to emphasize parts of a sentence include parallel structures and repetition—techniques that also help in paragraph coherence—and rhythms that call the reader's attention to important ideas. The end of a sentence provides emphasis as well; a reader naturally slows down when approaching the last part of a sentence and pauses slightly between sentences.

The following two paragraphs employ parallel structures, repetition, and rhythm for emphasis.

A. My professors, many of whom were to become very famous, did not tend to be philosophic and did not dig back into the sources of the new language and categories they were using. They thought that these were scientific discoveries like any others, which were to be used in order to make further discoveries. They were very much addicted to abstractions and generalizations, as Tocqueville predicted they would be. They believed in scientific progress and appeared (there may have been an element of boasting and self-irony in this) to be convinced that they were on the verge of a historic breakthrough in the social sciences, equivalent to that scored in the sixteenth and seventeenth centuries in the natural sciences. ... These teachers were literally inebriated by the unconscious and values. And they were also sure that scientific progress would be related to social and political progress.

Bloom, Allan. *The Closing of the American Mind.* Simon and Schuster, 2012.

Bloom employs the most common structural pattern of subject–verb–object in all his sentences, establishing a predictable rhetorical pattern that complements the predictability and uniformity of his professors that he wants to stress. Thus, *my professors*, the subject in the first sentence, is replaced by the pronoun *they* in the following three sentences; in the fourth sentence, *they* is the subject of two clauses. To avoid too many identical openings, Bloom continues with the same rhythm but varies the subject slightly: the last two sentences begin with *these teachers* and *and they*, respectively.

B. Tales about Pythagoras flew to him and stuck like iron filings to a magnet. He was said, for example, to have appeared in several

places at once and to have been reincarnated many times. Taken literally, this idea can be consigned to the same overflowing bin which contains the story that he had a golden thigh; but taken figuratively, it is an understatement. Pythagoras—or at least Pythagoreanism—was everywhere and still is.

Gottlieb, Anthony. *The Dream of Reason*. Norton, 2000.

The most obvious technique in this paragraph is the use of figurative language: Gottlieb uses a simile in the first sentence (*like iron filings to a magnet*) and a metaphor in the third (*overflowing bin*). He effectively uses sentence length and rhythm to make the paragraph more appealing. The paragraph is framed by short simple sentences that stress Pythagoras's importance. The middle sentences develop the main idea through examples. Gottlieb's final sentence, though the shortest, contains strong emphasis: the use of dashes allows the writer to repeat the name Pythagoras without seeming redundant, while heavy accents fall on the final two words.

Proofreading: Perfection *Is* Possible

In publishing, *editing* refers to the revising of a work before it is formatted, whether for a book, newspaper, magazine, journal, or other medium. *Proofreading* refers to the final check of the formatted material. While an editor is mainly concerned with improving a document, the proofreader looks for errors. The proofreader is the document's last line of defence before it is released. Ironically, poor proofreading may be the first thing noticed in the published document.

In spite of the importance of proofreading, student writers with an essay deadline usually neglect this stage. Exhausted from the final efforts of putting the essay together, students may think that tiny errors are unimportant compared to other parts of the process stressed throughout the term. However, distracting errors may strike your instructor in a completely different light. They could be seen as careless or a sign of a lack of effort. Your instructor could become annoyed by many small mistakes and even become more critical of other parts of the essay. An employer will also be concerned about the impression your poor work will have on the company's clients. They may wonder whether your carelessness is carried over to other aspects of your job and view your efforts more critically.

Whether or not proofreading is seen as tedious, it is best performed as a mechanical process. By taking a thorough and systematic approach to the essay at this stage, you can be more confident that the work of many hours, days, or even weeks will be more readable.

Proofreading Methods

Proofreading a printed copy of your essay will help you find more errors. A document may be read by two people, with the author reading the work aloud while the other follows the printed copy silently. This method works on the principle that two readers are twice as likely as one to spot

> **TIP**
> When you edit or revise, you try to improve your work's structure and readability or solidify your ideas; when you proofread, you try to catch all mistakes to provide a clean copy for your reader.

> **TIP**
> You may think that tiny errors are unimportant compared to other parts of the writing process. However, your instructor and future employer could see them as careless, a sign of a lack of effort.

errors—you will probably notice mistakes that you missed before. It may also be more enjoyable than working alone. Clearly, the approach works only if a second reader is available, both readers are knowledgeable about writing, and both are committed to the task. Another option is to use the read-aloud feature found in many word processing programs such as Word, Pages, and Google Docs. You can follow along in your writing while the computer reads the material to you. Sometimes hearing your words will help you find errors.

The method of reading forward involves reading the paper aloud or to yourself but more slowly and carefully than you would usually do, paying attention both to the words and to the punctuation. Because it can be hard to concentrate solely on the words, it's best to read through the essay at least once for meaning and then at least once again for spelling and other errors.

Reading backward is the method of reading your essay from the end to the beginning, word by word or sentence by sentence. This technique forces your attention on the writing; it works well for catching spelling errors. However, it is time-consuming, and you may miss some punctuation and other "between the words" errors, as well as words that depend on their context.

Another type of proofreading is to read syllabically: you read from the beginning, breaking every word into syllables. This method is faster than reading backward, works well for catching internal misspellings, and is quite effective for catching missing and extra words and for correcting word endings (which may be overlooked when you read forward). However, it is a slower method than reading forward word by word, requires some discipline to master, and can be hard on the eyes if done for a long time.

Guidelines for Proofreading

Follow these tips when proofreading:

- Remember that the time not set aside for proofreading can undo the work of several hours.
- Plan to let at least a few hours pass before you look at the essay for the final time (overnight is recommended).
- Having someone else go over the essay can be helpful but is no substitute for your own systematic proofing. Instructors are not likely to be sympathetic to the cry of baffled frustration, "But I had my roommate read it over!"
- As stated earlier, use a spell-checker but don't rely on it. A spell-checker will not catch the difference between *There house is over their, two* and *Their house is over there, too.*
- Do not rely on autocorrect. Look carefully at the suggested words and chose the correct one. Many students have included the word *defiantly* in their essays rather than the intended *definitely.*

- Experiment with the different proofreading methods discussed in this chapter and use the one(s) that works best for you. However, when you start proofreading with one particular method, use it until you finish reading.

Common Errors

Here are categories of typical errors to watch for and correct in your writing:

- All areas that require consistency—spelling, capitalization, abbreviations, hyphenation, numbers, internal punctuation, and other places where choices pertaining to the mechanics of writing may be involved.
- Proper nouns (especially unfamiliar names), acronyms, etc. Are all references to authors and titles spelled correctly?
- Middles and endings of words, for spelling and for agreement.
- Small words, such as articles and prepositions.
- Words that have different spellings but the same pronunciation (homophones): *to/too/two*, *their/there/they're*, *role/roll*, *cite/site*, *led/lead*, *manor/manner*, etc.
- Font style. Are italics, bold, and roman applied correctly and consistently and to all necessary words? Have you used italics for the titles of complete works, such as books and films, and put quotation marks around the titles of works contained in larger works, such as essays, articles, short stories, and poems?
- End punctuation (periods and question marks).
- Quotation marks. Are they applied appropriately? Are both opening and closing quotation marks present? Have double and single quotation marks been alternated correctly? Are periods and commas inside quotation marks and colons and semicolons outside? (Similar checks can be made for parentheses.)
- All citations, both in text and in the reference or works cited list. Check both for accuracy (author, title, journal name, date, and page numbers) and for consistency. Are all citations documented according to the style of your discipline—including capitalization, punctuation, and other conventions?

Essay Presentation

Your audience and purpose are relevant to how you present your essay; for example, a scientific or engineering report probably would look quite different from an essay for English class—the former might have headings, whereas the latter would probably not. A research essay must conform to the documentation style of your discipline; presenting a personal essay may mostly be a matter of following directions for title, typeface, margins, spacing, indentation, page numbering, and identifying information.

Document design can vary. If your instructor asks you to format your essay a certain way, you can be sure that you need to follow those guidelines or marks will be at stake. Therefore, if you are unsure about essay presentation, ask for help. Unless you are told otherwise, you can refer to the following, which is based on MLA guidelines:

- Most instructors require essays to be typed. Use good-quality white paper; print on one side. If you wish to conserve paper by printing on both sides, check with your instructor first.
- Leave 1-inch margins (2.5 cm) on all sides. The first page should include identification information positioned flush left (i.e., starting at the left margin). List information in the following order: your name and student ID, if applicable; instructor's name (use the title that your instructor prefers—e.g., Professor Robert Mills, Dr M. Sonik, Ms J. Winestock, etc.); course number and section, if applicable; and submission date. Double-space, then insert the essay's title, centred.
- Double-space your essay, including notes, works cited, and block quotations; this practice makes it much easier for the instructor to correct errors and add comments.
- Indent each paragraph one half-inch (1.25 cm)—do not use additional spaces to separate paragraphs, and leave a single space (not two spaces) after each period before beginning the next sentence.
- Number pages using Arabic numerals in the upper right-hand corner preceded by your last name; place this line about one half-inch (1.25 cm) from the top and flush right (you can create this kind of header automatically using *Insert* or a similar function in your word processing program). If you need to include prefatory pages such as a contents page or a formal outline, use lowercase Roman numerals (i, ii, iii) for them and insert a section break before the actual essay, so you can change the page numbers to Arabic numerals for the rest of the pages.
- A title page is usually optional, though some instructors require it. Position the essay's title down one-third of the page with your name about halfway down; include the course number, instructor's name, and submission date near the bottom of the page. All items should be centred. Begin your essay on the second page (numbered 1) under the centred title.
- Do not include any illustrations or colours other than black and white unless you use graphics directly relevant to your essay (e.g., charts or diagrams for a scientific study). Use a paper clip to attach the pages—some instructors ask for stapled pages—don't fold over a corner to keep them together. Don't use folders, clear or coloured, unless asked to. (If you do use a folder, the left-hand page margin should be slightly wider than the other margins to allow for the binding.)

- Prefer common fonts, such as Times New Roman, Arial, or Garamond (not Courier New or cursive ones). Use 12-point type size or the one required by your instructor. Do not justify lines to the margins in academic papers or reports (i.e., set the paragraph style to flush left and an uneven line at the right margin).
- Ensure that the text of your essay is easy to read. An essay printed in draft mode or from a cartridge that is almost out of ink or toner will be difficult to read.

TIP

Don't print your essay in draft mode; ensure that your cartridge has enough ink or toner. Otherwise, your essay will be hard to read.

Chapter Review Questions

1. Why is clarity important in writing?
2. Why is formal writing clearer than informal writing?
3. Find examples from business writing (such as advertising) that illustrate concepts discussed in this chapter, such as doubling up. Rewrite the samples so they are more formal and could be used in academic writing.
4. What are clichés? List examples other than those given in the chapter. Why should you avoid clichés in formal writing?
5. What is euphemistic language? Why are euphemisms confusing?
6. How are editing and proofreading different? Why are both important?
7. What are some things to look for when you proofread?
8. What message do you send to the reader if your paper has spelling mistakes or typos?
9. Why should you not rely solely on your spell-checker?
10. What are three different techniques you can use for proofreading?

Tense refers to the time when the action or condition expressed by the verb is taking, will take, or took place. There are four types of tense:

- simple
- progressive
- perfect
- perfect progressive

These forms further describe the aspect of the verb as to when its action began and its duration or completion.

The auxiliary (helping) verb for most forms determines the complete form of the verb. The auxiliary verb for the progressive tenses is *to be* (*is, was, will be*); for the perfect tenses, it is *to have* (*has, had, will have*).

Present Tenses

Simple Present (action or situation exists now or regularly):

I call	we call
you call	you call
he/she/it calls	they call

I usually *call* for the pizza; you *call* for it this time.

Present Progressive (action is in progress):

I am sending	we are sending
you are sending	you are sending
he/she/it is sending	they are sending

Mr Kahn *is sending* the package to you by courier.

Present Perfect (action began in the past and is completed in the present):

I have eaten	we have eaten
you have eaten	you have eaten
he/she/it has eaten	they have eaten

I *have eaten* the apple you gave me.

Present Perfect Progressive (action began in the past, continues in the present, and may continue into the future):

I have been hoping	we have been hoping
you have been hoping	you have been hoping
he/she/it has been hoping	they have been hoping

We *have been hoping* to receive news from the Philippines.

Past Tenses

Simple Past (action or situation was completed in the past):

I saw	we saw
you saw	you saw
he/she/it saw	they saw

Garfield *saw* the moon rise last night over his burrow.

Past Progressive (action was in progress in the past):

I was talking	we were talking
you were talking	you were talking
he/she/it was talking	they were talking

James and Beth *were talking* about storms when the hurricane warning flashed onto their smartphones.

Past Perfect (action was completed in the past prior to another action in the past):

I had finished	we had finished
you had finished	you had finished
he/she/it had finished	they had finished

Alex *had finished* the second assignment when the storm knocked out power to his computer.

Past Perfect Progressive (action in progress in the past):

I had been practising	we had been practising
you had been practising	you had been practising
he/she/it had been practising	they had been practising

The golf team sophomores *had been practising* for the tournament all summer, but when school started, their coach announced his resignation.

Future Tenses

Simple Future (action will occur in the future):

I will see	we will see
you will see	you will see
he/she/it will see	they will see

I *will see* the Rocky Mountains on my way to Vancouver.

Future Progressive (action will be continuous in the future):

I will be walking	we will be walking
you will be walking	you will be walking
he/she/it will be walking	they will be walking

Norm and Martee *will be walking* in the Marathon of Hope next Saturday morning.

Future Perfect (action will be completed in the future):

I will have gone	we will have gone
you will have gone	you will have gone
he/she/it will have gone	they will have gone

Sally *will have gone* around the moon several times before the ship leaves its lunar orbit.

Future Perfect Progressive (actions are ongoing up to a specific future time):

I will have been studying	we will have been studying
you will have been studying	you will have been studying
he/she/it will have been studying	they will have been studying

With the completion of this assignment, they *will have been studying* verbs for 13 years.

Remember that verbs can reflect mood (conditional, subjunctive) and voice (active, passive), and auxiliary verbs can be used to indicate conditions, such as necessity (*I should go*), obligation (*You must go*), and possibility (*He may go*).

Fix any verbs that are incorrect in the following passages.

A.

Drink up to boost brain health

Did you knew that the brain is 75 per cent water? It need water to replenish and ensure healthy cognitive functions and strong mental health. Drinking plentiful amounts of water daily helps ensure the brain cells could perform their many essential functions. Many people are misinterpreting the brain's signals for water as hunger, so it's a good idea to drink a glass of water whenever you will be feeling hungry to help stave off dehydration.

Everyone's ideal amount of water will differs depending on our overall health, how active we are, and where we live. According to the US National Academies of Sciences, Engineering, and Medicine, men need about 15 1/2 cups (3.7 L) and women 11 1/2 cups (2.7 L) of fluids each day. The fluids, however, can came from a combination of food and beverages, including water.

Adapted from Cook, Michelle. "Power Up Your Brain." Alive, July 7, 2020, www.alive.com/health/power-up-your-brain/.

B.

I remember a camping trip that I was going on with a few of my friends. We were very unprepared and run into a few mishaps along the way. The trip occurred during the rainy season, and we have not brought any firewood. We have a hard time getting the fire to start, even after we borrowed wood and an axe from the campers next door. Of course, we forgot to bring a can opener, so we had to try stabbing at the tins with a Swiss army knife to get them open. We spend the night around our Coleman stove, trying to keep warm.

That night made us realize how much we took nature for granted. In our homes every day we had many household appliances that made our lives easier for us. It is easy to forget that some people live in the world without these conveniences and relied on nature from dawn to dusk. This camping trip occurred a long time ago when I am much younger. But the memory of that long night in the nature stays with me ever since.

This appendix provides guidelines on some English idioms and the parts of speech. It also discusses articles, which can be confusing for EAL writers.

Adjectives

One-word adjectives usually precede the word(s) they modify, except predicate adjectives that follow linking verbs (see "Verbs" in Chapter 13). However, relative (adjectival) clauses follow the noun they modify and present special challenges for writers.

Adjectives as Participles

When a participle ending in *–ed* or *–en* precedes a noun and acts as an adjective, keep the ending it requires as a past participle:

> Although Patrick lived a **fast-paced** [not *fast-pace*] **life, he had the old-fashioned** [not old-*fashion*] **habit of stopping and reading a newspaper every day at work.**

Adjectives and Present versus Past Participles

For verbs related to feeling or emotion, use the present particle (ends in *–ing*) when the subject causes the feeling and the past participle (ends in *–ed* or *–en)* when the subject experiences the feeling.

> The surprise ending of the football game was **exciting**; the few fans left in the stadium were **excited**.

When you want to refer to a time in the past and relate it to today, you can use the adjective *ago* after the noun. To refer to a specific point in the past, you can give the date preceded by *on*. (See "Times and dates" in the "Prepositions" section of this appendix.)

> The first truly successful cloning of an animal occurred over **20 years ago**.

> The first truly successful cloning of an animal occurred **on 5 July 1996**.

Comparatives and Superlatives

Use the comparative of adjectives and adverbs when you want to compare one person or thing to another. Usually, the suffix *–er* is added if the quality being compared is one syllable, while *more* precedes a word of two or more syllables:

> **In British Columbia, summers are usually <u>drier</u> than they are in Ontario.**

> **According to <u>the most recent</u> statistics, it is <u>more dangerous</u> to drive a car than to take an airplane.**

Use the superlative of adjectives and adverbs when you want to compare more than two of something. The definite article is usually not used with comparisons, but it is used with superlatives (see "Articles—*A*, *An*, and *The*" in the "Adverbs" section of this appendix).

> **In my opinion, British Columbia is a <u>better</u> province than Alberta** [there are two provinces]; **in my friend's opinion, Alberta is <u>the best</u> of the western provinces** [there are four].

Few versus *a Few*

Both terms can precede nouns that can be counted, but *few* means "not many," and *a few* means "some."

> **<u>Few</u> Canadians know how to play cricket. However, <u>a few</u> people in my Facebook group said they would be interested in learning how to play it.**

Much versus *Many*

Use *much* before nouns that cannot be counted and *many* before countable nouns. (See Chapter 13 for count and non-count nouns.)

> **She didn't donate <u>much</u> money.**

> **Spotify features <u>many</u> different kinds of music.**

Plurals as Adjectival Phrases Concerning Distance, Money, and Time

When these kinds of plural nouns appear in hyphenated phrases before other nouns, they drop the final *s*.

> **a <u>10-kilometre</u> run** [not a *10-kilometres* run], **a <u>30-day</u> refund policy, a <u>70-year-old</u> man**

Relative (Adjectival) Clauses

A relative clause modifies the noun it follows (known as the antecedent). These clauses begin with a relative pronoun (usually *who*, *whom*, *that*, or *which*). Make sure you include the relative pronoun at the beginning of the clause. In the example, the complete relative clause is underlined, the relative pronoun is double-underlined, and the antecedent is italicized:

> **In China, there is a *high school* <u><u>that</u> was painted green</u> because green is considered a relaxing colour.**

When you use a phrase such as *in which* to introduce a clause, do not repeat the preposition at the end of the clause:

> **Happiness for some people is measured by their success in the society <u>in which</u> they live ~~in~~.**

Agreement with Relative Clauses

The antecedent of the relative pronoun determines whether the verb in the relative clause is singular or plural. In the following example, the relative pronoun is double-underlined, the verb is underlined, and the antecedent is italicized:

> **The Hyundai hybrid has a small *engine* <u>that</u> <u>consumes</u> less fuel than ordinary cars.**

Adverbs

Adverbs with Adjectives

Adverbs can modify adjectives, other adverbs, or verbs. Ensure that you always use the correct adverbial form. In the example, *environmentally* is the adverbial form:

> **The average Canadian household has become more <u>environmentally</u> conscious than in the past.**

The few adjectives that end in –*ly* (e.g., *friendly, fatherly, cowardly*) cannot be made into adverbs.

Comparative and Superlative of Adverbs

See "Comparatives and Superlatives" in the "Adjectives" section of this appendix.

Articles—*A, An*, and *The*

Indefinite articles precede some singular nouns, and definite articles precede some singular and plural nouns. Context often determines whether an article precedes a noun or whether it is omitted; idiom also can determine usage. Here are some guidelines for article use.

The Indefinite Article

Use the indefinite article *a* or *an* if you want to identify a general or nonspecific noun. Use *an* if the noun begins with a vowel that is not pronounced or with a silent *h*. Some vowels have both a strong and weak sound, such as the letter *u*. If the *u* is pronounced as ə as in *umbrella*, then use the article *an*. If it is a hard sound, as in *university*, use the article *a*.

> **When I was bird watching, I looked for <u>a</u> Rufus hummingbird.** [no specific bird is referred to]
>
> **I want to ride <u>a</u> unicorn.** [no specific unicorn is referred to]
>
> **I need to buy <u>an</u> umbrella.** [no specific umbrella is referred to]
>
> **When <u>the</u> hummingbird saw me, it darted into the trees.** [a specific bird is referred to]

The indefinite article is not used before most uncountable concrete nouns, nor do these nouns form plurals. It is easier to remember these nouns if you divide them into categories:

- Kinds of liquids: *beer, blood, coffee, milk, oil, soup, water, wine,* etc.
- Kinds of food: *bread, cheese, corn, flour, food, fruit, lettuce, meat, pasta, popcorn, rice, sugar,* etc.
- Names of languages: *Arabic, Dutch, French, Japanese, Mandarin, Vietnamese,* etc.
- Names of areas of study: *biology, economics, geography, mathematics,* etc.
- Names of gases: *hydrogen, methane, oxygen, ozone,* etc. (*air, fire, smoke,* and *steam* also belong here)
- Sports and games: *baseball, bowling, football, hockey, jogging, surfing, tennis,* etc. (But *baseballs* and *footballs*—the objects—are countable.)
- Others: *chalk, clothing, equipment, feedback, furniture, health, help, homework, housework, laughter, luggage, mail, money, research, scenery, soap, software, weather, wood, work,* etc.

However, if preceded by a word such as *piece* or *item,* such nouns may be countable: *a piece* (or *pieces*) *of chalk, an item* (or *items*) *of furniture, a glass of water.* As well, many nouns can be used adjectivally before countable nouns: *a cheese stick, a hockey game,* etc.

Some of the nouns in the list can be used in a countable sense if they can be divided into different types:

> **Red <u>wine</u> in moderation can be beneficial to one's health. Different <u>wines</u> are classified by their place of origin.**

Although *mail* is an uncountable noun, *email* can be used as a countable noun; thus, you can talk about receiving *an* email. As a noun, *email* can also be pluralized:

> **Flora was shocked to see that she had received more than a hundred <u>emails</u> over the weekend; as a result, she vowed to get rid of her <u>email</u> by the end of the week.**

See "Uncountable and Countable Nouns" in the "Nouns" section of this appendix.

The Definite Article

Nouns that refer to a specific person, place, or object are usually preceded by the definite article, *the*:

> **Please give me <u>the</u> pen on <u>the</u> table.**

A specific pen (distinct from other pens) on a specific table is requested.

> **Please give me <u>a</u> pen on <u>the</u> table.**

This request implies that there is more than one pen on the specific table.

> **Please give me <u>a</u> pen.**

Any pen from anywhere will do.

> **Young children, especially in <u>the</u> 3–5 age group, are always asking questions.**

Other age groups exist, making the reference specific.

Including Definite Articles before Nouns

1. *First versus second reference*: Use *a* when something is first mentioned and *the* when the same noun is mentioned again (it can now be identified).

   > **Mike found <u>a brown bottle</u> that had washed ashore. When he cleaned it up, he saw that <u>the bottle</u> had <u>a note</u> inside.**

2. *Nouns that refer to a species or class of objects*: Use the definite article before this group; an example is *the definite article* in this sentence. Here is another example:

   > **In her English class, Izumi studied <u>the argumentative essay</u> before <u>the research essay</u>.**

3. *Unique nouns*: If the noun has a unique identity, precede it by the definite article.

   - Specific eras or time periods: *the Industrial Revolution, the Age of Reason, in the twentieth century*, etc.
   - Unique celestial objects: *the sun, the moon, the North Star*
   - Newspapers, museums, theatres, and hotels: *The Vancouver Sun (newspaper), the Royal Ontario Museum, the Imax theatre, the Banff Springs Hotel*

4. *Superlatives*: See "Comparatives and Superlatives" in the "Adjectives" section of this appendix.

   > **I have found that <u>the best courses</u> at college are usually <u>the most challenging</u> ones, and they are taught by <u>the best teachers</u>.**

5. *Ordinals*: Ordinal numbers are *first, second*, etc.; cardinal numbers are *one, two*, etc.

   > **Maria was <u>the first</u> to cross the finishing line; Linden was <u>the second</u>. They finished one and two, respectively.**

Omitting Definite Articles before Nouns

When using nouns that fall into the following groups, omit the definite article in most cases.

1. *Before most plural nouns*:

   > **If <u>animals</u> have no consciousness, it is meaningless to discuss whether eating <u>meat</u> is immoral.**

   Animals is a plural noun; *meat* is an uncountable noun.

2. *Before proper nouns*:

   Canadians celebrate Thanksgiving in October; Americans celebrate this holiday in November.

   This general rule has many exceptions. The article is used with some national, social, and cultural groups (*the English, the Japanese, the middle class, the Indigenous Peoples*) and with some geographical names (*the Pacific Ocean, the United States, the Philippines, the Arctic*).

   Lonnie is a member of <u>the</u> Chipewyan First Nations and lives near Prince Albert in northern Saskatchewan.

3. *Before abstract nouns*: These nouns are usually uncountable and cannot be pluralized. Abstract nouns include *advice, anger, curiosity, employment, enjoyment, evidence, freedom, fun, health, information, intelligence, justice, knowledge, love, music, peace, pollution, reality, research, respect, truth, wealth, weather*, etc. The exception to this rule is that the article is used if a prepositional phrase follows the noun.

   <u>The reality of the situation</u>, unfortunately, is that <u>justice</u> does not always prevail.

   A prepositional phrase follows reality but not justice.

4. *Common nouns*: Using common nouns such *government, nature, society, internet,* and *media* often result in errors in article use.

   • *Government*: If you are referring to a specific government, use the definite article; otherwise, do not use *the*:

   <u>The government</u> [meaning, for example, the government of Newfoundland and Labrador] has no right to raise student tuition fees.

   • *Nature*: If you are referring to the natural world, the noun *nature* is not preceded by *the*. If the sense is of a quality, essence, or habit, *the* may be required.

   It has been <u>the nature</u> of previous generations [their habit] to take <u>nature</u> [the natural world] for granted.

   • *Society*: This term is not preceded by *the* if the reference is a general one. *Society* is usually singular and requires the singular verb form. If the reference is specific, *the* may be required (for example, if it is followed by a phrase that particularizes society):

   <u>Society</u> does not look kindly on those who fail to respect <u>its</u> rules.
   I find <u>the society of like-minded individuals</u> boring and unrewarding.

- *Internet/media*: When used as a noun, *internet* is preceded by *the*, as is *media* when it refers to *the news media* as a form of mass communication, such as television, radio, newspapers, and magazines; it usually takes a singular verb form when used this way.

With the rise of <u>the internet</u>, <u>the media has</u> become even a more powerful influence on <u>society</u>.

For article use with gerunds, see "Gerunds" in the "Nouns" section of this appendix.

Nouns

The following nouns often give students trouble:

Human: This noun can be used in the singular or the plural, but possessive forms should be avoided.

It is a <u>human</u> [not a *human's*] need to aim for perfection.

Humanity: *Humanity* is not preceded by the definite article (or possessive adjective) unless it refers to an inner quality (see "*Nature*" in the section "Omitting Definite Articles before Nouns" in this appendix).

One quality that <u>humanity</u> shares with other organisms is the need to solve problems.

She demonstrated <u>her humanity</u> [an inner quality] by forgiving her enemies.

Opinion; express an opinion: Don't say, "In my point of view," "As for myself," or "As far as I am concerned." The most direct way of stating your opinion is simply to say, "In my opinion" or "I believe that" and follow with a clause that states your opinion.

Every + Noun

Like *each one of, either one of*, etc., *every one of* is followed by a plural noun but a singular verb form. But when one of these words is followed directly by a noun, that noun and the verb will be singular, not plural:

Almost <u>every</u> drafting <u>course</u> in schools <u>involves</u> computers.

Using *every one of* would result in a plural noun in the *of* phrase: *Every one of the drafting courses*.

Gerunds

Gerunds are incomplete verb forms that act as nouns in a sentence (they end in *–ing*). They are always singular and are usually not preceded by articles.

<u>Learning</u> many new skills <u>is</u> enjoyable if you have the time for <u>it</u>.

Kind(s) of/Type(s) of + Noun

A singular noun follows *kind of* and *type of*; a plural countable or an uncountable noun follows *kinds of* and *types of* because more than one kind/type is referred to. Often, a demonstrative adjective—*this* or *that* (singular); *these* or *those* (plural)—precedes *kind/type*.

What <u>type of</u> car was Natalie driving?

Many <u>kinds of cars</u> are on the market today.

Uncountable and Countable Nouns

The following uncountable nouns are responsible for many writing errors:

- *Clothing*: As an uncountable noun, *clothing* is never preceded by the indefinite article and never forms a plural. *Clothes*, however, is a countable noun.

  Peobxple have used <u>clothing</u> to cover their body for thousands of years; however, we often choose our <u>clothes</u> for their fashion rather than their practicality.

- *Information, knowledge, evidence,* and *advice*: These words are uncountable abstract nouns. Thus, they are not preceded by *a* or *an* and are never plural.

  <u>Information</u> is available at the service desk.

- *Importance*: *An importance* or *importances* is incorrect. You can use *the importance* if a prepositional phrase beginning with *of* follows.

  Safety in automobiles is of <u>importance</u> to manufacturers and consumers.

  <u>The importance of</u> wearing seatbelts needs to be emphasized more.

- *Research*: As an uncountable noun, it is never plural. However, *researcher*, a person who does or conducts research, is a countable noun. As a verb, *research* is usually followed by a direct object (not by *about*). As an adjective, *research* can be followed by a plural noun: *research projects, research studies*.

  <u>Research</u> needs to be funded by the government.

  <u>The researcher</u> spent many days looking for his lost notebook.

  My goal is to <u>research</u> artificial intelligence.

  Many <u>research</u> studies are done at universities.

Some nouns can be either countable or uncountable depending on context.

In their youth, most people have at least 100,000 <u>hairs</u> on their head.

If you're determined, you could count the number of hairs!

Shaving your <u>hair</u> today is more often a matter of personal choice than of hygiene.

The sense here is of hair as a mass, therefore uncountable.

For examples of countable and uncountable nouns with articles, see "Articles—*A*, *An*, and *The*" in the "Adverbs" section of this appendix.

Prepositions

Despite, in spite of: Both act as prepositions, so a noun—not a clause—needs to follow each.

<u>In spite of</u>/<u>Despite</u> her best efforts to create interest in the performance, only a few people attended it.

Times and dates, referring to: The preposition used for time expressions varies according to context: "I will be there *for* Christmas." ("I will arrive sometime *on* or *before* Christmas"); "I will be there *during* Christmas" ("I will be there for the entire time").

For specific times:

He will arrive <u>at</u> 9 a.m. <u>on</u> Tuesday, 24 December.

For less specific times:

He will arrive <u>in</u> the morning. [or <u>in</u> the evening, <u>in</u> December, <u>in</u> 2022, but <u>at</u> night]

See "Verbs and Prepositions" in the "Verbs" section of this appendix.

Verbs

The following verbs sometimes give students trouble:

Conclude: There are a few ways to express a conclusion. In most cases, a clause should follow the verb:

One can <u>conclude that</u> commercialism destroys culture.

One can <u>come to the conclusion</u> that commercialism destroys culture.

One can <u>draw the conclusion</u> that commercialism destroys culture.

To announce the conclusion of your essay, use *In conclusion*, not *As a conclusion*.

Remember: When you are recalling something (for example, when you're writing about a past incident), use the present tense of *remember* but describe the action in the past tense.

I <u>remember</u> when I was little how I <u>thought</u> my parents <u>knew</u> everything.

Verbs as Modal Auxiliaries

Modals are a special category of helping verb that make the meaning of a main verb more precise. They are usually followed by the bare infinitive, without *to*. Here are some common uses of modals.

- *Can* expresses capability: **Clothing <u>can</u> really say a lot about a person.**
- *Could* expresses capability in the past tense: **When she lived near a lake, Nina <u>could</u> swim every day.**
- *Should* expresses necessity or obligation: **There <u>should be</u> [or <u>must be</u>] stricter gun laws in the United States.**
- *May* and *might* express possibility. *May* often conveys a stronger possibility than *might*:
  Since she has the prerequisites, Bianca <u>may</u> enroll in the second-year course.
  Although she worked late, she <u>might</u> decide to go to the party.
- *May* also expresses permission: **Students <u>may</u> bring beverages into the study area but not food items.**
- *Will* expresses probability: **Since she has the prerequisites, Bianca <u>will</u> enroll in the second-year anthropology course.**
- *Would* expresses a repeated action in the past: **When she lived near a lake, Nina <u>would</u> swim every day.**

Verbs and Nouns

Because nouns are sometimes formed from verbs and often look like them, they can be confused. Use a dictionary to ensure that you have used the required part of speech. Here are two sets of commonly confused words:

Belief, believe: *Belief* is a noun; *believe* is a verb. *Believe* is often followed by *in* or *that*, depending on whether a word/phrase (*in*) or a clause (*that*) follows:

> **She firmly <u>believed in</u> his innocence.**

> **She firmly <u>believed that</u> he was innocent; this was her true <u>belief</u>.**

Breath, breathe: *Breath* is a noun; *breathe* is a verb. You can *take* or *draw a breath*, meaning "breathe in." Somewhat idiomatically, to *take a deep breath* can mean to prepare yourself for a difficult task (whether or not a deep breath is actually taken).

> **The guest speaker, Madeleine, <u>took a deep breath</u> before she entered the crowded room. After she began speaking, she <u>breathed</u> normally again.**

Verbs and Prepositions

The following alphabetical list includes verbs that may be confusing, usually due to idiomatic prepositional use.

Agree/Disagree with: You agree or disagree with someone or with a person's views or opinions on something. Other prepositions can follow both these verbs, but use *with* in most essays where you argue a thesis.

> I **agree with** space exploration in general, but I **disagree with** those who want us to spend billions of dollars per year on something with no practical benefit for humanity.

Agreed followed by *to* means "to consent (to)."

> I **agreed to** give a speech on the merits of space exploration to my philosophy class.

Apply for, apply to: You apply for a loan, scholarship, position, or job; you apply to a place (such as a school) or situation:

> Joshua **applied to** several colleges before he **applied for** a student loan.

Attend, study at: *Attend* means "to be present at," as in attend a university, class, concert, or wedding. *To study at* refers to a place, such as a college.

> Before he decided **to study** at Red Deer College he **attended** some classes at the University of Alberta.

See "*Graduate from*".

Avoid, prevent: When you *avoid* something, you stay away from it; the verb is usually followed by a direct object (the thing that is avoided). When you *prevent* something, you take an action so that it does not occur; *prevent* can be followed by a direct object or by a direct object + *from* and a gerund phrase:

> You should **avoid people** when you are sick as this will **prevent others from catching your virus.**

Call/draw attention to: This verb is followed by a noun and means "to point something out." A noun or possessive adjective often precedes *attention*.

> The Intergovernmental Panel on Climate Change (IPCC) was founded in 1988 in order to **draw** world **attention** to the link between climate change and human activity.

To *pay attention to* means "to take note of or to look at closely."

> All Canadians should **pay attention** to the next IPCC report.

To *get attention*, meaning "to attract notice," is not usually followed by a preposition:

> After failing to **get** the teacher's **attention** any other way, Harmon shouted "Fire!"

See "*Pay (for)*" and "*Point out*".

Care: To care *about* means "to be concerned about" (see "*Concern*" later in this section).

She cares <u>about</u> good grades.

To *care for* or *take care of* means "to look after":

Thomas <u>took care of</u> his sister when his mother was working.

Commit: A person can commit a crime, a murder, an error, but a person commits perjury (no article). Another meaning of the verb *commit* is "to dedicate to" or "resolve to do something"; it is often followed by the reflexive pronoun and the preposition *to*.

After *committing* a serious crime, he considered *committing perjury* to protect a friend, but instead decided to *commit himself* to helping his friend and himself find a better life.

Compare, contrast: When you compare, you focus on similarities; when you contrast, you focus on differences. With either term, the direct object follows, then *with* or *to* and the indirect object.

In our class assignment, we were asked to <u>compare</u> the Canadian system of government <u>with</u> the system in another country.

In this construction, the grammatical subject (*Saskatoon*) is what is being compared:

<u>Compared to</u> the small town that I grew up in, Saskatoon seems like a big city.

The verb phrase *make a comparison* uses the preposition *between*:

He <u>made a comparison between</u> one political system <u>and</u> another.

Compete for, compete against: *Compete for* is used with a thing, and *compete against* is used with a person.

They <u>competed for</u> the honour of being named captain of the team.

Mohammed <u>competed against</u> his friend to see who could get the higher mark.

Concern: The meaning you want determines the preposition to use. *To be concerned about* means "to be troubled or worried about something." *To be concerned for* means "to be worried about (or, occasionally, something)."

She <u>was concerned about</u> the implications of the new driving regulations; specifically, she <u>was concerned for</u> her daughter, who would soon be getting her licence.

When it is not followed by a preposition, *concern* means "applies to" or "is relevant to":

> **The matter I have to discuss, Yuto, concerns your future with this organization.**

Consider, discuss, mention: When you consider something, you think carefully about it, usually in order to take some kind of action. *Consider*, like *discuss* and *mention*, is followed by a direct object—not by *about*. Unlike *discuss*, however, *consider* and *mention* may be followed by a clause beginning with *that*.

> **Before Yoshi decided to get married, he considered the matter by talking it over with his married friend Eizad. Then he discussed it with Sanjeet.**

> **Before Yoshi discussed his marriage plans with his fiancée, he mentioned to Eizad and Sanjeet that he was considering marriage.**

See "*Think*".

Depend, rely, count: These verbs can mean "have confidence in someone or something." They are followed by *on* + a noun that states who or what is depended/relied on and then may be followed by *for* + another noun that expands on the first:

> **Shaun depends on email for most of his business.**

> **Maheen relies on her friend Amy for fashion advice.**

Discuss: See "*Consider, discuss, mention*".

Encourage/discourage: You encourage someone *to* do something, but you discourage someone *from* doing something.

> **Raising tuition may discourage students from enrolling in other courses.**

> **The president of the students' union is encouraging all students to protest the tuition increase.**

Note that an infinitive follows *to*, but a gerund follows *from*.

Graduate from, to be a graduate of: In *graduate from*, *graduate* is a verb that refers to completing a program and receiving a diploma or degree. *To be a graduate of* is the noun form (the second *a* is a short vowel):

> **After Kasey graduated from college, she went to graduate school and became a graduate of UBC.**

Hire, hired by: To hire someone or a company is to give them a job or task. Employees are hired by their employers:

> **After applying for several positions during the summer, Teh was hired by another company.**

See "*Apply for, apply to*".

Know something, know someone: The former means to have information or expertise about something; the latter means to be acquainted with a person. When using *know someone*, follow the verb with the person's name.

> When I got <u>to know Tey</u>, I learned about computers, and I now <u>know</u> everything <u>about</u> them.

> Shelley <u>knows</u> that she has a test tomorrow.

Lack: As a verb, *lack* is followed by a direct object; as a noun, it is usually preceded by an article or other determiner (e.g., *its*, *that*, *this*, *your*) and followed by *of*:

> The first thing she noticed about the bedroom was <u>its lack of privacy</u>. The kitchen also <u>lacked</u> dishes and other utensils.

Lead to: This verb means the same as *result in* (see the entry later in this section). In both cases, a result or consequence follows the preposition.

> The cloning of animals, according to many people, is certain <u>to lead to</u> the eventual cloning of humans.

Look at/around/for/into/over:

> look at (examine): In my essay, I will <u>look at</u> solutions to the problem of homeless people.
> around: Dazed by the accident, he slowly sat up and <u>looked around</u>.
> for (search): Simon looked for his lost notes on his messy desk.
> into (investigate): After being laid off for the second time this year, Natalie began to <u>look into</u> self-employment.
> over (scan): She <u>looked over</u> her notes from the previous class.

Mention: See "*Consider, discuss, mention*".

Participate in: You participate *in* something—activities, sports, etc.:

> Dong Hun often <u>participates in</u> classroom discussions.

Pay (for): *Pay* means "to give (usually money) what is due for goods, services, work, etc." *For* + a noun may follow if you want to indicate what was purchased:

> She <u>paid</u> less than $80 <u>for</u> all her textbooks since she bought them used.

Point out: This verb means "to call attention to (something)." It is generally followed by a noun/pronoun or a clause beginning with *that*. One of the meanings of *to point* is "to indicate, to single out, using a finger"; it is followed by *to*.

> Ruji <u>pointed out</u> her sister among the bystanders.

Ruji <u>pointed out that</u> her sister was always late for a meeting.

Ruji <u>pointed to</u> her sister, who was standing in a crowd.

Refer: *Refer* is followed by *to* when the meaning is "to make a reference or to make mention of something." If a clause beginning with *that* follows, a noun such as *fact*, *idea*, etc., should intervene between the verb *refer* and the clause.

In his letter of recommendation, he <u>referred to</u> the many occasions in which Duy had demonstrated his sense of humanity and compassion. Specifically, he <u>referred to the fact that</u> Duy had often volunteered for work in local hospices.

Result in/result from: When you use the verb *result*, you must be careful about the preposition you use after it. To result *in* means that what follows the verb is a result or consequence; to result *from* means that what follows the verb is a cause.

Being convicted of the crime of murder <u>usually results</u> in a long prison term.

A prison term is the consequence.

Most murders in the United States <u>result from</u> the use of guns.

Guns are a cause.

Stress, emphasize: These terms mean the same thing and are usually followed by direct objects (not prepositions). But if you want to use the verb phrase *put stress/emphasis on*, note the preposition that is required. A *that* clause may also follow these verbs.

The writer <u>emphasized</u> the main point of her argument by providing examples.

The writer <u>put emphasis on</u> the main point of her argument by providing examples.

The instructor <u>stressed that</u> all students should arrive on time for class.

Think: This verb has many uses. *To think about* means to "reflect on," and *to think over* means to "consider"; note the placement of *it* in the example. Use *think* + a clause beginning with *that* if you want to refer to a belief or opinion.

William originally <u>thought that he would take a commerce class</u> in the second term, but when he <u>thought about it</u> [or <u>thought it over</u>], he decided to enroll right away.

Verbs and Their Subjects (Subject–Verb Agreement)

Always ensure that you use the singular form of any verb that has a singular subject and a plural verb for any plural subject. Remember that the third-person singular form of a verb usually ends in *s*.

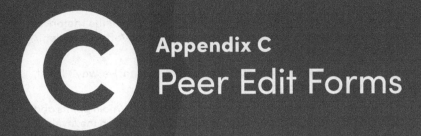

Appendix C
Peer Edit Forms

Formal Outline

The essay outline provides the structure for the essay. As an editor, you should pay special attention to the relationship among the parts (introduction, body paragraphs, conclusion), to the order of arguments (weakest to strongest? strongest to weakest? some other logical order?), and to the strength and effectiveness of each main point (Is each adequately developed? Is the claim supported?).

Instructions

Use the checkboxes to indicate that you have considered and evaluated the criteria. Add suggestions, comments, questions, and advice in the space provided.

Introduction

☐ What kind of formal outline is used: topic, sentence, or other (such as graphic)?

☐ Does the introduction attract your interest?

☐ Does it announce the topic?

☐ Does it contain a two-part direct thesis statement announcing the topic and commenting on the topic?

☐ Is the claim one of fact, value, or policy?

☐ Is the thesis statement interesting, specific, manageable, and clearly expressed?

Body Paragraphs

☐ Does each paragraph contain at least one main idea that can be easily identified as such? If not, which paragraph(s) doesn't do this?

☐ Does each paragraph contain at least two subpoints that help develop the main point? If not, which paragraph(s) doesn't?

☐ Has the writer provided support for their argument? If not, suggest ways that they could use kinds of evidence (e.g., examples, facts/statistics, personal experience, outside sources, etc.) to do so.

☐ Do the paragraphs appear to be organized using any of the rhetorical patterns discussed in Chapter 4 (e.g., definition, cause/effect, problem/solution, compare and contrast)?

☐ Are the main points ordered in a logical and persuasive way? If not, what is an alternative arrangement?

☐ Are there at least two levels represented in the outline (main points and subpoints)? Is parallel structure applied to main points and the levels of subpoints?

Conclusion

☐ Does it successfully summarize or restate the argument without sounding repetitious?

☐ Does it go beyond the introduction by enlarging on the implications of the thesis, urging a change in thought or call to action, or making an ethical or emotional appeal?

Final Comments or Suggestions

Writer's Name: _____

Editor's Name: _____

Argumentative Essay: First Draft

When editing a first draft, pay attention to its structure, argument, transitions, and grammar. Suggest ways for the writer to make points stronger and clearer.

Instructions

Use the checkboxes to show that you have considered and evaluated the criteria. Use the space provided to add suggestions, comments, and questions. In addition, underline, circle, or highlight possible grammar, spelling, usage, and stylistic problems.

Introduction

☐ Does the introduction function successfully?

  ☐ Is it interesting?

  ☐ Does it announce the subject and contain a thesis statement? Is the claim arguable?

  ☐ Does it suggest the main way the argument will be organized (e.g., definition, cause/effect, time order, division, compare and contrast, question/answer, etc.)?

☐ Does the writer establish credibility and trust? How?

Body Paragraphs

☐ Does the argument seem complete, and does the order of the paragraphs appear logical?

☐ Look at paragraphs individually. Are any too short or too long? Can any be divided into two paragraphs?

☐ Is each paragraph unified (relates to one main idea)? If not, which ones aren't?

☐ Is each paragraph coherent? If not, which ones aren't?

☐ Do paragraphs contain topic sentences?

☐ Is the order of the sentences natural?

☐ Are there appropriate transitions between sentences, helping you to see the relationship between sentences?

☐ Does the writer successfully use repetition, rephrasing, synonyms, or other devices to achieve coherence?

☐ Does each paragraph seem developed adequately?

☐ Are there different organizational methods used to develop the argument? Which ones? Are they effective?

☐ What kinds of evidence are produced? Are they used effectively? You don't have to refer to specific paragraphs—only note if they appear to be present to help support the thesis:

  ☐ examples, illustrations
  ☐ personal experience
  ☐ analogies
  ☐ precedents
  ☐ outside authorities/secondary sources
  ☐ other

☐ Are there points where the argument seems strained, weak, incomplete, and/or illogical? Are there any fallacies (e.g., cause/effect fallacies, fallacies of irrelevance, emotional/ethical fallacies)? (See Chapter 9 for fallacies.)

Conclusion

☐ Is the conclusion satisfying? Does it summarize and/or generalize?

Other Criteria

☐ Does the writer appear credible by

  ☐ conveying knowledge?
  ☐ being trustworthy and reliable?
  ☐ being fair?

☐ Is the opposing view acknowledged?

☐ Is the writer's voice objective?

☐ Are there any examples of slanted or biased language?

☐ Is the opposing view successfully refuted (as in the point-by-point method)?

☐ Are specific argumentative strategies—common ground, appeal to reader interest, concessions, emotional appeals—used? If not, could any of these be helpful?

☐ Are there any places where the language seems unclear or where a point is unclear due to the way it is expressed?

☐ If the writer uses sources, are they integrated smoothly and grammatically? Are all direct quotations, summaries, paraphrases, and ideas acknowledged?

☐ Are the sources cited and referenced correctly?

Final Comments or Suggestions

Writer's Name: _____

Editor's Name: _____

Research Essay: First Draft

Pay attention to a research essay's structure, argument, transitions, and grammar. Suggest ways for the writer to make points stronger and clearer. However, with this type of essay, you must also focus on the types of research used and the ways the writer integrates material from outside sources.

Instructions

Use the checkboxes below to demonstrate that you have considered and evaluated the criteria. Use the space provided to add suggestions, comments, and questions. Underline, circle, or highlight possible grammar, spelling, usage, and stylistic problems.

Introduction

☐ Is the introduction successful?

    ☐ Is it interesting?
    ☐ Does it announce the subject and contain a thesis statement with a claim of fact, a hypothesis to be tested, or a question to be answered?
    ☐ Does it suggest the main way the argument will be organized?
    ☐ Does the writer establish credibility and trust? How?

Body Paragraphs

☐ Does the essay seem complete, and does the order of the paragraphs appear logical?

☐ Look at paragraphs individually. Are any too short or too long? Can any be divided into two paragraphs?

☐ Is each paragraph unified (relates to one main idea)? If not, which ones aren't?

- ☐ Is each paragraph coherent? If not, which ones aren't?
- ☐ Do paragraphs contain topic sentences?
- ☐ Is the order of the sentences natural?
- ☐ Are there appropriate transitions between sentences, enabling you to see the relationship between sentences?
- ☐ Does the writer successfully use repetition, rephrasing, synonyms, or other devices to achieve coherence?
- ☐ Does each paragraph seem well developed?
- ☐ Has the writer used sources effectively? Note any exceptions.
- ☐ Do all the sources pass the CARS test (credible, accurate, reliable/reasonable, supported)?
- ☐ Does the writer use a sufficient number of sources? Is there an overreliance on one source? If so, which one?
- ☐ Does the writer show familiarity with the sources used?
- ☐ Do the sources appear to be relevant to the points discussed?
- ☐ Is each reference integrated smoothly into the essay, both stylistically and grammatically?
- ☐ Is the context made sufficiently clear in each instance?
- ☐ Do brackets and ellipses appear to have been used correctly?
- ☐ Are all sources cited? Identify any that may not be.
- ☐ Do the citations appear correct and consistent? Are they done using the proper style (MLA/APA)?
- ☐ Does the essay appear to be fundamentally focused on exposition (explaining) rather than argumentation (persuasion)?

Conclusion

- ☐ Is the conclusion satisfying? Does it summarize and/or generalize?

Other Criteria

- ☐ Does the writer appear credible by
    - ☐ conveying knowledge?
    - ☐ being trustworthy and reliable?
- ☐ Is the writer's voice objective?
- ☐ Are there any places in the draft where the language seems unclear or where a point is unclear due to the way it is expressed?

Final Comments or Suggestions

Writer's Name: _____

Editor's Name: _____

Exercise 13.2

1. The <u>children</u> built a large snow <u>fort</u>.
   common/concrete/count   common/concrete/count
2. The <u>doors</u> were slammed closed by the <u>wind</u>.
   common/concrete/count   common/abstract/count
3. The <u>women</u> present were all wearing <u>hats</u>.
   common/concrete/count   common/concrete/count
4. I would like five <u>glasses</u> of <u>water</u>, please.
   common/concrete/count   common/concrete/non-count
5. I bought a hard <u>drive</u> that has five <u>terabytes</u> of <u>memory</u>.
   common/concrete/count   common/abstract/count   common/abstract/non-count
6. I went to <u>Niagara Falls</u> yesterday.
   proper/concrete/count
7. I graduated from <u>Red River College</u> last <u>summer</u>.
   proper/concrete/count   common/abstract/count
8. My <u>job</u> as assistant <u>manager</u> is very challenging.
   common/concrete/count   common/concrete/count
9. <u>Legends</u> say that <u>King Arthur</u>'s <u>Knights</u> of the <u>Round Table</u> were loyal and chivalrous.
   common/concrete/count   proper/concrete/count   proper/concrete/count proper/concrete/count
10. <u>Learning</u> a new <u>language</u> is difficult.
    common/abstract/non-count   common/abstract/count
    For <u>example</u>, my <u>mom</u> is fluent in <u>Dutch</u>, but I can't understand it at all.
    common/abstract/count   common/concrete/count   proper/concrete/non-count

Exercise 13.3

1. Incorrect: Abiha and I
2. Incorrect: Greg and I
3. Correct
4. Incorrect: its

5. Incorrect: us
6. Correct: you and me
7. Correct: it
8. Correct: I (am)
9. Correct: himself
10. Correct: yourself

Exercise 13.4

1. linking
2. state of being
3. action
4. linking
5. action

Exercise 13.6

- Nouns: *Justin, Trudeau, Canada, prime minister, house, premier, background, son, Pierre, residence, 24 Sussex Drive, aspects, personality, lifetime, spotlight, fore, zeitgeist, comedian, John, Oliver, image, eve, election, search, choice, member, week, rehab, model, lobotomy, Johnny, Depp, twin, show, Last Week Tonight, March, 2012, psyche, fighter, senator, Patrick, Brazeau, match, opponent, nose, round*
- Pronouns: *who, he, his, you, him*
- Verbs: *is, has, was, are, lampooned, do, can, underwent, said, entered, beat*
- Adjectives: *elected, new, privileged, country, iconic, evolving, media, British, federal, Google, image, poor, boyband, sweater, model, evil, late-night, comedy, Canadian, much-loved, former, Conservative, charity, boxing, bloody, final*
- Adverbs: *newly, ahead, ever, literally*
- Prepositions: *in, of, after, to, on, from, before*
- Conjunctions: *however*

Exercise 13.7

1. I slept.
   Parts of Speech (POS): pronoun, verb
   Sentence Elements (SE): subject (*I*), verb (*slept*)
2. Henry bought a ball.
   POS: noun, verb, adjective (article), noun
   SE: subject (*Henry*), verb (*bought*), adjective (article; *a*), noun (*ball*)
3. Mr Safi gave the test to Joshua.
   POS: noun, verb, adjective (article), preposition, noun
   SE: subject (*Mr Safi*), verb (*gave*), direct object (*the test*), indirect object (*Joshua*)

4. Stacey is homesick.
   POS: noun, verb, adjective
   SE: subject *(Stacey)*, verb *(is)*, subject complement *(homesick)*
5. The bright red car drove quickly around the block.
   POS: adjective (article), adjective, adjective, noun, verb, adverb, preposition, adjective (article), noun.

SE: subject *(car)*, verb *(was driven)*, prepositional phrase *(around the block)*

Exercise 13.8

Complete subject = italic; complete predicate = underline

1. *Bob and his roommate Yan* <u>went to the movies</u>.
2. *Bob and Yan, who are big horror fans,* <u>really enjoyed the new superhero movie</u>.
3. *The hungry pair* <u>ate too much popcorn and drank too much pop</u>.
4. *Both Bob and Yan* <u>spent too much money</u>.
5. *Bob and Yan* <u>are now poor</u>.

Exercise 13.9

Simple subject = italic; simple predicate = underline

1. *Bob* and his roommate *Yan* <u>went</u> to the movies.
2. *Bob and Yan*, who are big horror fans, really <u>enjoyed</u> the new superhero movie.
3. The hungry *pair* <u>ate</u> too much popcorn <u>and drank</u> too much pop.
4. Both *Bob and Yan* <u>spent</u> too much money.
5. *Bob and Yan* <u>are now poor</u>.

Exercise 13.10

1. Tomorrow, (the class time) will be changed (for the rest) (of the semester).
   noun phrase adjectival adjectival
   S = *the class time*
2. (Some of the food) (in the fridge) (has spoiled).
   noun adjectival verb
   S = *Some of the food in the fridge*
3. The store (in the mall) (with the latest fashions) (has closed).
   adjectival adjectival verb
   S = *The store in the mall with the latest fashions*
4. A search (of the abandoned house) (turned up) several cartons (of stolen goods).
   adjectival verb adjectival
   S = *A search of the abandoned house*

5. (The 2022 hockey season) (will belong) (to the Leafs).
    noun verb adjectival
    S = *The 2020 hockey season*

Exercise 13.11

Dependent clause = underline; independent clause = italic

1. *I will meet you at the airport before the flight.*
2. <u>Because Stan likes ginger ale</u>, *I bought two flats of it.*
3. Yesterday, <u>while I was reviewing my finances</u>, *I noticed that I forgot to pay my electric bill.*
4. *I had to pay the bill with my credit card* and *I am now at my credit limit.*
5. *I need to go to the bank to apply for a loan*, and *I need to visit my parents* <u>because I need more money this month.</u>

Exercise 13.12

1. I <u>will meet</u> you <u>at the airport</u> <u>before the flight</u>.
2. Because Stan likes ginger ale, I bought two flats of it.
3. Yesterday, while I <u>was reviewing</u> my finances, I noticed that I forgot to pay my <u>electric bill</u>.
4. I had to pay the bill <u>with my credit card</u> and I am now <u>at my credit limit</u>.
5. I need to go <u>to the bank</u> to apply <u>for a loan</u>, and I <u>need to visit</u> my parents because I need <u>more money</u> this month.

Exercise 13.13

1. S
2. P
3. Complete sentence
4. Complete sentence; question structure
5. Complete sentence; command

Exercise 13.14

Italics show material added to make complete sentences. Other options exist for turning the fragments into complete sentences.

1. The store that opened on the weekend *had a really great sale today.*
2. The brilliant idea that came to me in the middle of the night *was lost when I woke up.*
3. A song that can get everyone dancing *is needed for the second dance at the wedding reception.*
4. The kind of doughnut that doesn't have a hole in the middle *is often called a Bear Claw or a Dutchie.*
5. The beach towel that was on the ground *needs to be washed.*

Exercise 13.15

Italics show material added to make complete sentences. Other options exist for turning the fragments into complete sentences.

1. The empty cup on the bench *belongs to Todd*; *I was surprised to see* the empty cup on the bench.
2. *The irate parent* signed his name to the bottom of the petition.

Exercise 13.16

<u>Underlining</u> shows material added to make complete sentences. Other options exist for turning the fragments into complete sentences.

1. Completing the test on time <u>is very important</u>. [–*ing*]
2. Huge tears rolled down his cheeks. [complete sentence]
3. Being that she worked late, <u>she had to make sure the office was securely locked</u>. [–*ing*] [A better sentence: Because she worked late, she had to make sure the office was securely locked.]
4. He promised to call her tomorrow to see if she was still all right. [add-on]
5. A murder of crows, along with a flock of sheep, <u>blocked the road</u>. [no predicate]
6. He must be guilty since he's already confessed. [dependent clause]
7. Walking beside the tracks, he eventually reached the town. [complete sentence]
8. <u>She was excited to be</u> introducing our next prime minister. [–*ing*]
9. <u>He likes science fiction</u>, for example, the reboot of the famous TV show *The X-Files*. [add-on]
10. Swimming on her back, <u>she eventually reached the shore</u>. [–*ing*]

Exercise 13.17

1. <u>When considering college or university</u>. [dependent] Many students must decide where to live. If they are going to school close to home, they may decide to continue living with their families.
2. <u>Listening to their parent's advice</u>. [–*ing*] However, if the school is far away and commuting is not possible, students must decide whether to live in the school residence or in an apartment. Residences are convenient.
3. <u>Especially if there is a meal plan available</u>. [add-on]
4. <u>Meal plans that are nutritious</u>. [add-on] Apartments might be a better idea though, especially if students need to work. Not all residences are close to where jobs are. Privacy might be an issue in residence. Not all students can get their own rooms. Apartments may provide privacy, but only if there is no need for roommates. Many factors need to be considered when choosing where to live.

Corrections:
1. When considering college or university, many students must decide where to live.
2. If they are going to school close to home, they may decide to continue living with their families, often listening to their parent's advice.
3 & 4. Residences are convenient, especially if there is a nutritious meal plan.

Exercise 13.18

1. They intended to eat at Benny's Bistro, but they saw a long line-up outside Benny's, so they went to Kenny's Kitchen instead. [compound]
   Alternative with minor changes: As soon as they saw a long line-up outside Benny's Bistro, they went to Kenny's Kitchen instead, even though they had intended to eat at Benny's. [complex]
2. Although there may be nearly 2 million kinds of plants in the world, and there are likely at least as many different kinds of animals, no one can know how many species have evolved, flourished, and become extinct. [compound-complex]

Exercise 13.19

1. I read two books in two days. I did nothing else but read. [run-on]
2. I couldn't use my laptop today. I forgot to plug it in before the battery was dead. [comma splice]
3. I was frightened during my first driving lesson: the instructor yelled at me. [run-on]
4. It's easy to punctuate sentences: just put a comma whenever you pause. [comma splice]
5. It was late when she finished watching the movie. She took a taxi home. [run-on]
6. Magazines are available for digital download. This is better for the environment. [comma splice]
7. Technology continues to evolve, but we can't always predict whether this is good or bad. [correct]
8. Humans are imitators. Conforming is something they are good at. [comma splice]
9. Many immigrants want to learn about Canadian culture. They take courses about it. [run-on]
10. Binge drinking is a serious problem. Many students engage in this behaviour. [comma splice]

Exercise 13.20

1. Problem: comma splice
   Correct: He managed to pass the year though he seldom did his homework. What will happen to him next year is anyone's guess.

2. Problem: fragment
   Correct: The opening ceremonies were delayed on account of rain.
3. Problem: fragment
   Correct: She has decided to work at a fast-food restaurant: not a great place for tips.
4. Problem: comma splice
   Correct: Movies provide entertainment for people; different people prefer different genres such as horror.
5. Problem: fragment
   Correct: She's been very happy since she bought the new tablet.
6. Problem: fragment
   Correct: The only way a person can learn is to pay attention to what is going on in class.
7. Problem: fragment
   Correct: He wished he could excel at sports, but he was happy cheering his team from the sidelines.
8. Problem: comma splice
   Correct: The concept that "bigger is better" is part of our culture. It is promoted by both advertisers and the media these days.
9. Problem: fragment
   Correct: I have trouble understanding the theory of relativity and its impact on our daily lives.
10. Problem: comma splice
    Correct: Justin Trudeau was the second-youngest person to become Prime Minister of Canada, but Joe Clark was the youngest.

Exercise 13.21

The "Freshmen 15" is not a recent phenomenon this refers to the weight students typically gain during their first year at college or university. [run-on] What concerns doctors now is the amount of weight gained during this time. In the 1970s and 1980s, students typically gained 5 pounds, now it is up to 15. [comma splice] This is a very unhealthy weight gain. Once the weight is gained. [fragment] It is very hard to lose. Because of this. [fragment] Cafeterias are starting to offer more nutritional meals with fewer calories. Student councils are beginning to be proactive and inform students of the dangers of excess weight gain. School gyms are offering more classes to help students battle this weight gain. In the future, many hope that the "Freshman 15" becomes non-existent.

Corrections:

The "Freshmen 15" is not a recent phenomenon. This refers to the weight students typically gain during their first year at college or university. What concerns doctors now is the amount of weight gained during this time. In the 1970s and 1980s, students typically gained 5 pounds, but now it is up to 15. This is a very unhealthy weight gain. Once the weight is gained, it is very hard to lose. Because of this, cafeterias are starting to offer more nutritional meals with fewer calories. Student councils are beginning to be proactive and inform students of the dangers of excess weight gain. School gyms are offering more classes to help students battle this weight gain. In the future, many hope that the "Freshman 15" becomes non-existent.

Exercise 14.1

1. While he was waiting for the bus, he read his graphic novel. (Sentence starts with a dependent clause)
2. Because he was hungry, he ordered hash browns, two eggs, bacon, and toast. (Sentence starts with a dependent clause, items in a series)
3. I would like to buy an electric car and a new bicycle after I graduate. (No comma needed)
4. Lions, tigers, and bears are not all found in the North American wilderness. (Items in a series)
5. While most of the class wants to leave early, John, however, does not. (Introductory phrase, word interrupting a flow)
6. The CN Tower was the world's tallest free-standing structure until the 1990s.
7. My white cocker spaniel, Trixie, is very spoiled. (Setting of an appositive)
8. The dusty pans in the damp, broken cupboard need to be replaced. (Coordinating adjectives)
9. "Stop," she yelled. (separating a quote from the rest of the sentence)
10. I wanted to buy his portrait, but it wasn't for sale. (Separating two independent clauses with a coordinating conjunction)

Exercise 14.2

1. Even though I had planned my trip for months, I had forgotten to pack essentials, so I had to buy them on my trip.
2. My trip included stops in Moscow, St. Petersburg, and Vladivostok before I returned home to Saint John, New Brunswick.
3. My sister, Tamara, came with me, despite being afraid of flying.
4. Her first flight was on May 30, 2001, but she never flew after that.
5. The flight attendant, who was fluent in English and Russian, was very kind to my sister on this trip.
6. Julie, the flight attendant, had worked for Air Canada for 15 years, but now she worked for KLM.
7. Julie said that, while Air Canada was a good company to work for, she wanted to live in Amsterdam.
8. My trip to Russia, while planned in detail, was full of surprises.
9. I did not expect such hot, humid weather in St. Petersburg.
10. Before I go to Russia again, I will study the language so that I can communicate with more people.

Exercise 14.3

1. Since the Peloton was introduced in February 2012, many people have decided to stop going to the gym, and they are exercising at home with the use of modern equipment and online classes. In addition to the Peloton, there are now smart exercise mirrors, online classes, and virtual running, cycling, swimming, or walking challenges. These tools seem to be an improvement over the older exercise equipment that people bought but didn't use. There are numerous stories of treadmills being used for storing clothing on, exercise bikes collecting dust in the corner, and exercise DVDs that are in an unused, dusty drawer. Because of the price of the newer equipment and the instant availability of classes online, experts say that people will exercise more than in the past. However, all of the above ignores the problem of staying motivated enough to continue an exercise program in order to get fit. If someone could invent a bottle of motivation and sell it at a reasonable price, Canadians might become fitter.

2. Autism is a much misunderstood problem. Often, children with autism are viewed as a "handful" and "hyperactive." Very little is known of its causes, and characteristics can vary, making a diagnosis difficult. In children, it is even harder because other children can exhibit some of the characteristics associated with autism. Although autism can cause many behavioural difficulties, autistic children can still live near-normal lives if they are surrounded by understanding caregivers. Working with autistic children can change a person and make one realize the need for better understanding and education. Treating autism can be difficult because often there is no feedback from the patient. Over the years, there have been many ideas of how to treat autism, but not all were correct and have at times made treatment problematic.

Exercise 14.4

Underlining shows words moved within a sentence.

1. One of my roommates rode her bicycle to school most of the time; therefore, she is more physically fit than I am.
2. SPCA officers work for but are not paid by the government; <u>in fact</u>, it is donations that provide their salary.
3. If homelessness continues to increase, it will be costly for taxpayers; homelessness, <u>moreover</u>, affects downtown businesses.
4. Although sailing is a popular sport among older people, younger adults cannot afford the price of boats.
5. Many young people, however, enjoy kayaking or paddle boarding.

Exercise 14.5

1. May flowers bring on my asthma; October leaf mould affects my allergies.
2. Every essay needs three parts: an introduction, a body, and a conclusion.
3. He travelled to the honeymoon capital of the world, Niagara Falls.
4. Mayumi tended to look on the good side of things; Glenn usually saw the bad side.
5. The following is not a rule for comma use: put a comma wherever you pause.
6. While I agree that studying math is important, I can't understand the use for algebra.
7. Marselina, who has a fine ear for music, can't sing a note.
8. Whenever I order designer clothing for my boutique, I shop in Toronto, Ontario; Buffalo, New York; and London, England.
9. The Online Dictionary defines animal cruelty this way: "treatment or standards of care that cause unwarranted or unnecessary suffering or harm to animals."
10. The tuition increase has affected many lower income families; therefore, there is an even greater demand for student loans.

Exercise 14.6

1. Swimming in the lake is one of the joys of a Canadian summer. In the winter, those who live close to a lake dream of warm days, picnics on the beach, the smell of suntan lotion, and the sound of waves rolling into shore. Swimming, however, is a skill that needs to be learned; one cannot simply go to the lake, swim, and be safe. Not knowing how to swim can lead to needless drownings. There are many Canadians who believe that the basic swimming skills need to be taught to all children, especially if they are going to spend any time near water. Because of this, organizations are trying to raise money to send children to swimming classes. Organizations fundraise so that parents have access to funds to pay for their children's swimming lessons. Some people feel that, as many refugees and immigrants come from areas where swimming was not possible, these children really need to learn the skills required to understand respect and swim in the water. With more children learning how to swim through this funding, the summer dream of spending the day in the lake safely is becoming attainable.

Exercise 14.7

1. Society's rules do not always correspond to behaviour.
2. My aunt and uncle's cottage is for sale; its list price is $450,000.

3. One's education should not depend on the financial resources of one's parents.
4. The school's biggest draw for new students was the brand-new recreation complex.
5. The city's buses run on natural gas; it's more cost-effective.
6. John's biggest complaint is about the school's expensive cafeterias.
7. Ryan's and Jessica's birthday is on the same day.
8. Apples, oranges, mangoes, and tomatoes are the store's specials today.
9. It's a shame that Lenny's parents weren't able to attend their son's graduation ceremonies.
10. I don't know whether this etching is theirs, but there's no doubt it's worth a lot in today's market.

Exercise 14.8

Corrections to the first two paragraphs are provided here.

Reader reaction was swift and impassioned. The site's traffic, which averages 65 to 70 million views each month, experienced an additional 50,000 page views within the first 10 days of the posting. The investigation drew more than 400 letters to the editor, hundreds of emails to the message boards, and more than 16,000 responses to an online poll.

The intensity of the response surprised veteran investigative journalist Wayne MacPhail, the article's author. Although the sheer volume of letters was unexpected, it proved to him that there was an audience for online journalism in Canada. MacPhail has experimented with hypertext reporting since the late 1980s, but, outside of "Spin Doctors," he believes that, by and large, newspapers have done a "woeful job" of building an audience for Web-based investigative reporting. . . .

Exercise 15.1

Gardening is becoming a popular hobby, as many people want fresh, organic vegetables and bright flowers they [option 1] can appreciate throughout the summer. There is also a movement to create a more natural habitat for wildlife. However, before pulling out a lawn, gardeners [option 2] must first make sure they know what to plant. Gardeners must consider things like whether plants are drought resistant or they need a lot of shade. Gardeners [option 2] must also plan their gardens [option 2] with care so that they can achieve the effect they dream of.

Exercise 15.2

1. Neither the film's director nor its producers were on hand to receive their prestigious award.
2. The child, as well as her parents, thinks the room is too small. (The child identifies as female.)

3. The student must study for his exam. (The student identifies as male.)
4. One should never expect to succeed in a career unless one is willing to persist—even against the odds.
5. Everyone who works during the year is obliged to file their income tax return.
6. Her set of baby teeth was complete when she was only 18 months old.
7. None of the company's products requires testing on animals.
8. Lining the side of the highway are a lot of billboards advertising fast-food restaurants.
9. Every specimen of the horned grebe has a distinctive tuft on each side of its/their head.
10. The maximum number of people allowed on this elevator is 30.

Exercise 15.3

1. Every person in the community should have the right to attend university and create new opportunities for themselves.
   or
   All people in the community should have the right to attend university and create new opportunities for themselves.
2. No errors.
3. The taste of Bob's burgers is excellent, but they could be better.
4. There have been a number of sales because it is "back to school" time.
5. Better public transportation and more bike lanes mean less pollution.
6. An unusual story by Neil Gaiman leaves the reader wanting to read more.
7. Use of rechargeable batteries is not as high as many would expect.
8. A group of students, parents, and teachers is forming as they disagree with the government's planned changes.
9. Everyone who has purchased tickets is eligible for the grand prize, but they must be a resident of Canada to claim their prize.
   or
   Everyone who has purchased tickets is eligible for the grand prize but must be a resident of Canada to claim the prize.
   or
   Those who have purchased tickets are eligible for the grand prize, but they must be residents of Canada to claim their prize.
10. No errors.

Exercise 15.4

Alex and his lawyer, Alan, left in Alex's limousine for Loonies Unlimited to buy Alex's landlady, Alice, a litre of light lemonade. She told them to also buy a litre of light lemonade for her long-time lodger, Alison. When they alighted at Loonies Unlimited, they were alarmed that Alex had left his loonie in his loft. So Alphonse, of Loonies Unlimited, allowed them only one litre of lemonade, along with a length of limp licorice, and he loudly lamented their laxness.

Exercise 15.5

Genetically modified foods have been engineered to flourish in harsh environments. *These foods* will help alleviate the need for usable farmland. Being able to plant these modified seeds will enable farming to occur on lands once considered unsuitable for growing crops. *Being able to use formerly unsuitable land* will be a major benefit to many nations in Africa, Asia, and South America where there is a shortage of food and available land.

Exercise 15.6

1. The daughter had long, brown hair down to her waist, but her mother said that the daughter had to cut it.
2. While Tom was sleeping soundly on the kitchen floor, Jim walked around him.
3. They lived as if nobody else mattered but themselves. Their lifestyle is a problem.
4. This tryout will be her chance to prove whether she is good enough to make the team.
5. The politicians have a responsibility to educate the public.
6. His attorney decided on a not-guilty plea. The attorney made the wrong decision.
7. Josh gave his car keys to Alan and told Alan to drive carefully.
8. The Taylors and the Smiths make delightfully odd couples and the friends of both couples agree.
9. The cat will eat only the most expensive kind of deluxe cat food. The cat is spoiled.
10. After hearing his children's protests for a long time, he finally agreed to take them along.

Exercise 15.7

1. The brochure says you must keep your seatbelt fastened when you are on a flight. [no reference]
2. Whenever a staff meeting is called, employees are required to attend. [no reference]
3. A popular proverb says that all good things must end. [ambiguous reference]
4. Pesticides are used on crops, and pesticides are our major ground water pollutant. [ambiguous reference]
5. During Roosevelt's Pearl Harbor speech, the president identified the United States as a peaceful and tolerant nation.
    or

During his Pearl Harbor speech, Roosevelt identified the United States as a peaceful and tolerant nation. [no reference]

6. I know the sign indicated "No Parking," but I went ahead and parked there anyway. An officer gave me a $20 fine. [no reference in both sentences]

7. Her first cat was a Russian Blue and her second cat was a Bengal. The Bengal was spoiled.

or

Her first cat was a Russian Blue and her second cat was a Bengal. The Russian Blue was spoiled. [ambiguous reference]

8. Despite being told that the deadline was May 23, Tom missed the deadline. [no reference]

9. Some psychologists and researchers believe in the "innate" theory of prejudice. According to this theory, ingrained prejudice is cross-cultural and awareness of race is one of the earliest social characteristics to develop in children. These findings may help account for the theory's popularity. [remote reference]

10. During the industrial age, with expanding factories and growing cities, people lived in a rapidly changing work environment. [no reference]

Exercise 15.8

1. We students need to fight for better public transportation.
2. With whom did you go to the dance?
3. Shia and I went surfing for the first time last week.
4. Shia fell off his board and knocked me off mine.
5. The gift card was for Maya and me.
6. As she entered the room, a mysterious feeling came over her.
7. Jeff Dunham, who is a famous ventriloquist, has many odd characters.
8. I can choose whomever I want to be in my group.
9. Between you and me, Professor Singh is a hard marker.
10. To whom are you texting?

Exercise 15.9

Informal: You can definitely learn a lot from educational TV; you can learn things that cannot be learned from written texts. If you are a major in commerce, for example, and if you watch the business news, you can understand the commerce textbook better by applying what you learn from the news. Similarly, watching sports programs can be exciting and can also give you a better understanding of the game. On the other hand, if you choose to watch comedy all the time, you are not going to gain any real benefits. In general, I think that comedies are meaningless.

Formal: Educational TV has many benefits and can teach people things they cannot learn from written texts. If students major in commerce, for example, and watch the business news, they can understand the commerce textbook better by applying what is learned from the news. Similarly, watching sports programs can provide people with excitement and also give them a better understanding of the game. On the other hand, if people choose to watch comedy all the time, they will not gain any real benefits as comedies, generally, are meaningless.

Exercise 15.10

1. Problem: misplaced
   Correct: A striped, pointed hat was on his head.
2. Problem: misplaced
   Correct: As we were leaving, he tearfully promised to visit us.
3. Problem: dangling
   Correct: Although Sam is unambitious and downright lazy, I have never known him to break his word.
4. Problem: dangling
   Correct: His ego was further inflated when he was awarded first prize in the Ben Affleck look-alike contest.
5. Problem: misplaced
   Correct: Every character has a purpose, big or small, in Shakespeare's play.
6. Problem: misplaced
   Correct: When asked what my favourite sport is, without any hesitation I usually say that it is running.
7. Problem: dangling
   Correct: Stepping out of the airplane, she thought the fresh air was most invigorating.
8. Problem: misplaced
   Correct: In his book, Gabriel Kolko describes peace in Vietnam after the war.
9. Problem: dangling
   Correct: As he opened the door unexpectedly, his eyes fell upon two of his employees sleeping in front of their computers.
10. Problem: misplaced
    Correct: Teacher Laurie McNamara posed for the photographer in the Cloverdale Elementary School hallway with Principal Dan Saunders, who gave her a kidney last month.

Exercise 15.11

1. It is exciting, as a serious snowboarder, to observe the growth of this sport.
2. Over the years, several world-class cyclists, such as Eddy Merckx and Greg LeMond, have had spectacular careers.
3. As he ran down the street without a care in the world, two pedestrians had to quickly move out of his way.

4. As I am a member of the Sikh community, my paper will be given a strong personal focus.
5. You will have a fully interactive website, built in mere minutes, for your business or for your personal use.
6. A mother and her daughter were recently reunited in a checkout line after 18 years.
7. Germany has built an extensive network of highways, known as the Autobahn, through its countryside.
8. When they look for employees today, employers are stressing verbal and written communication skills more than ever before.
9. Adolescents experience essentially the same depressive symptoms as adults do.
10. In captivity, this species of snake will eat frogs, mice, and small pieces of meat.

Exercise 15.12

1. I like toe socks because they are warm and comfortable, come in many colours and designs, and are the latest in sock fashions.
2. Yoga offers many benefits: it enables you to relax and reduce stress, to exercise regularly, and, through yoga classes, to meet people with similar interests.
3. Computers are important to students as they provide entertainment, cut down on homework time, and enable them to obtain a wealth of information quickly.
4. Disadvantages of having roommates are that they can create a lot of mess and invade your personal space, but having a roommate gives you someone to talk to about your problems.
5. The benefits of coffee include helping you wake up, improving your mood, and improving your concentration.

Exercise 15.13

1. A good journalist is inquisitive, persistent, and attentive. [series]
2. Music can directly affect your thoughts, emotions, and feelings. [series]
3. In this essay, I will be looking at and writing about the role of women in the military. [compounds]
4. Tiddlywinks is a game not only of considerable skill but also of strategy. [correlative conjunctions]
5. Television can affect children in a variety of negative ways since children often lack judgment, are naturally curious, and are easily influenced. [series]
6. When Jim has the choice of either jumping or staying on the doomed ship, he chooses to jump. [compounds]
7. Aman never has been and never will be good at golf. [compounds]

8. She not only was the best teacher I have ever had but also was very modest. [correlative conjunctions]
9. Physical education teaches children not only to work well together but also to be patient and to be disciplined. [series]
10. Although Nathanial Hawthorne and Mark Twain are two very different American writers, their works are nevertheless similar in many ways. (comparison)

Exercise 15.15

1. I was given two choices by my landlord: pay up or get out. (Focus is on the subject, so passive is fine.)
2. More than a thousand people were left homeless by recent flooding. (The reporter is unknown. Place the focus on the people.)
3. The dog was let out by her owner. (If the focus is on the dog, leave as passive.)
4. The band performed a concert in April. (The focus is the band, not the concert, so change to active.)
5. Beethoven's Third Symphony, *The Eroica*, originally was dedicated to Napoleon. (We don't know if Beethoven made the dedication, so leave as passive.)
6. Education needs to be seen by the government as the number one priority. (The focus is on education, not the government, so leave as passive.)
7. Marc returned the library books. (The focus is on Marc, so change to active.)
8. The city trucks plowed the streets after the snowstorm. (The focus is on the trucks, so change to active.)
9. Poverty in First Nations communities must be addressed by the federal, provincial, and First Nations' governments. (The focus is on poverty in First Nations communities, so leave as passive.)
10. Ian Rankin's book became an instant bestseller. (The focus is on Ian Rankin, so change to active.)

Exercise 15.16

1. *Identify the problems*: In my family, my father and sister play video games as much as me [c]. They [h] have become very complex, [b] and can even improve problem-solving in children. By progressing through increasing difficulty levels, it [e] can help childrens [g] thought processes. On the one hand, if the child goes straight to the hardest setting, it [f] may feel discouraged, [a] on the other, if the child tries to systematically progress through increasing levels, he [f] can learn the mechanics of the game step by step. This [d] can help in the study of math, as the child may be more likely to persevere with a problem until he [i] finds the solution.

Rewritten with corrections: In my family, my father and sister play video games as much as I do. Video games have become very complex and can even improve problem-solving in children. Progressing through increasing difficulty levels can help children's thought processes. On the one hand, if the child goes straight to the hardest setting, they may feel discouraged; on the other, if the child tries to systematically progress through increasing levels, they can learn the mechanics of the game step by step. This method can help in the study of math, as the child may be more likely to persevere with a problem until a solution is found.

2. *Identify the problems*: Having a job and earning one's livelihood is [b] a necessary goal in life, [h] it is one of the reasons you [g] acquire an education. At the place where I work [a] however, many people come in expecting to find a job lacking presentation skills [e]. Many are poorly dressed, do not know how to behave, and they may not speak grammatically [d]. Untidy, disorganized, and unprepared, [f] I still have to match them with a prospective employer. They lack the skills to present themselves to others and knowing [d] what to do in public. Although they may be highly intelligent people. [c]

Rewritten with corrections: Having a job and earning one's livelihood are necessary goals in life. They are among the reasons one acquires an education. At the place where I work, however, many people lacking presentation skills come in, expecting to find a job. Many are poorly dressed, do not know how to behave, and may not speak grammatically. They are untidy, disorganized, and unprepared, yet I still have to match them with a prospective employer. They lack the skills to present themselves to others and to know what to do in public, though they may be highly intelligent people.

Exercise 15.17

1. a. dangling modifier
   Correct: Written through the eyes of a young boy, the narrative shows us the perspective of the Indigenous Peoples.
2. c. more than one error (subject–verb agreement: the subject, *stresses*, should agree with the verb, *teach*; pronoun inconsistency: *you* is not the same person as the noun antecedent, *students*.)
   Correct: The daily stresses of students, such as project or assignment due dates, teach them to manage their time wisely.
3. b. pronoun reference error
   Correct: Parents sometimes push their children so hard to excel that these children lose interest altogether.
4. c. comma error
   Correct: My roommate thinks it would be better for society if all drugs were decriminalized.

5. d. parallelism error

   Correct: Contributors to homelessness include the lack of well-paying jobs, increasingly large families and, probably the most important factor, the cost of living in a large city.

Exercise 15.18

1. c. their

   Correct: Anorexia starts when a person decides to take control of their body weight.

   or

   Anorexia starts when people decide to take control of their body weight.

2. b. the semicolon

   Correct: There are three types of turbine engines used in aircraft: the turbojet, the turbofan, and the turboprop.

3. b. vendors

   Correct: Work songs and street vendors' cries are examples of traditional African American music styles.

4. c. to extend

   Correct: Reforms of the UN Security Council include abolishing the veto or extending the Council beyond the current five members.

5. c. who listened . . .

   Correct: Results from a recent study showed that patients suffering from osteoarthritis reported a 66 per cent reduction in their perception of pain by listening to music for 20 minutes each day.

Glossary

abstract ⑤, ⑩ An overview of your purpose, methods, and results; can include key phrases or whole sentences from the full work. Also a short summary that precedes most academic journal articles.

adjectival modifier ⑮ A word or phrase that functions as an adjective.

adjective ⑬ A word that describes a noun or pronoun; usually comes before the word it modifies but can also follow a linking verb, where it modifies the subject.

adverb ⑬ A word that modifies a verb, an adjective, an adverb, or a sentence.

adverbial modifier ⑮ A word or phrase that functions as an adverb.

agreement ⑮ The principle that a verb must agree with its subject, and a pronoun must agree with its antecedent, or the noun it replaces.

analogy ③ A comparison that helps the reader to better understand the original object.

anecdote ⑦ An incident or event that is used because it is interesting or striking.

annotated bibliography ⑤ A list that appears at the end of an essay or article and that summarizes similar works in the field of study. It includes a concise version of the content, focusing on the thesis statement and major points or findings, and can also include an appraisal of the study's usefulness.

antecedent ⑬ The noun that appears earlier in the sentence and that a pronoun replaces. The term can also refer to a preceding event, condition, or cause.

antecedent–consequent ④ A method of paragraph or essay organization that includes an antecedent (a preceding event, condition, or cause) and its consequence (result).

APA (American Psychological Association) style ⑫ A citation style used in the social sciences and some sciences; uses parenthetical in-text citations (which include the author's last name, year of publication, and page number) and a reference list.

apostrophe ⑭ A mark of spelling that indicates the possessive or shows where letters have been omitted in a contraction.

appeal ⑨ A call on reason, ethics, or emotion to persuade a reader that an argument is valid.

argument ⑨ An attempt to persuade your audience to change its mind or to see your point of view through claims of value or policy.

article ⑬ A word such as *a*, *an*, or *the*, which precedes and modifies a noun.

audience ② Your intended readers and their expectations.

authority ⑧ A specialist in a subject that can be used for support. An authority who is not an expert carries less weight.

block quotation ⑪ A method of setting off a large quotation (4 or more lines or 40 or more words) from the rest of the essay's text.

body paragraphs ④ The middle paragraphs of an essay that help prove the thesis by presenting facts, arguments, or other support.

Boolean operators ⑩ Terms such as AND, OR, and NOT, which are used to customize an online or database search.

brainstorming ④ Writing words, phrases, or sentences that you associate with a subject without stopping to edit your ideas.

case study ⑧ A carefully selected example that is closely analyzed in order to provide a testing ground for the writer's claim.

cause–effect ④ A method of paragraph or essay organization in which a writer might focus on one effect, which would be accounted for by one or more causes, or focus on one cause and consider one or more effects.

chronology ④ A method of paragraph or essay organization in which a writer traces a topic's development over time.

circular conclusion ⑦ A conclusion that reminds the reader of the thesis.

citation ⑩, ⑫ An acknowledgement of the source of a quotation, paraphrase, or summary; includes the author last name, publication date, and location in the text, using page or paragraph numbers. Parenthetical in-text citations point to a complete citation in a reference or works cited list.

claim ⑧ The assertion about your topic that appears in your thesis statement. See also *factual claim*, *value or opinion claim*, and *policy claim*.

clarity ⑯ In writing, work that is grammatical, concise, direct, precise, and specific.

classification ④ A method of paragraph or essay organization in which a writer focuses on a large number of items that can be organized into more manageable groups. See also *division*.

clause ⑬ A group of words containing both a subject and a predicate; can be independent or dependent. See also *independent clause* and *dependent clause*.

cliché ⑯ A word or phrase that, though often true, has become overused (e.g., *weak as a kitten*).

coherence ③ A body of writing that is easy to follow because its sentences are connected to each other.

collective noun ⑮ A noun that may be singular or plural, depending on context. If in doubt, consider it singular.

colloquialism ⑯ A word or an expression acceptable in conversation but not in formal writing.

comma splice (13) A major grammatical error in which a comma alone is used to separate two complete thoughts.

common ground (9) An argument strategy that shows an opponent that you share similar concerns or basic values.

comparison and contrast (4) A method of paragraph or essay organization that involves a writer finding logical criteria for comparison and then analyzing their similarities and differences.

complete sentence (13) A sentence that contains at least one subject and one predicate and expresses a complete thought.

complete subject (13) The subject of a sentence plus its modifiers.

complex sentence (13) A sentence that contains an independent clause joined to a dependent clause by a subordinating conjunction.

compound (15) Two of the same parts of speech acting as one grammatical unit.

compound-complex sentence (13) A compound sentence joined with a complex one.

compound sentence (13) A sentence that contains two or more independent clauses joined by a coordinating conjunction.

compound subject (15) Two nouns, two pronouns, or a noun and a pronoun acting as one subject.

concession (9) The acknowledgement that a point is valid; shows that you are fair and reasonable.

conclusion (7) The final paragraph of the essay that sums up what was said in the body paragraphs. See also *circular conclusion*, *spiral conclusion*, and *wrap*.

conjunction (13) A word that joins words, phrases, or clauses. See also *coordinating conjunction*, *correlative conjunction*, and *subordinating conjunction*.

conjunctive adverb (13) An adverb such as *however*, *therefore*, or *thus* that joins two independent clauses. It is preceded by a semicolon and usually followed by a comma.

connotation (1) The feeling or idea that a word creates.

coordinating conjunction (13) A conjunction that joins equal units, such as two independent clauses.

correlative conjunction (13) A two-part grammatical unit that joins parts of a sentence; both must be used to complete the sentence.

cost–benefit (4) A method of paragraph or essay organization in which a writer analyzes a topic's pros and cons.

credibility (8) Three factors contribute to credibility: knowledge of the topic, reliability/trustworthiness, and fairness.

critical response (4) A type of essay in which you think critically about a text and respond by sharing your views with others.

critical thinking (1) A series of logical mental processes that lead to a conclusion.

dangling modifier (15) A grammatical error in which a word or phrase modifies the closest noun, often giving the sentence an unintended meaning. See also *dangling participle* and *misplaced modifier*.

dangling participle (15) A dangling modifier that modifies nothing in the sentence, as the noun or phrase it should modify is absent. See also *dangling modifier*.

database (10) A collection of related data organized for quick access.

definition (3) Tells your reader what you will be discussing in your essay, helps you understand the topic better, and helps you organize your main points.

delayed subject (15) A sentence construction in which the subject appears after a prepositional phrase and the verb.

denotation (1) The literal meaning of a word.

dependent clause (13) A group of words that contains a subject and a predicate but expresses an incomplete thought. It needs more information to form a complete sentence. Compare *independent clause*.

description (4) Adds concrete, physical detail to an essay.

development pattern (4) The principle or method that determines how an essay or a paragraph will be organized.

diction (16) Related to word choices and level of language; formal and informal writing are examples of different kinds of diction. See also *usage*.

digital object identifier (DOI) (10) A number–letter sequence that begins with the number 10 and is often found on documents obtained electronically through databases; used in citations.

direct object (DO) (13) The receiver of the action of the verb.

direct quotation (11) A quotation that is used when the source and the exact wording are important. See also *block quotation*, *brackets*, *citation*, and *ellipsis*.

division (4) A method of paragraph or essay organization in which a writer breaks the subject into parts in order to better understand the whole. See also *classification*.

dramatic approach (7) A method of writing an introduction that is meant to catch the reader's attention in an interesting or thought-provoking way.

ellipsis (. . .) (11) A punctuation mark that indicates the omission of one or more words within a direct quotation. A fourth dot is added if you omit all the words up to and including the final period.

emphasis (16) The importance or stress placed on an idea. A word or phrase has greater or less emphasis depending on where it appears in the sentence.

empirical (8) Related to observing and measuring data under controlled conditions in order to reach a conclusion about a phenomenon.

euphemism (16) A word or phrase substituted for the actual name of something, usually to make it more acceptable or to give it dignity; an example of indirect writing.

evidence (8) Information, such as that gathered from books, journals, or personal experience, to give your claim more credibility. See also *hard evidence* and *soft evidence*.

example (3), (8) One of the best ways to support a point and clarify an abstract idea; uses concrete details to translate an abstract claim into something the reader can more easily understand.

expanded thesis statement (7) A thesis statement that gives more detail, such as the main points that will be covered in the essay. Compare *simple thesis statement*.

expert (8), (10) A person who is experienced or well educated and has published or produced significant work about a subject. See also *authority*.

exposition ⑨ Informing, explaining, describing, or defining a topic. An expository essay uses claims of fact.

factual claim ⑧ A claim that is proven by facts and figures or the results of relevant studies.

fallacy ⑨ A misleading or unsound argument or a misuse of an appeal to emotion.

faulty predication ⑯ The problem that occurs where a verb cannot be logically linked to its subject.

faulty reasoning ⑨ An error in thinking that can result from an invalid argument, a lack of proof for a claim, or an opinion that is not clearly separated from fact.

focused reading ① A close and detailed (i.e., word-by-word) reading of a specific, relevant passage. See also *selective reading*.

formal writing ⑯ Writing that features the rules of formal usage and correct grammar.

freewriting ④ Writing without stopping. It is important to let your ideas flow without editing or censoring them.

gender-inclusive language ⑮ The careful use of terms and grammatical forms that include all genders. When an antecedent is either a generic singular noun or an indefinite pronoun, the personal pronoun that follows must be gender inclusive.

generalization ⑨ A statement applied to all people or things in a large category. If there are many exceptions to the statement, the generalization is considered invalid.

hard evidence ⑧ Includes facts, statistics, and statements from authorities (experts).

helping (or auxiliary) verb ⑬ A verb that combines with a main verb to indicate tense.

hypothesis ⑧ A prediction or expected result of an experiment or other research investigation.

idiom ⑯ A phrase whose meaning is understood only within the context of the phrase, not by the meaning of the individual words.

illustration ⑧ A detailed example that usually takes the form of an anecdote or a brief narrative.

imperative sentence ⑬ A sentence that issues a command. Its subject, *you*, is always understood even though it is not expressed.

incomplete verb form (or base verb form) ⑬ A verb form ending in *-ing* that is mistaken for a complete verb.

indefinite pronoun ⑬-⑮ A pronoun that refers to an unspecified individual or group (e.g., *each*, *either*, *one*, or *everyone*). It is usually considered singular and takes a singular verb.

independent clause ⑬ A group of words that has a subject and a predicate and can therefore stand alone as a complete sentence. Compare *dependent clause*.

indirect object (IO) ⑬ A part of a prepositional phrase that usually tells for whom the action in the sentence is done.

indirect source ⑫ A source that is cited in another work.

inference ① A conclusion based on the evidence presented; the corresponding verb is *infer*.

interrogative pronoun ⑮ A pronoun, such as *who*, *whom*, *which*, and *what*, that introduces a question.

introduction ⑦ The opening of a document that presents the main idea (the thesis statement) and the main organizational pattern. See *logical approach*, *dramatic approach*, and *mixed quotation format*.

jargon ①, ⑯ Language that is specific to a field or a group; words or phrases that are used by certain professions, but these words are not always understood by others.

journal ⑩ A periodical that publishes the results of experts' research.

keyword ⑩ A word identified by an author or a cataloguer as important in an article.

linking verb ⑬ A verb that joins (links) a subject to a noun or an adjective that follows the verb.

logical approach ⑦ A method of writing an introduction that moves from a broad to a narrow focus.

looping ④ Underlining potentially useful words, phrases, or sentences and choosing the best one as a focus for more freewriting.

mechanics ④ In formatting, matters such as margin size, spacing between sentences, font size and type, and page numbers; in writing, it includes abbreviations, capital letters, hyphenation, and numbers.

mind mapping ④ A pre-writing strategy that involves circling words and phrases and connecting them to other words. Doing so allows you to see the relationship among thoughts.

misplaced modifier ⑮ An adjective, adjectival phrase, adverb, or adverbial phrase that is too far away in the sentence from the word it should modify, possibly giving the sentence an unintended meaning. See also *dangling modifier*.

mixed quotation format ⑪ A combination of significant words of the source (direct quotation) with paraphrasing.

MLA (Modern Language Association) style ⑫ In-text citations that include the author's last name and page or paragraph number(s).

modal verb ⑬ A verb that appears before the main verb to express necessity, obligation, possibility, or probability.

narration ③ The telling of a story; can be an effective way to introduce or reinforce your topic.

non-restrictive clause ⑭ A clause that contains information that can be left out of the sentence without affecting the meaning.

noun ⑬ The name of a person, a place, a thing, or an idea. See also *subject*.

noun phrase ⑬ A group of words that acts as a noun in a sentence and can be either the subject or an object.

outline ④ A representation of your points and supporting material. Creating an outline is an essential stage in essay writing, enabling you to see the arrangement of your ideas before you begin a draft.

parallelism ⑮ The principle that the elements in a sentence that have the *same grammatical function* are expressed in parallel structures.

paraphrase ⑤ Restating the source's meaning using only your own words and sentence structure. Paraphrase when you want to cite a small amount of material that is directly relevant to your point. Include the entire original though but rephrase it.

parentheses ⑪ A form of punctuation that may enclose text that explains or expands on something.

passive construction ⑮ A construction in which the subject of the sentence does not perform the action; the noun that receives the action is the subject and is placed at the beginning of the sentence.

peer review ⑩ The assessment of an article by experts in the field before publication.

periodical ⑩ A publication that is issued regularly, such as newspapers, magazines, journals, and yearbooks.

personal paragraph ③ An essay that focuses on an aspect of the writer's life or a relevant experience.

personal experience ⑧ A type of example that takes the form of direct experience or observation, which can often be effective in supporting a value or opinion claim.

personal pronoun ⑮ A pronoun that refers to persons. The *first person* refers to the one *doing* the speaking or writing; *second person* refers to the one *spoken to*; and *third person* refers to the one *spoken about*.

phrase ⑮ A group of grammatically linked words that lacks a subject, predicate, or both; functions as a single part of speech. See also *prepositional phrase*.

plagiarism ⑤, ⑪ The intentional or unintentional use of someone else's work as if it were one's own.

policy claim ⑧ A claim that is usually a call for action to fix a problem or improve a situation.

possessive ⑭ The case that indicates relationships such as ownership.

precedent ⑧ An example that refers to the way a particular situation was handled in the past.

preposition ⑬ A word or phrase that joins a noun or pronoun to the rest of the sentence, adding information.

prepositional phrase ⑬ A group of words that consists of a preposition and a noun or pronoun (the object of the preposition). The phrase can act as an adverb to modify a verb or as an adjective to modify a noun or pronoun.

primary sources ⑧, ⑩ Original sources, including literary texts, historical documents, surveys, questionnaires, and interviews. Compare *secondary sources*.

problem–solution ④ A method of paragraph or essay organization in which a writer focuses on a problem, a solution to a problem, or both a problem and a solution.

process ④ A method of paragraph or essay organization in which a writer focuses on the steps in a sequence.

pronoun ⑬ A word that takes the place of a noun in a sentence. See also *antecedent, agreement, pronoun reference, pronoun case, pronoun consistency,* and *relative cause*.

pronoun–antecedent agreement ⑮ The principle that a pronoun must agree with its antecedent in number.

pronoun case ⑮ The principle that a pronoun changes its form depending on its function in the sentence (e.g., *I/me, she/her, they/them*).

pronoun consistency ⑮ The principle that a pronoun must agree in number, gender, and person with its antecedent.

pronoun reference ⑮ The principle that each pronoun must refer clearly to a specific antecedent or preceding noun.

proposal ⑩ A description of a planned essay that announces the work's topic, purpose, and research sources.

purpose ② Your reason for writing, as well as how you approach the task.

question–answer ④ A method of paragraph or essay organization that involves a writer posing questions and explaining their answers. Questions such as Who? What? When? Where? Why? and How? can be applied to almost any topic.

questioning ④ A pre-writing strategy that helps you create a possible thesis as a specific question or series of questions that you will try to answer.

rebuttal ⑨ The part of an argument that raises the other side's points, usually to strengthen the argument and to appear fair.

reference ⑫ A citation that gives complete retrieval information for a source used in an essay.

reflexive pronoun ⑮ A pronoun that ends with *–self* (e.g., *himself*); can be used only if the person has already been referred to earlier in the sentence.

relative clause ⑮ A dependent clause that functions as an adjective, modifying the preceding noun. The clause usually begins with a relative pronoun.

relative pronoun ⑭, ⑮ A pronoun that introduces a dependent clause.

research ⑩ A stage of essay writing that involves finding out what others, especially experts, have written or said about a certain topic. Research requires using library resources and/or reliable online sources.

restrictive clause ⑭ A clause that contains information that is necessary for the reader to understand the sentence.

revising ⑯ A process that involves editing to achieve a polished final version.

run-on sentence ⑬ A major grammatical error in which two sentences are not properly separated.

scanning ① A reading strategy in which the reader looks for key words or sections of a text.

secondary sources ⑩ Works that comment on primary sources; include authoritative written sources (e.g., books and journal articles), oral presentations, and conference papers.

selective reading ① A reading strategy with a goal, such as scanning for main points or reading for details.

sentence fragment ⑬ A major grammatical error that consists of an incomplete clause or a dependent clause on its own.

signal phrase ⑤, ⑪ A phrase that indicates what follows is taken from another source.

simple sentence ⑬ A sentence that contains one subject and one predicate.

simple thesis statement ⑦ A thesis statement that announces the essay's topic and makes a comment on it. Compare *expanded thesis statement*.

slanted language (9) Language that reveals the writer's bias, affecting credibility. This language can take direct forms, such as accusation, or can be more indirect.

soft evidence (8) Evidence that indirectly supports your points and helps the reader understand them.

spiral conclusion (7) A conclusion that restates the thesis and leads the reader beyond it.

square brackets (brackets) (11) or Punctuation marks that, when used in a direct quotation, indicate a change or addition to the original passage.

style (16) The way that one writes.

subject (4) A broad category that contains several possible topics.

subject complement (SC) (13) A noun or an adjective that following the verb that gives more information about the subject.

subject–verb agreement (13), (15) The principle that a sentence's verb must match its subject in number (i.e., a singular subject requires a singular verb, and a plural subject requires a plural verb).

subordinating conjunction (13) A conjunction that joins a dependent clause, which contains less important information, to an independent clause, which contains more important information.

summary (5) A shorter rewritten version of an original work.

support (8) The use of ample and credible evidence in an essay.

synonym (1) A word that means the same thing as, and can therefore replace, another word. See also *connotation* and *denotation*.

syntax (15) The way words are put together into sentences in a language.

synthesis (10) The process of putting together ideas from different sources.

thesis statement (1), (4) The main point of your essay, or what you are trying to prove. A thesis statement can make a specific comment on the topic or tell the reader how you will approach it. See also *simple thesis statement* and *expanded thesis statement*.

tone (1), (16) The writer's attitude (e.g., subjective, objective, formal, or informal) to the subject matter.

topic (4) Narrower, or more focused, than a subject.

topic sentence (3) Usually the first sentence in a paragraph; introduces the paragraph's main idea.

transition (3) A word or phrase that connects ideas from one sentence or paragraph to the next.

unified paragraph (3) A paragraph that focuses on one central idea that is announced in the topic sentence and that all sentences relate to.

uniform resource locator (URL) (10), (12) The address of specific internet content.

usage (16) The customary and accepted way that a word is used. See also *diction*.

value or opinion claim (8) An ethical claim that appeals to the reader's principles or moral system.

verb (13) A word that conveys an action, a state of being, or a condition.

verb phrase (13) A group of words that acts as the verb in a sentence.

wrap (3) The last sentence of a paragraph that sums up the main point and recalls the topic sentence.

Index

Page numbers in *italics* indicate figures.

authors, anonymous or unknown: citing APA style, 209, 212; citing MLA style, 221
autocorrect, 356
auxiliary verbs, 241, 249, 312, 341, 360, 362, 405
avoid/prevent, 374

bandwagon (fallacy), 152
Banks, Brian, 144–5
Beal, Grace, 121
Beaudet, François, 48
because, 178, 244, 254; *reason...is*, 333
before, 243, 254, 372
belief/believe, 373
Benard, Laura, 156–7
beside/besides, 345
between/among, 345
bias, 17, 88, 335, 338; slanted language and, 153; in statistics, 140
bias/biased, 345–6
bibliographies: annotated, 85, 96, 403; as resource, 176; *see also* documentation; references; works cited
BioMed Central, 182
black hole constructions, 332–3
block organizational method, 106–7
block quotations, 403; in APA style, 207; in MLA style, 220
blogs and blog posts, 143; citing APA style, 216; citing MLA style, 228; as research sources, 184
body paragraphs, 63, 116–17, 118, 189, 403
book reviews: citing APA style, 214; citing MLA style, 226
books: citing APA style, 211; citing MLA style, 223, 225; reference, 180; as research sources, 176, 180
books, electronic: citing APA style, 215
Boolean operators, 181, 403
both, 291
both...and, 313
brackets, 196–7; *see also* parentheses
brainstorming, 67, 403
breath/breathe, 373
broad reference, 297–8
bulleted lists, 312
business writing. *see* workplace writing
Business Source Elite, 182
but, 40, 244, 248, 259, 264, 351
Butler, Mike, 201–2

call/draw attention to, 374
can, 372
capitalization: APA style, 210; MLA style, 222; of nouns, 237
cardinal numbers, 368
care, 374

CARS test, 18, 75, 140, 180, 183, 184
case, pronouns, 299–302, 406
case studies, 141, 403
cause–effect, as development pattern, 59, 139, 403
chapters, of works: citing APA style, 212; citing MLA style, 224
Chicago Manual of Style, The (CMS), 205
chronology, as development pattern, 58, 139, 403
circular conclusions, 130, 403
circular logic (fallacy), 152
citations, 171, 190, 192, 403; in-text (parenthetical), 197–8, 205, 206–10, 219–22; software for, 177, 178; styles of, 205–6; when not given, 337; *see also* documentation
cite/sight/site, 346
claims, 9, 137, 403; arguable, 154; factual, 137, 140, 405; policy, 137, 138, 140, 156, 406; SIM (specific, interesting, and manageable), 124, 127, 154–6; support for, 137; value or opinion, 137, 156, 407
clarity, 326–43, 403; direct writing and, 332–3; oral presentations and, 164; revising for, 74–5
classification, as development pattern, 59, 139, 403
clauses, 403; non-restrictive, 265, 266, 405; relative, 301–2, 330, 365, 366, 406; restrictive, 265, 266, 406
Cleave, Spencer, 157
clichés, 326, 342–3, 403
climax order, 72, 161
clincher statement, 85, 117, 129, 165
clothing, 371
coherence, 43–7, 56, 354, 403
collective nouns, 289, 292, 403
colloquialisms, 337, 403
colons, 193, 258, 276–7, 351
commas, 263–72
comma splice, 257–9, 271–2, 404
commit, 374–5
common ground, 155, 158, 404
common nouns, 369
companies, names of, 291; *see also* organizations
comparatives, 364–5
compare/contrast, 375
comparison and contrast: as development pattern, 61, 139, 404; parallelism and, 309, 312, 313–14; as type of essay, 106–9
compete for/compete against, 375
complex sentences, 248–9, 404
composing, 63, 72–4, 173–4; *see also* writing
compounds, 404; parallelism and, 312–13
compound subject, 288, 291–2, 404
"Computer Ergonomics" (Butler), 201–2
computers: composing on, 73; saving work and, 73–4; *see also* software
concern, 375

gender-inclusive language, 292, 405
general knowledge: citations and, 192
generalizations, 150, 405; hasty, 152
gerunds, 370
get attention, 374
glossaries, 21, 176
Golden Bull Award, 335
good/well, 346–7
Google Scholar, 184
government, 369
government documents: citing APA style, 214; citing MLA style, 226
graduate from/to be a graduate of, 376
grammar, 237; parts of speech, 237–44; sentences and, 246–59
graphs, in oral presentations, 164, 165
Gregg, Brian, 50–1
group, as author: citing APA style, 209, 212, 215; citing MLA style, 221, 224, 227
Gulli, Cathy, 76, 77–9

hard evidence, 140, 405
"Harnessing the Power of Nature to Fight Climate Change" (Banks), 144–5
hasty generalization, 152
headings, 6, 13, 75
Health Source: Nursing/Academic Edition, 183
helping verbs, 241, 249, 312, 341, 360, 362, 405
here is/are, 286
Herrera, Ivannia, 149
hire/hired by, 376
"Historical Influences on Québec's Traditional Desserts, The" (Donnelly), 232–4
Hoffman, D., 48
Holland, Eva, 15–16
homophones, 357
however, 43, 274
"How to Improve Memory" (Koca), 85, 103–5
human/humanity, 370
hyphens, 365
hypothesis, 141, 405

I/me, 28, 337
idioms, 337, 405
i.e., e.g., 346
IEEE Xplore, 183
"If Corporations Have Legal Rights, Why Not Rivers?" (Suzuki and Plotkin), 81–2
illusion/allusion, 344–5
illustrations, 141, 358, 405
importance, 371
in-class essays, 109–10
indefinite article, 366–7
indefinite pronouns, 239–41, 278, 280, 290, 292, 405

independent clauses, 243, 248–9, 405; parallelism and, 310; paragraph transitions and, 41; punctuation and, 258, 264–5, 273–5, 277; sentence variety and, 351–2; subordinating conjunctions and, 254
index cards, 177
indexes, 6, 180, 181, 185
indirect object, 246, 247, 405
indirect source, 405; citing APA style, 207, 214; citing MLA style, 220, 226
indirect writing, 326–7
inductive reasoning, 151
inferences, 5, 8, 20, 405
infinitive phrases, 353
informal writing, 28, 50, 280, 337
information, 371
informative approach, to writing, 33
in spite of/despite, 372
installation, art: citing APA style, 210
instead, 40
instructions, 103, 110
intensives, 331
interest level, audience and, 29
internet: citing APA style, 209, 214–16; citing MLA style, 221, 226–7; databases, 181–3; note-taking and, 177; research and, 176; source, 181–5; as term, 369–70; trustworthiness of, 183–4
interrogative pronouns, 302, 405
interviews: citing APA style, 207–8; citing MLA style, 229; as research source, 186
in-text citations: APA style and, 206–10; MLA style and, 219–22
introduction–conclusion inverted pyramid, *130*
introductions, 103, 119–27, 405; citing MLA style, 225; dramatic approach, 120; logical approach, 119–20; mixed approach, 121; organizational patterns, 119–21
inverted climax (dramatic) order, 161, 72
inverted pyramid, 119–20
is when/is where, 339–40
it, 296, 298
italics, 357
it's/its, 280, 347
it was constructions, 332–3

Jacobs, John, 49
jargon, 14, 33, 326, 405
joiners, 243–4
journals, 180, 186, 405; citing APA style, 211, 213, 215; citing MLA style, 223, 225, 227; peer-reviewed, 180, 184, 406; popular databases, 181–3

Kaminski, M., 5
Katt, Barclay, 94, 95, 108
keywords, 180–1, 405
Kimball, Meredith M., 88, 89

PowerPoint, 164, 165, 166
precedents, 141–2, 406
precision: clarity and, 326; logic and, 339–40; word choices and, 337–9
predicate, 248; complete, 247; missing, 251, 252; simple, 246
prediction (fallacy), 152
preface: citing MLA style, 225
prepositional phrases, 248, 249, 353, 406; beginning sentences with, 354; pronoun reference and, 296; subject–verb agreement and, 287, 288–9; wordiness and, 330
prepositions, 243–4, 287, 372, 406; verbs and, 373–8
pre-reading, 12–13
presentation: of essay, 357–9; oral, 163–7
present verb tenses, 360–1
Pressreader, 183
prevent/avoid, 374
pre-writing, 63, 64–70, 72
primary audience, 33–4
primary sources, 139, 171, 179–80, 406
problem–solution, as development pattern, 60, 139, 406
process, as development pattern, 58–9, 406
process essays, 103–5
progressive verb tenses, 360, 361, 362
Project Gutenberg, 180
pronoun–antecedent agreement, 291–3, 406
pronouns, 238–41, 406; case, 299–302, 406; consistency, 302–3, 406; demonstrative, 330; gender-inclusive, 240–1, 286, 291, 292–3; indefinite, 239–41, 278, 280, 290, 292, 405; interrogative, 302, 405; object, 239, 299–300, 301, 302; personal, 291, 299–300, 406; possessive, 239, 291, 300–1; problems with, 294–303; reference, 294–8, 406; reflexive, 239, 406; relative, 254, 265, 301–2, 333, 406; subject, 239, 299–300, 301, 302
proofreading, 75, 355–76
proper nouns, 238, 368–9
proposal, research, 171–2, 406
Proquest, 183
PsycArticles, 183
publication dates, 176
publisher, works without: citing MLA style, 224
punctuation: colons, 276–7; commas, 263–72; dashes, 278; with direct quotations, 195, 196; parentheses, 278; proofreading and, 357; semicolons, 273–6; *see also* apostrophes
puns, 340
purpose: of paragraphs, 47–50; of workplace writing, 33; of writing, 26, 406

qtd. in, 220
qualifiers, overused, 332

question–answer, as development pattern, 60, 406
questioning, as pre-writing strategy, 66–7, 406
questions: brainstorming and, 67; development patterns and, 57; revising and, 326
quotation marks: direct quotations and, 89, 92, 193, 207; double and single, 193; punctuation with, 268; proofreading and, 357
quotations: block, 193, 207, 220, 403; direct, 92, 193–4, 207, 219, 276–7, 404; mixed format, 194–5, 405; note-taking and, 176; punctuating, 196–7, 267, 276; signal phrases and, 195–6

radio series: citing MLA style, 229
reading: aloud and, 355–6; backward, 356; building vocabulary and, 21; CARS test and, 18; critical thinking and, 9; first, 14–15; focused, 6, 7, 405; forward, 356; pre-reading, 12–13; scanning, 6, 7; second, 16–18; selective, 6, 406; strategies, 4–7; syllabically, 356; writing and, 3–4
reason, appeals to, 140, 147, 148
reasonableness, CARS test and, 18
reasoning: deductive and inductive, 151; faulty, 151–3, 405
reason...is because, 333
rebuttals, 156–60, 161, 406
recall: in-class essays and, 109
red herring, 152
redundant writing, 328–9
refer, 377
references, 205, 406; software for, 177, 178; *see also* bibliography; documentation
references section: APA style and, 205, 210–16
reflexive pronouns, 239, 406
RefWorks, 177
relative clauses, 301–2, 330, 365, 366, 406
relative pronouns, 254, 265, 301–2, 333, 406
reliability, 140, 142, 143; CARS test and, 18
rely, 376
remember, 372
remote reference, 296
repetition, 43, 44, 352; emphasis and, 354
research, 63, 71, 171, 406; arranging and, 178–9; assimilating and, 178; composing and, 173–4; experts and, 175–6; finding and exploring sources, 171–2; internet, 181–5; library, 185–6; as life skill, 171–4; note-taking and, 176–7; organization and, 173; proposal, 171–2, 406; sources, 71, 179–86; strategies for, 178–9; synthesis and, 171, 172–3; as term, 371; topics and, 174–9
research essays, 171; organization and outlines, 188–9; peer edit form for, 382–3
restrictive clauses, 265, 266, 406
result in/result from, 378

television series: citing APA style, 209–10, 216; citing MLA style, 222, 229
templates: for argumentative essays, 161; for expository essays, 116–18
tenses, verb, 360–2
than/then, 313, 348
that, 297–8, 301, 330–1
the, 367–70
their/there/they're, 348
then/than, 40, 348
therefore, 243, 259, 267, 274–5
there has/have been, 286
there is/are, 286
thesaurus, 339
thesis, 65, 67, 69
thesis statement, 6, 38, 63, 64, 70, 122, 123–7, 407; checklist, 126; effective, 124–5; expanded, 123–4, 404; oral presentations and, 165; parallelism and, 311; simple, 123, 124, 406; summaries and, 89; in template, 116
they/them/their, 240–1
they're/there/their, 348
think, 378
third person, 299–300
this, 297–8
though, 265
thus, 243, 259, 274
time, 290, 365
time management, 109–10, 164
title pages, 358
titles (designations), 268
titles (of works), 12, 89, 291
to/too, 348
to be, 341, 360
to have, 341, 360
tone, 14, 34, 340, 407
topic, 64, 65, 66, 171–2, 407; researching, 174–9
topic sentence, 38, 41–2, 116, 118, 407
tradition (fallacy), 152
transitional phrases, 352; common, 274; independent clauses and, 273–5
transitions, 43, 407; between paragraphs, 41–2; between sentences, 39–41; oral presentations and, 164
translated works: citing APA style, 212–13; citing MLA style, 224
translation, 19, 86; dictionaries, 19, 44, 86
Trudeau, Justin, 341
Turnitin, 191
type of, 370–1

unified paragraph, 42, 56, 407
uniform resource locator (URL), 177, 184, 407; in APA style, 211, 214–15; in MLA style, 227

usage, 343, 407
usage/use, 348

vague reference, 297
Vahlis, Julianny, 79–80
value claims, 137, 156, 407
verb phrase, 249, 407
verbs, 241, 407; agreement with subject, 238, 286–91, 354, 378, 407; helping (auxiliary), 241, 249, 312, 341, 360, 362, 405; incomplete (base) form, 252–3; linking, 241, 287, 405; modal, 241, 249, 372–3, 405; mood and, 362; nouns and, 373; prepositions and, 373–8; redundancy and, 328–9; strong, 341; troublesome, 372–8; voice and, 362; weak, 333–4
verb tenses, 249, 360–2
Verhulst, Graeme, 141
very, 331
videos: citing APA style, 209–10, 216; citing MLA style, 222, 228
visuals, in oral presentations, 164, 165
vocabulary, 21; *see also* word choice
voice, active and passive, 316–18
volume, of multivolume work: citing APA style, 213; citing MLA style, 225

websites: citing APA style, 209, 212, 214–16; citing MLA style, 221, 226–8
weight, 290
well/good, 346–7
what, 254
when, 254, 339–40
where, 254, 339–40
whereas, 265, 275
which/whichever, 297, 301
which one of, 289
who/which/that, 266
who/whoever, 301–2
whom/whomever, 301–2
who's, whose, 348, 280
"Why Do We Still Put Young People in Solitary Confinement?" (Gulli), 77–9; critical response to, 79–80
Wikipedia, 184
will, 341, 373, 360, 362
Windsor, Hillary, 133–5
Wolchover, Natalie, 87–8
word choice, 43, 337–9
wordiness, 328; intensives, 331–2; phony phrases and, 330; redundant writing and, 328–9; unnecessary small words and, 330–1
word meanings, 18–21
word processing software, 178, 330, 356
words, confusing, 343–50